Certified Wireless Analys

Official Stu

(CWAP-403)

MW01223066

Certified Wireless Network Professionals

®

Errata, when available, for this study guide can be found at: www.cwnp.com/errata/

First printing: September 2018, version 1.0

ISBN: 9781729459485

In addition to the authors of this book, listed in the About the Authors section of the Introduction, CWNP would like to say a special thanks to all those involved in the development of materials for CWAP-403 from the Job Task Analysis (JTA) through to materials review and feedback. These individuals include Robert Bartz, Tom Carpenter, Adrian Granados, Brett Hill, Ravi Kiran Gundu, Manon Lessard, Peter Mackenzie, Martin Ericson, and R. David Paine III. If we have left out your name it is only because so many helped and not because you were not appreciated. Many thanks to all of you.

Table of Contents

Introduction

The Certified Wireless Analysis Professional (CWAP) is responsible for the capture and analysis of data related to wireless networks following troubleshooting principles and methodology. This professional has in-depth understanding of protocols, frame exchanges, and standards and the Physical Layer and MAC sublayer. This person is proficient in the use of spectrum and protocol analysis tools. The CWAP-403 exam tests the candidate's knowledge to verify his or her ability to perform the duties of a CWAP.

This book is a study guide for the CWAP-403 exam and a reference guide to help you master 802.11 wireless network analysis. With this book, you will be well-prepared for both the exam and real-life troubleshooting scenarios.

The CWAP-403 exam consists of 60 multiple choice, single correct answer questions and is delivered through Pearson VUE. The candidate can register for the exam at the Pearson VUE website (https://home.pearsonvue.com/). The candidate will have 90 minutes to take the exam and must achieve a score of 70% or greater to earn the CWAP certification. If the candidate desires to become a Certified Wireless Network Trainer (CWNT) the passing score must be 80% or greater. A CWNT is authorized to teach official CWNP courses for certifications in which they hold the CWNT credential.

Book Features

The CWAP Study and Reference Guide includes the following features:

- End of chapter Facts to Remember. These lists of important facts help you retain the information learned in the chapter.

- End of chapter review quizzes. These quizzes help you test the knowledge you've acquired from the chapter. Each chapter contains 10 quiz items.

- Notes with special indicators. The notes throughout the book fall into one of three categories as outlined in Table i.1.

- CWNP official glossary. A glossary of terms provided at the end of the book that helps you as a reference while reading.

- Complete coverage of the CWAP-403 objectives. Every objective is covered in the book and each chapter lists the objectives covered within.

Icon	Description
	Note: A general note related to the current topic.
	Defined Note: A note providing a concise definition of a term or concept.
	Exam Note: A note providing tips for exam preparation.

Table i.1: Book Note Icons

About the Authors

Tom Carpenter is the CTO of CWNP and has more than 20 years of experience in the Information Technology industry. He has written 18 previous books and developed more than 50 eLearning programs in the past fifteen years. He is a CWNE and holds several other industry certifications as well. As the CTO of CWNP, Tom is responsible for setting the direction for certifications and managing product development projects through their lifecycles. He can be reached at tom@cwnp.com and is heard on a monthly webinar series and the WLAN News Desk presented by CWNP and archived at YouTube on the CWNPTV channel. Tom lives in Ohio with his wife Julie and loves books and all things tech.

Landon D. Foster is a Wireless Architect and Analyst with Theatro Labs and a former US Marine. He lives in Fort Worth, Texas, and credits any success to his wife directly. He is immensely grateful to the WLAN community for its incredible openness and the generosity that it demonstrates daily. He can be found on Twitter at @AceHighWifi. Landon is on his way to becoming a CWNE.

Rowell Dionicio, CWNE #210, is a network engineer for a university on the U.S. west coast. He started focusing on Wi-Fi back in 2014 while at a managed service provider. In 2015, he created the Clear-To-Send podcast to get involved in the community and learn more about Wi-Fi by teaching others. When he's not working you can find him at a local sushi restaurant eating Hamachi. You can engage with him on Twitter @rowelldionicio where he encourages open communication and learning.

Bryan Harkins, CWNE #44, is an award-winning trainer and author who has been inspiring other IT professionals for over 20 years. He has designed and deployed wireless networks in places ranging from pig farms to submarines and most of the usual things in between. Bryan has been given the honor of speaking at several industry events around the world for groups including the Armed Forces Communications and Electronics Association, Secure World Expo and IP Expo. Additionally, he has served on the CWNE Advisory Board and the CWNE Round Table.

CWAP-403 Objectives

The CWAP-403 exam tests your knowledge against six knowledge domains as documented in Table i.2. The CWAP candidate should understand these domains before taking the exam. The CWAP-403 objectives follow.

Knowledge Domain	Percentage
Protocol Analysis	15%
Spectrum Analysis	15%
PHY Layers and Technologies	10%
MAC Sublayer and Functions	25%
WLAN Medium Access	10%
802.11 Frame Exchanges	25%

Table i.2: CWAP-403 Exam Knowledge Domains with Percentage of Questions in Each Domain

1.0 Protocol Analysis – 15%

1.1 Capture 802.11 frames using the appropriate methods and locations

1.1.1	Install monitor mode drivers
1.1.2	Select appropriate capture device
1.1.3	Select appropriate capture location
1.1.4	Capture for an appropriate amount of time based on the problem scenario
1.1.5	Scanning channels vs. capturing on a single channel
1.1.6	Capturing in roaming scenarios
1.1.7	Capture with portable protocol analyzers (laptops)
1.1.8	Capture with APs, controllers, and other management solutions
1.1.9	Capture with specialty devices such as handheld analyzers

1.2 Analyze 802.11 frame captures to discover problems and find solutions

1.2.1	Use appropriate display filters to view relevant frames and packets
1.2.2	Use colorization to highlight important frames and packets
1.2.3	Configure and display columns for analysis purposes
1.2.4	View frame and packet decodes and understand the information shown and apply it to the analysis process

2.0 Spectrum Analysis – 15%

2.1 Capture RF spectrum data and understand the common views available in spectrum analyzers

    2.1.1   Install, configure and use spectrum analysis software and hardware
- Configure Wi-Fi integration
- Save and export capture data

    2.1.2   Capture RF spectrum data using handheld, laptop-based and infrastructure spectrum capture solutions

    2.1.3   Understand and use spectrum analyzer views
- Real-time FFT
- Waterfall, swept spectrogram, density and historic views
- Utilization and duty cycle
- Detected devices
- WLAN integration views

2.2 Analyze spectrum captures to identify relevant RF information and issues

    2.2.1   Determine the RF noise floor in an environment

    2.2.2   Determine Signal-to-Noise Ration (SNR) for a given signal

    2.2.3   Locate and identify sources of RF interference

    2.2.4   Identify RF channel utilization

    2.2.5   Analyze a non-Wi-Fi transmitter and its impact on WLAN communications

    2.2.6   Overlapping and non-overlapping adjacent channel interference

    2.2.7   Poor performing or faulty radios

2.3 Analyze spectrum captures to identify various device signatures

    2.3.1   Identify frequency hopping devices

    2.3.2   Identify various 802.11 PHYs
- 802.11b
- 802.11g
- 802.11a
- 802.11n
- 802.11ac
- Channel widths

3.0 PHY Layers and Technologies – 10%

Extended Table of Contents

Chapter 1: 802.11—The Protocol

Objectives Covered:

1.5   Ensure appropriate troubleshooting methods are used with all analysis types

      1.5.1   Define the problem

      1.5.2   Determine the scale of the problem

      1.5.3   Identify probable causes

      1.5.4   Capture and analyze the data

      1.5.5   Observe the problem

      1.5.6   Choose appropriate remediation steps

      1.5.7   Document the problem and resolution

4.1   Understand frame encapsulation and frame aggregation

Wireless analysis professionals must know the 802.11 protocol well. When analyzing 802.11 network communications (Layer 2 frame exchanges and Layer 1 framing and modulation), the professional must understand the communications process. When analyzing 802.11 radio frequency (RF) signals, the professional must be able to differentiate between 802.11 signals and other RF signals and noise. This chapter begins the learning process with a brief description of what a wireless analysis professional does and needs to know and then moves on to review foundational material from your CWNA or other studies. Let's begin the journey.

 This chapter is mostly a review of CWNA materials. However, the sections titled *Basics of Network Frames—Data Link (MAC) Layer* and *Troubleshooting Methods* contain material that may appear on the CWAP exam as well. The CWNA materials are provided both for review and for those using this book as a reference to 802.11 analysis.

The Wireless Analysis Professional

A Certified Wireless Analysis Professional (CWAP) certified individual should be able to capture and analyze data related to wireless networks (wireless local area networks (WLANs)) following troubleshooting principles and methodologies. This professional should have an in-depth understanding of protocols, frame exchanges, and standards at the Physical layer and MAC sublayer. The CWAP must be proficient in the use of spectrum and protocol analysis tools. This book provides the knowledge required to perform the role of a CWAP. It also helps you to prepare for the CWAP exam. The journey begins with an understanding of the role played by a wireless analysis professional.

Tasks Performed

A CWAP or wireless analysis professional performs these common tasks:

- Troubleshooting specific WLAN problems in existing networks.
- Analyzing and optimizing the performance of an existing WLAN.
- Reviewing WLAN design documents to resolve potential future problems.
- Explaining 802.11 protocol operations.
- Using a protocol analyzer to evaluate 802.11 communications.
- Using a spectrum analyzer to evaluate both 802.11 and non-802.11 RF activity.

Skills Required

The wireless analysis professional must have knowledge and skills in four key areas:

- 802.11 protocol operations—understanding the details of how the 802.11 protocol operates is essential to skills development in the remaining three areas.
- Protocol analysis—the ability to capture and analyze frames and packets to determine the problems within a network and locate areas for improvement.
- Spectrum analysis—the ability to understand RF activity within an environment and its impact on 802.11 operations.
- Troubleshooting methods—understanding of common procedures used to understand, analyze, and resolve problems.

Foundations

To perform these tasks and gain these skills, the wireless analysis professional requires several foundational elements. This chapter provides the foundational knowledge of 802.11 that the CWNA needs to possess as well as additional information required for the CWAP exam and the task of wireless analysis in 802.11 networks. Later chapters go deeper into all the topics covered. These are the foundational elements we'll examine:

- Protocols and Communications
- The 802.11 Protocol
- Using RF to Communicate
- Basics of Network Frames
- Troubleshooting Methods

The remaining sections of this chapter follow this outline.

Protocols and Communications

A protocol, in computer networking, is a defined method used for communication between devices. The protocol works because both devices understand how to send and receive messages based on the protocol. Examples of protocols include 802.3 (Ethernet), 802.11 (Wi-Fi), Internet Protocol (IP), and Transmission Control Protocol (TCP). The Open Systems Interconnection (OSI) model is a networking reference model or framework used to describe and understand actual networking protocols. The OSI model is not implemented as a communications protocol but provides us with the language used to explain and understand protocols.

A *protocol* is a defined method used to accomplish some task. For example, an organization may have protocols for addressing customer complaints, or a military may have protocols defining how to act in war situations. A network protocol is similar, and many are defined for communications between and among devices on modern networks.

The OSI model is a seven-layer model consisting of the following layers and is represented in Figure 1.1:

- Layer 7: Application Layer
- Layer 6: Presentation Layer
- Layer 5: Session Layer
- Layer 4: Transport Layer
- Layer 3: Network layer
- Layer 2: Data Link Layer
- Layer 1: Physical Layer

The Institute of Electrical and Electronics Engineers (IEEE) 802.3 and 802.11 standard protocols operate primarily at Layers 1 and 2 of the OSI model. The Internet Engineering Task Force (IETF) IP and TCP standard protocols operate at Layers 3 and 4, respectively. IEEE protocols can be accessed from `cwnp.link/get802files`. IETF Request for Comments (RFCs), which define IETF protocols, can be accessed from `IETF.org`.

The OSI model will not be explained in extensive detail here. For more detailed information, go to `cwnp.link/osimodel`. The brief descriptions that follow should suffice for your understanding of the materials in the rest of this book.

Each layer of the OSI model is said to service the layer above it and the one below it, except for the two final layers, Layer 1 and Layer 7. Layer 1 is the final layer in transmission and Layer 7 is the final layer in reception. Layer 1 is responsible for receiving signals from the communications medium and transmitting signals onto the communications medium. Layer 7 receives data to be transmitted from the user-level applications and delivers data received to those applications.

As data moves down through the OSI model layers it is *encapsulated*, meaning that extra bits of information required for network communications are prepended and/or appended to it. On the receiving end, the received data is *decapsulated* as it moves up the layers until it is returned to the state of the original data the process on the sender intended to transmit to the receiver.

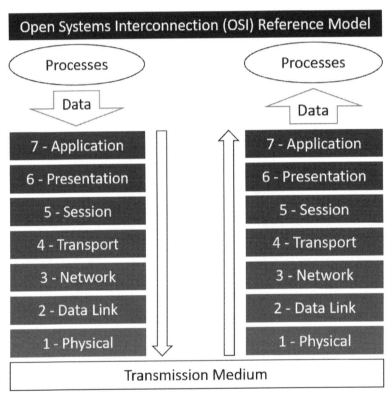

Figure 1.1: The Open Systems Interconnection (OSI) Reference Model

When considering modern networks, Layers 1 through 4 are the most important.

Layer 4 (Transport Layer) is typically TCP or User Datagram Protocol (UDP) communications today. TCP is a connection-oriented protocol, which means that it establishes a connection first (using a 3-way handshake) and then transmits data. UDP is typically implemented as a connectionless protocol and it sends data in a stream without acknowledgement. TCP is used when reliable delivery is required and UDP is used when unreliable or very fast delivery is required, such as in voice communications.

Layer 3 (Network Layer) is typically IP today, with the exception of Wide Area Network (WAN) protocols. In Local Area Networks (LAN) IP is the predominate protocol. It is also the primary Network Layer delivery protocol of the Internet.

Layer 2 (Data Link Layer) is either Ethernet or Wi-Fi on most LANs today. The Data Link Layer is divided into two sublayers: the Logical Link Control (LLC) upper layer and the Medium Access Control (MAC) lower layer. IEEE 802.2 defines the LLC that is used for Ethernet and Wi-Fi (among other standards). The MAC is defined by 802.3 and 802.11 specifically and provides for the data frame structures allowing local link communications. A local link is a connection that operates at Layer 1 and Layer 2, although it may carry a payload (data to be delivered) from upper layers of the OSI model.

This discussion is not focused on Storage Area Networks (SANs) and other network types that may implement non-IP protocols at Layer 3 and above. Such networks may also use different Layer 1 and Layer 2 protocols.

Given that the LLC sublayer is primarily the same for all the IEEE standards used in LANs, this guide further discusses the MAC sublayer only. The MAC sublayer for WLANs is defined in the 802.11 standard. This standard defines the frame formats used at the MAC sublayer, and they are a primary focus of this book and the CWAP exam. Three frame types are defined: management, control, and data/Quality of Service (QoS) data frames.

Frames are organized and meaningful collections of bits that are prepended and appended to upper-layer data within network communications or are self-existing at Layer 2 for network management and control purposes. Frame formats are defined for Layer 1 and Layer 2 of the OSI model in the 802.11 standard. Physical layer framing is used to prepare a receiver for an incoming Layer 2 frame. MAC sublayer framing is used to either communicate information about the WLAN or a WLAN link or to send data.

Layer 1 (Physical Layer) is also either Ethernet or Wi-Fi on most LANs today. The Physical Layer implements protocols for bit transmission and reception on the physical medium. The physical medium may be RF, light waves, fiber, or wires (cabling). Typical capabilities of this layer include encoding, modulation, demodulation, timing, and signal processing. Encoding is the process used to scramble and prepare the bits received from Layer 2 for transmission, and decoding is the opposite. Modulation is used to represent the bits on the physical medium through some form of change, such as phase or amplitude shifts in RF waves. Demodulation is used to read these represented bits from the physical medium. Network communications must be timed so that the receiver is synchronized with the transmitter. The preamble or training fields are used to accomplish this in 802.11 WLANs. Finally, signal processing is the phrase that defines the use of modulated carriers to represent information.

In 802.11 networks, the Physical Layer is divided into the Physical Layer Convergence Protocol (PLCP) and the Physical Medium Dependent (PMD). The PLCP is responsive for Physical Layer (PHY) framing and the PMD is responsible for sending and receiving bits on the RF medium. The PLCP adds preambles, training fields, and any other parameters required for receiving stations (STAs) to process the transmission correctly. Receiving STAs use the PLCP header information to understand the incoming transmission and synchronize their radios to receive the MAC sublayer data, which is the PHY payload, at the data rate defined in the PLCP header. A *header* is the information added by a layer, prepended to the upper layer data. That which is appended is sometimes called the *footer*, but the term *header* is used far more often than the term footer in relation to network communications. The following section, "The 802.11 Protocol," provides more introductory details of the PHY and MAC layers defined in the 802.11 standard. Figure 1.2 shows the structure of Layers 1–4 as described above.

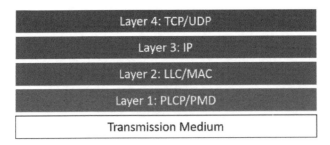

Figure 1.2: Layers 14 Detailed

The 802.11 Standard Protocol

The IEEE 802.11 standard protocol defines the MAC and PHY for communications on a LAN using RF as the transmission medium. The modern amendments to the 802.11 standard have added mesh support as well as other direct device-to-device communication methods. This section provides an overview of the implemented services and features of the PHY and MAC as defined in 802.11.

Using Radio Frequency to Communicate—Physical Layer

RF waves are used as the carriers of signals in 802.11 networks. Most WLANs operate on 2.4 GHz or 5 GHz today, but support for lower and higher frequency bands is included in the 802.11 standard. To enable the use of RF waves as carriers of data, wireless devices use modulation to impose data bits onto the RF waves.

The 802.11 standard defines the modulation methods used to communicate on WLANs. These include original methods defined in the 802.11-1997 standard as well as those added through the many amendments ratified since that time, leading up to 802.11ac and 802.11ax. Table 1.1 provides an overview of the various 802.11 PHYs still in use today.

Standard/Amendment	PHY Name	Maximum Data Rate (Rounded)	Supported Frequency Band
802.11-1997	DSSS	2 Mbps	2.4 GHz
802.11b	HR/DSSS	11 Mbps 2.4 GHz	2.4 GHz
802.11a	OFDM	54 Mbps	5 GHz
802.11g	ERP	54 Mbps	2.4 GHz
802.11n	HT	600 Mbps	2.4 GHz/5 GHz
802.11ah	S1G	350 Mbps	Sub-1 GHz
802.11af	TVHT	570 Mbps	Television Whitespaces
802.11ad	DMG	7 Gbps	60 GHz
802.11ac	VHT	7 Gbps	5 GHz
802.11ax	HEW	9.6 Gbps	2.4 GHz/5 GHz

Table 1.1: 802.11 PHYs Reviewed

As you can see from Table 1.1, the data rates vary greatly depending on the PHY in use. The earliest devices supported only 1 or 2 Mbps, but the newest devices coming to market today support nearly 10 Gbps as a maximum data rate. However, the real-world of WLAN performance results in average throughput available to wireless devices that is far less than the maximum data rate, because the medium is shared among all devices operating in the channel, and 802.11 management overhead consumes some of the air time as well.

The 802.11 PHYs are divided into two portions: The Physical Layer Convergence Protocol (PLCP) and the Physical Medium Dependent (PMD), as stated previously in this chapter. For this reason, at the PHY level, the header is called the PLCP header. The PLCP header includes information needed by the receiver to synchronize with the transmitter and to determine the data rate of the upper layer payload.

 A common misconception about 802.11 WLANs is that the data rate of the MAC frame is the rate at which the entire transmission is sent. The PHY information is sent at the lowest supported data rate in the BSS and then the MAC frame is sent at the data rate indicated. For example, the PHY information may be transmitted at 1 Mbps in 2.4 GHz networks, while the MAC frame is then sent at 144.4 Mbps.

Table 1.1 also provides a mapping of amendments to the PHYs that the IEEE introduced. Table 1.2 provides a mapping of PHY acronyms to PHY names.

PHY Acronym	PHY Name
DSSS	Direct Sequence Spread Spectrum
HR/DSSS	High Rate DSSS
OFDM	Orthogonal Frequency Division Multiplexing
ERP	Extended Rate PHY
HT	High Throughput
S1G	Sub-1 GHz
TVHT	Television Very high Throughput
DMG	Directional Multi-Gigabit
VHT	Very High Throughput
HEW	High Efficiency Wireless

Table 1.2: PHY Acronyms Mapped to Names

At the PHY layer, important communication methods are used including modulation, coding, streaming, and beamforming. Whatever the Data Link layer desires to send, the

8

PHY must perform these methods or a subset of them to make the actual communications happen.

Modulation is the process of imposing bits on the transmission medium. With wireless, the medium is RF waves. Therefore, something about the RF wave must be changed or manipulated to represent bit changes. The property that is manipulated is amplitude and/or phase in the common modulation methods used within 802.11.

 Modulation is the process of imposing bits on a transmission medium, such as RF. Something about the medium is manipulated to represent bit values in the transmission.

The *phase* of an RF wave is a comparison between that wave and another wave. If the phase is the same, they are said to be *in phase*. If the phase is different, they are some degree *out of phase*. To modulate bits, for example, the phase can be shifted by 180 degrees to indicate a change in bit value. The phase shift can occur within a time window the receiver is expecting. If a shift does not occur, the receiver can assume that, for the next time window, the bit value stays the same. This example is a simple one, but it illustrates how phase can be used for modulation. Figure 1.3 illustrates the concept of phase shift keying (PSK), which was described.

The amplitude of an RF wave is the strength of the wave. An increase in amplitude means the strength or power of the wave has increased. An increase in amplitude is also called gain within a transmission path. A decrease in amplitude indicates that the strength or power of the wave has decreased. A decrease in amplitude is also called loss within a transmission path.

Amplitude can be used to modulate bits by increasing or decreasing the amplitude at the transmitter by some amount. For example, if the amplitude increases by some percent, this can represent a change from a 0 to a 1. If the amplitude is then decreased to the original value, this can represent a change from a 1 to a 0. If in the time window observed no change in amplitude occurs, the bit can be assumed to remain the same as the previous value. This description of modulation is an example of amplitude shift keying (ASK). ASK is illustrated in Figure 1.4. In both Figures 1.3 and 1.4, note that the shifts occur in Time Window 3 and Time Window 4.

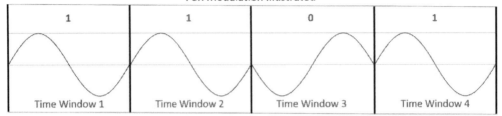

Figure 1.3: Phase Shift Keying (PSK) Modulation

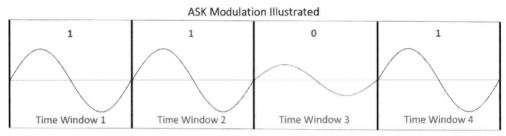

Figure 1.4: Amplitude Shift Keying (ASK) Modulation

Both PSK and ASK are used in 802.11 modulation methods, though not exactly as described in the preceding text. Even with higher–data-rate modulation methods, PSK and ASK are still used. Quadrature Amplitude Modulation (QAM) uses both ASK and PSK together. A very important concept to remember is this: higher-data-rate transmissions require more complex modulation methods and increased signal quality for proper demodulation. This concept is the reason data rates decrease as the signal quality decreases and increase up to the maximum data rate supported in the link as the signal quality increases. You'll find additional information about modulation will be covered in Chapter 3.

Coding, or encoding, is the process of scrambling the bits in some way before transmission. The bits sent are not the same as the meaningful bits intended to be received at the MAC layer. Instead, they are encoded bits to provide resiliency in communications. Coding is used before modulation in RF transmissions and decoding is used after demodulation in RF receptions. Because the process of transmitting the desired bits involves both modulation and coding every time, the phrase *Modulation and*

10

Coding Scheme (MCS) is used to define a particular transmission method that is a combination of both.

To understand how coding works, consider a simple example. This example is not identical to the coding implemented in 802.11 but it helps to understand the concept. In this example coding scheme, a 1 is represented by the bits 01010101 and a 0 is represented by the bits 10101010. Therefore, the coding scheme is a 1/8 ratio, where every desired bit to be transmitted requires 8 bits of actual transmitted bits.

That's an extreme example, but you can see that if the coding rate is at a ratio where many more bits are used to send the data than the actual data length, the ultimate data rate will be decreased. For example, if 5 transmitted bits are sent to accomplish the transmission of 3 desired bits, the data rate will be lower than it would be if 5 transmitted bits are sent to accomplish the transmission of 4 desired bits. Therefore, to accomplish higher data rates, more complex modulation methods and higher ratios of desired bits to transmitted bits must be achieved. In the 802.11 standard, these combinations of coding and modulation methods are defined in MCS tables.

MCS tables were first introduced with the 802.11n (HT) amendment to the standard. Before 802.11n, the available data rates were fewer in number and did not require such a structure. With the release of 802.11n and the PHY amendments after it, MCS tables make it easier to understand the many different data rates available. Figure 1.5 shows the MCS table from the 802.11ac (VHT) PHY for a single spatial stream transmission at 20 MHz, and Figure 1.6 shows the MCS table for two spatial streams in a 20 MHz transmission.

The following should help you decipher the MCS tables as they are presented in Figure 1.5, Figure 1.6, and the 802.11 standard:

- R – The coding rate used.
- N – Placeholder for the word number. For example, N_{SP} represents the number of spatial streams.
- BPSCS –Bits per single carrier
- SD – Complex data numbers per spatial stream per symbol.
- SP – Pilot values per symbol.
- CBPS – Code bits per symbol.
- DBPS – Data bits per symbol.

- ES – Binary Convolutional Code (BCC) (a type of coding) encoders for the data field.
- GI – Guard interval.
- ns - nanoseconds

From Figures 1.5 and 1.6 you can see that the data rates vary based on the modulation and coding scheme within a specific bandwidth and number of spatial streams. The modulation acronyms listed in the tables represent the following:

- BPSK (Binary Phase Shift Keying): Modulation that uses two phase shifts.
- QPSK (Quadrature Phase Shift Keying): Modulation that uses four phase shifts.
- QAM (Quadrature Amplitude Modulation): Modulation that uses phase shifts and amplitude shifts.

BPSK uses two phase shifts to represent 1 or 0. QPSK uses four phase shifts to represent 00, 01, 10, and 11. For this reason, when the coding rate is the same, QPSK effectively doubles the data rate of BPSK. Note in Figure 1.6 that BPSK with a 1/2 coding rate results in 13 Mbps and that QPSK with the same coding rate results in 26 Mbps. As previously mentioned, when you improve the coding rate, the data rate improves. Note that QPSK with the better coding rate of 3/4 provides 39 Mbps, which is 50 percent more than that provided by QPSK with the 1/2 coding rate.

VHT-MCS Index	Modulation	R	N_{BPSCS}	N_{SD}	N_{SP}	N_{CBPS}	N_{DBPS}	N_{ES}	Data rate (Mb/s)	
									800 ns GI	400 ns GI (See NOTE)
0	BPSK	1/2	1	52	4	52	26	1	6.5	7.2
1	QPSK	1/2	2	52	4	104	52	1	13.0	14.4
2	QPSK	3/4	2	52	4	104	78	1	19.5	21.7
3	16-QAM	1/2	4	52	4	208	104	1	26.0	28.9
4	16-QAM	3/4	4	52	4	208	156	1	39.0	43.3
5	64-QAM	2/3	6	52	4	312	208	1	52.0	57.8
6	64-QAM	3/4	6	52	4	312	234	1	58.5	65.0
7	64-QAM	5/6	6	52	4	312	260	1	65.0	72.2
8	256-QAM	3/4	8	52	4	416	312	1	78.0	86.7
9	Not valid									
NOTE—Support of 400 ns GI is optional on transmit and receive.										

Figure 1.5: MCS Table: 1 spatial stream 20 MHz bandwidth

VHT-MCS Index	Modulation	R	N_{BPSCS}	N_{SD}	N_{SP}	N_{CBPS}	N_{DBPS}	N_{ES}	Data rate (Mb/s)	
									800 ns GI	400 ns GI
0	BPSK	1/2	1	52	4	104	52	1	13.0	14.4
1	QPSK	1/2	2	52	4	208	104	1	26.0	28.9
2	QPSK	3/4	2	52	4	208	156	1	39.0	43.3
3	16-QAM	1/2	4	52	4	416	208	1	52.0	57.8
4	16-QAM	3/4	4	52	4	416	312	1	78.0	86.7
5	64-QAM	2/3	6	52	4	624	416	1	104.0	115.6
6	64-QAM	3/4	6	52	4	624	468	1	117.0	130.0
7	64-QAM	5/6	6	52	4	624	520	1	130.0	144.4
8	256-QAM	3/4	8	52	4	832	624	1	156.0	173.3
9	Not valid									

Figure 1.6: MCS Table: 2 spatial streams 20 MHz bandwidth

Spatial streams also impact the data rate. Figure 1.5 shows data rates for a single spatial stream and Figure 1.6 shows data rates for two spatial streams. Most clients implement either one or two spatial streams today, with a few implementing three spatial streams. As 802.11ax devices come to market, four stream laptops will be seen, but tablets and phones will mostly continue to use one or two spatial streams to conserve battery life. The key item of note is that doubling the spatial streams doubles the data rate if the frequency bandwidth (20 MHz in the figures) remains the same.

Beamforming was introduced with 802.11n and continues to be supported in 802.11ac and 802.11ax. Beamforming uses antennas and waveform phases strategically to increase the signal strength of the received signal. Higher data rates require better signal quality. Therefore, beamforming is yet another method used to impact data rates. To understand this, you should recall the concept of dynamic rate switching (DRS) from the CWNA materials.

DRS changes the data rate based on the ability of the remote device to receive transmissions and other potential factors considered in the wireless chipset, such as the signal strength of the frames received from the remote device. For example, a device transmitting at 144 Mbps that fails to receive acknowledgements for some number of transmitted frames may switch down to 130 Mbps on the next transmission to that same STA. DRS is dynamic in relation to the environment, but it is not dynamic in relation to the data rates it selects. The data rates are fixed for each PHY operating within a specific bandwidth and with a set number of spatial streams. Stated differently, a STA will never drop from 144 Mbps to 143 Mbps. It will always drop to the next or another of the predetermined data rates available in the MCS tables for the specific PHY.

It is essential to understand that actual throughput will be far less than the data rate of a link. Figure 1.7 illustrates this reality. Each STA will use a data rate for communications based on the link quality (signal strength versus noise, known as the signal-to-noise ratio (SNR)). However, the STA can only communicate when air time is available. Management overhead (including co-channel interference (CCI)), non-Wi-Fi interference, and other STAs communicating all reduce the available airtime. Therefore, throughput within the link will be far less than the data rate of the link even if throughput is measured at the MAC layer instead of the Transport Layer, where throughput is typically measured.

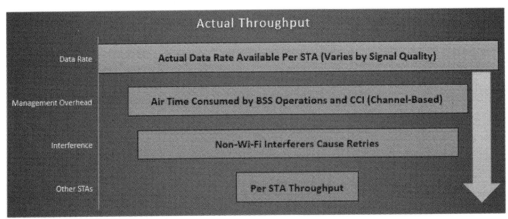

Figure 1.7: Actual Throughput versus Data Rates

802.11 Physical Layers

Today's 802.11 is very different from the one ratified in 1997, which we now call 802.11-Prime. Nine PHYs have been specified since that time. This section provides a brief review of the PHYs still potentially in production environments today. Frequency Hopping Spread Spectrum (FHSS) is not addressed in this section. It was available in 802.11-Prime but was not the PHY that was adopted the most in early 802.11 network installations, so you are very unlikely to see it live in an environment today.

802.11-Prime

The oldest PHY still supported by modern 802.11 devices is *Direct Sequence Spread Spectrum (DSSS)*, and it was included in the first ratified 802.11-Prime standard. DSSS uses a channel 22 MHz wide and operates only in the 2.4 GHz band. Each channel is assigned based on a channel center frequency, such as 2.412 GHz for channel 1, and uses 11 MHz on either side of the center frequency. Therefore, channel 1 would use the range from 2.401 to 2.423 for the 22 MHz channel and channel 6 would use 2.437 as the center frequency and range from 2.426 to 2.448.

Like all PHYs introduced before 802.11n (HT), DSSS supports only one spatial stream. It is a SISO (single-input/single-output) PHY. The transceiver (transmitter/receiver) sends one stream of data or receives one stream of data at a time. 802.11n and 802.11ac, as well as future PHYs, support multiple streams for transmission and reception using MIMO (multiple-input/multiple-output), greatly increasing the available data rates.

Remembering the supported data rates for DSSS is simple. Only two data rates are supported: 1 Mbps or 2 Mbps. By today's standards, this PHY is very slow. However, the DSSS PHY is supported by all 802.11 devices that operate in the 2.4 GHz band, including the newest 802.11n , 802.11ac, and 802.11ax devices. It is important to remember that the PHY preamble and headers will be transmitted at these low data rates regardless of the data rate at which actual Layer 2 frame data is transmitted—even in PHYs capable of a higher data rate within the 2.4 GHz band unless a G-only or N-only mode is implemented, and this mode is effectively disabled on Orthogonal Frequency Division Multiplexing (OFDM) data rates (the rates of 1 and 2 Mbps for DSSS and 5.5 and 11 Mbps for HR/DSSS (discussed in the next section)).

In summary, the DSSS PHY supports data rates of 1 or 2 Mbps. It operates in the 2.4 GHz band and supports only a single spatial stream. All DSSS transmissions use a 22 MHz channel width.

802.11b

The *High Rate/Direct Sequence Spread Spectrum (HR/DSSS)* PHY was released with the 802.11b amendment in 1999. It introduced more advanced modulation techniques, allowing for data rates of 5.5 and 11 Mbps while still supporting the DSSS data rates of 1 and 2 Mbps. HR/DSSS uses the same 22 MHz wide channels as DSSS and supports only a single spatial stream. Like DSSS, HR/DSSS operates only in the 2.4 GHz frequency band.

All newer PHYs operating in the 2.4 GHz frequency band are designed to be backward-compatible with earlier PHYs in the same band. An HR/DSSS device can communicate with a device that supports only DSSS. Additionally, an HT PHY device can communicate with a DSSS PHY device if they both operate in the same 2.4 GHz frequency band and the network configuration allows for it. We'll explore the details of the HT PHY shortly.

 WLAN administrators may disable backward compatibility by disallowing lower data rates. However, that is a configuration constraint and not a radio or device constraint. With all data rates enabled, newer 2.4 GHz 802.11 devices can communicate with all older devices.

It is unlikely you will see actual 802.11b (HR/DSSS) or 802.11-Prime (DSSS) devices in most production WLANs (though, in some rare cases, they do still appear); however, this does not mean the PHY will not be used. If you allow the low data rates and a better AP is not available to which the client can roam (for example, an AP with a stronger signal), the client could fall back to these data rates depending on the client chipset and software. Instead, however, with proper configuration, the worst-case scenario for an HT (802.11n) device in 2.4 GHz should be MCS 0, assuming no 802.11b/g devices are in use, which operates at 6.5 Mbps (as a single-stream 20 MHz communication), 13 Mbps (as a two-stream 20 MHz communication), or 19.5 Mbps (as a three-stream 20 MHz communication) as the lowest data rates. These rates can be raised even higher when enabling the short Guard Interval (GI).

 Even though 802.11n (HT) supports 40 MHz channels in 2.4 GHz, they should never be used. The available frequency space in 2.4 GHz is not sufficient for the use of 40 MHz channels.

802.11a

The *Orthogonal Frequency Division Multiplexing (OFDM)* PHY was the first to support 5 GHz band operations. This PHY was made available through the 802.11a amendment in 1999. In addition to 5 GHz band support, OFDM was the first to use 20 MHz channels instead of 22 MHz channels. All modern PHYs that are based on OFDM use 20 MHz channels or some factor thereof. For example, they may use 20 MHz or 40 MHz channels (as well as 80 and 160 MHz). 802.11a was the first PHY amendment to use OFDM modulation and the PHY is named after the modulation. All PHYs introduced since 802.11a also use OFDM modulation but have a different PHY name to clearly differentiate them from 802.11a OFDM.

OFDM still uses one spatial stream, but with enhanced modulation, it supports data rates of 6, 9, 12, 18, 24, 36, 48 and 54 Mbps. Notice that it does not support 1, 2, 5.5 or 11 Mbps. OFDM operates in 5 GHz and has no need to be backward-compatible with DSSS or HR/DSSS.

802.11g

The *Extended Rate PHY (ERP) (802.11g)* was introduced in June of 2003 to bring the OFDM modulation down into the 2.4 GHz band. The ERP PHY uses the same OFDM modulation used in 802.11a 5 GHz devices and uses 20 MHz channels but operates in the 2.4 GHz band. There are some slight differences in the way the PHY was implemented, but it is enough to know that it provides the same basic functionality that OFDM provided in 5 GHz.

Operating in 2.4 GHz, all ERP devices (which are also called 802.11g devices based on the amendment that defined ERP) support backward compatibility with HR/DSSS and DSSS PHY devices. This fact is another difference from the OFDM PHY in 5 GHz. The OFDM PHY required no backward compatibility, as it was the first PHY introduced in 5 GHz. To accomplish backward compatibility, ERP (802.11g) devices still support the DSSS data rates of 1 and 2 Mbps and the HR/DSSS data rates of 5.5 and 11 Mbps. In addition, they support the same data rates as OFDM (802.11a) of 6, 9, 12, 18, 24, 36, 48, and 54 Mbps. To be clear, the ERP PHY supports only the data rates of 6, 9, 12, 18, 24, 36, 48, and 54 Mbps, but all devices implementing the ERP PHY also effectively implement the DSSS and HR/DSSS PHYs so that the 1, 2, 5.5 and 11 Mbps data rates are also supported.

802.11n

The *High Throughput (HT)* PHY was introduced in the 802.11n amendment in October of 2009 and offers several advantages over older PHYs. HT provides wider channels by combining two 20 MHz sections into a 40 MHz channel. Thus, it provides either 20 MHz or 40 MHz channels. An AP offering a 40 MHz channel can still service 20 MHz clients on its primary channel. The second 20 MHz section is known as the secondary channel.

The primary channel will be one of the defined channel numbers, such as 1, 6, 11, 36, or 44. Then the secondary channel, which provides the total of 40 MHz, will be the 20 MHz range above or below the primary channel. When using the 20 MHz above the primary channel, it is referenced as a +1 configuration. When using the 20 MHz below the primary channel, it is references as a -1 configuration. When a device connects to an AP offering a 40 MHz channel and the connecting device supports only a 20 MHz channel, it will communicate with the AP using the primary channel. The 40 MHz client devices can use the entire 40 MHz channel. Remember, do not use 40 MHz channels in 2.4 GHz, because the available frequency bandwidth is insufficient to support multiple BSSs on different channels with 40 MHz widths.

Wider channels result in higher data rates even with no additional features. However, the HT PHY also introduced the capability to use multiple spatial streams through *Multiple Input/Multiple Output (MIMO)*. MIMO takes advantage of RF propagation behaviors to send multiple concurrent streams of data from the transmitter to the receiver. The HT PHY supports up to four spatial streams; however, most devices support from one to three spatial streams when using the HT PHY today.

Another first for the HT PHY was the fact that it operates in either 2.4 GHz or 5 GHz. More channels are available in the 5 GHz band, so it is the preferred band, but many devices operate only in 2.4 GHz (even some of the newest devices being sold), so it must continue to be supported in nearly all implementations. It is important to know that HT devices may be 2.4 GHz-only, so as a WLAN administrator, you should select equipment with great care. It is best to select devices that support the 5 GHz bands whenever possible.

Finally, the HT PHY offers many more data rate possibilities than earlier PHYs. The actual data rates available will depend on the channel width (20 MHz versus 40 MHz), the number of spatial streams, and the modulation and coding used. Some additional factors impact the available data rates, such as the GI. The maximum data rate achievable with the HT PHY, assuming a 40 MHz channel and the highest modulation and coding rate, is 600 Mbps. Most HT or 802.11n devices support maximum data rates of 150, 300, or 450 Mbps because the devices support from one to three spatial streams, but the standard allows for up to 600 Mbps.

It is beneficial to know that 2.4 GHz devices will support maximum data rates of 72.2, 144.4, and 216.7 Mbps (sometimes these numbers are rounded to 72, 144, and 217 Mbps) because they will only support 20 MHz channel widths in a proper implementation. While the 2.4 GHz devices could be configured to support the higher data rates offered by 40 MHz channels, they should not be. When using 40 MHz 2.4 GHz channels in a multi-AP deployment, the degradation in performance due to channel overlap is not worth the gains offered by 40 MHz channels. If you haven't noticed yet, CWNP is opposed to the deployment of 40 MHz channels in 2.4 GHz enterprise deployments. However, in 5 GHz standard deployments, 40 MHz channels can be beneficial, depending on the type of network being deployed.

802.11ac

The *Very High Throughput (VHT)* PHY, introduced 2013, moves 802.11 networks even further than the HT PHY. The VHT PHY now supports additional channel widths of 80 MHz and 160 MHz (though 160 MHz channels should not be used in enterprise deployments, and 80 MHz channels should rarely be used). The base channel width is still 20 MHz, but two, four, or eight 20 MHz portions may be used to form the wider channels.

With the wider channels comes higher data rates, but VHT (802.11ac) also adds support for more spatial streams. A VHT device can use up to eight spatial streams. The first devices that were released supported three spatial streams, but devices are now on the market supporting four spatial streams. Whether we will see eight spatial streams is yet to be seen, simply because the general trend in client devices is to stay with fewer spatial streams, which reduces battery consumption and therefore extends battery life.

It is very important to know that the VHT PHY works only in the 5 GHz frequency band. There is no support for VHT in 2.4 GHz, unlike the HT PHY. The primary reason for this decision to limit VHT to the 5 GHz band was simply the lack of frequency space for wider channels in 2.4 GHz. Some vendors indicate that they have implemented 256-QAM (a new modulation introduced with VHT) in the 2.4 GHz band. They typically allow this because the chipset they use supports it. However, given that this is not according to the standard, you cannot assume that client devices will also support it. You should not plan on gaining the advantages of 256-QAM in 2.4 GHz even if the APs implemented allow for it.

Finally, VHT devices can achieve a maximum data rate of 6933.3 Mbps; however, this data rate would require eight spatial streams. Because 802.11ac devices implement no more than four spatial streams today, the real-world peak data rate is 3466.7 Mbps. To achieve this data rate, the AP and client must both support four spatial streams and use a 160 MHz channel. Given the reality that few 802.11ac APs, properly deployed, will be implemented with channels configured with a bandwidth of more than 40 MHz, it is more likely that you will see maximum data rates of 800 Mbps for four spatial streams on a 40 MHz channel.

 The term *chipset* refers to the radio and filters that provide 802.11 communications. The chipset is typically installed on a printed circuit board (PCB) that includes antenna connectors or onboard antennas. Drivers interface with the chipset to communicate on the WLAN or allow for protocol analysis using the features of the chipset.

Always remember that the data rate available for a link is constrained by the less capable device in the link. For example, if an AP is configured with a 40 MHz channel and supports four spatial streams, a four–spatial-stream client supporting a 40 MHz channel could potentially connect with a data rate of 800 Mbps (according to the standard). However, a single-stream 40 MHz client will connect to the same AP with a maximum data rate of 200 Mbps. As you can see, the real world is often very different from marketing literature and even from the potential of the 802.11 standard.

802.11ax

The *High Efficiency Wireless (HEW)* PHY is defined in 802.11ax, which is in draft at the time of this writing but is mature enough to know the major features that will be in the ratified amendment. This section provides an overview of these features.

Orthogonal Frequency Division Multiple Access (OFDMA) is a new modulation introduced to the 802.11 standard with the 802.11ax amendment. OFDMA has been used in other networks and brings useful new features to the 802.11 WLAN. The most exciting feature is what you might call sub-channelization. It is the ability to divide the channel into multiple resource units (sub-channels) that can be used to transmit or receive to or from multiple STAs concurrently. All previous modulations used the entire channel to communicate between STAs. This behavior was even true for multi-user MIMO (MU-MIMO). Figure 1.8 illustrates the difference between OFDM and OFDMA. The image represents frames sent from an AP to four different STAs. With OFDM and no MU-MIMO, each frame must be sent in succession. With OFDMA, a portion of the frequency bandwidth can be assigned to each STA and all four frames can be sent concurrently. It will take more airtime (at the same data rate) to send all four frames concurrently (given that less bandwidth is used for each frame), but it will take far less time than sending each frame at full bandwidth in succession.

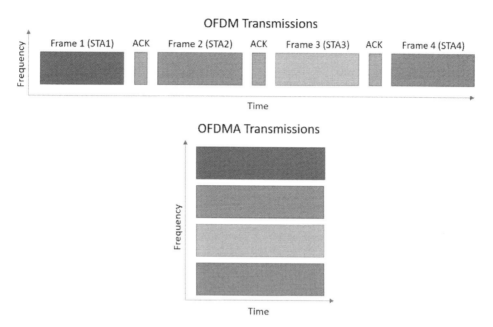

Figure 1.8: OFDM Compared with OFDMA

1024-QAM is also introduced with 802.11ax. 802.11ac supported 256-QAM, and this higher modulation rate increases the number of bits that can be represented in a symbol, effectively increasing the data rate. However, it will require excellent signal-to-noise ratio to function and will only work within short distances. Figure 1.9 shows the constellations for 256-QAM and 1024-QAM. You can see why a better signal is required as the modulation rates go higher. The target becomes smaller and smaller and the receiver must be able to process the received signal in a low noise environment to perceive the appropriate target.

A *constellation* is used to show the targets for a modulation method. Higher modulation rates have more targets in the constellation and lower error allowances because each target is closer to another. The target represents a waveform based on phase and amplitude.

Uplink MU-MIMO is added to the standard with 802.11ax as well. 802.11ac introduced downlink-only MU-MIMO, which was not very advantageous in production networks. Time will tell what impact uplink MU-MIMO will have, but it is available as of the 802.11ax amendment.

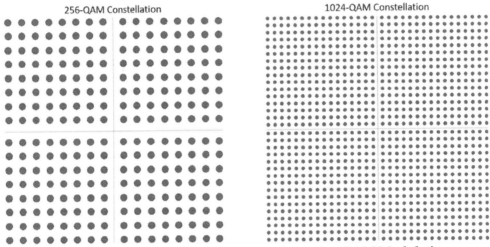

Figure 1.9: Constellations for 802.11ac and 802.11ax QAM Modulations

Target Wake Time (TWT) is a new power save scheduling ability for 802.11ax, OFDMA-only STAs. The clients request a sleep schedule from the AP, and they can then wake when required based on the schedule; this way, they don't have to wake at predefined intervals individually assigned to each STA. TWT was first introduced in 802.11ah but is more likely to see wide use with the ratification of 802.11ax.

 Some have mistakenly referenced TWT as target wait time, but the standard defines it as target wake time. Given that it defines the duration the STA can wait before waking, one can see where the confusion enters.

To allow it to acknowledge communications of varied signal strengths, 802.11ax implements BSS coloring. Each BSS is assigned a color (identifying bits in the PHY layer communications), and BSS transmissions matching the current STA's BSS color are considered active transmissions at a weaker signal level than those that do not match the current STA's BSS color. Clearly stated, when a signal is received with the same BSS color as the receiving STA, a lower signal strength threshold is used to defer to the signal and remain silent. When a signal is received with a different BSS color than the receiving STA, a higher signal strength threshold is used to defer to the signal and remain silent. For example, the matching BSS color threshold could be -90 dBm and the non-matching BSS color threshold could be -75 dBm. The actual signal thresholds may be configurable in enterprise systems, and the exact method used at higher layers to process this data is not defined in the 802.11 standard but is instead left to the vendors to control.

Finally, 802.11ax operates in both the 2.4 GHz and 5 GHz frequency bands, unlike 802.11ac, which was 5 GHz-only. This dual-band allowance brings the efficiency gains of 802.11ax into the 2.4 GHz band, which is very congested and will eventually benefit from these gains. The benefit will be eventual because the clients and APs must support 802.11ax to achieve any of the benefits referenced in this section. At the time of writing, very few draft-based 802.11ax devices were available. By the year 2020 or 2021, we will begin to see more benefit from the new features of 802.11ax.

802.11ad

The *Directional Multi-Gigabit (DMG)* PHY is seeing some traction in consumer wireless routers and client devices. For example, at the time of writing, a few vendors have released laptops supporting the DMG PHY, which was ratified in 802.11ad. This PHY operates in the 60 GHz frequency band and is a high data rate, low range specification. It specifies three modulation methods:

- Control modulation

- Single Carrier (SC) modulation

- OFDM modulation (this mode is defined as obsolete and may be removed in a later version of the standard)

The DMG PHY supports the range 57–64 GHz worldwide and 57–66 GHz in Europe. The specific areas supported within these ranges varies by regulator domain.

802.11af

The *Television High Throughput (TVHT)* PHY is not tested on the CWAP exam, because of the limited hardware available for deployment at this stage. This PHY is designed to take advantage of unused frequencies in the bands often used for television and other broadcasts. Because it is designed to use such spaces, it supports very narrow channel widths of 6, 7, or 8 MHz depending on the regulatory domain in which it operates. Additionally, the channel widths of 6, 7, or 8 MHz (called Basic Channel Units BCUs) can operate as 1, 2, or 4 BCUs. Therefore, with two 7 MHz BCUs, the total frequency space available for the transmissions would be 14 MHz.

The maximum data rate supported, with the use of four 8 MHz BCUs (32 MHz of frequency space), is 568.9 Mbps. This data rate is accomplished with four spatial streams. Like 802.11n devices, TVHT devices can use from one to four spatial streams.

Finally, TVHT operates in the frequency range from 50 MHz to 790 MHz and uses frequency space as allocated by the operating regulatory domain.

802.11ah

The *Sub-1 GHz (S1G)* PHY was designed with long range, low data rate communications in mind and is defined in the 802.11ah amendment. It is ideal for Internet of Things (IoT) and industrial automation and monitoring networks. The S1G PHY operates on 1, 2, 4, 8, or 16 MHz channels, and it appears likely that more devices will use the 1, 2, and 4 MHz channels as the likely use cases do not warrant the higher data rates.

The maximum data rate supported no the S1G PHY is 346.6667 Mbps. This rate is based on a 16 MHz channel and four spatial streams. Given the desire for extended battery life and little need for high data rates, as devices are released supporting the S1G PHY, we are likely to see many single stream devices. Such devices, operating on a likely maximum of 4 or 8 MHz channels, will achieve a maximum data rate of 8666.7 Kbps for a 2 MHz single stream device or 20,000 Kbps (20 Mbps) for a 4 MHz single stream device.

The actual frequencies used will vary greatly by regulatory domain, but will all be lower than 1 GHz. Some will operate in the 700 MHz range, others in the 900 MHz range, and still others in between.

 Much more detail about the 802.11 PHYs is available in later chapters of this book. This section was intended to provide a review of CWNA materials and introduce several new or more advanced concepts than those tested on the CWNA exam.

Basics of Network Frames—Data Link (MAC) Layer

Network frames operate at Layer 2 of the OSI model. They are used to provide for communications within a LAN based, most typically, on Medium Access Control (MAC) addresses. IEEE 802.11 networks are no different. As a wireless analysis professional, you should understand the basics of frames, before moving on to explore the details of 802.11 frames, which are covered later in this book. These basics include the concepts of encapsulation and frame aggregation.

Encapsulation

As data moves down through the OSI model it is encapsulated for delivery. Each layer of the OSI model can be conceptualized as communicating with the peer layer in the target STA. For example, the Network Layer communicates with the Network Layer and the Data Link Layer communicates with the Data Link Layer. Each layer depends on the layer beneath it to provide the communications. For example, an IP packet destined to 192.168.1.12 from 192.168.1.13 depends on the Data Link Layer for MAC address-based communications even if the to IP addresses are on the same subnet. The Data Link Layer encapsulates the Network Layer IP packet by prepending frame header information and appending a Frame Check Sequence (FCS) for error detection in the transmission.

 Encapsulation is the process of enclosing upper-layer information into the current layer's delivery format. For example, IP packets encapsulate TCP datagrams or messages and 802.11 frames encapsulate IP packets.

Within Layers 1 and 2, the service data units (SDUs) go by specific names, which you should be familiar with: The MAC Service Data Unit (MSDU) and MAC Protocol Data Unit (MPDU) exist at Layer 2 (specifically, in the MAC sublayer of the Data Link Layer). The PLCP Service Data Unit (PSDU) and PLCP Protocol Data Unit (PPDU) exist at Layer 1 (specifically, in the PLCP sublayer of the Physical Layer).

The terms service data unit (SDU) and protocol data unit (PDU) come directly from the OSI reference model document, ISO-IEC 7498-1, corrected edition June 16, 1996. This document defines the SDU and PDU as follows:

- **Service Data Unit (SDU):** an amount of information whose identity is preserved when transferred between peer-(N+1)-entities (*layer peers*) and which is not interpreted by the supporting (N)-entities (*lower layers*).

- **Protocol Data Unit (PDU):** a unit of data specified in an (N)-protocol and consisting of (N)-protocol-control-information and possible (N)-user-data.

In these definitions, (N) is a placeholder for a layer. For example, if you were considering the Network Layer, where IP operates, the PDU definition would be, "a unit of data specified in a Network Layer protocol (IP) and consisting of IP control information and possible IP user data (IP packets)."

Beginning with this definition, it is easier to understand the SDUs and PDUs in the context of 802.11 communications. All OSI model layers have SDUs and PDUs. Sublayers, such as the MAC sublayer of the Data Link Layer, can also have SDUs and PDUs. The MSDU and MPDU are indeed the SDU and PDU of the MAC sublayer for 802.11. The LSDU and LPDU, which are the LLC sublayer SDU and PDU, are defined in the 802.2 standard and are used whenever the LLC is used with any 802 specifications.

Figure 1.10 shows the location of the SDUs and PDUs in 802.11 implementations. The MSDU and MPDU reside at Layer 2. The MSDU contains the information provided to the MAC sublayer from above that requires service by the MAC sublayer; hence the name *service data unit*. After the MAC sublayer has prepended the frame header information and appended an FCS (remember, encapsulation), it is an MPDU. The MPDU is sent to the PHY Layer, specifically the PLCP sublayer, and is considered the PSDU by the PLCP. To be clear, the PSDU is the MPDU from the perspective of the PHY. The PLCP sublayer appends the appropriate PHY Layer header information and sends it to the PMD for transmission as a PPDU.

PPDUs are sent on the RF medium and they contain MPDUs in every case. However, MPDUs do not always contain upper-layer information. For example, a Beacon frame is sent out, by default, approximately every 102.4 milliseconds (ms) on the wireless medium. This Beacon frame contains no upper layer payload data. It is a Layer 2 frame that originates from the AP and provides information about the Basic Service Set (BSS) offered by the AP. In this case, the MPDU is transmitted inside of a PPDU, but the MPDU itself contains, for example, no IP packet information.

In summary, it is accurate to say that an MPDU can contain an MSDU and a PPDU contains a PSDU. The MSDU is encapsulated by the MAC sublayer to become an MPDU and the PSDU is encapsulated by the PLCP sublayer to become a PPDU.

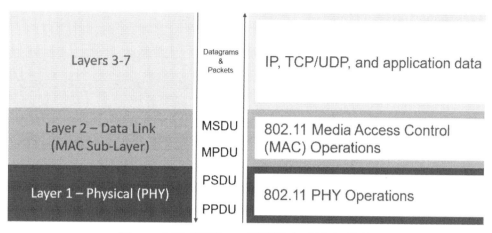

Figure 1.10: SDUs and PDUs in 802.11 STAs

Frame Aggregation

In addition to the concept of encapsulation, the wireless analysis professional should know that 802.11 frames can be aggregated. Frame aggregation was introduced in 802.11n (HT) and continues to be supported in newer PHYs such as 802.11ac (VHT) and 802.11ax (HEW).

Frame aggregation is the process of combining multiple MSDUs or MPDUs into a single PPDU transmission. Two types of aggregation exist: Aggregated-MSDU (A-MSDU) and Aggregated-MPDU (A-MPDU).

An A-MSDU combines multiple MSDUs into a single MPDU. For example, multiple UDP datagrams encapsulated into IP packets can be assembled into an A-MSDU. The A-MSDU ends up containing multiple IP packets, and they are all passed down to the PHY layer as a single A-MSDU-based MPDU. Figure 1.11 illustrates the concept of an A-MSDU. A-MSDU is potentially supported by 802.11n PHYs, where it was first introduced, as well as later PHYs.

When A-MSDU is used, one MAC header is created for all of the MSDUs in the A-MSDU. This structure saves on frame overhead because one MAC header is all that is required. Given that a MAC header can be 40 bytes in size, combining just two MSDUs together saves 40 bytes of transmission time; three MSDUs would save 80 bytes, and so forth. Of course, 40 bytes of MAC overhead assumes that the optional Address 4 field in the frame is used (you will learn more about the frame formats in later chapters). If this field is not used, the MAC header is still 36 bytes in size and the A-MSDU format can provide improved efficiency.

The A-MSDU is built by combining multiple MSDUs, called A-MSDU subframes, into a single MPDU. A-MSDU subframes have a minimal header that is 14 bytes long including a destination address field (6 bytes), a source address field (6 bytes), and a length field (2 bytes). The size constraints imposed on an A-MSDU vary depending on the PHY. For example, the maximum size of an A-MSDU in 802.11n is 7,935 bytes. The limit in 802.11ac is 11,454 bytes.

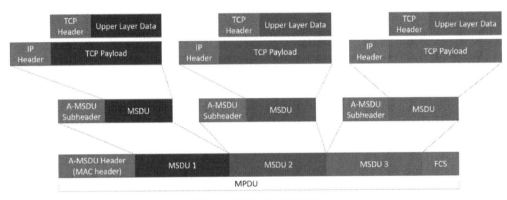

Figure 1.11: A-MSDU

802.11ac made a significant change in that all frames transmitted via the 802.11ac (VHT) PHY were required to be A-MPDU frames regardless of the number of MPDUs or MSDUs in the frame. The difference between A-MSDU and A-MPDU is that A-MPDU combines one or more MPDUs together in a single transmission, but each MPDU has a full MAC header. An MPDU delimiter is placed between each MPDU in the A-MPDU as well. The MSDUs combined into an A-MPDU can be either traditional MSDUs or A-MSDUs. Figure 1.12 illustrates the A-MPDU model.

The maximum size of an A-MPDU in 802.11n is approximately 64 kB (65,535 bytes/octets). The maximum size in 802.11ac is approximately 1 MB (1,048,575 bytes/octets). In some APs, this maximum size can be adjusted. The wireless engineer may choose to change the maximum size to optimize a BSS or channel. For example, if a channel is occupied by many VoIP phones, and several 802.11ac computer clients communicate with large A-MPDUs, it could result in decreased voice performance because of the lengthy air time consumption of the clients sending large A-MPDUs. Reducing the maximum size could provide optimization in such networks.

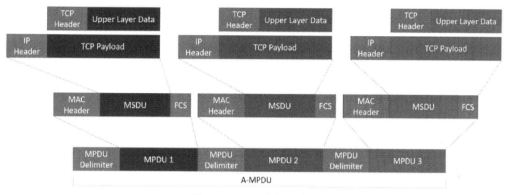

Figure 1.12: A-MPDU

For 802.11n APs, the supported values are these:

- 8,191 bytes
- 16,383 bytes
- 32,767 bytes
- 65,535 bytes

For 802.11ac APs, the supported values are these:

- All 802.11n values
- 131,071 bytes
- 262,143 bytes
- 524,287 bytes
- 1,048,575 bytes

 All MPDUs in a given A-MPDU must be addressed to the same receiver. This allows STAs receiving the A-MPDU to look at the MAC header of the first MPDU in the A-MPDU and determine if the transmission is targeted for them or another STA.

Services Provided by 802.11 Devices

802.11 devices are defined as providing services that allow for communications at Layer 1 and Layer 2. These services are the station service (SS) and the distribution system service (DSS).

The SS is a set of services that support transport of MSDUs between STAs within a BSS. The SS is in all STAs, including APs, mesh gates, portals and clients. The services provided by the SS include these:

- Authentication
- Deauthentication
- Data confidentiality (encryption)
- MSDU delivery
- Dynamic Frequency Selection (DFS)
- Transmit Power Control (TPC)
- Timer synchronization with higher layers (Quality of Service (QoS) facility only)
- QoS traffic scheduling (QoS facility only)
- Radio measurement
- Dynamic STA enablement (DSE)

The DSS is the set of services provided by the distribution system (DS) for communications between APs, mesh gates, and the portal of an extended service set (ESS). The DS is the system or network through which the STAs with the DSS (APs) interconnect or, more specifically, through which the BSSs interconnect. The DS Medium (DSM) is the medium used by the DS, for example Ethernet cables, RF mesh, and so on.

The services provided by the DSS include:

- Association
- Disassociation
- Distribution
- Integration
- Reassociation
- QoS traffic scheduling (QoS facility only)
- DSE
- Interworking with the DS (in a mesh)

Keep in mind that when a controller-based architecture is used, some of these DSS services may reside in the controller instead of the AP. Because many controller-based architectures use a split-MAC model, portions of the DSS are in the controller and portions are in the AP.

Figure 1.13 reproduces Figure 4-14 from the 802.11-2016 standard and illustrates the concepts of the SS, DSS, and DS. Note that STA 1-6 all have the SS, but not all have the DSS. However, STA 2 and STA 3 are APs and, therefore, have both the SS and DSS. Note the cloud-like DS that interconnects BSS 1 and BSS 2 to form an ESS.

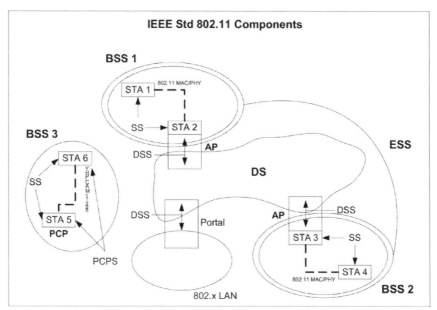

Figure 1.13: The 802.11 Services Illustrated.

Control, Management, and Data Planes

The control plane, management plane, and data plane are conceptual planes that include different types of communications. The control plane is about network control protocols like routing protocols and switching protocols, along with WLAN solutions like radio resource management (RRM) and automated radio management (ARM). The management plane is focused on managing the devices and monitoring them, such as WLAN configuration and monitoring. The data plan is focused on user data transfer.

31

Consider RRM as an example and how it relates to the different planes. In the control plane, RRM operates. In the management plane, RRM is configured. In the user plane, data is sent on a WLAN that uses RRM for radio configuration management.

As another example, in the control plane, APs are controlled by a controller through some protocol such as Lightweight Access Point Protocol (LWAPP) or Control and Provisioning of Wireless Access Points (CAPWAP). They are configured in the management plane through the controller interface. Users utilize these APs to transfer data.

Dividing the network into control, management, and data planes helps to understand how the network works and how it is managed and operated.

Troubleshooting Methods

The networking industry has developed troubleshooting methodologies (processes and tools) to assist the wired and wireless analyst with problem resolution. When you understand these methodologies, you can better troubleshoot a problem and ensure that the proper steps have been taken as you work toward resolution. This section reviews the processes recommended by a few vendors and discusses industry methods commonly used as well as the CWAP exam objectives-based troubleshooting method.

Industry Troubleshooting Methods

We will review industry troubleshooting methods first. During this review, you will see that most vendors recommend similar processes. While these processes are generic to all networking, including wireless, they provide beneficial guidance to the wireless analyst. The industry troubleshooting methods referenced here are for your information, but they are not tested on the CWAP exam.

The Cisco Troubleshooting Process

Cisco defines a specific troubleshooting model at `cwnp.link/ciscots`. This basic model is their recommended troubleshooting process and can be applied to wired and wireless problems. In this book, the focus is primarily on wireless troubleshooting, but some wired troubleshooting must be introduced as well because the wireless network depends heavily on services that are typically provided by the wired network.

The Cisco troubleshooting process is as follows:

1.   Define a clear problem statement with symptoms and potential causes.

2. Gather the facts to help isolate the possible causes.
3. Consider possible problems based on the facts discovered.
4. Create an action plan based on the remaining potential problems and the most likely cause.
5. Implement the action plan.
6. As changes are made, gather results.
7. Analyze the results and determine whether the problem has been resolved.
8. If the problem is not resolved, create a new action plan based on the next most likely cause and proceed with steps 5–8. Repeat until resolved or escalated.

Each of these steps is considered in detail in the pages that follow. For our purposes, a common WLAN problem will be analyzed. The scenario is common, though simple: a user connects to the WLAN, but receives a message indicating that the connection is limited. The user cannot browse the Internet or even access local network resources. Using the Cisco process, we will analyze this connection problem.

1. Define a clear problem statement with symptoms and potential causes.
The first step is to define a clear problem statement. A problem statement should plainly state the problem experienced by the user and any related symptoms that would be helpful in the troubleshooting process. This problem statement will become the foundation for the troubleshooting process. Without it, the wrong problem may be solved, or the problem may be incompletely solved. The problem statement is essential— even if it exists only in the analyst's mind.

Many organizations have documentation systems in which analysts are expected to document problem statements such as the ones discussed here. If such a system does not exist, the analyst must still go through this thinking process to ensure that she is addressing the appropriate problem. Users will often use phrases to describe a problem that the analyst can easily misinterpret. The problem statement, when created using steps 1–3 of Cisco's process, can help to remove any misunderstandings between the user and the support analyst.

At step one of this process for the scenario in question, the following problem statement (repeated in part from above) will suffice:

> A user connects to the WLAN, but receives a message indicating that the connection is limited. The user cannot browse the Internet or even access local

network resources. This may be caused by a misconfiguration or a network problem.

2. Gather the facts to help isolate the possible causes.
Now that you have a problem statement, you can further clarify the details and improve on the statement. This step involves the use of open-ended questions and possibly some verification procedures.

Open-ended questions are those that cannot properly be answered with a yes or no response. For example, most questions that begin with *are, was, were, is, will, do, can,* and *may* are answered with a yes or no response. However, most questions that begin with *who, when, where, why, how,* and *what* cannot be answered with just a yes or no response. In general, open-ended questions solicit more useful information from the user. Here are some example fact-gathering questions for the scenario in question:

- When did the problem begin?
- What changes have been made to the system recently, if any?
- What are you trying to do that is failing?
- How are you trying to do it?

Consider the following four answers to the preceding questions, in the same order the questions are listed:

- It started happening yesterday afternoon.
- I haven't made any, but Fred worked on my computer yesterday.
- Access my email and two Internet Web sites.
- I use Outlook for email, and I was using Chrome as the Web browser.

An additional important question to ask in all such scenarios is a yes or no question: Are any other users experiencing the problem? We will assume, in this scenario, that no other users on the same subnet are experiencing the problem.

In addition to questioning the user, the analyst should attempt to replicate the problem at the user's computer if possible. In a scenario like this, going through the steps the user would normally take allows the analyst to verify the process and to view any error messages or notifications that may appear. In this scenario, when the analyst repeats the process, the notification in Figure 1.14 is displayed.

This page can't be displayed

- Make sure the web address https://www.google.com is correct.
- Look for the page with your search engine.
- Refresh the page in a few minutes.

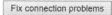

Figure 1.14: Internet Browser Error

Additionally, when the analyst attempts to access other Web sites, the same error is displayed. An exclamation mark is also shown periodically on the wireless client icon in the Notification Tray of Windows as shown in Figure 1.15.

Figure 1.15: Network Notification Icon with Error

3.- Consider possible problems based on the facts discovered.
After gathering the facts, the analyst can then list likely causes of the problem. With a list of potential causes, the analyst can prioritize them in order of most likely and work through them to resolve the problem. The list will come from experience, vendor literature (FAQs, troubleshooting guides, support videos, and so on), internal documentation of past problems, and information shared by peers. For the given scenario, the following list includes common causes of such problems:

- Supplicant misconfiguration
- Improper static IP settings
- DHCP pool depletion
- DHCP server unreachable
- Improper DHCP pool settings
- DNS server failure or misconfiguration

Based on experience and other sources of information, the analyst may determine the following as the most likely order of causality:

1. DHCP server unreachable
2. Improper static IP settings
3. Supplicant misconfiguration
4. DNS server failure or misconfiguration
5. DHCP pool depletion
6. Improper DHCP pool settings

Finally, with the list generated, you can consider the facts gathered more closely to see if any can be eliminated. For example, it is not likely to be a DHCP pool settings problem, as other users on the subnet have functioning connections. This fact also rules out DNS server failure or misconfiguration, as well as most scenarios that would result in the DHCP server being unreachable (due to router failure or DHCP server failure). These further considerations result in the following prioritized list:

1. Improper static IP settings
2. Supplicant misconfiguration
3. DHCP pool depletion

4. Create an action plan based on the remaining potential problems and the most likely cause. With a refined and prioritized list, the analyst is ready to create an action plan for the most likely cause. In this case, the most likely cause is improper static IP settings (which may not be the most likely cause in all environments). The plan of action may look something like this (assuming that DHCP should be in use instead of static IP configuration):

1. Check the IP settings on the client adapter to verify appropriate settings.
2. If configured for static IP settings, change the configuration to use DHCP.
3. Save the changes.
4. Verify network connectivity.

The action plan, as illustrated in the preceding four steps, is simply the list of actions you will take to resolve the issue if the problem had the candidate root cause. In some cases, an action plan will be more complex and involve many more steps. In such scenarios, documenting the action plan becomes more important because you can more easily reverse the steps if they do not resolve the problem. In production environments, standard configurations are often used. If a device has been configured differently than the standard, it may indicate the need for user education. The user needs to understand the ramifications of making unauthorized changes. Additionally, configurations may be locked down so that changes cannot be made without an administrative password.

5. Implement the action plan.

Now that the action plan is documented, or at least fully developed in your mind, you can implement it. This step involves performing the actions in sequence to verify a theoretical cause.

6. As changes are made, gather results.

As the action plan's steps are taken, results must be gathered. For example, when changing from static to DHCP configuration, did the Internet connectivity begin working? Did the device receive an IP configuration set correctly from the DHCP server?

7. Analyze the results and determine whether the problem has been resolved.

After completing the steps in the action plan, the analysis must verify that all problems are resolved. For example, in this scenario, are both Web sites and the email application working? If the Web sites are working, but the email application is not, it could indicate that the IP configuration is only part of the overall problem. It may also reveal that additional changes were made, such as the email server settings, which prevent the email application from working properly.

8. If the problem is not resolved, create a new action plan based on the next most likely cause and proceed with steps 5–7. Repeat until resolved or escalated.

If the problem was resolved, in step 7, the analyst should document the problem and solution in detail and close the trouble ticket, if such a support system is in use. If the problem is not resolved, the next most likely cause should be considered, and an action plan created. In this scenario, it was determined that the next most likely cause was supplicant misconfiguration. The supplication settings could be verified, and if the problem is still not resolved, the third most likely cause should be considered, and so on.

In the end, this process will lead to either a solution or escalation. If you have exhausted all possible software and configuration settings about a given problem, a hardware failure could be related. In some organizations, the wireless analyst would not be responsible for hardware failures and the problem would be escalated to the hardware group. Now, let us move from Cisco's process to Microsoft's.

The Microsoft Troubleshooting Process

Microsoft's recommended troubleshooting process is at `cwnp.link/mstshoot`. The process is divided into five phases as follows:

- **Phase 1:** Discovery—Gather information about the problem.
- **Phase 2:** Planning—Create a plan of action.
- **Phase 3:** Problem Reproduction—Reproduce the problem or determine that you cannot reproduce it. If you cannot reproduce the problem, then you might not have enough information to confirm that there is a problem.
- **Phase 4:** Problem Isolation—Isolate the variables that relate directly to the problem.
- **Phase 5:** Analysis—Analyze your findings to determine the cause of the problem.

The Microsoft methodology will not be explored in as much detail as the Cisco methodology was. This decision does not mean one process is better than the other, but both are represented here simply to expose you to variances in vendor methodologies. For example, notice that the Cisco methodology suggests creating an action plan after listing likely causes. The Microsoft methodology suggests creating the action plan before problem reproduction and isolation. However, when the Microsoft methodology is studied in more detail (at the URL provided previously), defining possible causes is part of Phase 1.

Additionally, the Microsoft methodology is very focused on finding solutions to problems that occur on a larger scale. For example, if you have deployed 10,000 computers running Windows 10 and find that 1,500 of them are having the same problem, it is very beneficial to reproduce the problem and ensure that the reproduced problem is consistently caused by the same collection of settings and actions. With such assurance, the analyst can then come up with a plan to repair all 1,500 problem clients and trust that the plan will work even on such a large scale. For this reason, the Microsoft methodology places greater emphasis on reproduction of the problem (though the Cisco methodology could include this) and not on creating a list of likely causes.

CompTIA Methodologies

The A+ objectives (220-902) list the following steps for a troubleshooting methodology:

1. Identify the problem.
2. Establish a theory of probable cause (question the obvious).
3. Test the theory to determine cause.

4. Establish a plan of action to resolve the problem and implement the solution.
5. Verify full system functionality, and if applicable implement preventive measures.
6. Document findings, actions, and outcomes.

As you can see, the A+ recommended methodology is very similar to the Cisco and Microsoft methodology, with some areas of additional action. The extra recommendation to "implement preventive measures" is an excellent idea, which is an often-overlooked step that leads to a much more stable environment when executed. It is important to have a standard configuration and to also ensure that the standard configuration evolves as needed. Many troubleshooting methodologies overlook this action.

The Network+ objectives (N10-005) list the following steps for a troubleshooting methodology:

1. Identify the problem.
2. Establish a theory of probable cause.
3. Test the theory to determine cause.
4. Establish a plan of action to resolve the problem and identify potential effects.
5. Implement the solution or escalate as necessary.
6. Verify full system functionality, and if applicable implement preventive measures.
7. Document findings, actions, and outcomes.

The Network+ methodology includes the process of escalation. This is, in part, because A+ is mostly focused on single-machine troubleshooting and Network+ is focused on troubleshooting parts of a system. Network troubleshooting is more complex in many cases as you must consider local systems, devices along the route of communication, and the end systems involved in the transaction.

 The preceding methodologies were covered to expose you to general troubleshooting concepts. You will be tested against the CWAP-403 objectives related to troubleshooting methods covered in the following section and not against the above-mentioned methodologies specifically. However, where the above methodologies include similar steps, the concepts still apply.

CWAP-403 Objectives and Troubleshooting

The CWAP exam objectives list the following troubleshooting actions:

- Define the Problem
- Determine the Scale of the Problem
- Identify Probable Causes
- Capture and Analyze the Data
- Observe the Problem
- Choose Appropriate Remediation Steps
- Document the Problem and Resolution

All these actions are documented in the following sections. The focus will be on an example problem that is more complex than that covered in the preceding Cisco troubleshooting methodology section. The problem reported is as follows:

> *After a recent upgrade of the Windows 10 operating system, several dozen laptop computers are now experiencing connection problems. The computers are all the same model, which includes a two-stream 802.11ac chipset. Before the upgrade, all the systems worked as expected. Now, the systems are periodically losing their connection to the WLAN and must be rebooted before they can reconnect.*

Using this scenario, you will explore the CWAP objectives-based troubleshooting actions.

Define the Problem

In the scenario provided, the problem is well-defined. However, it is not uncommon to begin with an overly simplified statement like, "the laptops keep losing their connection." In such cases, you must gather more information. Have configuration changes occurred on the laptops? In this case, you know that they were recently upgraded. However, it is important to determine what the upgrade entailed. Was it a complete operating system upgrade from one version of Windows to another or was it an upgrade within the existing version? Did the upgrade modify the networking subsystem in any way? Were specific changes made to the wireless supplicant or drivers within the operating system? Answering these questions helps to more clearly define the problem.

Given that the problem is periodic in nature and that rebooting the client with no changes to the APs or infrastructure allows for reconnection on a consistent basis, it is not likely an AP or infrastructure issue. Additionally, the fact that the laptops were all recently upgraded to a new version of Windows 10 or at least applied some updates to the operating system, it already indicates a likely problem on the client. The next step is to determine the scale, which will help further narrow the eventual list of likely causes.

Observe the Problem

It is often helpful to observe the problem as it happens. In this case, you can use one of the laptops in question to see what occurs when the connection is lost. Furthermore, you can verify that a reboot is required to reconnect. While user reports are helpful in troubleshooting problem scenarios, it does not replace the value gained form observing the problem.

Additionally, the problem can be observed, when it is related to wireless communications, by capturing the frame exchanges and analyzing them to verify proper operation and potential problems. Therefore, observing the problem is something that may occur immediately after or within the step of defining the problem and it may occur after capturing data that can be analyzed.

Determine the Scale of the Problem

The scale of the problem indicates how widespread the issue is on the network. For example, is it impacting a single user, a subnet, a BSS, a mobility domain, an entire campus, or the entire network at large?

In the scenario provided, the scale seems to be all the laptops of a given model that have been upgraded. However, this fact is not specifically stated in the original problem statement. The next step, therefore, is to verify this scale. Is the problem occurring on all laptops of this model that have been upgraded? Is it only occurring with some laptops of this model that have been upgraded? If it is occurring with all laptops of the specified model, it is practically certain that something changed during the upgrade that caused the problem. If it is occurring with only some laptops of this model, and others of the same model have also been upgraded without the problem, more investigation will be required. What is different on the laptops experiencing the problem from those not experiencing the problem?

For the purposes of this scenario, assume that all laptops of the specified model that have been upgraded are experiencing the same problem. With the problem defined and the scale of the problem explored, you can identify probable causes.

Determining the scale of the problem is one of the most important steps in troubleshooting network problems. Knowledge of the problem scale allows you to diagnose the problem properly and find a resolution.

Identify Probable Causes

The ability to identify probability grows as knowledge and experience increase. Knowledge of how Wi-Fi works and of how the devices and operating systems work will help the analyst to identify probable causes. Experience improves the analyst's predictions as to the most likely causes.

Two factors indicate a few probable causes in the scenario defined:

- The problem is occurring on all laptops of a specific model.
- All the problem laptops have been upgraded recently.

These two factors indicate a problem with the Windows 10 upgrade on those specific laptops. While this reality may have seemed obvious from the clear original problem statement, such problems do not always begin with such clarity. Defining the problem and the scale of the problem leads to this clarity in such cases.

Based on these factors, you may determine that the probable causes are:

- Faulty drivers installed during the upgrade.
- Bugs in the new Windows wireless drivers.
- Implementation of an 802.11 feature that is incompatible with the infrastructure.

If you determine that faulty drivers are the most likely cause, you can begin capturing and analyzing data related to this. But among these three probable causes, you should identify the most likely, second most likely, and, given that there are only three, third most likely. Then you can capture and analyze data related to the issue.

Capture and Analyze the Data

With the problem clearly defined through investigation and observation, the analyst may need to capture data for analysis. At least three data sources may be used in the capture process:

- Frame captures from the wireless networks
- Spectrum captures from the RF domain

- System captures including system logs, debug logs, trace logs and error reports

Frame captures require the use of a protocol analyzer or an infrastructure-based capture solution. 802.11 frames may be captured using a computer-based protocol analyzer with the appropriate adapter. This capture method is useful when you want to capture near the client experiencing the problem or anywhere other than the AP location. The frames can also be captured with infrastructure-based solutions, which may be integrated or overlay. An integrated solution captures the frames within the APs or controllers and provides a view of the frame exchanges from the perspective of the APs. An overlay solution captures based on the location of the sensors. Neither integrated nor overlay infrastructure solutions provide you with a localized view of the frame exchanges for each client device. As you can see, both infrastructure-based and computer-based capture are beneficial.

Spectrum capture requires the use of a spectrum analyzer. Like protocol analysis, spectrum analysis may be performed using a computer-based analyzer or infrastructure (integrated or overlay) solutions. The same issues with infrastructure-based spectrum analysis exist as with infrastructure-based protocol analysis—it does not show you the spectrum activity as seen at specific locations, but only at available locations based on the sensors or APs used for spectrum capture. Many organizations provide both to their analysts, and both are beneficial.

System captures allow you to capture logs of events occurring or having occurred in a system. System logs can be used to view past events, such as driver upgrades or errors that have occurred. Debug or trace logs, which must typically be enabled as they consume system resources when running, can show more details about specific events such as Wi-Fi activities like connections and wireless subsystem errors. In the scenario provided here, the system captures are likely to reveal more useful information than either protocol (frame) or spectrum captures.

After you locate the appropriate data, it must be analyzed to identify the source of the problem. Investigate protocol captures to identify behaviors on the WLAN. Investigate spectrum captures to locate potential sources of interference. Investigate system logs to identify specific error messages or logged changes to the system. In this scenario, you evaluate the System Event Logs in Windows 10 and see that an update was installed related to the networking layer of Windows. After researching online, you determine that several other organizations are experiencing problems with this update. You determine that the most likely cause of the problem is a bug in the new Windows wireless drivers. You are now ready to select an appropriate remediation plan.

Choose Appropriate Remediation Steps

After the most likely cause is determined, you can select a remediation plan. The plan will vary based on the assumed cause. Remediation actions are many and varied with WLAN problems, but there are eleven common solutions:

- Modify drivers: install newer drivers or install older drivers.
- Update AP firmware.
- Reconfigure client devices.
- Reconfigure APs.
- Extend or replace the DHCP pool.
- Remove or work around interference sources.
- Upgrade older client devices.
- Replace faulty cabling.
- Evaluate and repair design problems.
- Report the problem to the appropriate vendor.
- Turn on the wireless adapter in the client device.

While this list may seem obvious at times, it is surprising how often the problem is resolved with one of these actions and, yet, how often troubleshooters fail to act on them. This list is not intended to be a top ten list. It is merely an experiential list of common problems on WLANs. Many times, the problem is not a wireless problem at all, and such issues may require escalation to the wired networking group if the wireless administrators lack proper access.

In the scenario presented, the most likely remediation actions would be to modify drivers or report the problem to the appropriate vendor, in this case working with Microsoft to identify the problem caused by the update.

Document the Problem and Resolution

The final step in any quality troubleshooting methodology is documentation. Many organizations use a database system called a trouble ticket tracking system or something similar. The problem, actions taken, resolution, and principles should be documented. A principle (or lesson learned) is a more general concept that may apply to other situations. For example, while simple, the fact that an upgrade can cause connection problems is a general principle. The specific kind of problem caused (cannot connect, slow performance, and so on) is a unique case of the general principle.

Chapter Summary

In this chapter, you reviewed 802.11 operations including the MAC and PHY layers. You explored troubleshooting methodologies and looked specifically at the CWAP objectives troubleshooting actions. In the next chapter, you will begin exploring the details of the 802.11 MAC layer.

Facts to Remember

The following facts are important to remember from Chapter 1:

- 802.11 defines operations at the MAC sublayer of the Data Link Layer and the Physical Layer.
- The MSDU is received by the MAC sublayer and encapsulated into an 802.11 frame as an MPDU.
- PPDUs are transmitted onto the RF medium. They contain one or more MPDUs.
- 802.11 networks use both PSK and ASK modulation techniques.
- Higher modulation rates require better signals—higher SNR.
- The throughput for WLAN clients is always less than the connection data rate because of management overhead and other communicating STAs on the shared RF medium.
- 802.11ax adds the OFDMA modulation to the 802.11 family of PHYs and it increases the highest modulation rate to 1024-QAM.
- 802.11ad operates at 60 GHz and 802.11ah operates below 1 GHz.
- To increase efficiency, all 802.11ac frames are transmitted as A-MPDUs even when the frame includes only one MPDU.
- Remember that you must clearly define the problem and the scope of the problem before you can effectively identify probable causes.

Review Questions

1. What is the unit name received at the MAC sublayer of the Data Link Layer?

    a. MSDU

    b. MPDU

    c. PSDU

    d. PPDU

2. Which one of the following is a sublayer of the 802.11 PHYs?

    a. MAC

    b. LLC

    c. PMD

    d. UDP

3. Which kind of modulation is not used by 802.11 devices today?

    a. PSK

    b. FSK

    c. ASK

    d. OFDM

4. What modulation method uses both ASK and PSK?

    a. BPSK

    b. QAM

    c. QPSK

    d. DSSS

5. In addition to the coding rate, modulation and number of spatial streams, what impacts the data rate?

    a. Use of A-MPDU

    b. TCP segment size

    c. IP payload size

    d. Channel bandwidth

6. What common modulation method is used in all 802.11 PHYs starting with 802.11n and later?
   a. DSSS
   b. HR/DSSS
   c. ERP
   d. OFDM

7. In addition to OFDMA, what is introduced in 802.11ax?
   a. Target Wake Time
   b. Dynamic Rate Switching
   c. Short Guard Interval
   d. Aggregated MPDU

8. What is the generic term for a unit received by a layer from the layers above it for processing in the OSI Reference Model?
   a. PDU
   b. SDU
   c. Segment
   d. Packet

9. What is a constraint of an A-MPDU assembly?
   a. All MPDUs must be targeted to the same TCP port on the same machine.
   b. All MPDUs must be targeted to the same IP port on the same machine.
   c. All MPDUs must be targeted to the same 802.11 STA.
   d. All MPDUs must be part of the same application stream.

10. What action is taken after defining the problem, determining the scale of the problem, and identifying probable causes?
    a. Capture and analyze the data
    b. Document the problem and resolution
    c. Choose appropriate remediation steps
    d. Escalate the problem

Review Answers

1. The correct answer is A. The MAC Service Data Unit (MSDU) is received by the MAC sublayer and processed into an 802.11 frame called an MPDU before being passed to the PHY.

2. The correct answer is C. The 802.11 PHYs are divided into the Physical Layer Convergence Protocol (PLCP) and the Physical Medium Dependent (PMD). The PLCP is responsible for creating and processing PLCP headers and the PMD is responsible for transmitting and receiving bits onto and from the RF medium.

3. The correct answer is B. Frequency Shift Keying (FSK) is not used in 802.11 devices. Both Phase Shift Keying (PSK) and Amplitude Shift Keying (ASK) are used in Quadrature Amplitude Modulation (QAM) modulation methods.

4. The correct answer is B. Quadrature Amplitude Modulation (QAM) uses both phase shifts and amplitude shifts for modulation. It is used by all OFDM PHYs and by OFDMA in 802.11ax.

5. The correct answer is D. Of the listed items, only the channel bandwidth impacts the data rate. The other items may impact the throughput accomplished at a given data rate, but they do not alter the data rate.

6. The correct answer is F. OFDM modulation is used by 802.11n, 802.11ac, 802.11ad, 802.11ah, and 802.11af. It will also be available in 802.11ax as well as OFDMA. OFDM was also used with 802.11a and it is also the name of that PHY. DSSS, HR/DSSS and ERP are used in 802.11, 802.11b and 802.11g respectively.

7. The correct answer is A. TWT is a new power save scheduling ability in 802.11ax for OFDMA communications. DRS has always been in 802.11. A-MPDU was introduced with 802.11n as was the short GI.

8. The correct answer is B. Each layer receives service data units (SDUs) from the layer above it. After processing at the current layer, the SDU becomes a PDU.

9. The correct answer is C. All MPDUs in an A-MPDU must be targeted to the same 802.11 STA or receiver. They are not required to be part of the same stream or destined to the same IP or TCP port on that machine.

10. The correct answer is A. After identifying the probable causes, you should capture and analyze the data to validate the problem or observe the problem.

Chapter 2: Protocol Analysis

Objectives Covered:

1.1   Capture 802.11 frames using the appropriate methods and locations

1.2   Analyze 802.11 frame captures to discover problems and find solutions

1.3   Understand and apply common capture configuration parameters available in protocol analysis tools

1.4   Utilize additional tools that capture 802.11 frames for the purposes of analysis and troubleshooting

Although they share many things conceptually, the wireless 802.11 protocols have enough differences from the wired 802.3 protocols to require additional tools for diagnostics and an additional skillset to implement them and understand how they are being used. Network administrators have used various tools to analyze traffic on wired networks and mistakenly believe 802.11 protocol analysis to be the same. They quickly learn that starting from the contention methods used to the capture methods used for complex diagnosis of wireless communication issues such as roaming, 802.11 protocol analysis is quite different.

Remember that 802.11 communications occur at the Physical and Data Link layers of the OSI model. Layers 3 and higher are merely encapsulated by wireless transmissions and are diagnosed on the wired network when encryption and 802.1X authentication are in use on the WLAN. 802.11 based networks have vastly different architectures, methods of transmission, modes of operation, packet formats, sources of interference, and vulnerabilities than those found in wired communications. This difference is due, in no small part, to the use of a shared unbounded medium, the RF, versus the use of an unshared bounded medium of cables in 802.3 networks. A new skillset is required to be learned when making the transition from wired to wireless analysis. The skillset includes an understanding of the protocols, frame types, header information and the tools used to capture and analyze the traffic. Knowing what should be happening and being able to compare that knowledge with a capture of what is really happening will assist you in network verification and troubleshooting. Gathering information about what is happening in your service set area at Layer 2 can require specialized hardware and software. Within this chapter you will begin to learn about the analysis of 802.11 communications.

Capturing 802.11 Frames

As stated above, 802.11 communications, although similar, are not the same as 802.3 communications. There is no management port on a switch to which you can connect and simply capture every frame being sent onto the medium. Wireless traffic is not segmented by using a switch. It is segmented by using a different frequency, more commonly called a channel. The transmissions are in the air and not contained within a known set of cables, switches and routers.

To capture wireless transmissions, you must have protocol analysis software and a wireless network adapter that works with the software. The wireless adapter must be in monitor mode. Monitor mode means that the wireless adapter has been configured to capture traffic that is destined for any MAC address and not just its own. This is accomplished by using the required driver that works not only with the adapter but also with your protocol analysis software.

 Know that promiscuous mode and monitor mode are not the same thing. Promiscuous mode allows you to capture all frames on a network to which you're connected. Monitor mode allows you to capture all frames from all networks in the channel without having a network connection.

You can also use existing APs as part of infrastructure protocol analysis, if supported. Another method is to use a distributed and dedicated group of sensors, APs or purpose-built radios configured for protocol analysis only. See Figure 2.1 for a look at some of the various capture options. Additionally, you, or your capturing radios, must be within hearing range of the signals you wish to capture, since the air has no management port to use like that found on a switch.

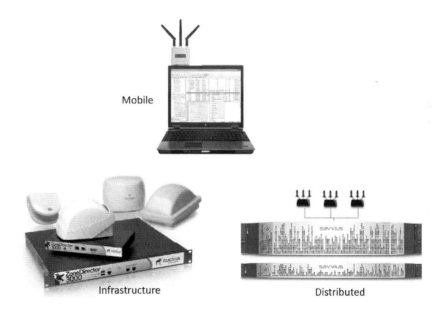

Figure 2.1: Various protocol capture options

Within this section, you will learn about capturing wireless frames using the appropriate methods and locations. We will discuss:

- Installing monitor mode drivers
- Selecting the appropriate capture device(s)
- Selecting the appropriate capture location(s)
- Capturing for an appropriate amount of time based on the problem scenario
- Scanning channels versus capturing on a single channel
- Capturing in roaming scenarios
- Capturing with portable protocol analyzers (laptops)
- Capturing with APs, controllers, and other management solutions
- Capturing with specialty devices such as handheld analyzers

Installing Monitor Mode Drivers

Wireless adapters, just like wired adapters, each have their own MAC addresses. When listening for traffic that is destined for them, they examine the TO address found in the headers of all detected frames. If the address matches the adapter address, the adapter realizes that the frame is intended for its use. It passes the frame up to the next Layer for continued processing. The same thing happens on a wired network at Layer 2.

In wireless communications, if the adapter reads the TO address and it does not match its own, it will not begin to process the frame but will set its Network Allocation Vector (NAV) value and use the value to set its backoff timer, a time in which the adapter will assume the medium is busy and will not attempt to contend for the medium until this counter reaches zero. This is part of the collision avoidance method used by 802.11 communications and is perfectly fine, if all your doing is using the network. However, if you need to analyze the traffic, this is of no assistance.

By using drivers that will work with the adapter and the protocol analysis software, you can place the adapter in monitor mode. This means that the adapter will be able to gather all detected frames and pass them up to the protocol analysis software. Not all adapters will work with every protocol analysis application. Software vendors publish a list of supported adapters that they have certified to work with their software as shown in Figure 2.2. If you are going to be using more than one protocol analysis tool, it is a good idea to have dedicated cards for each one you use. Each analysis application will have its own driver requirements. If you are using the same card with multiple protocol analysis software products, you will need to install the driver for the adapter every time you change tools. Repeatedly changing the driver can cause hardware failure. It is easier to simply buy the required cards and label them by the appropriate analysis software.

Model	Band	Driver
Savvius WiFi Adapter for Omnipeek (3-stream, 802.11n) *	a/b/g/n (3-stream 11n)	MediaTek v5.1.12.48 (32 and 64-bit drivers)
Savvius WiFi Adapter for Omnipeek (2-stream, 802.11ac) *	a/b/g/n/ac (2-stream 11n/11ac)	MediaTek v5.1.12.48 (32 and 64-bit drivers)

Figure 2.2: Adapter and driver requirements Savvius Omnipeek

Protocol analysis begins with determining what will be the right hardware and software to use. Several choices exist. However, they are all combinations of the same three basic things:

1. The operating system you are using
2. The protocol analysis software and drivers
3. The required hardware

It is simple to start with the operating system you will be using if you already have a laptop. Some tools only work on Windows based platforms. If you like these tools and already have a Windows laptop, you are ready to select the adapters. Other tools work on Mac and some others on Linux. Some work on multiple platforms, provided you install the matching version of the software. The same holds true for these. If you have them and like the software that will run on them, you are ready to select the adapters.

Additionally, The MAC OS X operating system can perform protocol captures natively, using the integrated adapter. The OS and hardware choices made vary by preference and budget. Native analysis software may or may not be able to give you all you need. The important things to remember here are that you need to make sure that the software you want to use will work with the OS you choose, and the adapters chosen must work with both the software and OS. Rely on the software vendors published supported OS and hardware list when making your selections.

Once you have your choices in hand, you will need to install the software and required drivers. Some software packages will want to tie the license to an adapter or system board during installation. If this is the case, many vendors will allow you to use a removable adapter for licensing. They will also allow you to use the license across many laptops, if the adapter to which the license is attached is connected to the laptop being used. This allows you to send just the adapter to others for use versus having a dedicated laptop to share.

Most licensed analysis software will check for licensing at startup. Having the license attached to an adapter allows the software to be used by many administrators but only by one at a time. This works well if you only need one person at a time doing the work. If more than one person may need to conduct protocol analysis at the same time, simply buy more licenses and adapters. During installation, you will be asked for your key, as with most software. You will also find that the software looks for supported adapters. If one is not present, you will get an error message. This may halt installation until a supported device is detected. You may also be able to install without a supported adapter and be prompted to insert one when you launch the software. Simply stated, for mobile captures, remember to make sure your adapters are supported by the OS and your capturing software.

If you are going to be using an infrastructure or distributed method of capture for your protocol analysis, there is usually some firmware and or licensing involved. Some versions require you to install an application on the computer you are using for analysis. Others allow you to access the protocol analysis tools using a browser. You may encounter some of the same compatibility issues here as when using mobile analysis software. Ensure that your OS is supported and, if using a browser to access the tools, that it is supported and using the correct version.

For the infrastructure method, you will need to ensure that the access points you are using for protocol analysis support this function. Not every AP model will support the same functions. In addition to ensuring the AP models used support this, you will also need to ensure that all these APs are running the correct version of firmware to enable the functions to work. You will also need to make sure that you have the proper licenses installed on your controller or WNMS to allow you to use the functions.

Another concern is Java. Some older tools only worked with a specific version of Java. If you update Java to work with other applications, the protocol analysis tool may no longer work without rolling back the Java version. Most modern tools, mobile or other, usually work without any trouble in a browser or a self-contained application without the need for Java runtimes.

Many issues occur because you are using adapters, browsers and operating systems in ways they were not initially intended to be used. To avoid any issues, follow the manufacturers requirements when installing and using any protocol analyzer.

Selecting the Appropriate Capture Device

As stated above, you will need to either be in the same location as the traffic you need to capture while conducting mobile protocol analysis or use infrastructure devices, APs, to do your capturing in the required areas or have a distributed protocol analysis solution. The adapters and APs used today are generally dual band. So, it is an easier choice to make so far as the hardware is concerned. However, you must remember that the adapters or APs you use must also support the protocols you wish to analyze.

For example, an 802.11n radio can detect an 802.11ac signal but will not be able to decode all of the traffic. If you are supporting newer APs and stations, you will need a newer radio for the analysis of your traffic. Newer radios can analyze older transmissions, due to backwards compatibility, but older radios are not able to analyze newer radio transmissions.

The MIMO support matters too. When selecting a radio for your captures, you must ensure that the adapters you select support the same number of spatial streams and the PHY/MAC layers you wish to capture or better. You will not be able to diagnose problems faced by 3X3:3 radios using a 1X1:1 radio. If your capturing radios do not have the ability to decode the number of spatial streams used by the radios transmitting the frames you are capturing, you may be able to capture some information (such as beacon frames), but not the detailed information needed for analysis.

Beyond the frequencies, protocols and spatial streams supported, the method of capture will dictate the type of device or devices you use. If you have the need to monitor your airspace constantly, a distributed solution or infrastructure solution would be the best choice. If you need to monitor only when a problem is suspected, the infrastructure or the mobile method will work well for you. The method of capture and the required device(s) you select will be based upon your needs, time and budget.

Often a combination of methods is used across an enterprise. When using a distributed method, if you need to examine traffic, simply log into the system and navigate to the desired sensor's captures. When using an infrastructure method, it is a similar process. However, you should be aware that using an APs radios strictly for protocol analysis will disrupt the service an AP is providing to the clients in that service set area. Some infrastructure solutions allow you to time slice between AP and protocol analysis functions. This disrupts clients to a lesser degree but misses many transmissions you may need in your analysis.

 It is often assumed that infrastructure capture solutions are best because they are built into the APs and controllers or management software. However, infrastructure captures do not see what the client sees, and they have the additional problem of taking the AP radio offline for protocol capture so that they cannot service clients. A tri-band AP with a software configurable radio as the extra radio may work well to resolve the client service issue.

Selecting a mobile method of capture will require someone with the analysis software running on the required hardware and OS to be in the physical area where the traffic you are trying to capture is being transmitted. This may be perfectly fine within the building in which you work but can be extra travel when the wireless traffic is in another facility. In situations like this, it is not uncommon to see a hybrid capture method used, a small sampling taken via an infrastructure or distributed method followed by an onsite visit by an IT staff member for a mobile capture and customer discussions. There are advantages and disadvantages to each solution. The solution that is chosen as best can vary by location, budget or preference.

Selecting the Appropriate Capture Location

Obviously, you will need to capture the desired traffic within hearing range. However, you can optimize your capture by selecting better locations from which to conduct your captures. You may want to capture near the clients that are having problems or producing suspect behavior. This can mean that you capture right next to the devices or users, if allowed in the area. Some areas may require clearance and or an escort, just like when you conduct physical surveys. Some areas require special safety gear be worn if you are to enter that space. Being close to the client devices that are having trouble will expose your tools to the same problems to which the client device is exposed. This can help you determine if the problem is being caused at Layer 1 or Layer 2 faster than gathering your information from a location closer to the AP.

If several clients are having troubles, you may want to capture from an area close to the AP in addition to capturing near clients. By capturing in both locations, near clients and near the AP, you may be able to find a solution faster than capturing from only one location.

The type of problems being reported should guide you in selecting your capture locations. If only one station is having trouble, capture near it. If several clients are reporting issues, you should capture near the AP and near some if not all the clients until you find the source of the problem.

Often the first capture you perform will yield the answers you seek. If not, you need to capture from other locations and or for longer time periods. Persistent problems are more quickly diagnosed than intermittent ones. You be able to use multiple locations and methods of capture, when available, until the problem is diagnosed.

Most interfaces used in protocol analysis from an AP or dedicated sensor will have a greater receive sensitivity than client adapters. Therefore, captures made from an infrastructure AP or sensor will gather more information than captures from a mobile method, even when they are in the same proximity. This means that you may need to visit a location with your mobile solution for the last mile of device discovery or analysis from the client locations and may need to apply additional filters while reviewing captures from APs or sensors.

Your captures should not only be based upon physical location but should also be based upon channels used within that area. If you are having trouble in a service set, you may want to lock your analyzer on the same channel used by the AP and stations. If you are working in 2.4 GHz, you can lock your analyzer on a single channel but still see traffic transmitted on adjacent overlapping channels, provided you are close enough to the transmitting radios. When you are examining frames, you should see two channels in a captured frames analysis, the first channel seen is the channel on which your adapter was when it captured the frame. The second, seen in the frame body, is the channel the frame says it was transmitted upon. Figure 2.3 shows an example of this. If the frame is truly being transmitted on an overlapping adjacent channel you should be able to correct the problem by adjusting your channel use plan. If you simply detect the frame while your adapter is on an overlapping adjacent channel and see that the AP is on a proper channel and you do not detect any overlapping interference, you can eliminate this as a potential issue. The illustration below depicts a capture taken on channel 3 of a transmission made on channel 1.

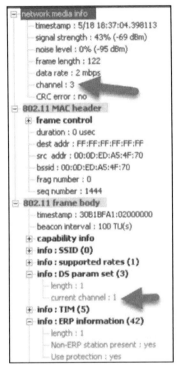

Figure 2.3: A beacon frame transmitted on CH 1 but captured on CH 3

Before you begin your capture, you will need to determine the best method of capture, the best location(s) for capture and whether or not you will lock onto specific channels or scan all channels while capturing.

When troubleshooting roaming issues, it is helpful to have multiple adapters, each locked on a channel being used by a different AP in the area within the band you are

60

analyzing. For example, in an area with three APs to which a client may roam in 2.4 GHz you could have one adapter locked on CH 1, one on CH 6 and the third on CH 11. This allows you to capture the entire roaming process. If you are only scanning on a single channel, troubleshooting roaming issues takes longer and is harder to do well.

Keep in mind, for the best results you should try to have your radios used in capturing the frames as close to the devices involved in transmitting the frames as possible and on the same channel(s). This may or may not be possible based upon the method of capture available: mobile, infrastructure or distributed. You may need to capture from many client locations and AP locations to get the best information to use in your diagnosis. To determine the best place from which to capture you will need to make some determinations such as, the types of frames you need to capture, capture scope of BSS or ESS, is the capture for a specific station or AP, or if the capture is for a roaming device.

You will also need to determine which physical areas will provide the best perspective of the packets: the client side or AP side of the conversations. You will need to determine if you need only one side of the conversation or both sides. You will need to know if the capture is for design, troubleshooting or baselining the network. When you are analyzing a mobile client's traffic, you will need to move along with the client. Knowing the APs in the roaming path and their channels is required for better analysis of roaming issues. You should use multiple adapters each locked on the appropriate channels to capture to troubleshoot roaming issues, as discussed above. Localized problems are more easily diagnosed. Problems spanning an enterprise will require diagnostics in several locations, both stationary and mobile.

Capturing for an Appropriate Amount of Time

Some problems only occur occasionally and others last for extended periods of time. If the problem you are diagnosing occurs at the same times over and over, that is when you should be conducting your frame captures. If the problem is persistent, you can capture at almost any time you like, within reason, to diagnose the trouble.

While we are discussing the time to capture, an important thing for you to do before beginning any capture, short or long, is to sync your capture devices with the same NTP server as your network. Your frame capture will need to be collated with debug captures, and with other wired and/or wireless captures and service logs. Having your timestamps out-of-sync will make the collation much more difficult.

One common problem is authentication failure. Although this can happen anytime users or devices try to connect, the peak times are at the beginning of shifts and returning from breaks. Obviously, you should capture during these peak authentication times to find the source of authentication problems impacting multiple users.

If only one person or device is having trouble connecting, the problem is most likely being caused by that device or user. To capture these frames, you will need to be near the user or device at the time they are trying to connect. This diagnosis is normally completed in a matter of seconds. When using PSK, the most likely cause for a single user or devices failure to authenticate is the use of the wrong PSK as seen in Figure 2.4. When using 802.1X authentication there are several other possible causes for the authentication failure. With any method of authentication, the time it takes to capture the required frames for diagnosis is very short, a matter of seconds. These are simple problems. Things that either work or do not work, like authentication, are easily diagnosed. You know what should be happening and how things are configured. You can compare that information to what you find in a capture, allowing you to pinpoint the problem very quickly.

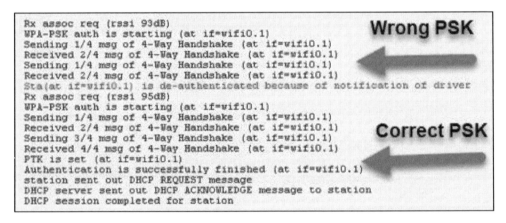

Figure 2.4: A failed PSK authentication followed by a successful PSK

Problems that go on for longer time periods will take more time to diagnose. What if users complain that the network is slow? First, you need to define slow. You will need to know what the capacity of the network is that they are using along with the airtime utilization, client types, protocols used, MIMO versions supported, any throttling used in the RF profiles on the APs, and several other pieces of information beyond what the users call "slow". Once you know what the network is designed to support, you can begin running your captures to see what is happening in the space.

In scenarios requiring longer captures, infrastructure and distributed capture methods are convenient. Without them, you may need to spend a great deal of time onsite using a mobile method to diagnose the problem.

Remember, when troubleshooting it is a good idea to "work up the stack". This means that you start your diagnosis at the bottom of the OSI model and work your way to the top. If there is no Layer 1 problem, such as a wireless camera or other interference source flooding the medium, you should move up to Layer 2 analysis and conduct a frame capture. Sometimes, it is not a Wi-Fi issue but rather a DNS, DHCP or firewall issue. Some problems are quickly found while others take a great deal of time to diagnose.

If you see that the problem has a source on the wired network, you may need to show and explain your capture to a wired administrator. A common wired side problem that gets blamed on Wi-Fi is running out of IP addresses in the DHCP scope. A wireless capture will show the Probe Request, Probe Response, Authentication process and the Association process. After these occur, you should see a DHCP request from the wireless client followed by a DHCP response from the DHCP server. When the server is not available, there is no response. If it is available but out of addresses, you will see a negative DHCP response. Your capture of this process is very similar to that of a wired stations DHCP process, with the addition of the APs transmissions. The wired administrator should be able to see this and solve the problem on the wired side of the network. Diagnosis of this problem takes only a few moments longer than diagnosing an authentication failure.

Scanning Channels and Single Channel Captures

There will be times when you need or want to scan all or multiple channels and times when you need or want to scan a single channel. Both techniques have their uses. When scanning multiple channels, you are missing traffic being transmitted on the channels you are not scanning as you cycle through the channels. However, you are collecting some information about all the channels being scanned. This is a common and useful technique used in survey work and routine security checks. The thought is, you are scanning all channels and the longer you scan the more likely you are to find problems and security issues not only on the channels you know you are using but, on all channels, used within your airspace.

If you need to examine what you have captured for a single channel after capturing on all or multiple channels, you can apply a channel filter to your view after saving the capture. On the other hand, when you only scan a single channel, no matter the band, you gather the most information possible about the use of that channel in that space. The image in Figure 2.5 below shows selecting a single channel for scanning. However, you gather no information whatsoever about any other channel being used in that space.

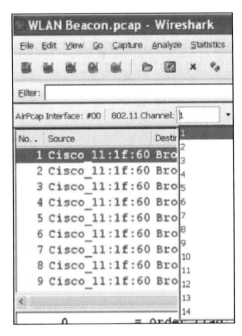

Figure 2.5: Selecting a single 2.4 GHz channel for capturing while using Wireshark

How do you decided what to do, scan all channels, a set of channels, or a single channel? The choice should be based upon your reason for being in that space capturing frames. For example, if a station is having trouble connecting, you may want to scan all channels so that you can capture any of that station's probe requests. They could be probing for the wrong SSIDs. By capturing all channels, you will be able to gather more information about the way this station is trying to connect. You could also decide to scan only the channels used by the APs that are within that space to diagnose the connectivity issue. You could also decide to only scan the channel used by the AP which is physically closest to the station having problems with connectivity. There is no absolute answer.

Another multiple channel scanning scenario is the diagnosis of roaming problems. This requires multiple adapters for best results. Although each adapter may be locked on a single channel, you are still scanning multiple channels, just using multiple adapters scanning one channel each. This method allows you to capture the entire roaming process as the client device moves throughout the area. If you were only capturing frames on a single channel, you would miss a lot of valuable information. Scanning a single channel while troubleshooting roaming issues is a mistake many make. This is often the case when they do not fully understand the need to capture on multiple channels. It also occurs when the person conducting the capture does not have enough adapters to conduct the capture or they are lacking a USB hub to allow their laptop to accommodate multiple adapter use. Selecting multiple channels, all channels or a single channel for your capturing should be based upon the frames or events you are trying to capture and the tools available for your use: mobile or stationary (APs and sensors).

Capturing in Roaming Scenarios

One of the best things about using Wi-Fi is that we are no longer required to be tethered to a desk or other stationary location. Unfortunately, as we move about we may lose connectivity or face other problems such as near far problems or hidden node issues. To avoid things like these, we co-locate multiple APs in our designs. This means the mobile stations will need to roam from AP-to-AP and channel-to-channel.

When troubleshooting roaming issues, you will need to capture on multiple channels simultaneously and when using a mobile protocol analysis tool, move with the client devices for which you are diagnosing problems. The additional component of a truly mobile station means you will need to be more creative in your capturing and diagnosis. You will need to scan on a minimum of two channels at the same time. Scanning on three channels, 1, 6 and 11, in 2.4 GHz is common practice. Figure 2.6 shows three adapters using a USB hub configured to capture on three channels simultaneously.

You may need to scan on more channels in a very high density 5 GHz deployment. Some applications are more sensitive to roaming issues. Data transmissions may not experience problems with a 300 ms roam time, but voice transmissions require a 150 ms roam time or less. The type of client and traffic can play a large role in diagnostic requirements.

Figure 2.6: Multiple USB adapters and USB hub configured for the capture of roaming events

Barcode scanners traveling through a warehouse on a forklift may make hard roams, disconnecting and reconnecting as if it is their first time connecting to the ESS. This is usually not an issue, because their users must find what they need to scan when they stop and get off of the forklift. By the time they have done that, their device will have connected. The user most likely will not experience any trouble working. However, a person walking while using a wireless phone may drop calls or experience such poor voice quality that the phone is unusable to them. If the devices connect and perform as desired while stationary, you could be facing roaming issues.

Some phones do not roam well when using 802.1X authentication. You can quickly determine the authentication method used by capturing an authentication process if you are not able to examine the configuration of the APs. If this is not an issue or if these devices are using PSK, there could be other problems, requiring analysis.

If you are capturing on a single channel, you will miss a large portion of the roaming process. If you are scanning all channels, you will miss a lot too, because you are off channel too long scanning unused channels. When gathering information about roaming stations, it is a best practice to use multiple adapters. Each adapter should be locked on separate channels used within the physical area where the problem exists. If there are too many APs in the area, the station could be roaming excessively. You should lock your adapters on the channels used by your APs with the strongest signals in the physical area.

The main criteria stations use when roaming within an ESS is AP signal strength, specifically the RSSI values calculated by the station of the APs. The station will normally connect to the AP it detects with the greatest RSSI value unless it is a sticky client. With multiple adapters configured to capture only on the channels used in the physical area and each adapter locked to a single channel, you will be able to capture the entire roaming process. By being able to capture the entire roaming process, you can diagnose problems faster and determine to which APs your clients are trying to roam.

 Sometimes roaming problems are not a client issue. Load balancing configurations on APs can create roaming problems if not configured properly. Stations may want to roam but the APs are making it difficult by ignoring the reassociation requests too long before allowing the roam to occur.

What are some of the causes of roaming issues that you can find using protocol analysis? One cause is legacy client device use. Many legacy client devices tend to remain connected to the first AP with which they associate, so long as that AP is seen, even if they must use the lowest supported data rate to do so. These clients are commonly referred to as sticky clients because they sick to the first AP with which they connect as long as possible. When mobile clients have slow connections as they move about, they may not have roamed when they could have. To diagnose this problem using protocol analysis, simply capture frames going to or coming from the client device near the station or the AP and look for the data rates used in transmission. If the traffic between the two is being transmitted at the lower rates, you may have a sticky client problem. Although both the AP and station may support the highest rates offered by the protocol used, the distance from the AP may have caused the station to use dynamic rate switching and to have selected a lower data rate to remain connected instead of roaming away to another AP with which it could use a higher data rate. See Figure 2.7 for an example of distance and rate use.

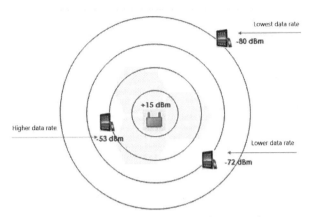

Figure 2.7: Clients at different distances and signal strengths use varying data rates

One way to mitigate this problem is to disable the support of lower data rates on the APs. This configuration will force the clients to roam to other APs as they move too far from the original AP. This roam may or may not be a smooth transition. You can also reduce the transmit power on the APs, disabling the client stations ability to hear the APs at greater distances and forcing them to roam away sooner. The stations may be forced to make a hard roam if your network is not designed correctly to support roaming.

Additionally, to solve this problem, you should also verify that the clients in this situation are using the most current firmware. Vendors of sticky clients often address the roaming aggressiveness of the stations in firmware updates, causing the stations to roam more aggressively and not stay connected at lower rates when a better connection exists. Although you can try to influence roaming behaviors by configuring data rates, load balancing and other things on the APs, the decision to roam is made by the client.

Sticky clients are only part of the problem. Poor design is another, often larger, part of the problem. Remember, the number one problem in wireless networking is poor design. The design must accommodate roaming by having sufficient APs with the right overlap of their BSAs so that clients can seamlessly roam.

What if the client station is over roaming? Excessive roaming can be caused by the roaming aggressiveness setting in the client station being set too high. Older client software had a sliding bar, allowing the user to make this adjustment. This option was a bad thing, because most users have no idea of how Wi-Fi works. Letting them touch this was a mistake. Most client devices do not allow the user to adjust this setting anymore.

However, the aggressiveness setting could be set too high in the firmware. If you see a station roaming too often, especially if their physical location is not being changed enough to warrant a roam, you should verify that the station is using the most current firmware and check with the cards manufacturer for known issues.

Additionally, you should conduct a frame capture of the beacon frames being sent out from the APs in the area. Within the beacon frame you will find both the supported and basic data rates. The basic data rates are the ones for which support is required to allow stations to connect with the APs. If the minimum basic, required, data rate is too high, this will cause excessive roaming. Too many administrators think that increasing the minimum basic data rate will solve all their problems and in changing it will set it too high. Be sure to keep this setting in balance. In most cases, disabling 1 and 2 Mbps in 2.4 GHz and disabling 6 Mbps (or 6 and 9 Mbps) in 5 GHz is enough. See Figure 2.8 for an example of changing the minimum basic data rates.

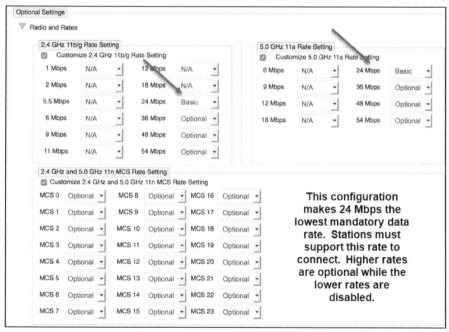

Figure 2.8: Data rate configuration, Aerohive

A lack of overlapping coverage can also cause roaming issues. When conducting protocol analysis to find the root cause of roaming issues you may find clients that never send a reassociation request but make hard roams, disconnections from one AP and brand-new connections to others, in certain areas of the network. Hard roams that are not caused by poor data rate configurations are often caused by poor design. Your capture, as you follow the client, will show them sending a disassociation frame to the original AP, followed by probe requests. As they move into the range of the next AP, that AP should respond to the probe requests. You will then see the usual authentication and association frame exchanges. This is a hard roam. If it were a regular roam, you would see the client station send a reassociation frame to the next AP and make a smooth transition.

Clients may move into areas where there is no usable coverage between APs, no overlapping coverage cells. This could also be blockage, such as walls, shelves, trucks, or other impediment sources. The users may not have reported any problems in this area before. However, if the devices used or the intended use of the network has changed, such as going from barcode scanners only to a voice network, the new devices or applications used may have exposed the problem. The resolution of this problem is redesign.

Years ago, people used to state that a percentage of overlap is required for roaming or bridging. However, there was no accurate way to prove a percentage of coverage overlap. It is better to plan for a given signal strength in the desired space that matches the intended use of the network, including the strengths from neighboring APs at a level to allow fast transitioning from one BSS to another as the applications require. Voice, for example, requires a 150 ms roam time, or less, and is more susceptible to roaming problems than data transmissions.

When troubleshooting roaming issues, validate the design, capture traffic on the channels used by neighboring APs around your test client at the same time using multiple adapters, look for noise sources if indicated, and verify the configuration of the WLAN APs and clients, including firmware. You can use integrated or distributed capturing methods to help solve roaming issues. However, it is best to use a multi-adapter capturing method on a mobile device like a laptop as you accompany the roaming device through the problematic area. Roaming issues, like most wireless problems, are usually caused by poor design or client drivers.

Capturing with Portable Protocol Analyzers

As you learned earlier, there are many types of devices you can use for protocol analysis, from handheld specialized devices to access points. The most commonly used device for protocol analysis is a laptop with the analysis software, wireless cards and drivers installed. Why is this the most common devices used? Most if not all administrators have a laptop. They may or may not have a specialized device or a WLAN with distributed sensors or protocol analysis abilities for their use. With a laptop, all you need to do is obtain and install the preferred software and compatible adapters. Laptops are also portable, like most of the client devices that you will be troubleshooting.

Some protocol analysis software only works on one OS. Others have OS specific versions. As long as you are running the correct version of the OS for the protocol analysis software you have chosen and have the correct license to use, you should not encounter too many issues. You should also ensure that the hardware requirements are met for installation, such as the correct processor and the correct amount of RAM being installed.

 Except for Wireshark, most protocol analyzers that are Wi-Fi-specific (OmniPeek, CommView for Wi-Fi, and Wi-Fi Analyzer Pro) are designed for Windows. Many engineers run these applications in a virtual machine on MacBooks with USB adapters to perform captures. You may capture using Wireshark natively on the MacBook and then simply pass the PCAP file to the commercial software in a virtual machine.

Your next concern should be the use of supported adapters. Sometimes you must install the adapter and have it recognized by your OS prior to installing the protocol analysis software. During the installation of the protocol analysis software, a check for compatible adapters is to be expected. Some packages will halt installation until you insert a compatible adapter. Others will continue installation but warn you that the software will not function as desired without a compatible adapter. You may have software that requires a proprietary adapter from the same company as the software. Compatibility issues should be found, and their resolutions determined prior to buying the software or hardware you intend to use.

Some protocol analysis applications, like CommView for Wi-Fi, provide internal installation engines to install the appropriate adapter. They may also switch from a connectivity driver (that which ships with your adapter) to the monitor mode driver at application launch time and then switch back to a connectivity driver at application exit. Though, at times, this feature seems to fail for various reasons.

You will also need to ensure that the laptop you intend to use has the correct port types or adapters needed to allow the wireless cards you intend to use to connect to the laptop. For example, your wireless cards may have USB 2 connectors, but your laptop may only have USB C ports. In this case you will need a USB to USB C adapter to use your wireless card with your laptop. This is increasingly common, since laptops have evolved to support USB C, often exclusively, but wireless cards have not evolved yet.

Most non-administrative users rely solely on the integrated wireless adapters found in their laptops. Administrators have more complex needs. What if your laptop does not have enough USB ports for you to use all the cards for which you have a simultaneous need? You can use USB hubs to allow more cards to be used in your work. These are often attached to the back of the laptop using hook and loop fasteners as in Figure 2.9, children's locking blocks as in Figure 2.10 or a purpose-built device such as a Hub Holster, see Figure 2.11 for an example from hubholster.com. You should use a method of attaching your USB hub that both securely holds it on the laptop and prevents the hub or adapters from dangling or swinging about as you are conducting your analysis.

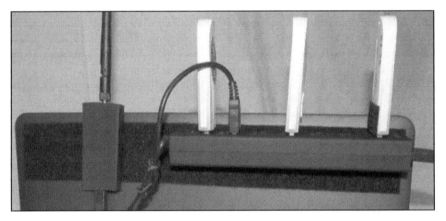

Figure 2.9: USB hub attached using hook and loop fastener

Figure 2.10: USB hub attached using children's locking blocks

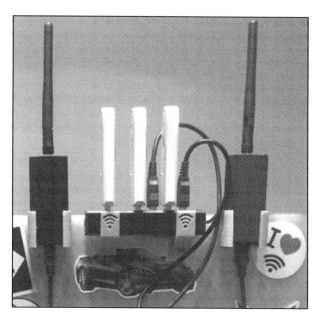

Figure 2.11: USB hub holster from hubholster.com

When using a USB 3 hub or USB 3 adapter for analysis, be aware of the USB 3 interference issue in 2.4 GHz. USB 3 can generate significant RF interference in the 2.4 GHz band ranging from less than 2-3 dB change in the noise floor to more than 20 dB change in the noise floor. This interference can massively impact capture performance. See the CWNP demonstration video on YouTube at: cwnp.link/USB3interference.

Using a laptop for analysis is not only the most commonly used method but is also more versatile. You can have different software packages installed allowing you to conduct more testing and capturing than when using a dedicated handheld. You can use different radios for testing if needed without switching devices or begin wired analysis by connecting to the wired network. There are a few drawbacks here too, most of which can be easily overcome.

Walking about carrying a laptop with several adapters connected will make you look like you are up to something, like hacking. The same thing occurs when you are conducting a physical site survey. You can quickly explain what you are doing and present ID if needed.

People may bump into you or your adapters causing damage. This one can largely be avoided by watching out for others as you walk about.

One of the more irritating things you will encounter when using this method of information gathering is that your body attenuates RF signals. This attenuation may cause you to miss frames or not be able to read them due to a decrease in signal strength (they will result in CRC errors in the capture, which will always occur anyway, but body attenuation can increase it). This is also a problem faced when conducting physical site surveys. The same mitigation technique can be applied in both situations. Simply stop and turn as you progress through areas.

In addition to being used in mobile capturing, you can also run the analysis on a laptop from a stationary position, such as placing the laptop on a desk, filing cabinet or other fixed location.

An additional concern is holding the laptop for extended periods of time while you conduct your captures or analysis. To take the weight away from your hands and arms, you could use a cart or a harness, see Figure 2.12, just like when you conduct a physical site survey.

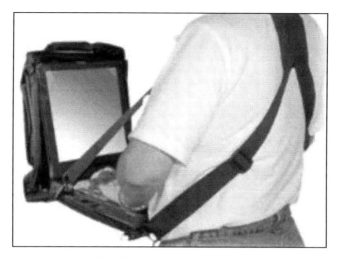

Figure 2.12: The Panasonic InfoCase, a harness and carrying case all-in-one

You also need to be aware that all the adapters you are using will be draining your battery. It is a good idea to have an extra battery or plan to stop and recharge as needed when you are conducting analysis for extended periods of time, a problem infrastructure or distributed capturing does not face.

One last but important caution, avoid using a wireless connection when you are capturing frames. Your adapter with which you are transmitting may cause problems capturing as needed. The noise created from your adapter being so close to your capturing adapters will make hearing other transmissions on that channel and any adjacent channels difficult. You should use a separate device for testing the connectivity and transmitting. This will allow you the best opportunity to capture what you need as efficiently as possible. Although laptop use for protocol analysis requires more truck rolls (the need to go onsite) and time than fixed solutions, like distributed sensors and APs, it is usually the most convenient, mobile, and cost-effective method used today.

Capturing with APs, Controllers, and Other Management Solutions

Using fixed solutions for protocol analysis has several advantages. You do not need to travel to perform protocol analysis, reducing costs and time needed to locate and solve problems. It does lack the mobility needed to troubleshoot some problems like failed roams and has additional licensing and hardware requirements that can be costly, if not required. The cost associated with the hardware and licensing required is argued to be recouped quickly by reducing truck rolls and helping to increase uptime by allowing you to solve problems faster from remote locations.

Some solutions will allow you to capture and store your information in a standard PCAP format. This option allows you to conduct the capture remotely but still do the analysis with familiar laptop-based tools. Other tools, knowing that a network administrator or help desk employee may not be a skilled analysis professional, allow a capture to be triggered based upon event alarms or even manually and will present the person analyzing the capture with a simple user interface having the analysis done for them and plain language used to describe what the system believes to be the issue. See Figures 2.13 and 2.14 for examples of remote capturing.

Some APs in an infrastructure may be deployed to act only as sensors for capture. This configuration would allow them to act as if they were part of a distributed solution. However, the distributed solutions often have more advanced analysis tools, a better user interface for protocol analysis, and are quite often from the same vendors that also make popular laptop-based solutions, reducing the learning curve for many administrators already familiar with the other tools.

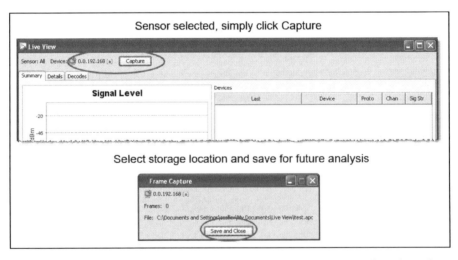

Figure 2.13: Beginning a remote capture using Extreme Networks AirDefense

Status/Log Messages

Order log entries by [Log Message Time ▾]   Level [Detail ▾]   Line [100 ▾]

```
DETAIL   Send message to RADIUS Server(10.5.2.2): code=1 (Access-Request) identifier=5 length=174,   User-Name=user-1 N
DETAIL   RADIUS: EAP start with type peap
DETAIL   Receive message from RADIUS Server: code=11 (Access-Challenge) identifier=5 length=64
DETAIL   Sending EAP Packet to STA: code=1 (EAP-Request) identifier=9 length=6
DETAIL   received EAP packet (code=2 id=9 len=8D) from STA: EAP Reponse-PEAP (25)
DETAIL   Send message to RADIUS Server(10.5.2.2): code=1 (Access-Request) identifier=6 length=261,   User-Name=user-1 N
DETAIL   RADIUS: SSL negotiation, receive client hello message
DETAIL   Receive message from RADIUS Server: code=11 (Access-Challenge) identifier=6 length=1100
DETAIL   Sending EAP Packet to STA: code=1 (EAP-Request) identifier=10 length=1034
DETAIL   received EAP packet (code=2 id=10 len=6) from STA: EAP Reponse-PEAP (25)
DETAIL   Send message to RADIUS Server(10.5.2.2): code=1 (Access-Request) identifier=7 length=187,   User-Name=user-1 N
DETAIL   RADIUS: SSL negotiation, send server certificate and other message
DETAIL   Receive message from RADIUS Server: code=11 (Access-Challenge) identifier=7 length=646
DETAIL   Sending EAP Packet to STA: code=1 (EAP-Request) identifier=11 length=584
DETAIL   received EAP packet (code=2 id=11 len=193) from STA: EAP Reponse-PEAP (25)
DETAIL   Send message to RADIUS Server(10.5.2.2): code=1 (Access-Request) identifier=8 length=373,   User-Name=user-1 N
DETAIL   RADIUS: SSL connection established
DETAIL   Receive message from RADIUS Server: code=11 (Access-Challenge) identifier=8 length=107
DETAIL   Sending EAP Packet to STA: code=1 (EAP-Request) identifier=12 length=49
DETAIL   received EAP packet (code=2 id=12 len=6) from STA: EAP Reponse-PEAP (25)
DETAIL   Send message to RADIUS Server(10.5.2.2): code=1 (Access-Request) identifier=9 length=187,   User-Name=user-1 N
DETAIL   RADIUS: SSL negotiation is finished successfully
DETAIL   Receive message from RADIUS Server: code=11 (Access-Challenge) identifier=9 length=90
DETAIL   Sending EAP Packet to STA: code=1 (EAP-Request) identifier=13 length=32
DETAIL   received EAP packet (code=2 id=13 len=34) from STA: EAP Reponse-PEAP (25)
DETAIL   Send message to RADIUS Server(10.5.2.2): code=1 (Access-Request) identifier=10 length=215,   User-Name=user-1
DETAIL   RADIUS: PEAP inner tunneled conversion
DETAIL   Receive message from RADIUS Server: code=11 (Access-Challenge) identifier=10 length=113
DETAIL   Sending EAP Packet to STA: code=1 (EAP-Request) identifier=14 length=55
DETAIL   received EAP packet (code=2 id=14 len=8) from STA: EAP Reponse-PEAP (25)
DETAIL   Send message to RADIUS Server(10.5.2.2): code=1 (Access-Request) identifier=11 length=269,   User-Name=user-1
DETAIL   RADIUS: PEAP Tunneled authentication was rejected
DETAIL   Receive message from RADIUS Server: code=11 (Access-Challenge) identifier=11 length=96
DETAIL   Sending EAP Packet to STA: code=1 (EAP-Request) identifier=15 length=38
DETAIL   received EAP packet (code=2 id=15 len=38) from STA: EAP Reponse-PEAP (25)
DETAIL   Send message to RADIUS Server(10.5.2.2): code=1 (Access-Request) identifier=12 length=219,   User-Name=user-1
DETAIL   RADIUS: rejected user 'user-1' through the NAS at 10.5.2.2.
BASIC    Authentication is terminated (at if=wifi0.1) because it is rejected by RADIUS server
```

Figure 2.14: Invalid user credentials found as source of authentication failure using Client Monitor from Aerohive

Disadvantages are found in using infrastructure protocol analysis too. First, the APs being used as sensors are not able to service clients unless they have a dedicated radio for use as a sensor. Most deployed APs are dual-band and not tri-band, which makes it a challenge to dedicate a radio to monitoring. Taking a radio out of service mode and placing it into monitor mode (or sensor mode) will force clients to roam to other APs or may even prevent those located within the service set area from being able to connect, if there is not adequate redundant coverage in the WLAN to allow for this use without adversely impacting the users. Second, while a few may include this functionality, most vendors charge a per AP or per radio fee to license the sensor features. This solution is not mobile like laptop or purpose-built handheld device solutions. Most users of a fixed solution, infrastructure or distributed, also use a portable solution to resolve this issue. You can use the fixed solution to solve many problems remotely and to help locate the areas in which problems may require truck rolls, reducing the time it takes onsite to resolve issues. This hybrid method of protocol analysis in troubleshooting is very effective.

Capturing with Specialty Devices

Although they are often more expensive than laptop-based tools and are not always upgradable, handheld devices that are purpose-built for protocol analysis are great tools to use as well. They capture the same information and are also configurable for your captures as well as also being mobile. They are often more efficient since they do not have the compatibility or driver issues found in laptop protocol analysis. See Figure 2.15 for an example.

Handheld analyzers can provide fast, simple, and accurate isolation and troubleshooting. They can be a ruggedized device, are lightweight, and easy to use. These can be stored at remote locations and used by less experienced people to gather information as needed, since you basically just need to make sure they are charged and the user knows how to turn them on in order to use them. Some offer a one-click diagnosis of the captured information with a suggested problem source based upon the captured information. Connectivity to a centralized test results management platform is also available from some, making it even easier for people with less experience to capture the information you need for you and allow you to review it through the centralized platform.

Figure 2.15: AirCheck G2 wireless tester from NETSCOUT

Some devices offer active testing as well as passive capturing. See Figure 2.16 for an example. Some do not connect to an AP at all. They simply look for things such as available transmit time. This is determined by examining the use of the medium on a channel.

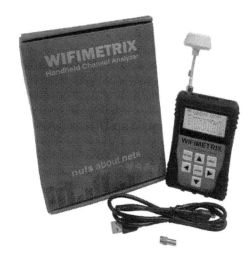

Figure 2.16: WIFIMETRIX from nutsaboutnets.com

Some handheld diagnostic tools may be different sizes than others and or have a different level of functionality, just like laptop-based tools. Many people use both laptop-based and handheld tools in the field. It is simply a matter of choosing the right tool or tools for the job at hand. The size of the display limits the amount of information you can view at once, so some of these devices will also connect to a laptop for use, making them a more specialized wireless card for protocol analysis or simply improving what their users can see. Some handheld devices are a bit larger, tablet size in fact, but offer more functionality. These tools can provide analysis from the edge of the network all the way to the data center by performing both wireless and wired analysis. See Figure 2.17 for an example. The key is to select the best tool for the job you are performing. Do not limit your thinking to the use of only one tool type. There are even tee-shirts that can simply detect Wi-Fi, though, thankfully, they don't perform advanced analysis of the wearer.

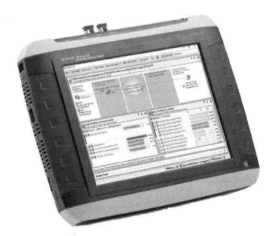

Figure 2.17: OptiView XG Network Analysis Tablet from NETSCOUT

Analyzing Frame Captures

Unless you are just examining Wi-Fi, protocol use for fun, you are most likely trying to validate a network or are involved in troubleshooting. Honestly, when everything is working or when no one is reporting a problem, you are usually busy doing something else. However, when you start protocol analysis you have a need to solve a problem.

After you have learned how wireless devices communicate when using a given protocol or technology, you can recognize anomalous behaviors. If you know that a frame of a certain type is to be followed by a frame of another type or some variant of interframe spacing and your capture shows something else happening, you know there is a problem. Diagnosing wireless problems comes down to knowing what is supposed to be happening and comparing that to what is happening. In later chapters of this book, you will learn in-depth details of what is supposed to be happening. Within this section we will cover the following topics:

- Using appropriate display filters to view relevant frames and packets
- Using colorization to highlight important frames and packets
- Configuring and displaying columns for analysis purposes
- Viewing frame and packet decodes and understanding the information shown and applying it to the analysis process
- Using multiple adapters and channel aggregation to view captures from multiple channels

- Implementing protocol analyzer decryption procedures
- Viewing and using captures statistical information for analysis
- Using expert mode for analysis
- Viewing and understanding peer maps as they relate to communications analysis

Display Filters

No matter how long you capture, display filters allow the user of a protocol analysis application to configure the software to only display what they desire. Filters can be applied both before and after conducting frame captures. If you know the exact frame types you wish to capture, setting up a filter before you begin capturing can make diagnostics easier, because all you will need to view is the frames you believe to be suspect. However, you should capture as much information as possible when using protocol analysis.

Some problems are immediately identifiable and are persistent. Others take more analysis and are intermittent. Protocol analysis applications will let you determine how long they should capture. You can set a specific duration as well as scheduling a start and end time for capturing.

As mentioned above, it is a good idea to sync your device with the NTP service used by the network for which you are conducting the analysis. You can also filter the display by time. The reason you should capture as much as possible is that you may need to know more about what is happening than just that in the frames you believe to be suspect.

Having more information, the first time you capture frames, is of more use in the future. You can always apply a filter after the capture to see just the frames you believe to be in question. You can filter on many things, MAC address, protocol, channel, frame type, frame sub-type, To DS, From DS or any one of the many components of the capture you are analyzing. If you apply a filter before the capture, you may be missing information of critical importance in diagnosing the issue(s) at hand, by limiting what is stored in your software. Remember, all the Layer 2 information gathered by your adapter can be used for your analysis and much of it for filtering.

Many problems have more than one cause. If you are looking for the one cause you think to be the source of the issues and are incorrect in your guess, you will need to conduct more captures, waste time, and possibly miss the cause completely if it is from an intermittent source.

We will now examine some of the more commonly used filters. In Figure 2.18, you see that there are no filters in use. Notice that there are multiple frame types and subtypes contained within this capture. This is the best configuration to use when you are either uncertain of the cause of any troubles or if you are simply gathering information for a network health analysis. Not all captures are conducted for troubleshooting.

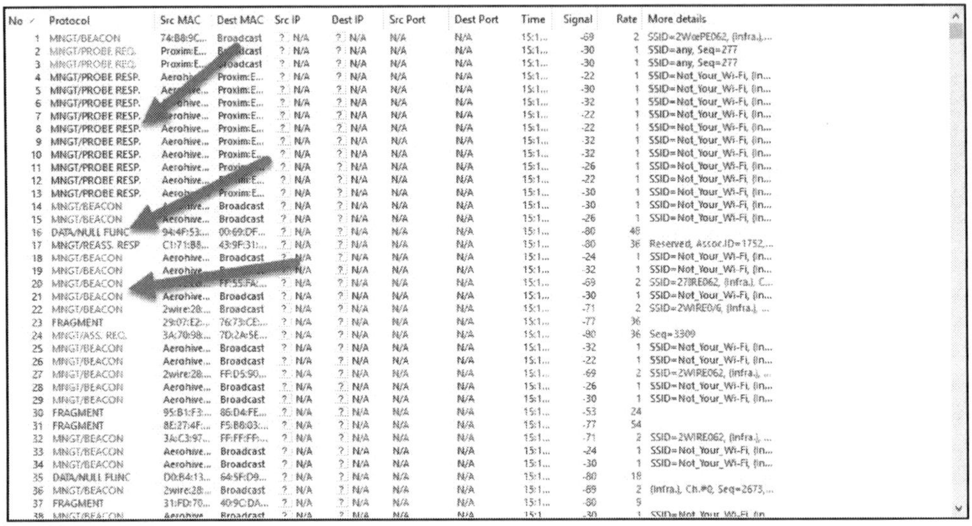

Figure 2.18: A frame capture without any filters using CommView for WiFi

Should you have a need to only see frames of a certain type you can apply a filter either before or after your capture, as discussed above. Figure 2.19 illustrates configuring a pre-capture filter to only capture management frames. Notice that only the Management frame enablement icon is selected.

Figure 2.19: A pre-capture filter set to only capture Management frames using CommView for WiFi

You can also select to only capture Data frames or only capture Control frames or combinations of frame types up to and including capturing all frames if desired, simply by selecting the frame type. You can also apply filters based upon the device versus the frame type. This can be done by applying a MAC address filter as seen in Figure 2.20. You will need to select the MAC filter option followed by entering the required address and any other information your capturing tool needs. Once you apply the MAC address filter, your protocol analysis tool should only display traffic coming from or going to that device MAC address.

Figure 2.20: Filtering your capture by the MAC address of the desired device using CommView for WiFi

Protocol analyzers also support highlighting or colorization as well as filtering. The highlighting feature allows you to define colors for packets or frames which match your defined criteria. The use of colors within the frame capture, see Figure 2.21, allows those frames to be quickly identified by their assigned colors as you browse through your captured frames.

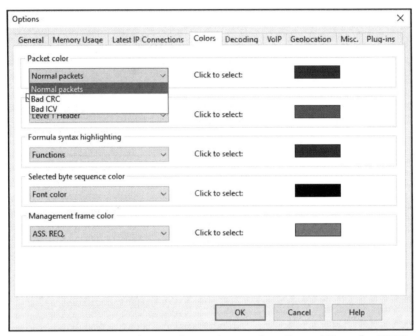

Figure 2.21: Frame color configurations using CommView for WiFi

Simply having the ability to configure filters and highlight devices or frame types in your capture will not ensure that they have been implemented properly. You must know not only how to apply filtering but when to use properly assigned filters. For example, if you are diagnosing authentication problems, you can apply a frame filter specifying that only authentication frames be displayed. You can filter further, if needed, by adding a MAC address filter displaying just the frames from a specific device. With such a configuration, you would only be shown authentication frames to or from a certain device. This type of advanced filtering strategy will greatly reduce the time it takes you to troubleshoot authentication problems for a single client.

Figure 2.22 illustrates a capture of a failed PSK authentication followed by a successful PSK authentication of a single client. The display filter used was set to show traffic going to and coming from a specific client device, since it was the one having trouble authenticating. You should know that the number one reason PSK authentication fails is the use of the wrong PSK. In the illustration below, you can see that the client station does not get through the third phase of the four-way handshake. This indicates the wrong PSK was used. When the correct PSK is used, the station completes the four-way handshake, is authenticated, associated, and begins the DHCP process, making it successfully to Layer 3.

```
21:57:04  000E3B330A53  001977066610  02-A-066600  BASIC  Rx assoc req (rssi 93dB)
21:57:04  000E3B330A53  001977066610  02-A-066600  INFO   WPA-PSK auth is starting (at if=wifi0.1)
21:57:04  000E3B330A53  001977066610  02-A-066600  INFO   Sending 1/4 msg of 4-Way Handshake (at if=wifi0.1)
21:57:04  000E3B330A53  001977066610  02-A-066600  INFO   Received 2/4 msg of 4-Way Handshake (at if=wifi0.1)
21:57:08  000E3B330A53  001977066610  02-A-066600  INFO   Sending 1/4 msg of 4-Way Handshake (at if=wifi0.1)
21:57:08  000E3B330A53  001977066610  02-A-066600  INFO   Received 2/4 msg of 4-Way Handshake (at if=wifi0.1)
21:57:09  000E3B330A53  001977066610  02-A-066600  BASIC  Sta(at if=wifi0.1) is de-authenticated because of notification of driver
22:05:18  000E3B330A53  001977066610  02-A-066600  BASIC  Rx assoc req (rssi 95dB)
22:05:18  000E3B330A53  001977066610  02-A-066600  INFO   WPA-PSK auth is starting (at if=wifi0.1)
22:05:18  000E3B330A53  001977066610  02-A-066600  INFO   Sending 1/4 msg of 4-Way Handshake (at if=wifi0.1)
22:05:18  000E3B330A53  001977066610  02-A-066600  INFO   Received 2/4 msg of 4-Way Handshake (at if=wifi0.1)
22:05:18  000E3B330A53  001977066610  02-A-066600  INFO   Sending 3/4 msg of 4-Way Handshake (at if=wifi0.1)
22:05:18  000E3B330A53  001977066610  02-A-066600  INFO   Received 4/4 msg of 4-Way Handshake (at if=wifi0.1)
22:05:18  000E3B330A53  001977066610  02-A-066600  INFO   PTK is set (at if=wifi0.1)
22:05:18  000E3B330A53  001977066610  02-A-066600  BASIC  Authentication is successfully finished (at if=wifi0.1)
22:05:18  000E3B330A53  001977066610  02-A-066600  INFO   station sent out DHCP REQUEST message
22:05:18  000E3B330A53  001977066610  02-A-066600  INFO   DHCP server sent out DHCP ACKNOWLEDGE message to station
22:05:18  000E3B330A53  001977066610  02-A-066600  BASIC  DHCP session completed for station
```

Figure 2.22: Frame capture of failed PSK authentication followed by successful PSK authentication

This was an example of knowing which frame types needed to be analyzed to troubleshoot the issue at hand and which filter(s) to apply. How often will users state that they typed in the correct key, when they really did not, or the key has been changed without their knowing? This capture lets you quickly know that it is a wrong PSK issue.

As mentioned earlier, if you do not suspect that the problem is detectable by filtering for a specific frame type, do not use capture filtering. Simply capture all frames and apply a display filter when you are finished.

Another example of when to use filters is troubleshooting devices that are not able to connect on their own. Users are accustomed to turning on a device and having it automatically connect. However, if the user has recently cleared their network history, updated firmware or hardware or replaced a device, their device will not be able to automatically connect. In many cases, the probe request frames from this device will be null-probes, see Figure 2.23, probe frames without an SSID in them. If this is the case, the user should be presented with a list of the SSIDs to which they can connect when using a manual connection. Then, they may face authentication issues as above. However, they may not know how to do this, and you will need to see what SSIDs their device is trying to find, if any. Filtering on their MAC address and further filtering by the probe request frame type will allow you to see the SSIDs, if any, their device is trying to find. If they are not probing for the correct SSIDs, they will not automatically connect to the desired network. Given that you are unsure of the exact issue, using a display filter may be best in this scenario.

MNGT/PROBE REQ.	2A:FC:53:F9:22:1C	Broadcast	? N/A	? N/A	N/A	N/A	17:2...	-49	1	SSID=any, Seq=3457
MNGT/PROBE REQ.	2A:FC:53:F9:22:1C	Broadcast	? N/A	? N/A	N/A	N/A	17:2...	-49	1	SSID=any, Seq=3458
MNGT/PROBE REQ.	2A:FC:53:F9:22:1C	Broadcast	? N/A	? N/A	N/A	N/A	17:2...	-45	1	SSID=any, Seq=3459
MNGT/PROBE REQ.	2A:FC:53:F9:22:1C	Broadcast	? N/A	? N/A	N/A	N/A	17:2...	-45	1	SSID=any, Seq=3460

Figure 2.23: A client searching for any SSID using null-probes, probe requests without specifying an SSID

Colorization

Being able to make the information gathered easier to read and relevant portions of the capture easier to find are integral parts of protocol analysis software. One way that this type of software allows you to do this is using colors in identifying desired frame types or other pieces of information. You can assign a specific color to a frame type, making it more easily identified in your capture weather you are filtering by frame type or not.

Within Figure 2.24, broadcast frames are highlighted using coloring. The capture has not been filtered by frame type. Figure 2.25 illustrates the default coloring rules found in Wireshark. Other protocol analysis tools have their own default settings. You may find them useful or want to customize the color representations to make them easier for you to see or to place your own emphasis on the frames within your captures. Highlighting the frame types you wish to see in different colors allows them to be quickly identified, even when surrounded by frames of different types in the display interface.

The colorizing, color coding, of packets and filtering packets are important configuration tasks that will make decoding the information easier and faster for you when using protocol analysis. Using these features properly allows you to more quickly locate the data you need for analysis. Any unfiltered capture of WLAN frames can include thousands of entries. You must know how to organize and filter the capture to locate and solve problems quickly.

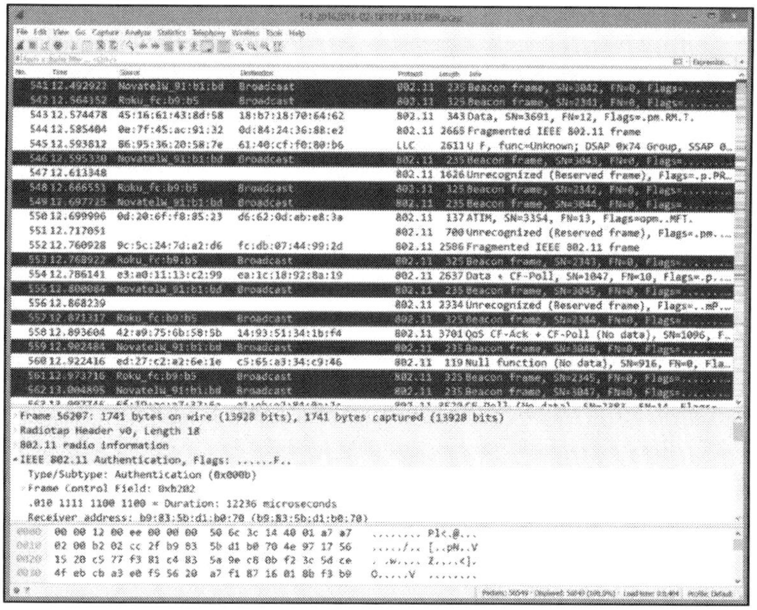

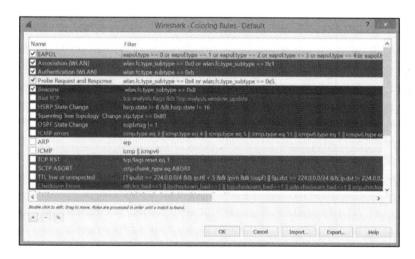

Figure 2.24: Broadcast frames highlighted by using a specific color for them using Wireshark

Figure 2.25: Wireshark default coloring rules which you can change if desired

Display Columns

Being able to sort frames based upon source, destination type and other criteria will allow you to analyze your captures more efficiently. Changing or using columns is part of this function. As seen in Figure 2.26, you can choose which columns you feel you need to display. You can display information about the nodes, packets, channels and more. The key is to display only what you need to display. This will reduce the time it takes to diagnose problems or analyze your capture. Just like many of the optional configurations found in protocol analysis, there is no right or wrong here, so long as you display what you need. Every capture may have different configuration needs to show you what you need to see as efficiently as possible. Some of the display configurations are simply a matter of preference while others are a matter of necessity.

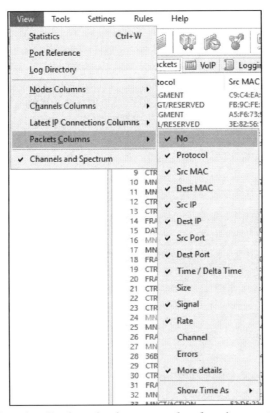

Figure 2.26: Changing the displayed columns under the view options in CommView for WiFi.

Viewing Decodes

When you understand wireless frame formats and types, it is easy to tell what type of frame you have captured and know for what purposes that frame is used. Within the protocol analysis display, you will see the source of the frame and its intended destination. You will be able to determine if the frame is going to or coming from the distribution system. Knowing how the specific frames are supposed to be used, their sources and destinations, and how they fit within 802.11 communications will allow you to determine if they are normal traffic being used properly, anomalous traffic, or indications of communication problems.

In 802.11 communications, there is a specific order in which communications must occur, timings and spacings between frames. Many of the things that happen in 802.11 communications either do not happen at all in 802.3 communications or happen in a different manner than in 802.3 communications. You must be able to identify the process that is occurring within your capture and be able to compare that to what the expected behavior is to effectively diagnose any problems.

For example, unicast 802.11 frames are to be followed by an interframe space and an acknowledgement frame. If a client device is trying to send a data frame through the AP to a station on the wired network or even to another wireless client through the AP, the AP should acknowledge the reception of the data frame to let the transmitting station know that it was received. If after the acknowledgement timeout threshold has expired and the transmitting station has not received an ACK, it will assume the AP did not receive the frame. It will then begin the retransmission process. It will multiply a pseudorandom backoff timer against a slot time, which varies in size based upon the modulation technique used. It will then use the Duration value in any frames it sees being transmitted to set the value for its Network Allocation Vector, another logical backoff timer. When all timers have been counted down to zero, the station will conduct a Clear Channel Assessment, CCA, to determine if the medium is idle. If the medium is idle, the station will try to send the same frame to the AP again. If the medium is busy, the station will use the duration value found in the header of the detected frame to count down another backoff timer before transmitting the frame. When that counter has expired, and the station has conducted another CCA without detecting a transmission, it will transmit the frame to the AP again. Stations will do this up to 32 times before they determine that the frame is undeliverable. So, when you are analyzing the traffic in this scenario, you are expecting an ACK and normal behavior, like the station was on the first attempt to deliver the frame. However, just like the station, you do not see it.

There are several reasons the AP could have missed the frame. It could have collided with traffic from a hidden node, it could have collided with non-802.11 interference, the station could have roamed too far away making the transmission too weak for the AP to decode, or the AP could be down, among other things. Using protocol analysis, you should be able to determine the cause of the problem. A small percentage of retransmissions is usually deemed to be normal. When the station transmits the frame the second time and beyond, you will see that the retransmission bit in the frame header is turned on, set to 1. There is no indication in any frame of what number retransmission a frame is, just that it is or is not a retransmission.

Figure 2.27 shows a normal first transmission of a frame. It is a QoS data frame coming from the distribution system (DS) through an AP. You can see that the exit from the distribution system bit is set to 1, meaning that it is a From DS transmission. Notice that the information in the header states that it is not a retransmission. This frame should be followed by interframe spacing and an ACK from the destination MAC address. A high percentage of retransmissions could indicate a Layer 1 noise problem. If you have conducted spectrum analysis and not found an interferer in the area, you should look to your protocol analysis for the answer. The frame headers give you a great deal of useful information when diagnosing problems such as this one. If you see frames from different radios with the same timestamp being transmitted and not acknowledged, you have a hidden node problem: two or more radios are unable to see each other's traffic when conducting their CCA. They assume the medium is idle and transmit. Their frames collide. Any receiving radio will see this as a corrupt transmission and will not acknowledge the frame, since the data within the frame is most likely unusable.

The information in the header of all wireless frames is in clear text, even when the strongest encryption possible is used to protect the data. It holds invaluable information you can use in protocol analysis. Information found here includes the addressing for the source and destinations, the directionality of the transmission (meaning is it going to or coming from the DS), the frame type and subtype, duration value, whether or not it is a retry, if QoS is used, channel used to transmit, protocol version, if the frame is fragmented, the fragment number if fragmented, power management information and more. Newer protocols have more information in the header than older ones.

```
¶ 802.11 MAC Header
    ⬡ Version:              0 [0 Mask 0x03]
    ⬡ Type:                 %10   Data [0 Mask 0x0C]
    ⬡ Subtype:              %1000   QoS Data [0 Mask 0xF0]
⊟ ¶ Frame Control Flags:    %01000010 [1]
    ⬡                         0... .... Non-strict...der
    ⬡                         .1.. .... Protec...Frame
    ⬡                         ..0. ....No...re Data
    ⬡                         ...0 ....ower Management - active mode
    ⬡                         .... 0... This is not a Re-Transmission
    ⬡                         .... .0.. Last or Unfragmented Frame
    ⬡                         .... ..1. Exit from the Distribution System
    ⬡                         .... ...0 Not to the Distribution System
```

Figure 2.27: A data frames first transmission, the retransmission bit is off, set to 0. This is not a retransmission.

Figure 2.28 illustrates basic 802.11ac MAC frame header components. Because newer PHYs change the frame formats, you should be using an adapter that supports at least the protocols used you wish to decode or newer. You may only want to see the Beacons or some other low data rate frame but using an adapter that is able to decode the protocol captured will allow you to also decode the encapsulated data, if you can decrypt the frame.

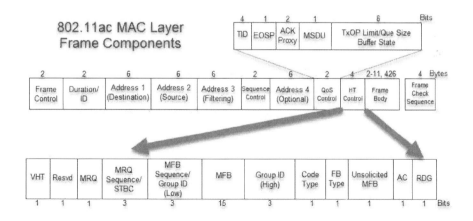

Figure 2.28: Basic components of an 802.11ac MAC Layer frame

More information about the frame structure and contents will be discussed later in this study guide. If you can decrypt the transmission, there is nothing about a frame you are

91

unable to learn using protocol analysis. Some tools even allow you to reconstruct entire transmissions and view the data. You should be familiar with basic 802.11 frame components and their usage. This will allow you to know within which part of a captured frame to look for the desired information. Additionally, you should spend some time using protocol analysis software gathering your own traffic for analysis. This will give you practice using frames of a known type and source thus enabling you to more quickly identify the important elements of your captures in the field when diagnosing problems or validating networks.

 Being prepared for the CWAP exam means known the 802.11 protocols and frame exchanges well. There is no better preparation for this than viewing and analyzing as many frame captures as you can. Getting hands-on experience will go a long way toward helping you to retain this information.

Multiple Adapters and Channel Aggregation

As you learned earlier, using multiple adapters is of great benefit when troubleshooting roaming issues. Multiple adapter use has additional applications beyond troubleshooting roaming. When all the adapters are in use, you can capture on both the 2.4 GHz and 5 GHz bands simultaneously, reducing the time it takes to capture relevant traffic within an area for physical survey and protocol analysis work alike. The adapters can be locked on individual channels, locked on bands or allowed to operate in monitor mode on all channels and bands.

Using multiple adapters can also improve your protocol analysis of bonded channel use. Access points typically can bond using wider channels than supported by most clients. You should capture across the entire aggregate channel, bonded channel. This will let you know if you are really getting the most from the bonding. In high-density deployments you may not be using any bonded channels. However, neighboring networks could be using it. By listening on all channels, you may discover bonded channel use of which you were not aware. Only scanning the bands and channels you know you are using, limits your discovery of things like overlapping channel interference, neighboring device detection and rogue detection.

Within your protocol analysis software, you will need to configure each of the adapters you are using for your capture as desired, locked on a band, locked on a channel or scanning everything, to get the desired results from your capturing efforts. Figure 2.29 below shows 13 adapters configured to capture traffic on separate channels simultaneously.

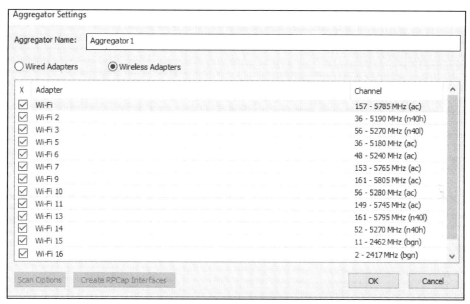

Figure 2.29: Savvius OmniPeek Aggregator settings for 13 adapters each set to capture on a separate channel

Decryption Procedures

Given that most enterprise WLANs use some form of encryption, most WLAN analysts spend much of their time using a protocol analyzer viewing the information about the frames they have captured. However, if you have the encryption keys or shared keys for your network traffic, you can use protocol analysis software to rebuild traffic, allowing you to not only analyze the traffic but also to see the actual transmitted data, including replaying voice traffic.

You will need to enter the shared keys into the tool as seen in Figure 2.30 below to allow your protocol analysis software to decode the frames you have captured. The dynamic nature of WPA encryption doesn't allow simply knowing the WPA passphrase to let you decrypt traffic after simply entering the correct passphrase. To decrypt WPA-encrypted traffic, your protocol analyzer must be running and capturing packets during the key exchange phase of authentication (key exchange is carried out using the EAP over LAN, EAPOL protocol), also called the four-way handshake. It is important that all the EAPOL key exchange packets be successfully captured for decoding the payload of WPA encrypted frames. A damaged or missing EAPOL piece of the exchange will make it impossible for you to decrypt packets being sent to/from the given station. Should this be the case, you will need to capture the next EAPOL conversation between the AP and desired station. This is an important distinction in the way WEP traffic is decrypted. WEP traffic can more easily be decoded by simply entering the correct key, one of the many reasons WEP has long been abandoned. More information about authentication and encryption types can be found in the CWSP course.

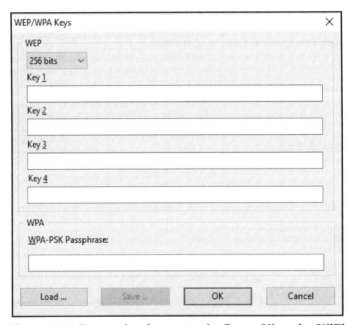

Figure 2.30: Encryption key entry in CommView for WiFi

Once you have the keys and the captured frames you can rebuild the transmissions to reveal the transmitted data, viewed webpages, or even replay a voice call using an MP3 player. To begin the process, select the desired frame and choose to reconstruct the traffic. The terms used to do this will vary among software packages used. Figure 2.31 below shows you the beginning of the process.

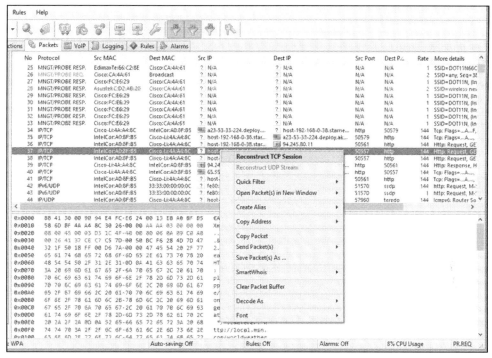

Figure 2.31: Reconstructing a TCP session using CommView for WiFi

If WPA-Personal or WPA2-Personal are being used, most protocol analyzers allow you to enter the PSK so that you can decrypt the traffic. It is important that you have permission before you begin, in writing if possible. Always check the privacy policies of an organization before decrypting traffic, even if it is where you work. Even running a capture without authorization may be against policy.

The procedures involved in decrypting and viewing wireless transmissions are very similar if not the same across protocol analyzers. When using shared key authentication, you must capture the authentication process to make sure that you have the correct keys. Simply using the known PSK will not allow you to decode the frames in the same manner as used in legacy WEP decodes. If all the stations are already associated when you begin, you will not be able to decrypt. You will need to wait for the station for which you are decoding to reconnect. You can force this or simply wait. Once you have captured the authentication process for the desired station, you can conduct your capture. You then need to enter the PSK into your protocol analysis software. The decoding can be done in real-time or post-capture for analysis. You must select the traffic you wish to reconstruct and tell the software to do so. There are also many free utilities available to decode wireless frames.

Why would you want to decrypt data on your own network? You should be able to access the data directly on the servers and stations alike. You may need to verify that the correct data is moving within the frames as part of a network assurance test. Just because something is being transmitted, does not ensure that the correct things are being transmitted. This combined with the access logging on the network can help validate the transmissions. You will not be doing this very often since network administrators can verify data access on the network and its devices using log files. You spend the bulk of your time using protocol analysis looking with the Layer 2 information.

Statistical Information

Protocol analyzers capture a lot of information about the behavior of your WLAN devices. This can be overwhelming if you need to sort through all of it to find the information for which you are looking. You can apply filters in the display to assist you, as you learned above. However, the filters alone are not enough. If you need to determine the percentage of retries in a network, you could do that by hand. The same holds true for failed authentications, average frame counts, and other valuable statistics. Why do all of that by hand when the protocol analysis software can do it faster and more accurately than you can?

You can even use it to generate reports. The statistical views can be graphical as well as in simple chart form. These visualizations of your captures will help you understand what is happening on the network faster than poring over the frames. They will also allow you to present your customer with a deliverable they are more likely to understand. Figure 2.32 is a general information visualization of network statistics. *Figure 2.33* show you packet sizes, useful if you believe there are clients passing relatively large frames. Traffic by device MAC address can be seen in Figure 2.34.

Some protocol analyzers offer more charts and graphs than others. The key here is in knowing that they can gather and display the relevant information much faster than you could using display filters as well as presenting the statistical information in a more easily digested format benefiting both you and your customers. You can find and solve problems by looking at the frames. Explaining what you have found and why it is a problem is made easier using the statistical analysis tools within your protocol analysis software.

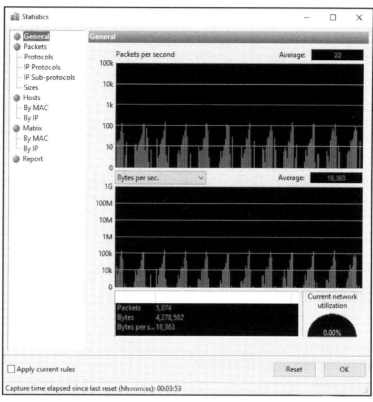

Figure 2.32: General statistics and network utilization in CommView for WiFi

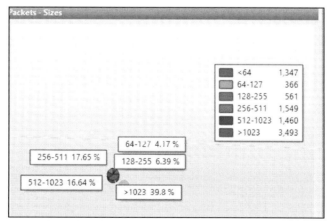

Figure 2.33: Packet sizes by percentage captured in CommView for WiFi

MAC/Alias	/	Pkts Sent	Pkts Rec.	Bytes Sent	Bytes Rec.	B-casts	M
2E:BB:58:51:1D:2E		0	7	0	2,191	0	0
5A:23:8C:75:E8:24		1	0	169	0	1	0
2wire:D3:C6:F2		14	0	3,304	0	14	0
2wire:D3:C6:FB		6	0	714	0	3	3
Aerohive:41:6B:80		69	18	42,073	2,918	0	0
Aerohive:00:60:E4		15	0	4,447	0	11	0
Aerohive:00:60:E0		5	0	2,170	0	5	0
Aerohive:00:60:C0		1	0	110	0	0	1
Aerohive:00:60:D4		748	73	230,940	1,851	466	0
AlpsElec:23:E6:C7		0	28	0	8,764	0	0
Apple:0F:E9:F0		0	3	0	78	0	0
Apple:9F:2B:80		0	4	0	108	0	0
Apple:95:48:6D		19	21	2,066	4,478	0	3
Apple:32:E4:9B		4	6	525	2,521	3	0
Apple:68:07:E8		23	54	3,281	35,663	13	0
AsrockIn:73:02:48		81	63	11,288	24,224	1	2
Broadcast		0	556	0	166,123	0	0
Cybertan:D1:AA:DC		101	62	25,316	7,663	0	0
GemtekTe:34:77:A8		0	3	0	939	0	0
GroupedMulticast		0	27	0	4,242	0	0
HonHaiPr:05:94:08		63	23	4,916	6,051	37	0
LiteonTe:B1:82:97		0	6	0	1,878	0	0
Proxim:50:41:81		0	108	0	61,074	0	0

Figure 2.34: Traffic by device MAC address in CommView for WiFi

Additionally, protocol analysis software often has reporting ability. You can use that to generate targeted reports as well as general reports based on the same information found in your captures. Again, this will be a much faster and more accurate way for you to compile the information you wish to save for future discussion and to present to your customers as part of your deliverables. Figure 2.35 is an example of the statistical reporting. More than looking at a few frames is required for statistical analysis. Use the features within your protocol analysis tools to help you see the statistical information faster and in a more easily read and explained format.

Expert Modes

Expert modes or displays are often a presentation of the anomalies found by protocol analysis in your capture files. The expert modes exist to have a better display of rarely detected behaviors or just notable network behaviors. Having an expert view allows both novice and expert users to find network problems faster, compared to scanning the captures manually.

Figure 2.35: A statistical report generated in OmniPeek

The amount of additional information displayed in an expert mode or view will vary based upon the protocols being used. More commonly used protocols will display more information. Expert modes will often allow you to track events and provide possible symptoms and remedies. You will have the same captured frames for your analysis in standard or expert modes. For many, the expert modes are more than they need; however, the diagnosis of complex problems is often made easier when you are able to get suggestions from the software instead of doing everything on your own. Figure 2.36 shows the expert mode analysis of Application Layer traffic using OmniPeek.

Peer-Maps

One of the reasons you analyze wireless traffic is to better understand your traffic patterns. Are you stations mostly downloading video or data or are the using station to station voice calls, uploading large files or some combination of all traffic types? It is important to know which stations are communicating with each other as well as just knowing what types of traffic exist on your networks. Peer maps can be used to illustrate these connections.

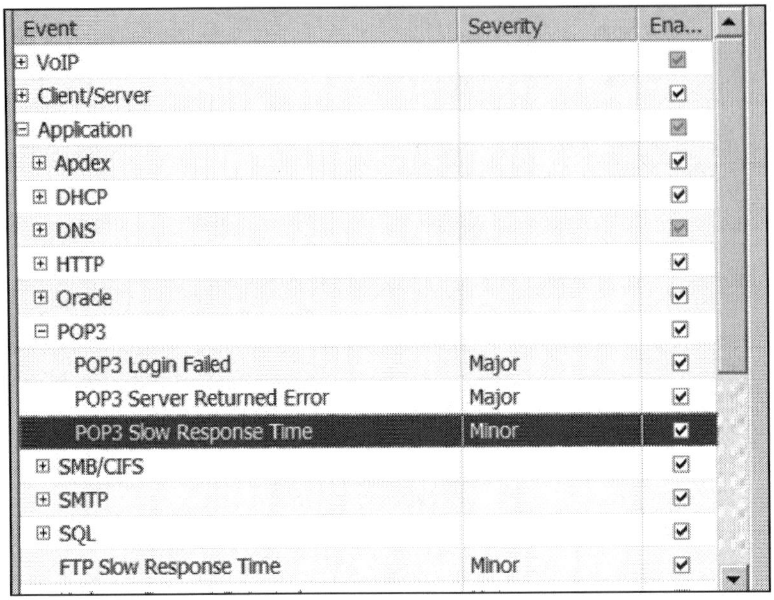

Figure 2.36: Application Layer analysis using the expert mode in OmniPeek

Network maps have been used for years in wired networking to show workgroups and client server model networks. It helps us know which devices connect through which switches and routers to get to which resources. The same type of knowledge is useful in wireless communications. You need to know which peers are communicating with each other to understand traffic low within your WLAN. Figure 2.37 shows a peer map by IP address. Figure 2.38 shows a peer map by MAC address. Both mappings are useful in understanding your traffic patterns, improving your network or even in troubleshooting.

It is important to remember that Layer 3 information is encrypted on WPA and WPA2 WLANs. If you cannot decrypt the communications, you cannot view IP peer maps from a wireless capture. However, you may be able to capture at the wired egress/ingress of the AP or controller to build IP peer maps, even when encryption is used on the wireless link. The only remaining task would be to map IP addresses to wireless client STAs as opposed to wired nodes. If you can do this, you can generate peer maps based on IP. The peer maps can be created within known the STAs holding the IPs, but it will be more challenging for you to determine which of the peers are wireless and which are wired instead.

100

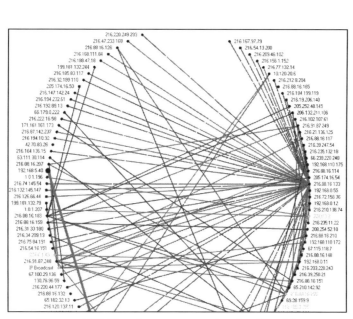

Figure 2.37: Peer to peer mapping by IP address

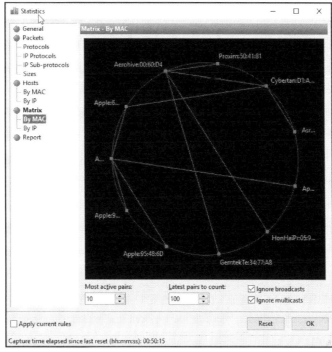

Figure 2.38: Peer to peer mapping by MAC address

Capture Configuration Parameters

Protocol analysis is a very powerful tool. You can use it for many things from assisting you in designing a new network to helping you when troubleshooting an existing network. To make its use more productive and to save what you have captured, you must know how to apply and configure the features within the tool. In this section we will discuss:

- Saving to disk
- Packet slicing
- Event triggers
- Buffer options
- Channels and channel widths
- Capture filters
- Channel scanning and dwell time

Saving to Disk

Once you have completed your capture, you will need to save the gathered information for analysis. Protocol analysis software allows you to determine where you save your capture files. As with most software, you select to save the information. You will need to stop any running capture to save it. Then you will be asked where you wish to save your files. You can store them locally, on the network, in the cloud or in a combination of locations. Many protocol analyzers allow you to configure them to save to disk during capture, but it is important to ensure that your system can write to the disk as fast as the capture happens or that appropriate capture buffers are in use.

Storing the capture, even after you have diagnosed any issues and solved any problems is important. You may wish to review the files for historical analysis when similar problems exist, of use them for training or documentation purposes. Once saved, the capture files can be reopened an analyzed at a future time. You may have only enough time to run a capture and need to examine it later. You may not be the one needing to conduct the analysis. You could then save the file and share it with the correct person. Also, when using a distributed or integrated capturing tool, you may need to save any captures on the network because the APs and sensors have limited storage which could be overwritten later or lost if the device loses power. Figure 2.39 shows the beginning of storing a capture.

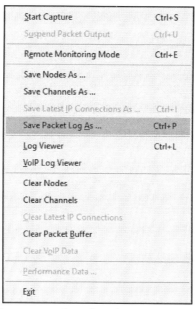

Start Capture	Ctrl+S
Suspend Packet Output	Ctrl+U
Remote Monitoring Mode	Ctrl+E
Save Nodes As ...	
Save Channels As ...	
Save Latest IP Connections As ...	Ctrl+I
Save Packet Log As ...	Ctrl+P
Log Viewer	Ctrl+L
VoIP Log Viewer	
Clear Nodes	
Clear Channels	
Clear Latest IP Connections	
Clear Packet Buffer	
Clear VoIP Data	
Performance Data ...	
Exit	

Figure 2.39: Configuring the storage location for your capture files using CommView for WiFi

Packet Slicing

Packet slicing, also called packet truncating, is used when you feel the capture will be too large. Figure 2.40 shows this option in OmniPeek. Here you can limit each packet to a specific size. What this means is that you get all the frame headers, but the actual data payload is not captured. As mentioned earlier, most protocol analysis is for troubleshooting or planning not for decrypting the contents of the frames. It is about gathering the Layer 2 data, which is in the frame headers. Slicing the captured frames to only include the headers reduces the capture size and will still get you the Layer 2 information that you require. If you are not interested in the payload of the frames, packet slicing will allow you to get what you need while saving disk space. Consider setting the slicing value to 400 bytes or so to ensure that you still capture large Beacon frames and other larger management and control frames in their entirety.

Remember, if encryption is in use, the IP payloads are not of any value to you anyway, given that, in most cases, you cannot decrypt the traffic on enterprise WLANs. As stated previously, when WPA-Enterprise or WPA2-Enterprise are in use, the frames from the wireless link cannot be decrypted. Even when Personal configurations are used, you can only decrypt frames for which you have the 4-way handshake in the capture, which is not likely to be the case for most of the transmissions within the channel.

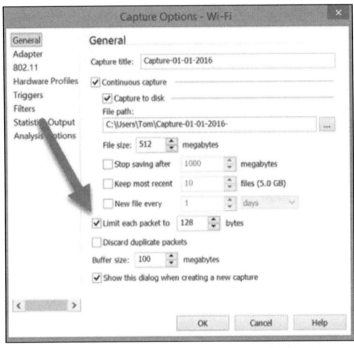

Figure 2.40: RF Packet slicing and other analysis options

Event Triggers

Many problems are inconsistent. They occur and by the time you are in place to begin your analysis, they have stopped. There may also be some network health issues that are not seen as a problem by the user but are indications of potential network issues such as slowness or excessive contention. While you are using an integrated or distributed capturing system, you can set event triggers to begin captures when a specified event occurs. You can also use event triggers in laptop-based protocol analysis software to begin truncating frame captures when events such as your capture equaling a configurable size or to stop capturing when the file reaches a configurable size.

Buffer Options

Buffers are used to store the captured packets/frames in memory as they are captured by your protocol analysis tool. The buffers size is limited by the amount of RAM in your computer. When the capture file size exceeds available space, it can be over written causing you to lose your information. The capture may be configured to stop when the buffer is full, causing you to lose any future captures. To prevent these incidents from happening, you can also choose to save the information to disk when the buffer is full. Some software may allow you to save directly to disk. If you are using an infrastructure or distributed system, you can set the captures to save on the controller, WNMS or on a server. These options give you the ability to capture for longer periods of time without the worry of losing information.

 It is recommended that you use a laptop with fast processors and at least 8 GB RAM to perform laptop-based capture and analysis. The fast processor will help with the CPU load required to do real-time expert analysis and statistics and the large amount of RAM will ensure you have sufficient buffer space.

Channels and Channel Widths

As you learned earlier, you can capture on all channels or only on a single channel or set of channels. You will need to use a capturing radio that can gather information at the desired channel width. For example, you need to capture the payload of frames being transmitted on a 160 MHz wide channel using 802.11ac adapters that support this channel width. Data will be found on all eight of the 20 MHz wide OFDM channels combined to make this 160 MHz wide channel. You will not be able to do this by using an 802.11n radio, since 802.11n only uses 80 MHz wide channels or smaller and doesn't understand all of the details of 802.11ax frames, without missing information. You will need an 802.11ac radio for this capture, as such clients become available.

When using bonded channels, Management frames are transmitted on the base channel or primary channel. Data is distributed across the other bonded. If you simply need to know what is happening in management and control frames from the primary channel and do not need the data frames, you could just monitor the one primary channel. However, you will miss events such as neighboring transmissions on the other channels.

Another important thing to remember is that when using modern channels bonding, the bonded channels may or may not be directly adjacent. 160 MHz channels can be non-contiguous 80+80 channels. Also, if an AP using bonded channels detects interference or other Wi-Fi on a bonded channel, it may discontinue using that channel, reducing the total channel width, or select another channel to use, based upon vendor implementation. These are all normal behaviors that may impact your devices. Being able to find and visualize these things in a protocol analyzer is very useful. Seeing these problems here may indicate that you should follow up with some spectrum analysis. Please review multiple adapter use above if needed. Remember that you can select the channels you wish to scan on a per adapter basis within you protocol analysis tool.

Capture Filters

As you learned previously, protocol analyzers support filtering the traffic during the capture. Since you will only be capturing the desired frames, this allows you to limit the size of your capture file. Capture filters occur while the data is being captured. If the detected frame does not match the capture filter settings, it will be ignored and can never be recaptured. Applying capture filters is the best way to limit the trace files to only those frames that are necessary, reducing the size of your capture file, but the loss of information bust be considered.

Capture filters, when properly applied, can be very useful, as you learned earlier. So, what types of filters are commonly used when conducting protocol analysis? Some of the more commonly used capture filters include channel, protocol, source or destination MAC address, To and From DS filtering, frame type, frame sub-type, time, retransmissions, frame size and authorized and or unauthorized device. When to use the filters and which filters to use is dictated by the type of information you are trying to gain by conducting your capture. As mentioned earlier, unless you know the specific thing you want to find, it is a good idea to capture all traffic. You can sort out the desired frames using display filters after you are finished capturing frames.

If you know the channel or channels being used, locking your adapters on them is not a bad idea, which may be thought of as a type of filtering because you a filtering to a given channel. This will give you more information in a shorter time since the adapters do not need to go off channel to scan. You can still capture all frame types for sorting later.

It cannot be said enough, if you apply any filtering during your captures, you will miss things you may need later. There is no RF rewind option allowing you to go back in time to remove the filter and get what you want. You will need to start a new capture with the filters removed. If you are trying to filter as you capture simply to save disk space or buffer space, don't. You can increase the size of your buffer, move the storage location or use packet slicing (truncating) to achieve this goal and still capture everything of importance. The application of filters prior to capturing will not save time. Capturing additional frames will not slow down the process. Capture it all and sort/filter the capture when you are ready to begin your diagnosis unless you are absolutely certain you will never need the uncaptured data.

Channel Scanning and Dwell Time

Protocol analyzers allow you to select an individual channel to scan per radio or scan them all and any combination between. When scanning all channels, on a single radio, there is no way to scan all the channels at the same exact time. They are usually scanned in order from the lowest to the highest in each band. If using a single radio to scan both bands, 2.4 GHz and 5 GHz, you will miss information on one band completely while scanning the other and will miss information on all other channels while scanning a single channel. The sweep usually scans all 2.4 GHz channels and then all 5 GHz channels, if scanning both bands. Over time, you gain enough information to have a good idea of what is happening within an area, although you are still missing a lot of information.

These tools allow you to select the channels you wish to scan, as we have discussed at length in this chapter. You can also determine how long the radio scans each channel. This setting is the dwell time. In fact, your analysis radio is acting like a frequency hopper, only passively since it moves across multiple channels to listen. As you probably know, Frequency Hopping Spread Spectrum, FHSS, networking was abandoned due to its inefficiencies. To improve the throughput of a legacy FHSS network, we would increase the dwell time, the time the radios stayed on a single frequency. The same theories that were used to improve FHSS can be applied when you are scanning multiple channels using a single radio in protocol analysis. You can increase the dwell time to gain more information per channel scanned or decrease the dwell time to scan the channels faster.

An adjustment you can make using protocol analysis that you could not do in the old FHSS networks is to increase the dwell time on individual channels while leaving others at the default. For example, if you are using an infrastructure or distributed system, you can set your scanning pattern to scan all channels for security but to spend more time on the channels you know are being used in your WLAN to increase the amount of information about those channels for security and network assurance alike. This is a happy medium between locking on channels and scanning them all.

Of course, should targeted analysis be required, you can always lock channels to only those desired and adjust the dwell time as needed to obtain the right information. Figure 2.41 is an example of channel and dwell time configuration found in a distributed system. In this software the dwell time is called Channel Scan Time and is in milliseconds. To enable or disable scanning on a channel you can check or uncheck the box next to the desired channel. Adjusting the dwell time per channel is done by typing in the millisecond value or using the up and down arrows. Use channel selection and dwell times as needed. They should not be used in every capture only used sparingly as required by your needs.

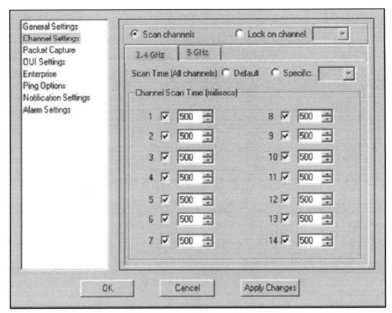

Figure 2.41: Channel and dwell time configurations within a distributed analysis system

Additional Capture Tools

Protocol analyzers are not the only tools you can use to gather information to be used in analysis or troubleshooting your WLAN. There are several tools from simple handheld devices to distributed spectrum analysis systems. Within this section we will discuss some of these including:

- WLAN scanners and discovery tools
- Protocol capture visualization and analysis tools
- Centralized monitoring, alerting and forensic tools

WLAN Scanners and Discovery Tools

WLAN scanners and discovery tools are often low-cost items or freeware. These range from something as simple as a key chain or tee shirt, see Figure 2.42, that will illuminate to alert the user to the presence of Wi-Fi, to things approaching the complexity of analysis software.

Figure 2.42: Wi-Fi discovery clothing from thinkgeek.com

Such items as seen above are usually just a novelty and are conversation starters. More serious discovery and scanning tools exist that are low-cost items as well. Acrylic WiFi Home, see Figure 2.43, is a scaled down version of a professional tool which runs on Windows platforms and gives you a lot of information in an intuitive user interface.

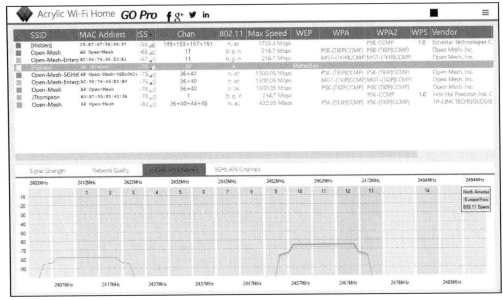

Figure 2.43: Acrylic WiFi Home

Another such tool is Cain & Abel. This tool, in addition to discovery, also has a limited key cracking ability. It does not have many useful graphics and is an older tool. So, its use may be found more on the detection and cracking end of analysis. Figure 2.44 shows this tool.

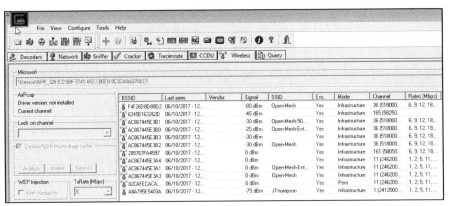

Figure 2.44: Cain & Abel

A popular free tool that can be used not only for discovery but also be used in a limited manner for Wi-Fi design is HeatMapper from Ekahau, Figure 2.45. This is a very scaled down version of their professional tool, Ekahau Site Survey and Site Planner.

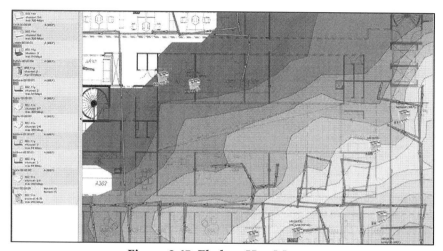

Figure 2.45: Ekahau HeatMapper

LizardSystems WiFi Scanner, Figure 2.46, offers a free edition of their application for personal use. It offers discovery, graphic tools and reporting as well.

Access Agility has many Wi-Fi tools, offered a very low cost, which work on Apple iOS devices and Windows based devices as well, see Figure 2.47.

Such tools are also available for handheld devices such as phones. One popular tool that is available for free through a download from the iTunes store is the Airport Utility, see Figure 2.48. This tool will display the APs, channels, SSIDs, signal strengths and more information as detected by your devices. Many people use this utility to verify the detection of access points by mobile clients.

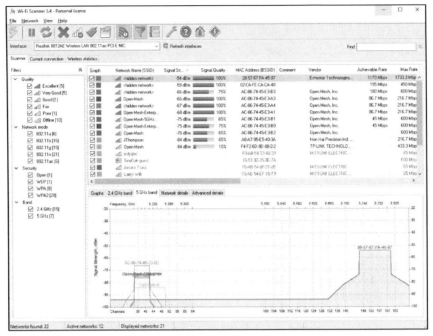

Figure 2.46: LizardSystems WiFi Scanner

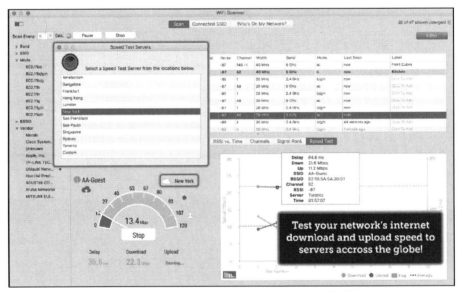

Figure 2.47: Wi-Fi Scanner from Access Agility

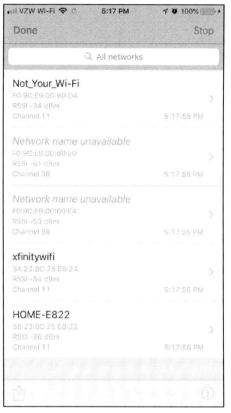

Figure 2.48: The Airport Utility from Apple

You can even use the built-in network discovery tools or your operating system to simply find networks in your airspace. These, however, are lacking a great deal of information you would need in analysis, such as MCS rates in the Windows environment. Simply knowing the SSIDs in an area may be all a user wants. Professionals need more information to troubleshoot and analyze traffic. The tools you choose are largely determined by the job at hand. If you simply need to verify that Wi-Fi or an SSID exists in each space, freeware on your phone may be enough. If you need to fully diagnose and troubleshoot Wi-Fi, you will need a protocol analyzer and a spectrum analyzer. If you need some of the more complex features but not all of them, there are many low cost or free alternatives available across many platforms. The key is in knowing what you need, how to capture it and how to analyze the capture.

Visualization and Analysis Tools

Protocol capture visualization and analysis tools are built into protocol analysis, spectrum analysis and design software, see Figure 2.49 below. These tools make it easier to explain what is happening on the WLAN to those not familiar with Wi-Fi. They are excellent to use in making reports for your own use or for the deliverables you will share with your customers. You can even visualize things beyond coverage and signal strength such as airtime utilization, as seen in Figure 2.50, channel use, client density and interference. You can sort and view frames by type in protocol analysis. However, being able to see the impact of the events you have captured in a graphical representation or even in a nice chart, helps IT professionals and users to more quickly understand what is happening within a given space. Just like choosing the proper display filters and configurations for analysis, you will need to select the proper visualizations. You can examine a channel use graphic or chart to see where the channels are being used and or any overlap that exists. Unfortunately, these views are not going to show you channel utilization, how much the air time is being used on a given channel. For that and other more specific information you will need to select the proper visualization to see the information you require.

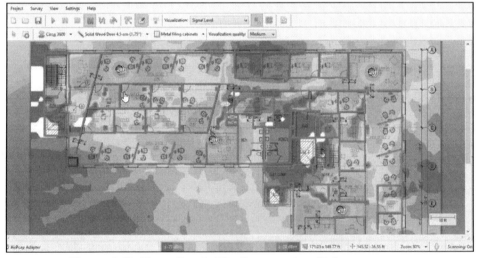

Figure 2.49: TamoGraph Site Survey visualizing coverage

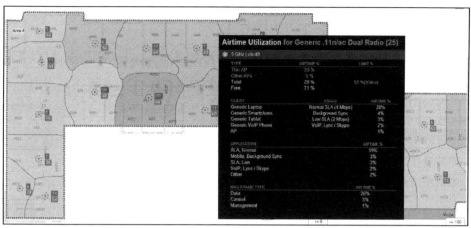

Figure 2.50: Airtime Utilization displayed both in a graphic and in a chart using Ekahau Site Survey

In addition to visualizing your captured information in more useful ways, you will also need to be able to use these visualizations as part of your analysis. For example, your frame capture has revealed a high percentage of retries. You know that there is either noise or a contention problem in the airspace in which you have conducted your capture. To begin analyzing the problem, you can use a visualization of retries on the map for the area. This will give you a look at the specific locations in the WLAN where the problem is most injurious to your network health. Knowing that, you can determine which radios, client or AP, that are being impacted the most or may be the source of the problem. You can then go into that area and look for noise using a spectrum analyzer, to determine if the problem is RF related. If you find the noise source, like a camera, microwave, or alarm system, you can mitigate the problem. If you do not find noise in the space to be the cause, you can start to examine the time stamps of transmitted frames that are sent but not acknowledged by devices in the area to locate the hidden nodes responsible for the undesired behavior or any other problem cause. Visualizations are helpful to even the most experienced analyst, since they reduce the amount of time it takes to analyze the information, deduce the problem(s) and develop solutions.

Chapter Summary

Knowing the structure of wireless frames and the ins and outs of wireless communications using given protocols is a must for WLAN administrators, designers and troubleshooters. Being able to capture and analyze the frame exchanges in a WLAN allows you to troubleshoot communication problems and validate network configurations and performance. In all these endeavors, protocol analysis allows you to compare the knowledge you have about how a network or device should be communicating and how they actually are communicating. The delta between these two is a spotlight shining on the problems experienced, performance impediments and other issues found in wireless networking. The tools and methods chosen for use in protocol analysis are largely dictated by the issues experienced and the information you wish to obtain. Remember, diagnose problems in an ascending manner from the bottom of the OSI model to the top. Protocol analysis is most often used in problem resolution. Knowing what should be happening, capturing frames as needed and comparing the two to determine a course of action is a great way to solve WLAN issues faster, plan WLAN use better and reduce downtime.

Facts to Remember

- You must have a compatible adapter that works with the protocol analysis software you wish to use to perform frame captures.
- Monitor mode is used to capture all 802.11 frames on a channel and monitor mode drivers are required to perform this action.
- Infrastructure-based capture options often exist and use the AP radios to capture the frames.
- When using an AP to capture frames it cannot concurrently act as an AP.
- Many configuration options are available in protocol analysis software including buffer sizes, save to disk, filtering, and more.
- The frame decode view interprets the bits in the capture frames so that they are presented as meaningful information to the analyst.
- In the packet/frame list view, many columns are available, and you can customize which columns are displayed based on your analysis needs.
- Visualization and analysis tools include such tools as site survey tools and Eye P.A. from Metageek.
- When using packet slicing (or truncating), remember to set it to 400 bytes to ensure larger management and control frames are fully captured.

Review Questions

1. What is the best reason to have dedicated adapters for each of the protocol analysis programs you are using?

    A. It allows you to capture frames across different PHYs.

    B. It allows you to capture frames across different channels.

    C. Repeatedly capturing with the same adapters can cause corrupted frames.

    D. Repeatedly changing the adapters driver can cause hardware to stop working.

2. What is one of the concerns faced when conducting a frame capture using the infrastructure method?

    A. The capture will only be on a single channel.

    B. The AP used may support different technology than the stations.

    C. The AP used will not be able to support clients while acting as a sensor.

    D. The capture will gather too much information since you are using an AP.

3. What is the best reason to use multiple adapters locked on different channels when conducting protocol analysis?

    A. To make it easier to diagnose roaming issues

    B. To capture the desired traffic faster

    C. To capture traffic from MIMO devices

    D. To capture information transmitted in the SIFS

4. When using a mobile protocol analysis solution, a laptop, what are the two most important things you must consider? (Choose the single best answer.)

    A. The OS support and the adapter support

    B. The screen size and the installation time

    C. The battery life and the hard drive space

    D. The PHY and MIMO support of the adapter

5. What is the largest advantage using a distributed or an infrastructure-based method of protocol analysis has over using a mobile method?

    A. They cost less than a mobile based method.

    B. They reduce truck rolls and save time.

    C. They require less training to use than mobile methods.

    D. They capture more information than mobile methods.

6. What can be used to allow you to see only the frames transmitted by a specific station in your analysis?

    A. MAC locking

    B. IP locking

    C. Display filtering

    D. Packet segregation

7. You are looking through a frame capture for the beacon frames sent by a specific AP to which users are connected. You see data and control frames from the AP but you are not able to see any beacon frames from that AP. What is the most likely cause of this problem?

    A. The user traffic is taking all of the air time and the AP is unable beacon.

    B. The AP is configured not to transmit beacon frames.

    C. You have misconfigured a display filter.

    D. The beacon interval on the AP is set to too great a value.

8. In addition to display filters, what to protocol analyzers offer to make finding frames of different types easier?

    A. Highlighting or colorization

    B. PHY structure recognition

    C. MIMO decoding

    D. Frame regeneration

9. True or False: The duration for which an infrastructure-based protocol analyzer remains on a single channel is not changeable when scanning multiple channels.

    A. True

    B. False

10. What is an advantage to using an expert view in a protocol analysis tool?

    A. Ensuring only professionals see the important information

    B. Finding network problems faster

    C. Creating a complex deliverable for your customer

    D. Presenting only the information needed in the interface

Review Answers

1. The correct answer is D. If you are using the same card with multiple protocol analysis software products, you will need to install the driver for the adapter every time you change tools. Repeatedly changing the driver can cause hardware failure.

2. The correct answer is C. While acting as a sensor, access points are in listen-only mode and will not be able to support client access.

3. The correct answer is A. By using multiple adapters locked on the channels used by neighboring APs you can capture the entire roaming process of client STAs. This makes diagnosing roaming issues much easier than capturing on a single channel at a time.

4. The correct answer is A. Although many things are important when selecting and using protocol analysis software, the top two are the support for the OS and support for the adapter.

5. The correct answer is B. The largest advantage found in using distributed or infrastructure methods of capture is that the AP or sensors are already in the locations where problems exist. There is no need to travel to the remote locations to gather the needed frames for initial analysis.

6. The correct answer is C. Display filtering allows you to select the frames you wish to see while hiding others within your capture.

7. The correct answer is C. A display filter is most likely set to not show management frames. Beacon frames are management frames.

8. The correct answer is A. Protocol analyzers also support highlighting or colorization as well as filtering. The highlighting feature allows you to define colors for packets or frames which match your defined criteria.

9. The correct answer is B. You can adjust the amount of time a sensor or AP scans a single channel, even when scanning multiple channels. This is often done to spend more time on the channels you are using than on off channels. This is even done when using a Wireless Intrusion Prevention System, WIPS, for the same reason.

10. The correct answer is B. Having an expert view allows both novice and expert users to find network problems faster, compared to scanning the captures manually.

Chapter 3: The Physical (PHY) Layer

Objectives Covered:

3.1 Understanding and describing the functions of the PLCP and PMD sublayers

3.2 Applying the understanding of PHY technologies (including PHY headers, preambles, training fields, frame aggregation and data rates) to captured data

3.3 Identifying and using PHY information provided in pseudo-headers within protocol analyzers

3.4 Recognizing the limits of protocol analyzers in capturing PHY information including NULL data packets and PHY headers

3.5 Using appropriate capture devices based on an understanding of PHY types

Many administrators and engineers overlook the examination of Layer 1 information, focusing only upon Layer 2 information. This may be due to their experience analyzing wired traffic or due to a lack of understanding the value of Layer 1 analysis. When analyzing 802.11 based communications in troubleshooting, pre-design site survey or network assurance, many people only focus on the Layer 2 information that can be seen in a packet capture. This information is very valuable and often points to the issues as desired. However, it only tells part of the story.

Because 802.11 communications use both Layer 1 and Layer 2, you really need to examine what is happening at both layers to get the whole story. A commonly used abbreviation for the Physical layer of the OSI model in wireless networking or a specific networking implementation is PHY. In describing the function of different physical technologies (DSSS, FHSS, OFDM, HT, VHT, etc.) in 802.11, the PHY is divided into two sublayers called the Physical Medium Dependent, PMD, and the Physical Layer Convergence Procedure, PLCP. The function of the Physical Layer, PHY, is to provide a mechanism for transferring MAC Layer Protocol Data Units, MPDUs between two or more stations, STAs. Within this chapter we will explore the functions used in Wi-Fi transmissions as they relate to the PHY.

The PLCP and PMD Sublayers

802.11 communications are similar to communications found in 802.3. However, due to the unbounded and shared nature of the medium used by Wi-Fi, the RF in the air, there are a few differences, even at Layer 1. Too many people assume the only things they need to understand about wireless transmissions are contention and noise, but this is not the case.

The MAC and PHY sublayer usage in Wi-Fi communications is defined within the 802.11-2016 standard in part 11: Wireless LAN Medium Access Control (MAC) and Physical Layer (PHY) Specifications. There are many functions at the Physical layer that you will need to understand to be a successful wireless professional. Most network training does not teach that the PHY has sublayers nor do they even mention sublayers existing beyond the Data Link layer. The PHY is also divided into two sublayers, much like the Data Link layer is divided into two distinct sublayers: The LLC and the MAC. The Physical Layer Convergence Procedure (PLCP) sublayer exists at the top of the PHY. The lower portion of the PHY is where the Physical Medium Dependent (PMD) sublayer resides.

The PLCP sublayer prepares the frame for transmission when it takes a frame from the Media Access Control (MAC) sublayer of the Data Link layer and creates the PLCP Protocol Data Unit (PPDU). The Physical Medium Dependent (PMD) sublayer then modulates and transmits the frame as bits. So, you can already see that the importance and function of these sublayers must be understood in 802.11 analysis. Within this section we will discuss the important roles of the PLCP and the PMD sublayers of the PHYs. You will learn what they are and what they do for us in wireless communications.

The Physical Layer Convergence Procedure (PLCP)

The Physical Layer Convergence Procedure, PLCP, until renamed in 802.11-2007 was called the Physical Layer Convergence Protocol. Some writings still use the older term. The PLCP performs important tasks of which many are not aware. When a station needs to transmit, it prepares the transmission starting at the top of the OSI model and passes the information through the various layers and sublayers formatting and encrypting it along the way. When that information reaches Layer 2 it has the MAC sublayer information, such as the MAC address, added. The MAC sublayer refers to an 802.11 frame as the MAC Protocol Data Unit or MPDU. When a frame is received, changing the directionality of the frames travel to up the OSI model versus down the OSI model the Physical layer refers to the frame as a Physical layer Service Data Unit or PSDU. The two terms are both correct. The term you should use to describe the encapsulated payload should reflect the sublayer from which the traffic is received and the direction of reception. Transmissions should be referred to as MSDU as they pass through the MAC sublayer of Layer 2 down and become an MPDU and as PSDU when passing through the PLCP sublayer of Layer 1 up. It can be confusing. Just remember that both terms refer to Layer 3 and up payloads as they are encapsulated or unencapsulated in transmission or reception by Layer 1 and Layer 2.

When the PLCP sublayer receives the MPDU from the MAC sublayer, the appropriate PLCP Preamble & PLCP Header are added to the now called PSDU to create the PLCP Protocol Data Unit, PPDU. The MAC layer communicates with the PLCP sublayer via primitives (a set of "instructive commands" or "fundamental instructions") through a service access point (SAP). When the MAC sublayer instructs it to do so, the PLCP prepares MPDUs for transmission. The PLCP minimizes the dependence of the MAC sublayer on the PMD sublayer by mapping MPDUs into a frame format which can then be transmitted by the PMD.

The PLCP also passes received frames up to the MAC sublayer upon reception from the PMD.

For transmission, the PLCP prepends a PHY-specific preamble and header fields to the MPDU that contain information needed by the Physical layer transmitters and receivers. The 802.11 standard refers to this composite frame (the MPDU with an additional PLCP preamble and header) as a PLCP protocol data unit (PPDU). The MPDU is also called the PLCP Service Data Unit (PSDU) and is typically referred to as such when referencing physical layer operations.

The frame structure of a PPDU provides for asynchronous transfer of PSDUs between stations. As a result, the receiving station's Physical layer must synchronize its circuitry to each individual incoming frame. The improvements within the 802.11 standard have given us different formats for the headers based upon the different modulation types, which allow us to have the speeds we do today versus the speeds offered in the original 802.11-1997 version of the standard.

The basics remain the same. A payload from Layer 3 and up is encapsulated at Layers two and one for transmission and unencapsulated at Layers one and two for reception. The information and format of the headers may change based upon protocol use but the intended functionality remains the same. There is no mention of the PLCP in Part 11: Wireless LAN Medium Access Control (MAC) and Physical Layer (PHY) Specifications of the 802.11-2016 standard. PPDU, however, is used quite extensively. So, PLCP is still there but as part of the PPDU discussion rather than being discussed on its own as in previous versions of the 802.11 standard.

The 802.11-2016 standard defines the PPDU as the unit of data exchanged between two peer PHY entities to provide the PHY data service. Each channel width defined in the 802.11-2016 standard, 20 MHz, 40 MHz, 80 MHz and 106 MHz, has its own requirements of the PPDU, because the things that need to happen at the PHY for each width vary. Different PHYs are defined as part of the 802.11-2016 standard. Each PHY can consist of the following protocol functions:

- A function that defines a method of mapping the MPDUs into a framing format suitable for sending and receiving user data and management information between two or more STAs.

- A function that defines the characteristics of, and method of transmitting and receiving data through, a wireless medium (WM) between two or more STAs.

The protocol reference model for the IEEE 802.11 architecture is shown in Figure 3.1. Most of PHY definitions in 802.11-2016 contain two functional entities: the PHY function and the layer management function. Additionally, the 802.11-2016 standard presents an architectural view which emphasizes the separation of the system into two major parts. They are the MAC sublayer of the Data Link layer and the PHY. These two major parts are intended to correspond closely to the lowest layers of the ISO/IEC basic reference model of Open Systems Interconnection (OSI) (ISO/IEC 7498-1:1994). The layers and sublayers are also depicted in Figure 3.1 below along with the PHY service which is provided to the MAC sublayer entity at the STA through a service access point or SAP, called the PHYSAP, as shown in Figure 3.1.

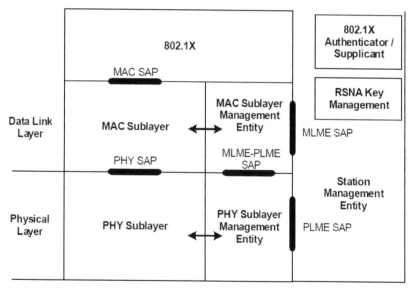

Figure 3.1: A portion of the ISO/IEC basic reference model covered in the 802.11-2016 standard

The services provided by the PHY to the MAC sublayer are specified and described in an abstract way by the 802.11-2016 standard and do not imply any particular implementation or exposed interface. The primitives, the instructions and data directly understandable, associated with communication between the MAC sublayer and the PHY, fall into two basic categories:

- Service primitives that support MAC peer-to-peer interactions, Figure 3.2
- Service primitives that have local significance and support sublayer-to-sublayer interactions, Figure 3.3

Due to a lack of direct relevance of PHY service primitives to protocol analysis, they will not be explained in detail in this text. The charts below are for your personal reference. Should you desire to know more about the relevance of primitives, you can consult the 802.11-2016 standard, where they are expounded upon in greater detail. Figure 3.4 illustrates the parameters used by one or more of the PHY SAP service primitives.

Primitive	Request	Indication	Confirm
PHY-DATA	X	X	X

Figure 3.2: The PHY SAP peer-to-peer service primitives

Primitive	Request	Indication	Confirm
PHY-TXSTART	X		X
PHY-TXEND	X		X
PHY-CCARESET	X		X
PHY-CCA		X	
PHY-RXSTART		X	
PHY-RXEND		X	
PHY-CONFIG	X		X
PHY-TXBUSY		X	
PHY-TXHEADEREND		X	

Figure 3.3: The PHY SAP inter-(sub)layer service primitives

Several service primitives include what is called a parameter vector. This is a list of parameters that may vary depending on the PHY type being used. Figure 3.5 lists the minimum parameter values required by the MAC or PHY in each of the parameter vectors, covering important things like data rate and channel usage. There is a lot of required information found in the headers of wireless transmissions. This information, which is added by the transmitting STA, provides any receiving STAs with the details needed to process the frame. The receiving STAs need to understand the simplest of things like data rate to begin the demodulation of the payload of the frame. If the transmitting and receiving STAs do not use or support the same PHY type, they will not be able to communicate. The primitives used, by PHY used, determine the parameter vectors used and their associated values.

Parameter	Associated primitive	Value
DATA	PHY-DATA.request PHY-DATA.indication	Octet value X'00'–X'FF'
TXVECTOR	PHY-TXSTART.request	A set of parameters
STATE	PHY-CCA.indication	(BUSY, [channel-list]) (IDLE)
RXVECTOR	PHY-RXSTART.indication PHY-RXEND.indication	A set of parameters
RXERROR	PHY-RXEND.indication	NoError, FormatViolation, CarrierLost, UnsupportedRate, Filtered
IPI-STATE	PHY-CCARESET.request PHY-CCARESET.confirm	IPI-ON, IPI-OFF
IPI-REPORT	PHY-CCA.indication PHY-CCARESET.confirm	A set of IPI values for the preceding time interval
PHYCONFIG_VECTOR	PHY-CONFIG	A set of parameters
TXSTATUS	PHY-TXSTART.confirm	A set of parameters
STATE	PHY-TXBUSY.indication	IDLE, BUSY

Figure 3.4: PHY SAP service primitive parameters

The STATE parameter, as seen in Figure 3.4, can have one of two values: BUSY or IDLE. The parameter value is said to be BUSY if the assessment of the channel(s) by the PHY determines that the channel(s) are not available. If the channel(s) are available, the value of the parameter is said to be IDLE. When performing the PLCP functions, the 802.11-2016 standard specifies the use of state machines. Each state machine performs one of the following functions:

- Carrier Sense/Clear Channel Assessment (CS/CCA)
- Transmit (Tx)
- Receive (Rx)

Parameter	Associated vector	Value
DATARATE	TXVECTOR, RXVECTOR	PHY dependent. The name of the field used to specify the Tx data rate and report the Rx data rate may vary for different PHYs.
LENGTH	TXVECTOR, RXVECTOR	PHY dependent
ACTIVE_RXCHAIN_SET	PHYCONFIG_VECTOR	The ACTIVE_RXCHAIN_SET parameter indicates which receive chains of the available receive chains are active.
OPERATING_CHANNEL	PHYCONFIG_VECTOR	The operating channel the PHY is configured use.
SECONDARY_CHANNEL_OFFSET	PHYCONFIG_VECTOR	Enumerated type: SECONDARY_CHANNEL_NONE indicates operation in 20 MHz HT STAs. SECONDARY_CHANNEL_ABOVE indicates operation in 40 MHz with the secondary channel above the primary. SECONDARY_CHANNEL_BELOW indicates operation in 40 MHz with the secondary channel below the primary.
ANT_CONFIG	PHYCONFIG_VECTOR	Indicates which antenna configuration(s) is to be used when receiving packets and which configuration is to be used when switching configurations during the reception of a packet. Values are implementation dependent.
GROUP_ID_MANAGEMENT	PHYCONFIG_VECTOR	Specifies membership status and STA position for each of the group IDs as described in 9.6.23.3
PARTIAL_AID_LIST_GID00	PHYCONFIG_VECTOR	Includes the list of partial AIDs, of which the STA is an intended recipient, associated with group ID 0. The settings of the PARTIAL_AID are specified in 10.20).
PARTIAL_AID_LIST_GID63	PHYCONFIG_VECTOR	Includes the list of partial AIDs, of which the STA is an intended recipient, associated with group ID 63. The settings of the PARTIAL_AID are specified in 10.20).
LISTEN_TO_GID00	PHYCONFIG_VECTOR	When true, indicates to the PHY not to filter out PPDUs with GROUP_ID field equal to the value 0.
LISTEN_TO_GID63	PHYCONFIG_VECTOR	When true, indicates to the PHY not to filter out PPDUs with GROUP_ID field equal to the value 63.

Figure 3.5: Vector Descriptions

Carrier Sense/Clear Channel Assessment

CS/CCA, is used to determine the state of the medium, BUSY or IDLE. The CS/CCA procedure is executed while the receiver is turned on and the station is not currently receiving or transmitting a packet. The CS/CCA procedure is used for two specific purposes. It is used to detect the start of a network signal that can be received (CS), and to determine if the channel is available prior to transmitting a packet (CCA). The CCA is part of the collision avoidance method used in 802.11 communications.

As you learned earlier, the MAC sublayer passes a frame to the PLCP for transmission when needed. The transmit procedure is invoked by the CS/CCA procedure immediately upon receiving a PHY-TXSTART request (TXVECTOR) from the MAC sublayer. The Transmit (Tx) is used to send individual octets of a frame. Carrier Sense Multiple Access with Collision Avoidance, CSMA/CA, is performed by the MAC sublayer with the PHY PLCP in the CS/CCA procedure prior to transmitting.

An additional parameter we must discuss for transmission is the idle power indicator or IPI-REPORT parameter. This is present if dot11RadioMeasurementActivated is true and if idle power indicator reporting has been turned on by the IPI-STATE parameter. The IPI-REPORT parameter provides a set of IPI values for a time interval. The set of IPI values is used by the MAC sublayer for radio measurement purposes. The IPI values are recent values observed by the PHY entity since the generation of the most recent PHYTXEND, confirm, PHY-RXEND.indication, PHY-CCARESET.confirm, or PHY-CCA.indication primitive, whichever occurred latest, according to 802.11-2016.

If the STATE of the medium is IDLE or when, for the type of PHY in operation, CCA is determined by a single channel, the channel-list parameter is absent. Otherwise, it carries information or sets indicating which channels are in use and therefore BUSY. The channel-list parameter in a PHY-CCA indication primitive generated by a VHT STA contains at most a single element. Figure 3.6 through 3.8 shows the members of this information or set. When using bonded channels, to get the higher speeds all bonded channels must be used. If one is BUSY, the remaining channels may be used but you will not achieve the higher data rates offered by the given protocol due to the reduced channel size. The assessment of the STATE of each channel is conducted prior to transmission. In a high-density deployment area, you may never find that all the bonded channels are available, IDLE, with the result being throughput and data rates below the expected values.

channel-list element	Meaning
primary	In an HT STA that is not a VHT STA, indicates that the primary 20 MHz channel is busy. In a VHT STA, indicates that the primary 20 MHz channel is busy according to the rules specified in 21.3.18.5.3. In a TVHT STA, indicates that the primary channel is busy according to the rules specified in 22.3.18.6.3.
secondary	In an HT STA that is not a VHT STA, indicates that the secondary channel is busy. In a VHT STA, indicates that the secondary 20 MHz channel is busy according to the rules specified in 21.3.18.5.4. In a TVHT STA, indicates that the secondary channel is busy according to the rules specified in 22.3.18.6.4.
secondary40	Indicates that the secondary 40 MHz channel is busy according to the rules specified in 21.3.18.5.4. In a TVHT STA, indicates that the secondary TVHT_2W channel is busy according to the rules specified in 22.3.18.6.4.
secondary80	Indicates that the secondary 80 MHz channel is busy according to the rules specified in 21.3.18.5.4.

Figure 3.6: Channel list parameter elements as defined by 802.11-2016

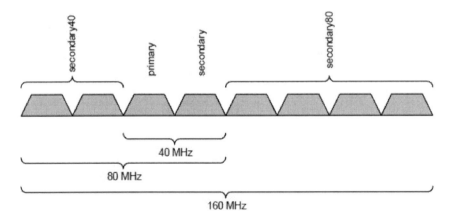

Figure 3.7: The channel-list parameter element for 40 MHz, 80 MHz, and 160 MHz channel width

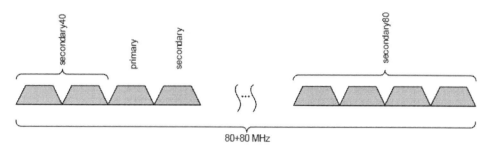

Figure 3.8: The channel-list parameter element for 80+80 MHz channel width

Many of the procedures carried out by the PLCP are just expected, based upon the BSS configuration, data rates, channel width, etc., and cannot really be directly analyzed. Some can be verified within a frame capture and protocol analysis. However, many of the operations are truly beyond the scope of protocol analysis and are therefore not displayed in a capture.

The reception of wireless transmissions is a similar process, just in reverse from the transmission. When you ship something to another person, you need to box up the shipment: encapsulate it. You need to address the package with both to and from addressing. You need to determine the manner of shipping, overnight or standard delivery for example, like the data rates and channels. On the receiving end, the same things happen in reverse, address verification and opening the package, de-encapsulating.

Receive (Rx) is used to receive individual octets of the frame. The receive procedure is invoked by the PLCP CS/CCA procedure upon detecting a portion of the preamble sync pattern followed by a valid start frame delimiter, SFD, and PLCP Header. Oddly, the preamble and PLCP header are not truly "received". Reception and acknowledgement are part of the MAC sublayers duties.

The PHY bits have three parts with which you should be familiar. They are the Preamble, the Header and the PSDU. The Preamble contains two important pieces, the Synchronization (Sync) field and Start Frame Delimiter (SFD) field. The Sync field alerts the receiver that a potentially receivable signal is present. This basically says the RF signal is not noise but rather an 802.11 transmission. Without this field receivers would have a very difficult time determining what is an 802.11 signal and what is just noise. This field consists of a string of 0s and 1s. When the Sync is detected, receivers will begin their synchronization with the incoming signal. Often, receivers may not receive the entire Sync field. They only hear a portion of it. This is not a problem, since the Sync field is a continuous stream of 0s and 1s. What is important for this procedure is that the receiving STA synchronizes before the Start Frame Delimiter, SFD arrives.

The SFD field denotes the beginning of a frame. The pattern of 1's and 0's in the SFD will vary based upon the type of preamble used, long preambles, for legacy transmissions, or short preambles, used in newer transmissions. Most APs and RF profiles in use today allow the administrator to select the lengths of the preambles used. Shorter preambles are more efficient. So, many administrators select to use them exclusively. This works well unless you must support legacy clients or clients in 2.4 GHz that due to their distance from the AP are forced to use legacy modulation techniques and data rates, like those found in 802.11-1997 networks. When supporting a mixture of legacy and modern client types, most configurations will allow you to select to support both long and short preambles. In fact, the 802.11g amendment made support for both mandatory to allow for legacy client support. You can easily determine preamble support of an AP by viewing the Capability Information fixed field of a Beacon frame from the AP in question. You can view an 802.11b long preamble in Figure 3.9 and an 802.11b short preamble in Figure 3.10 for comparison, both of which, by todays use of 802.11, are legacy formats.

Orthogonal Frequency Division Multiplexing, OFDM, introduced a different structure, see Figure 3.11 for an example. Additionally, the HT PHY introduced the concept of three PPDUs with differing structures which will be discussed later. The information found and used in the header is to ensure that the receiving STAs recognize the transmission as an 802.11 signal and know how to process any transmissions intended for their use. Without the PLCP/PPDU information the signals may as well be noise, because 802.11 as defined would not work. Frames often collide with noise and are rendered unusable by the receiving STAs. Such frames are discarded and are not acknowledged. We will discuss more about the frame structures used by different protocols later. You should be able to identify the protocol used and the data rates used during protocol analysis. A basic description of the primary function of the PLCP sublayer is that it provides a mechanism for transferring MPDUs between two or more nodes over the PMD sublayer.

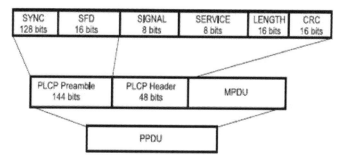

Figure 3.9: 802.11b Long Preamble format (Legacy)

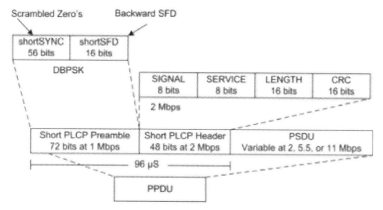

Figure 3.10: 802.11b Short Preamble format (Legacy)

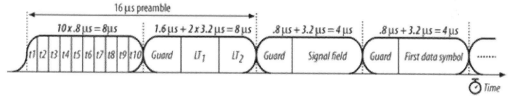

Figure 3.11: OFDM PLCP format

The Physical Media Dependent (PMD) Sublayer

The lesser revealing functions involved in network communications occur at the bottom of the OSI model. Unfortunately for the PMD, that is where it resides. So, there is not as much to discuss here, although what occurs here is vital to 802.11 communications. The PMD sublayer is the service within the PHY responsible for transmitting and receiving bits onto and off of the medium. It is where data is converted into modulated bits: 0's and

1's represented by changes in RF wave characteristics. To provide this service in Wi-Fi, the PMD interfaces directly with the wireless medium and provides modulation and demodulation of the frame transmissions.

The PLCP or PPDU, as used in 802.11-2016, and PMD sublayers communicate using primitives, through a SAP, to govern the transmission and reception of frames. The PMD sublayer uses complex coding techniques that vary with the protocol in use and signal strengths; remember dynamic rate switching causes a change in data rate used and also in the corresponding modulation scheme/coding technique. Here, in addition to data rates, signal strengths used determine the modulation techniques capable stations use such as Binary Phase Shift Keying (BPSK) or Quadrature Amplitude Modulation (QAM).

In 802.11 based communications, the PMD functions define the characteristics of, and method of transmitting and receiving frames via the wireless medium between two or more STAs. The protocol used may require the definition of a unique PLCP. If the PMD sublayer already provides the defined Physical Layer services, the PLCP function might be null. The PHY contains three functional entities: the physical medium dependent function, the physical layer convergence function, and the layer management function. The PHY service is provided to the MAC entity at the node through a SAP as shown in Figure 3.1 called the PHY_SAP. A set of primitives might also be defined to describe the interface between the PLCP sublayer and the physical medium dependent sublayer called the PMD_SAP. Simply stated, the PMD sublayer is responsible for the modulation/demodulation and encoding/decoding of 802.11 transmissions.

PHY Technologies and Captured Data

There is a lot more happening at the PHY than most people will ever need to know, unless they are Wi-Fi professionals. Within this section, we will learn how to apply the knowledge and understanding of what happens at the PHY as it relates to the protocols used in 802.11 communications. You will learn more about applying what you know concerning the headers, preambles, training fields, frames, frame aggregation and data rates used in 802.11 based networking to your captured data in protocol analysis. We will focus upon:

- Direct Sequence Spread Spectrum, DSSS
- High Rate Direct Sequence Spread Spectrum, HR/DSSS
- Orthogonal Frequency Division Multiplexing, OFDM
- Extended Rate Physical OFDM, ERP-OFDM

- High Throughput OFDM, HT-OFDM
- Very High Throughput OFDM, VHT-OFDM

The 802.11 standard and our uses of the technologies found therein are constantly evolving. There are more protocols being developed to increase the efficiency of our airtime utilization. However, at the time of this writing the above protocols are the most commonly used. As the newer uses of 802.11 begin being used, you will have a solid understanding of Wi-Fi use, but will need to add an understanding of the new uses to be able to analyze them.

 As a CWAP, it is important to know that you cannot capture everything about the PHY. Some information is passed up through the drivers, but much of it is lost and simply guessed or not made available in protocol analyzers.

Direct Sequence Spread Spectrum

Why use spread spectrum transmission rather than using a narrow band transmission? Narrow band transmissions require more power. Given the relatively small size of mobile devices and their need to conserve battery life, this was a problem that the use of spread spectrum addressed. The term spread spectrum refers to the expansion of signal bandwidth which occurs when a key is attached to the communication channel. Specifically, spread spectrum means an RF communications system in which the baseband signal bandwidth is intentionally spread over a larger bandwidth by injecting a higher frequency signal. By taking the same data and transmitting it using more frequency space, the transmissions can take place using a much lower power level than when using a narrowly focused signal. This allows the use of the wireless devices for a longer period as the battery life is extended. The spreading of signals across a larger portion of the spectrum allows the same data rates as well. Spreading the signal across a larger portion of the spectrum directly results in less space for us to use in the unlicensed frequency ranges. That overallocation of spectrum is well offset by the ability for many users to share the enlarged frequency band.

Direct Sequence Spread Spectrum (DSSS) was defined for our usage in 802.11-1997 and can still be found in use today due to legacy devices and design. Legacy devices will always haunt us. They are already owned and are usually not slated to be replaced until they no longer function. You cannot escape the confines of budget.

Poor design is the number one cause of wireless networking problems. If you do not need to support legacy devices, why support legacy protocols and data rates which use less efficient means of communication that slow down your network? You can learn more about WLAN design in the Certified Wireless Design Professional (CWDP) materials, but for now, know that "designing out" lower data rates can be helpful.

DSSS defined data rates of 1 and 2 Mbps. These seem rather sluggish by todays usage and demands. In 1997, when introduced, they were faster than the internet connections used by most people and were only deemed to be slow when used for LAN resource access. Also, the use of Wi-Fi in the enterprise at the time was not widespread. These rates were quite acceptable in warehousing, retail and logistics as well as in the few and novel deployments of Wi-Fi that existed in the enterprise and small office home office (SOHO) environments.

DSSS coding/modulation used in 802.11-1997 is Barker code with Differential Binary Phase Shift Keying (DBPSK) for 1 Mbps and Differential Quadrature Phase Shift Keying (DQPSK) for 2 Mbps. Phase-shift keying (PSK) is a digital modulation process. It conveys data by modulating/changing the phase of a constant frequency reference signal. DBPSK is a modulation scheme where bits are represented by a change in BPSK state. A 0 means no change; a 1 means change. In Quadrature Phase Shift Keying (QPSK), information is conveyed by the Absolute Phase of each symbol. In contrast, DQPSK conveys information by establishing a phase of one symbol which is relative to the previous symbol. Figure 3.12 illustrates the difference.

PPDUs vary in formation based upon the technology used. In Figure 3.13 you can see the construction of the DSSS PPDU. Notice that the PPDU contains the MPDU. The DSSS PPDU uses a long preamble with the header, and the MPDU (PSDU) as specified in the 802.11-1997 standard. Both the preamble and the header are transmitted at 1 Mbps when using the long preamble format. The MPDU is transmitted at the data rate specified by the transmitting device, 1 or 2 Mbps. As you learned earlier, the preamble enables the receiver to synchronize to the incoming signal before the actual content of the frame arrives. The header provides vital information about the frame, allowing the receiving STA(s) to begin processing the transmission.

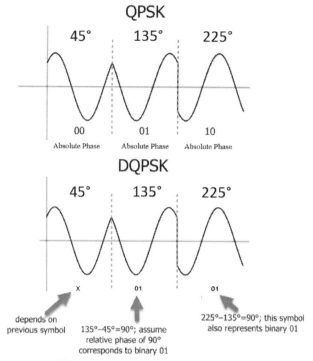

Figure 3.12: QPSK versus DQPSK

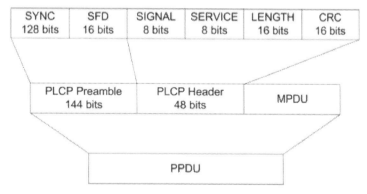

Figure 3.13: DSSS PPDU structure (Long Preamble)

Remember, the Preamble contains two important components, the Synchronization (Sync) field and Start Frame Delimiter (SFD) field. The Sync field alerts the receiver that a potentially receivable signal is present and what they have detected is not just noise.

When using DSSS, the data rates of 1 and 2 Mbps severely limit the throughput available. You will find many networks that support operation in 2.4 GHz will have these rates disabled. They will not allow any original 802.11 stations to connect, because these rates do not appear as supported in neither the beacon frames nor in any probe response frames. Disabling these data rates will also force clients at a significant distance from the AP to roam away faster or completely disconnect when they can no longer receive a strong enough signal to use the higher rates supported within the service set.

Other important things to know about DSSS transmission are that they use a 10μ (10 microsecond) Short Interframe spacing (SIFS) and a 20μ Slot Time. The importance of both are discussed later in this book. Although DSSS is a legacy method of communications in Wi-Fi and is extremely slow when compared to more modern methods, having an understanding of DSSS, its rates, its preamble and its limitations will help you better understand more modern uses of 802.11 signaling.

High Rate/DSSS

If something works, making it go faster must be better, right? In 802.11-1999 a faster implementation of DSSS was introduced. It is called High Rate Direct Sequence Spread Spectrum, HR/DSSS. The HR/DSSS PHY is the enhanced physical layer as defined by IEEE 802.11b. HR/DSSS is a data rate extension of the original 802.11 and is backwards compatible with DSSS transmissions. Like the original 802.11 DSSS, HR/DSSS operates in the 2.4 GHz band. It supports the same technologies and data rates of 1 and 2 Mbps to allow legacy DSSS stations to communicate with the newer HR/DSSS stations. Both DSSS and HR/DSSS use 22 MHz wide channels in the 2.4 GHz spectrum.

HR/DSSS added two higher data rates, 5.5 and 11 Mbps. By the time HR/DSSS was introduced, Wi-Fi adoption was increasing, and the users were demanding more from their use of wireless communications. HR/DSSS achieves these "higher rates" by using a more complex code than the 802.11 primes barker code. HR/DSSS uses Complementary Code Keying (CCK). DSSS transmissions multiply the data being transmitted by a "noise" signal. This noise signal is a pseudorandom sequence of 1 and −1 values, at a frequency much higher than that of the original signal.

Due to a likelihood of noise interference, DSSS uses a sequence of chips, see Figure 3.14. As DSSS spreads transmission across a frequency range, it sends a single data bit as a string of chips, also called a chip stream. With redundant data being sent, if part of the signal is lost, due to collision with noise, the data may still be understood. The chipping code process expands each data bit into a string of bits. CCK uses an 8-chip pseudorandom number, PN, along with using different PNs for different bit sequences. CCK can encode 4 bits of data with 8 chips (5.5 Mbps) and can encode 8 bits of data with 8 chips (11 Mbps) see Figure 3.15. Both the 5.5 Mbps and 11 Mbps data rates use DQPSK modulation, the same modulation used by DSSS at 2 Mbps.

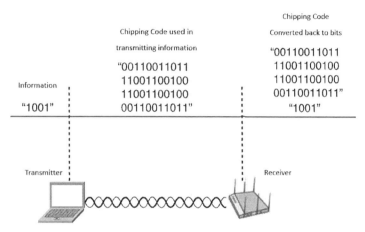

Figure 3.14: Chipping code used in HR/DSSS with CCK

	Data rate (Mbps)	Encoding	Chip length	Bits encoded	Modulation
HR/ DSSS	5.5	CCK coding	8	4	DQPSK
HR/ DSSS	11	CCK coding	8	8	DQPSK

Figure 3.15: HR/DSS Encoding, Chip length, Bits used and Modulation

To further improve our use of the medium, HR/DSSS stations, when communicating with other HR/DSSS stations, use a short preamble. See Figure 3.16 for an example. It is important to note here that, even though HR/DSSS uses a short preamble of 72 bits versus the 144 bits of a long preamble, the PLCP Preamble and the PLCP Header are still transmitted at 1Mbps for backwards compatibility with 802.11 Prime. The payload, the PPDUs, are transmitted at data rates based upon radio abilities and frame component, typically 2, 5.5 or 11 Mbps. The PLCP Header remains at its previous length of 48 bits but is now transmitted at 2Mbps.

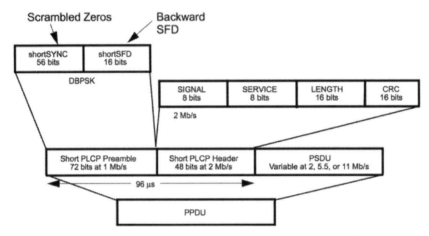

Figure 3.16: HR/DSSS Structure (Short Preamble)

If a legacy 802.11 Prime STA is in use, this short preamble format cannot be used. In that scenario, APs must indicate when Long Preamble Only clients, either 802.11 Prime or 802.11 HR/DSSS with Long Preamble in use are present within the BSS. This means that all stations and the AP must use long preambles. The PSDU will then be transmitted at either 2, 5.5, or 11 Mbps. The ability to support legacy devices is normally part of each improvement in 802.11 usage to increase the improvements adoption rate. This allows network owners to update the infrastructure without requiring the clients also be updated. It also allows newer client stations to connect to legacy APs and stations.

In a mixed legacy and new device service set, you will find that overall throughput is somewhere between the speeds offered by the technologies and not as fast as the speed offered by the newer technology alone. Part of troubleshooting a "slow" WLAN is knowing the client technologies in use and their impact on the network due to backward compatibility requirements for their continued usage. HR/DSSS is quite a bit faster than DSSS due to the speed enhancements of more efficient encoding, CCK versus Barker, and the shorter preamble offered.

Orthogonal Frequency Division Multiplexing

Orthogonal Frequency Division Multiplexing (OFDM) was also introduced in 1999. It was introduced as 802.11a. OFDM is used for modulation in wireless networks with many of the PHYs, but only one PHY is named OFDM and that is the 802.11a PHY. OFDM is not considered to be a spreading technology. It is a frequency-division multiplexing (FDM) scheme used as a digital multi-carrier modulation method. OFDM works by splitting the radio signal into multiple smaller signals that are then transmitted simultaneously at different frequencies to the receiver. These smaller signals are transmitted as sub-carriers within the OFDM channel.

There are 52 sub carriers per channel when using the 802.11a OFDM PHY. OFDM channels are only 20 MHz wide versus the 22 MHz width of DSSS channels. Originally, in 802.11 transmissions, OFDM was only found in 5 GHz with 802.11a. Today, variations of OFDM can be found in both 2.4 GHz and 5 GHz. OFDM, as introduced in 802.11a, gave us data rates of 6, 9, 12, 18, 24, 36, 48 and 54 Mbps. These data rates were much more appealing than the slower data rates of even HR/DSSS. The higher data rates were available largely due to the use of Quadrature Amplitude Modulation or QAM. QAM is a signal in which carriers are shifted in phase by 90 degrees and are modulated. The resultant output consists of both amplitude and phase variations. Since both amplitude and phase variations are present it may also be considered a mixture of amplitude and phase modulation.

QAM can be used in both analog and digital formats. Wi-Fi uses the digital, because it can carry higher data rates than ordinary amplitude modulated schemes and phase modulated schemes. As found in phase shift keying, the number of points at which the signal can rest, the number of points on the constellation, is indicated in the modulation format description. For example, 16 QAM uses a 16-point constellation whereas 64 QAM uses a 64-point constellation. See Figure 3.17 for a 16-point constellation example. In 256 QAM, each quadrant has 64 points, adding to both the speed and complexity of use. The larger constellations yield higher data rates.

The constellation points in QAM are arranged in a square grid. The grid has equal vertical and horizontal spacing. The most common forms of QAM use a constellation with the number of points equal to some power of 2 such as 4, 16 or even up to 256 QAM in 802.11ac. The details of how either BPSK or QAM work are quite complex beyond the scope of the CWAP exam. You should know, however, that there are different modulations used at different data rates and with different PHYs. You should know the names of these modulation techniques, their data rates and where they are used.

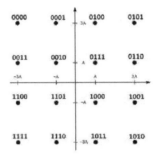

Figure 3.17: A 16 QAM Constellation

By using more points on the constellation, it is possible to transmit more bits per symbol. This increase comes with a cost. The points are closer together and they are more susceptible to noise and data errors. This susceptibility to noise usually means you will need smaller cells and cleaner environments to get the highest data rates. Data capacities of modulation types in bits per symbol and error margin can be seen in Figure 3.18.

MODULATION	BITS PER SYMBOL	ERROR MARGIN		COMPLEXITY
OOK	1	1/2	0.5	Low
BPSK	1	1	1	Medium
QPSK	2	$1 / \sqrt{2}$	0.71	Medium
16 QAM	4	$\sqrt{2} / 6$	0.23	High
64QAM	6	$\sqrt{2} / 14$	0.1	High

Figure 3.18: A summary of types of modulation with data capacities

Modulation techniques used with data rates per sub-carrier and total data rate vary based upon signal strength and dynamic rate switching. In Figure 3.19 you can see the various modulation techniques used with data rates per sub-carrier in OFDM and total data rate.

OFDM and 802.11a were not widely adopted at first, despite the more efficient use of air time and the use of QAM. This was because it worked in 5 GHz only and enterprise deployments as well as personal use deployments were heavily invested in DSSS and HR/DSSS which only worked in 2.4 GHz. It simply came down to the budget winning out over technology. You will find, even years after it was ratified and made part of the 802.11 standard, the term 802.11a is still used in the industry, just like 802.11b. Often people will refer to their networks by the 802.11 amendments they support versus the spectrum used. In addition to the higher speeds, using the 5 GHz band gave OFDM users a significant advantage, since the 2.4 GHz band was and still is heavily used to the point of being over populated with both 802.11 and non-802.11 RF energy.

Modulation Technique	Data rate per subchannel (Kbps)	Total Data Rate (Mbps)
BPSK	125	6
BPSK	187.5	9
QPSK	250	12
QPSK	375	18
16-QAM	500	24
16-QAM	750	36
64-QAM	1000	48
64-QAM	1125	54

Figure 3.19: Modulation techniques used with data rates per sub-carrier and total data rate

How are these 52 OFDM subcarriers used? The majority, 48, are for data. The remaining 4 are pilot subcarriers with a carrier separation of 0.3125 MHz (20 MHz/64). Each of these subcarriers can be either BPSK, QPSK, 16-QAM or 64-QAM. The total bandwidth is 20 MHz per channel with an occupied bandwidth of 16.6 MHz. The symbol duration is 4 microseconds. This value includes a guard interval of 0.8 microseconds.

Each of the subcarriers can be represented as a complex number. The time domain signal is generated by taking an Inverse Fast Fourier Transform (IFFT). A fast Fourier transform is an algorithm that samples a signal over a period and divides it into its frequency components. These components are single sinusoidal oscillations at distinct frequencies each with their own amplitude and phase. Correspondingly the receiver down converts, samples at 20 MHz and conducts a Fast Fourier Transform (FFT) to retrieve the original coefficients.

The advantages of using OFDM include reduced multipath effects in reception and increased spectral efficiency. The modulation used with sub-carriers varies depending on the data rates as seen in Figure 3.19 previously. Although the data rate per sub-carrier is relatively low, the data is sent simultaneously over the subcarriers in parallel. OFDM is a form of multicarrier modulation. An OFDM signal consists of several closely spaced modulated carriers each responsible for a portion of the transmission. Combining the use of sub-carriers and QAM is how the higher data rates found in OFDM transmissions are achieved. The OFDM PHY structure is not the same as the earlier PHY structures. See Figure 3.20.

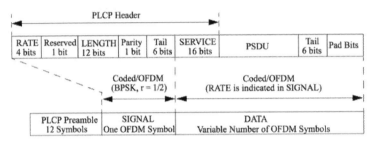

Figure 3.20: OFDM Frame Structure

Extended Rate PHY

People saw and liked what OFDM did for data rates and throughput in 5 GHz when introduced in 1999 and wanted that same speed increase in 2.4 GHz. In 2003, to achieve this, ERP/OFDM was introduced. ERP was to extend the rates offered by OFDM into the physical space of 2.4 GHz while also providing a method of backwards compatibility with the DSSS and HR/DSSS devices that existed in the space. See Figure 3.21 for a comparison of the rates, modulations and frequencies used in HR/DSSS, OFDM and ERP/OFDM.

	HR/DSSS	OFDM	ERP with variants
Standard approved	July 1999	July 1999	June 2003
Maximum data rate	11 Mbps	54 Mbps	54 Mbps
Modulation	CCK	OFDM	OFDM and CCK
Data rates	1, 2, 5.5, 11 Mbps	6, 9, 12, 18, 24, 36, 48, 54 Mbps	CCK: 1, 2, 5.5, 11 OFDM: 6, 9, 12, 18, 24, 36, 48, 54 Mbps
Frequencies	2.4–2.497 GHz	5.15–5.35 GHz 5.425–5.675 GHz 5.725–5.875 GHz	2.4–2.497 GHz

Figure 3.21: Frequencies, rates and modulations compared, PBCC information is not included since PBCC has long been abandoned.

144

This backwards compatibility, which did not impact our use much when using DSSS and HR/DSSS devices in the same network, really degrades performance when mixing ERP and DSSS or HR/DSSS devices. When introduced in 2003, there were four implementations possible:

- **ERP-DSSS-CCK:** This PHY is the same as used that used with HR/DSSS. Direct sequence spread spectrum is used here along with CCK. The performance is that of a legacy HR/DSSS network.
- **ERP-OFDM:** This PHY uses OFDM to enable the provisioning of the same data rates in 2.4 GHz that were introduced by OFDM in 5 GHz.
- **ERP-DSSS/PBCC:** This PHY was introduced for use with HR/DSSS and initially provided the same data rates as the DSS/CCK layer, but the data rates were extended to provide 22 and 33 Mbps. As its name indicates, it uses DSSS technology for the modulation combined with Packet Binary Convolutional Coding, PBCC, for the data. PBCC has long since been abandoned.
- **DSSS-OFDM:** This PHY uses a combination of DSSS and OFDM - the packet header is transmitted using DSSS while the payload is transmitted using OFDM. See Figure 3.22.

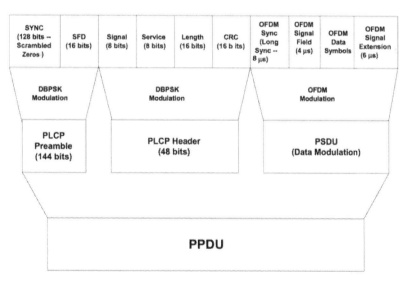

Figure 3.22: DSSS/OFDM Frame format

When using DSSS/OFDM, as in Figure 3.22, the PLCP Preamble and PLCP header very closely resemble that of DSSS and HR/DSSS with a long preamble and using 1 Mbps data rates for backwards compatibility. The OFDM Sync field (preamble) and the OFDM Signal Field are both transmitted at 6 Mbps, just like when using standard OFDM. The OFDM Data Symbols, the actual payload, can be transmitted using defined rates from 6 to 54 Mbps.

The ERP PHY uses elements from DSSS and OFDM as needed to support legacy and newer stations alike. The higher data rates offered by OFDM are achievable using ERP if all the stations and the AP in a service set support them. If a protection mode is in use, the overall throughput will be degraded. 802.11g was an amendment to 802.11 and was ratified in 2003. It clearly states that APs should signal to all associated stations in the BSS to use protection mechanisms when a non-ERP station associates with the AP. This means that in your nice ERP/OFDM world if you are allowing DSSS clients to connect, you must use a protection method which will cause all transmissions within the service set to use preambles readable by non-ERP stations. If the ERP stations were using OFDM preambles the non-ERP stations would not be able to use them. The stations would see each other's traffic as noise, not 802.11 signaling.

There are two protection modes, RTS-CTS and CTS-to-Self. In RTS-CTS, stations, after a positive CCA, send an RTS frame to the AP. The AP responds with a CTS frame to that station's MAC address. All other stations hearing the CTS will set their NAV value using the Duration value in the CTS, even if they did not see the RTS from the original sending client. This way all stations DSS and ERP alike will defer. In CTS-to-Self, a station after a positive CCA will transmit a CTS frame without a preceding RTS frame. All stations hearing this frame will set their NAV value based upon the duration value found in the CTS frame. This may seem to be a more efficient choice, but hidden nodes would not see the frame and would not differ. RTS-CTS assumes all stations can hear the AP and would defer when hearing the CTS frame. APs should use CTS frames to gain control of the medium, but client stations have to begin with the RTS frame. In reality, even most APs use the full RTS-CTS communication.

Either method used will impact the network with up to a 50 percent loss in throughput. Look for mixed mode issues in 2.4 GHz if the users complain about a slow network. The use of protection can be caused by clients that support ERP/OFDM if they are at a long distance from the AP and have used dynamic rate switching to stay connected but have dropped down into DSSS data rates. This is one reason people turn off the support of

146

lower data rates and or all DSSS and HR/DSSS data rates (1, 2, 5.5 and 11), when there are no DSSS only clients on the network.

To determine if a service set is in mixed mode, some legacy and some new stations in use, you can capture a beacon frame and look for the ERP information element Non-ERP station present to be turned on (its bit set to 1). If the legacy station is associated with this AP, the Use Protection element will also be enabled (its bit set to 1). See Figure 3.23 below.

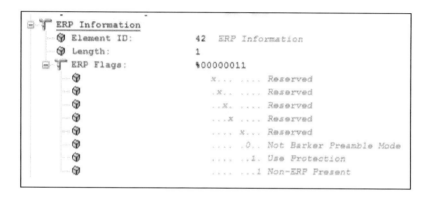

Figure 3.23: Frame capture of a beacon frame telling stations to use protection because a non-ERP station is associated

Figure 3.24 illustrates the ERP information element. Some ERP access points keep this bit turned on once enabled, even if the legacy station disassociated, until the AP is rebooted. This causes many networks to always be operating in protection mode. You can set the mode of operation to DSSS only (802.11 and 802.11b), ERP/OFDM only (802.11g) or mixed mode (also called b/g mode) as seen in Figure 3.25. Most newer APs ship with mixed mode enabled, even when using newer technologies like High Throughput OFDM, HT-OFDM or 802.11n.

Figure 3.24: The ERP information element

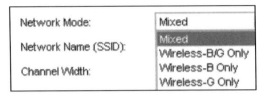

Figure 3.25: Network mode selection on an ERP/OFDM access point

An issue with backwards compatibility is that it not only impacts the service set where the non-ERP station is associated but it also impacts adjacent service sets on the same channel that hear the beacon from the first AP or ad-hoc station in some situations. If an ERP AP hears a beacon from an AP in which the supported data rates contain only DSSS or HR/DSSS rates, it will enable the Non-ERP Present bit in its own beacons, forcing the enablement of protection mechanisms in its BSS. This allows legacy and newer APs and ad-hoc stations to coexist in the same physical space on the same channel, an evil that may be unavoidable in densely populated areas.

Additionally, when an ERP AP hears a management frame that is not a probe request where the supported rates include only DSSS or HR/DSSS rates, the Non-ERP Present bit may be set to 1. So, your neighbors could force your all ERP BSS into protection mode, slowing you down or vice versa. The throughput will not be great, but everyone is able to function. For more information about the protection mode ripple, when one BSS causes others to use protection, go to https://cwnp.link/ProtectionRipple to read a CWNP whitepaper on the topic.

Backwards compatibility saves some money, since you do not need to update all the client devices when upgrading the APs. However, it also has a cost. That cost is the overhead created when supporting a mixed mode of operation. You are not going to get the higher rates offered by the newer APs and the users may be frustrated. It is preferred that the stations be updated as well, if the budget allows. If not, expectations need to be set correctly from the start. Additionally, you will need to know that legacy clients exist in the BSS when troubleshooting to eliminate the overhead created in supporting them as a "problem".

High Throughput
High Throughput OFDM (HT/OFDM or simply HT) was introduced in 2009 and increased the data rate up to 600 Mbps while adding support for transmit beamforming and Multiple Input Multiple Output (MIMO). HT is still referred to by many as 802.11n,

due to marketing and human nature. HT operates in both the 2.4 GHz and 5 GHz spectrums. It also has backwards compatibility to support the existing client base. However, in this case the backwards compatibility, like HT its self, exists in both bands.

Early release clients only supported 2.4 GHz, since at the time of HT's release into the market most WLANs were 2.4 GHz-only. As 2.4 GHz became even more crowed due to the widespread adoption of Wi-Fi, more and more people started using 5 GHz, but in HT and bypassing the use of the then ten-year-old OFDM. This led to dual band HT clients becoming prevalent in the market. However, most of these clients had an affinity for 2.4 GHz to connect to legacy networks. This could be changed in the client software to prefer 5 GHz on many client devices. Today, most dual band devices ship with a preference for 5 GHz.

The HT PHY raised concerns for the first time that the wired network may not be able to keep up with the speeds of the data wireless APs were pushing through them. Many wired networks were on 100 Mbps while HT offered data rates of up to 600 Mbps. People began to upgrade their wired infrastructure to support gigabit transmissions.

So, what is the magic in HT that makes it so much faster than the 54 Mbps offered by OFDM? It is due to several things. First, HT/OFDM reduced the per-packet overhead at the MAC layer by allowing multiple MSDUs to be combined into a single PHY-layer burst. HT had two methods of frame aggregation, a method of combining multiple frames into a single frame transmission. This aggregation reduced the contention by allowing what normally took multiple contentions, transmissions and acknowledgements into a single contention and transmission.

Additionally, HT uses Block Acknowledgements, a way to acknowledge all of the MSDUs within the aggregated frame with a single ACK frame. More about this process can be found in the other chapters of this book.

HT optionally allows a more efficient Low-Density Parity-Check (LDPC) encoder decreasing the time needed for error checking. The details of LDPC are beyond this text and more suited to programing than protocol analysis.

HT also uses a shorter guard interval between symbols, again, increasing the speed. HT can use an 800-nanosecond guard interval, like the original OFDM and ERP/OFDM, but also supports a 400-nanosecond guard interval optionally available called the Short Guard Interval (SGI).

Increasing the number of subcarriers used in the default 20 MHz physical channel also helped to increase speeds beyond the original OFDM. HT/OFDM uses 64 subcarriers versus the 52 used in OFDM.

Although channel bonding was used in some niche' deployments of legacy ERP/OFDM, it became mainstream in HT. HT offers the ability to bond two 20 MHz channels into a single 40 MHz wide channel. Management and control frames are transmitted on the primary channel with data frames using both bonded channels. When troubleshooting an HT network, look for channel bonding being used in 2.4 GHz. This is problematic and should not be done, due to the limited number of non-overlapping channels, overpopulation, and noise existing in that spectrum. There can also be problems in 5 GHz when using bonded channels upon which other networks exist within the space. If there is a problem using a bonded channel, due to other networks etc. in either band, the service set will only use the primary 20 MHz wide channel. Users will complain about slower connectivity, not knowing they are only using half of the channel width they thought to be available. More information about channel planning and bonded channel use can be found in the CWDP materials.

Another improvement to speed in HT comes from using MIMO. MIMO allows multiple streams to be transmitted on the same channel simultaneously and takes advantage of multipath, which was a problem for Single Input Single Output (SISO) networks. A common implementation problem occurs when users apply SISO polarization versus MIMO polarization, providing the wrong coverage for the technology being used.

A misconception is that all HT radios are created equally. They are not. Some support more MIMO streams than others. If the clients are 1X1:1 MIMO and the AP is 3X3:3, the stations are not as efficient as the AP allows them to be and will not be able to get the higher data rates expected. This is like using a 10 Mbps Ethernet card in a client connected to a gigabit switch using CAT 6 cable. The limiting component is the client device not the network.

So, it's really not magic making HT faster. It's a combination of newer technologies being applied.

The structure of HT MAC frames is similar to, but of course not exactly the same as, that of OFDM frames, see Figure 3.26. The HT maximum MSDU size is still 2304 octets or bytes, just like used in OFDM. However, the support for frame aggregation discussed earlier uses Aggregate-MSDUs (A-MSDUs) allowing for a total data size of up to 7935 octets or bytes based upon on the station's capabilities. VHT/OFDM, discussed later, supports even larger A-MSDU sizes. An A-MSDU is an aggregation of more than one MSDU which is transmitted in a single frame. Within the aggregation, each MSDU is still limited to the original 2304 bytes.

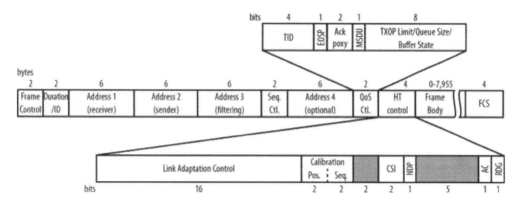

Figure 3.26: HT MAC Frame Format

HT defined new formats defined for the PLCP, greenfield and mixed mode. HT uses a legacy format which duplicates the 20 MHz legacy packet format in two 20 MHz halves of a 40MHz wide channel. When an HT device is communicating with legacy devices, it uses a legacy mode as in Figure 3.27. Using this legacy mode, the frames are transmitted using the legacy OFDM format. When operating with both legacy and HT devices, Mixed Mode, the packets are transmitted using a preamble compatible with legacy OFDM. The legacy Short Training Sequence, the legacy Long Training sequence and the legacy signal description are all transmitted so they can be decoded by legacy OFDM devices. The rest of the frame uses a new MIMO training sequence format.

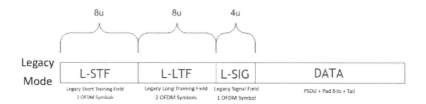

Figure 3.27: HT PLCP Legacy Mode Format

HT has information elements used for indicating when only HT stations are present, greenfield mode, and when non-HT stations are present, mixed mode. The mixed mode format is used to allow fair contention with legacy stations. It has a header they can read and uses data rates they can understand. The HT frame does vary slightly from an OFDM frame. The most notable differences are an increase in size to allow for frame aggregation, an optional HT Control subfield, and the use of the QoS Control field for block acknowledgment.

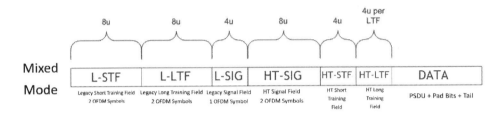

Figure 3.28: HT PLCP Mixed Mode Format

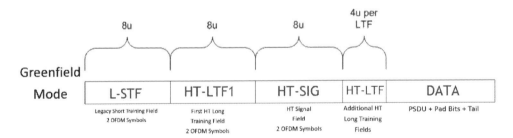

Figure 3.29: HT PLCP Greenfield Mode Format

HT STAs, APs and clients alike, identify themselves as HT STAs by including HT Capabilities Elements, see Figure 3.30, in management frames such as beacons, probe requests, probe responses, association requests, association responses, reassociation requests and reassociation responses. This lets other involved devices know that the sending device can use HT technologies. The HT Capabilities Information Field Format can be seen in Figure 3.31. A sample of station declaring its HT capabilities can be seen the frame capture in Figure 3.32.

Element ID	Length	HT Capabilities Info	A-MPDU Parameters	Supported MCS Set	HT Extended Capabilities	Transmit Beamforming Capabilities	ASEL Capabilities
Bytes: 1	1	2	1	16	2	4	1

Figure 3.30: HT Capabilities Element Format

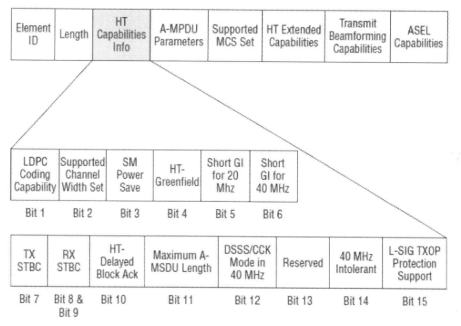

Figure 3.31: HT Capabilities Information Field Format

```
HT Capabilities Info: 0x19ee
.... .... .... ...0 = HT LDPC coding capability: Transmitter does not support receiving LDPC coded packets
.... .... .... ..1. = HT Support channel width: Transmitter supports 20MHz and 40MHz operation
.... .... .... 11.. = HT SM Power Save: SM Power Save disabled (0x0003)
.... .... ...0 .... = HT Green Field: Transmitter is not able to receive PPDUs with Green Field (GF) preambl
.... .... ..1. .... = HT Short GI for 20MHz: Supported
.... .... .1.. .... = HT Short GI for 40MHz: Supported
.... .... 1... .... = HT Tx STBC: Supported
.... ...01 .... .... = HT Rx STBC: Rx support of one spatial stream (0x0001)
.... ..0. .... .... = HT Delayed Block ACK: Transmitter does not support HT-Delayed BlockAck
.... 1... .... .... = HT Max A-MSDU length: 7935 bytes
...1 .... .... .... = HT DSSS/CCK mode in 40MHz: Will/Can use DSSS/CCK in 40 MHz
..0. .... .... .... = HT PSMP Support: Won't/Can't support PSMP operation
.0.. .... .... .... = HT Forty MHz Intolerant: Use of 40 MHz transmissions unrestricted/allowed
0... .... .... .... = HT L-SIG TXOP Protection support: Not supported
```

Figure 3.32: HT Capabilities Information seen in frame capture

HT also introduced another Control Frame type called a Control Wrapper, see Figure 3.33. It is used to carry other control frames, except other Control Wrapper frames, with

153

an HT Control field. If an HT device is capable of advanced HT features such as beamforming, this allows control frames to leverage those additional features.

```
⊞ Frame 2019: 3063 bytes on wire (24504 bits), 3063 bytes captured (24504 bits)
⊞ 802.11 radio information
⊟ IEEE 802.11 Control Wrapper, Flags: op...M.T
  Type/Subtype: Control Wrapper (0x0017)
⊟ Frame Control Field: 0x74c5
  .... ..00 = Version: 0
  .... 01.. = Type: Control frame (1)
  0111 .... = Subtype: 7
⊟ Flags: 0xc5
  .... ..01 = DS status: Frame from STA to DS via an AP (To DS: 1 From DS: 0) (0x01)
  .... .1.. = More Fragments: More fragments follow
  .... 0... = Retry: Frame is not being retransmitted
  ...0 .... = PWR MGT: STA will stay up
  ..0. .... = More Data: No data buffered
  .1.. .... = Protected flag: Data is protected
  1... .... = Order flag: Strictly ordered
  .010 1010 1000 1010 = Duration: 10890 microseconds
```

Figure 3.33: HT Frame capture of an HT Control Wrapper frame

As stated earlier, there are many similarities between HT and previous technologies. You will need to know the differences. The differences focus on making transmissions more efficient when possible while providing backwards compatibility for legacy stations. As you just learned, there is a capabilities field in HT frames. This is so stations know how to work with each other. The frame capture in Figure 3.32 above illustrates this. That is so the stations know there is something different, but they can work together.

Another item that is similar but with a differing implementation is the protection mode use. HT, like ERP/OFDM, must be backwards compatible with legacy devices. Much like the ERP information element in an ERP beacon, HT beacons tell stations whether or not they need to use a protection mode. They accomplish this by using the "Operating Mode" and "Non-greenfield STAs Present" fields in the HT Information Element. You should look for this information in captured beacons.

There are four protection modes, 0-3, in HT. Mode 0 is used if all stations in the BSS are 20/40 MHz HT capable or if the BSS is 20/40 MHz capable or if all stations in the BSS are 20 MHz HT stations in a 20 MHz BSS. This is called greenfield mode. Mode 1 is used when there are non-HT stations or APs using the primary or secondary channels but are not part of the BSS. This is called Non-Member Protection mode. Mode 2 is used when only HT stations are associated in the BSS and at least one 20 MHz HT station is associated. Mode 3 is used when one or more non-HT stations are associated in the BSS and is called Mixed Mode.

By determining if protection is in use and if so the mode specified, you are able to determine if legacy stations are causing an HT network to use legacy rates and older technologies. Legacy stations will cause a performance loss for HT deployments, although having them is perfectly normal. Customers complain they are not getting the speeds promised by the new APs when this occurs. You can simply capture a beacon from an HT AP and determine if this is the case. When looking for HT specific behaviors, use your protocol analysis tool and examine the HT information elements.

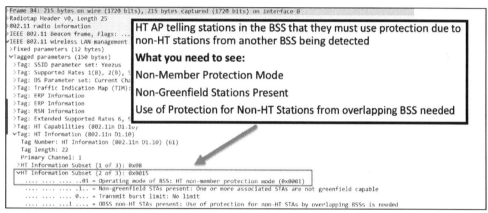

Figure 3.34: HT protection mode 1 in use found in beacon frame

Very High Throughput

Just like HT improved on OFDM, VHT improves upon HT. Again, there will be some similarities and differences. However, the basic rules are the same. VHT also uses MIMO and has mechanisms for backwards compatibility. Since VHT devices are required to co-exist with existing legacy devices in 5 GHz, OFDM and HT, and because VHT devices support wider channels, VHT devices send the same preamble in each 20 MHz bonded channel so that all 802.11 devices hearing the transmission will be able to synchronize with the frame being transmitted. This attempt to coexist introduces a new problem. It causes a high Peak to Average Power Ratio (PAPR), which reduces the efficiency of power amplifiers.

VHT can use 160 MHz wide channels versus the 40 in HT and 20 in OFDM. Since VHT can use such wide channels, it does not operate in 2.4 GHz. Dual band VHT devices are really HT in 2.4 GHz and VHT in 5 GHz. Customers may wonder why their new VHT client is not any faster than their old HT client. It can be much faster when connecting in 5 GHz to a VHT AP.

Much like HT, many stations fail to support all VHT's improvements. The battery life of a station is short when compared to an AP plugged into AC power. So, they usually do not support the larger implementations of MIMO like 8X8:8. Ii was the same for HT stations and APs. VHT is the next evolution of HT in a similar fashion to HR/DSSS being the next evolution of DSSS. So, HT and VHT have a lot in common.

Let's take a look at the magic VHT uses to improve what HT offered. First the VHT PHY introduces faster data rates, just like all of the evolutions we have discussed. VHT devices that can make use all the improvements will be able to attain data rates of almost 3.5 Gbps. One such improvement that allows this to be accomplished in VHT is the use of 256 QAM. 256 QAM can represent more data than the 64 QAM used in HT. This requires a very good connection and can only be used in most environments over short distances.

Secondly, VHT supports more spatial streams than HT does using MIMO. HT only supported 4 streams. VHT supports 8. HT devices never really used 4X4:4 MIMO beyond a few enterprise APs having the ability. Most likely we will not see VHT reach 8X8:8 either.

Lastly, VHT introduces Multi User MIMO (MU-MIMO). This concept allows the AP to transmit to multiple client stations, up to 4, simultaneously. In reality, it does add the gains many hoped it would add because MU-MIMO requires to many factors to be just right for it to work extremely well in most scenarios.

So, there is the new magic. VHT is an improvement over HT but the delta between the two is nothing like the delta between OFDM and HT. Remember from our discussion of HT, HT used an 800-nanosecond guard interval with an option for a 400-nanosecond guard interval. VHT also uses a 400-nanosecond short guard interval. All the modifications and new features found in VHT are necessary to meet its goals. More information about the basics of VHT can be found in the CWNA materials.

Now we will examine the frame structure of VHT transmissions. The VHT PHY is still based on the OFDM PHY and it maintains the same basic modulation, interleaving and coding architecture of HT.

Figure 3.35 shows you the VHT mixed format PPDU. The L-STF and L-LTF contain the information needed to detect the signal, perform frequency offset estimation, timing synchronization, etc. Remember, just as in HT, the L stands for legacy. Within the details of the sequences, you will find that the 20 MHz signals are the same as the legacy OFDM and HT preamble fields. Having them formed this way allows all 802.11 devices hearing the signal to synchronize with the signal. The next portion, the L-SIG field, contains information regarding the length of the rest of this frame, not to be confused with the duration field which is always about what comes after the frame, such as IFS and ACK frames. Reading the L-SIG field allows devices detecting the frame, including the legacy OFDM and HT devices to know a frame of a specified length is being transmitted.

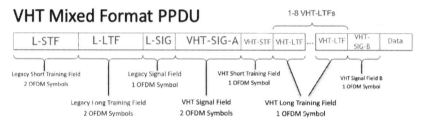

The first 3 fields are the same as an HT format PPDU

Figure 3.34: VHT Mixed Format PPDU

There are two OFDM symbols in the VHT-SIG-A field. The first symbol is modulated using BPSK to allow legacy HT devices to believe that it is a frame from an OFDM station. The second symbol also uses BPSK. However, it uses a rotation of 90° allowing any detecting VHT device to see frame this as a VHT transmission. The information contained in the bits of these two symbols includes important VHT details such as bandwidth mode, Modulation and Coding Scheme, the number of space time streams, etc. The legacy fields and the VHT-SIG-A fields are duplicated over each 20 MHz channel using the appropriate phase rotation.

The next field is the VHT Short Training Field, VHT-STF. Its primary use is to improve automatic gain control estimation in a MIMO transmission. The next field or fields, 1 to 8 may be used, are the VHT Long Training Fields (VHT-LTFs). These fields are used for estimating the MIMO channel and equalizing the received signal. The number of LTFs sent is greater than or equal to the number of spatial streams per user.

The last field of the VHT preamble is the VHT-SIG-B. The VHT-SIG-B uses BPSK modulation. It provides information on the length of the useful data in the packet. When using MU-MIMO, the VHT-SIG-B field provides the MCS.

After the VHT preamble the data symbols are transmitted which are also using phase rotation in the upper 20 MHz bonded channel(s). The VHT-SIG-A symbols contain 24 bits each. 8 of these bits are used for the Cyclic Redundancy Check (CRC) and 6 are used as tail bits for the encoder. The remaining 34 bits are needed for VHT devices to read the VHT packet. The format for Single user VHT SIG-A can be seen in Figure 3.35 below. Remember, MU-MIMO can support up to four users. When multiple users are present, some of the VHT-SIG-A fields are modified to signal user specific information. Figure 3.36 shows the number of bits per field with bits that are intended for a specific user.

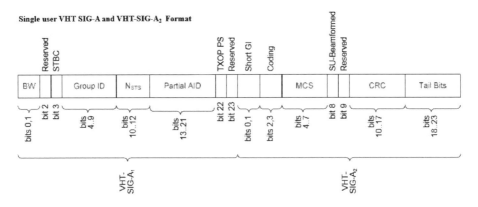

Figure 3.35: The Single user VHT SIG-A and VHT-SIG-A2 Format

The VHT-SIG-B, the last portion of the VHT preamble and uses BPSK modulation. It provides information on the length of the useful data in the packet. VHT Signal B field is also used to set up the data rate. The VHT Signal B field is designed to be transmitted in a single OFDM symbol. Therefore, it has different lengths based upon the channel width. The VHT-SIG-B field contains 26 bits in a 20 MHz channel use, 27 bits in a 40 MHz channel use and 29 bits in 80 MHz and 160 MHz channels. Its format varies based upon whether the packet is for a SU-MIMO, Figure 3.37, or for a MU-MIMO, Figure 3.38

transmission. The length field is a measure of the length of the Data field payload of the physical layer frame, in four-byte units. Notice that there is no CRC within the VHT Signal B field. To detect errors in the VHT Signal B field, there is a CRC at the beginning of the Data field.

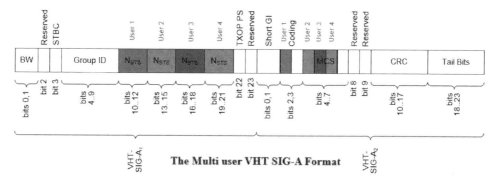

Figure 3.36: The Multi user VHT SIG-A Format

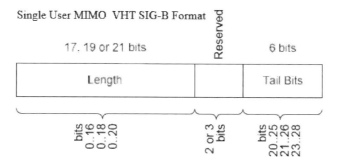

Figure 3.37: SU-MIMO VHT-SIG-B Format

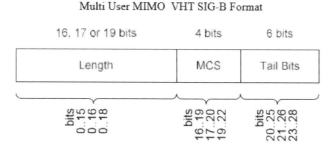

Figure 3.38: MU-MIMO VHT-SIG-B Format

159

The last field, the Data field is the payload of the physical layer frame. Shown in Figure 3.39 below is the format of the Data field, where the CRC mentioned earlier resides. Since the Data field is transmitted following the header, it is transmitted at the data rate found in the physical layer header.

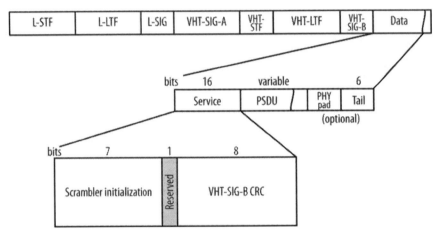

Figure 3.39: The data field of a VHT frame

The VHT information elements vary from those of an HT transmission as do the frame formats, to get the much higher data rates promised. However, the basics are the same, preamble and payload. As you have learned here, the VHT frame format has been designed with backwards compatibility in mind. To meet this requirement, the VHT frame format is constructed similarly to an HT mixed mode format. However, unlike HT, VHT has only one frame format. Only a slight change in frame appearance from HT is made, but it is significant in the implementation of VHT. Understanding the frame structure will assist you when conducting protocol analysis of VHT frames.

PHY Information in Pseudo-Headers

Now that you have learned more about the information found in 802.11 PHYs, we will discuss how to use that information in troubleshooting and network validation. Protocol analyzers allow you to capture transmissions. However, you must know how to use that information. You can analyze the captured information to determine what is happening in your WLAN. You then can compare what is happening to what is expected to be happening. The delta between the two is where you will find users complaining because their devices are not behaving as they believe they should. Finding the root cause of a wireless problem is easily done by applying your knowledge of wireless behaviors when analyzing what you have captured. Within this section, we will cover the following topics:

- Pseudo-header formats
- Radiotap
- Per Packet Information (PPI)
- Signal strength
- Data rate and MCS index
- Length information
- Channel center frequency or received channel
- Channel properties
- Noise

Pseudo-Header Formats

Some header types are called pseudo-headers because they are not actually transmitted with the frame. They are used to convey information within a single device. They do however contain additional radio information about the frame. These pseudo headers are supplied by the driver or the operating systems wireless subsystem. Pseudo-header formats vary based upon their intended use. You can filter captures based upon header type to show only the desired information.

Radiotap is used in 802.11 frame injection and reception. The radiotap header format is used to supply additional information about frames from the driver to applications such as libpcap, in Linux, or WinPcap, in Windows. Protocol analysis software may use libpcap and/or WinPcap to capture packets. I some newer versions, radiotap is used to transmit packets on a network at the link layer. It can also be used to enumerate network interfaces for their possible use with libpcap or WinPcap. It is also used to take information from applications to the driver for transmission. A radiotap capture format starts with a radiotap header, see Figure 3.40. Radiotap fields are strictly ordered. The *it_version* field indicates which major version of the radiotap header is in use. The *it_pad* field aligns the fields onto natural word boundaries. The *it_len* field indicates the entire length of the radiotap data. The *it_present* field is a bitmask of the radiotap data fields that follows the radiotap header. More in-depth information about radiotap can be found at www.radiotap.org should you want to learn more about its structure.

```
struct ieee80211_radiotap_header {
        u_int8_t        it_version;     /* set to 0 */
        u_int8_t        it_pad;
        u_int16_t       it_len;         /* entire length */
        u_int32_t       it_present;     /* fields present */
} __attribute__((__packed__));
```

Figure 3.40: Radiotap capture format

The **Per Packet Information (PPI)** header is a general and extensible meta-information header format. It was originally developed to provide HT radio information, but it can be used to handle other information as well. The role of PPI is to address restrictions in legacy methods of limited scope, a restriction to the use of specific elements in a single domain, rigidity, an inability to add new elements or causing difficulty in their addition, and the use of fixed data link types (DLTs), supporting only one data link type per format. PPI data elements are formatted as type-length-value triplets. This formatting allows for future expansion of the header and offers backward compatibility. Per-packet DLTs can be implemented by using an empty PPI header.

The PPI header format can be seen in Figure 3.41. PPI packet headers contain a packet header followed by zero or more fields. This removes any requirement that a supplemental data exists for every packet captured. It also allows you to save packets with multiple DLTs in a single capture file. The PPI packet header structure can be seen in Figure 3.42. The fields include the *pph_version*, version of the PPI header, the *pph_flags*, an 8-bit mask that defines the behavior of the header, the *pph_len*, the length of the entire PPI header and the *pph_dlt*, which contains the data link type. Case Technologies has published a white paper for developers which goes into detail for the use of PPIs in applications. You can find that whitepaper here: https://cwnp.link/ppipaper.

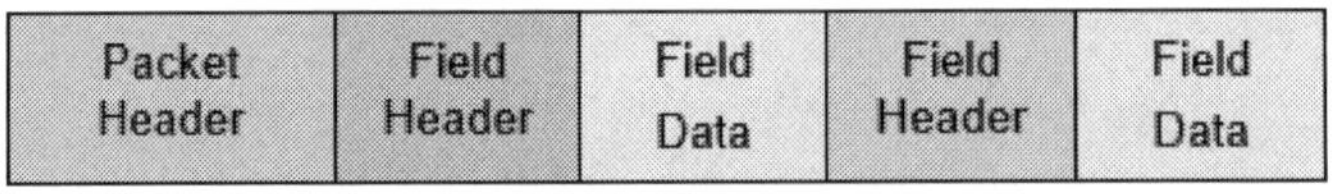

Packet Header	Field Header	Field Data	Field Header	Field Data

Figure 3.41: PPI header format

```
typedef struct ppi_packetheader {
    u_int8_t pph_version;        /* Version.  Currently 0 */
    u_int8_t pph_flags;          /* Flags.    */
    u_int16_t pph_len;           /* Length of entire message,
                                  * including this header and TLV
                                  * payload. */
    u_int32_t pph_dlt;           /* Data Link Type of the captured
                                  * packet data. */
} ppi_packetheader_t;
```

Figure 3.42: PPI Packet Header Structure

Signal Strength

By the time you are ready to study protocol analysis in Wi-Fi, you know what signal strength means. You know about transmit power, received signal strength and its impact on data rates and modulation types used. You also know about the effects of dynamic rate shifting as caused by changes in RSSI values. Within this context, you will need to know that protocol analysis can be used to determine if any issues are related to RSSI values.

In analysis you can see the signal strength with which a frame was captured. This should let you quickly see if any slowness is due to RSSI values and rate shifting. You can also use this knowledge to determine if connectivity problems are related to RSSI value. For example, if an AP is configured to require higher data rates to connect and your client is too far from the AP to be able to use the data rates it requires, the client will not connect.

Signal strength is a used in calculating the signal-to-noise ratio, SNR. If the SNR is too low, some applications will fail. The data rate used by a station is determined in part by the ability of the receiver to demodulate the signal. Higher data rates require more separation between the 802.11 signal and any other RF "noise" in the environment. To be used reliably voice traffic should be at least 33 dBm over the noise floor. This separation is referred to as the SNR. Therefore, to achieve higher data rates the client STA must be close enough to the AP to have a high SNR.

Signal strength and noise can be found under the Radiotap header within a capture of a frame as in the capture of the beacon frame seen in Figure 3.43 below. The signal strength found in beacon frames is used by client stations as part of their criteria for selecting an AP with which to connect or to which to roam. This is an important element to examine when troubleshooting connectivity and roaming problems. There is no industry standard for the calculation of RSSI values or roaming criteria. Each chipset manufacturer determines how their chips calculate RSSI values and how their devices make roaming decisions. You can apply filters to your captures allowing you to only see frames above or below the desired signal strength.

```
˅ Radiotap Header v0, Length 26
      Header revision: 0
      Header pad: 0
      Header length: 26
   ˃ Present flags
      MAC timestamp: 2407696744
   ˃ Flags: 0x10
      Data Rate: 1.0 Mb/s
      Channel frequency: 2437 [BG 6]
   ˃ Channel flags: 0x00a0, Complementary Code Keying
      SSI Signal: -47 dBm
      SSI Noise: -87 dBm
      Antenna: 0
      SSI Signal: 40 dB
 ˃ 802.11 radio information
 ˃ IEEE 802.11 Beacon frame, Flags: ........C
 ˃ IEEE 802.11 wireless LAN management frame
```

Figure 3.43: Signal strength in dBm under the Radiotap Header

Data Rates and MCS Index

The data rate used to transmit a wireless frame is also available for viewing when using protocol analysis. Various modulation schemes and coding rates are defined within the 802.11 standard and are represented by a Modulation and Coding Scheme (MCS) index values. These can also be seen in protocol analysis.

As mentioned above, when stations select a data rate to use the signal strength plays a large role in their choice. This is in addition to the advertised data rates found in a beacon from the AP. Some data rates are mandatory, basic, and others are supported, optional. So, based upon what the AP tells stations it requires and supports and the RSSI values the stations calculate for the signals coming from the AP, a station will select a data rate to use.

Lower data rates use less efficient modulation and coding while higher rates use more efficient methods. Channel width and number of special streams supported will impact data rates as well. For example, both an AP and STA may support VHT and its higher rates and more efficient modulation and coding schemes. If the AP is only configured to use a 20 MHz channel or is only a 3X3:3 MIMO device, the data rates at the upper limits of the standard will not be attainable.

More commonly, the AP will support larger MIMO configuration than the stations will. It is common to see a 3X3:3 AP supporting 1X1:1 or 2X2:2 stations. So, when users are complaining that the magic VHT AP and STAs are not getting the lightning fast speeds offered in VHT, you can verify the configured abilities of the AP by examining the data rates supported in the beacon frames, the data frames sent and examine the MCS information elements to verify the configuration and usage by the stations. The stations using lower rates could be farther away and using lower data rates due to dynamic rate switching. A nice chart covering HT and VHT MCS, data rates, special streams, channel width and VHT MCS index can be found at http://mcsindex.com.

In Figure 3.44 below, under the VHT Information you can see the channel width is 20 MHz, the MCS Index is 6 (64-QAM with ¾ coding), MIMO support is 2X2:2, and the data rate used was 117 Mbps. This capture makes it clear that although the devices support VHT, the configuration, physical construction and signal strength used will not allow the devices to use the higher data rates and more efficient modulation offered in VHT.

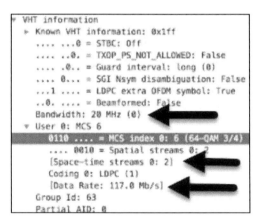

Figure 3.44: The VHT Information Elements showing Bandwidth, MCS, Spatial Streams and Data rate used

Things like this are great evidence for you to use in troubleshooting or in network validation as you try to explain such complex things to wired experts or even non-IT people. One of the many great things about Wi-Fi is that the frames tell you, in clear text, everything about themselves, except what is in encrypted payloads. A frame using a more complex PHY will have a larger story to tell than a frame using a less complex PHY.

Length Information

The length information should not be confused with the value found in the duration field. The duration field is about the time it should take for everything following a frame to complete, such as SIFS, ACK and DIFS. In pseudo header elements the length information gets its value from libpcap/WinPcap, which in turn gets the value from the underlying capture mechanism, which should get the value from the device driver, which ultimately gets the value from the radio hardware. Here, the length information is the length of the pseudo header you are analyzing. Figure 3.45 shows you the radiotap header length.

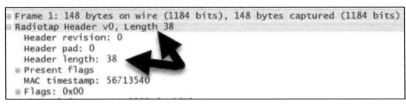

Figure 3.45: The Length information for a radiotap header

Channel Frequencies Used

An 802.11 channel is defined by its center frequency. As you know, 802.11 transmissions are broadband not narrow band, meaning they use a large portion of frequency space as a single channel versus using a single frequency as the channel. OFDM channels are 20 MHz wide. Channel bonding uses two or more of these 20 MHz wide channels to increase the data rate. When you are conducting a frame capture, your adaptors are gathering information as configured, on a single channel or on multiple channels. Within the capture, you can see the channel upon which the frame was captured as well as the channel upon which the frame tells you it was transmitted. It is easy to mistakenly identify the channel in use from mis-reading the frame, since in more than one place a channel value can be found.

In 5 GHz space the channels are considered to be non-overlapping. So, both information elements, the channel your radio was on when it captured the frame and the channel upon which the frame says it was transmitted, should be the same. This is not the case in 2.4 GHz, due to the overlapping of channels. It is possible to be physically close enough to the transmitting radio to decode the frames from an overlapping channel. If this is the case, you will see two channels in your capture, the one on which the capture was made and the one the frame is telling you it was transmitted upon. If you really want to know what is happening in your airspace, trust the frame. The transmitting device has encoded the channel it used in transmission into the frame. See Figure 3.46 for an example of a frame having been captured on an overlapping channel. The capture was made on channel 3 but the frame was transmitted on channel 1.

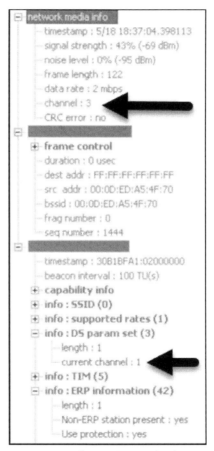

Figure 3.46: A frame capture made on CH 3 of a frame transmitted on CH 1

Channel Properties

The channels used in 802.11 networking have distinct properties. They each have a center frequency and a known width. Channels have been assigned numbers to make it easier for people to understand them. For example, knowing you are on channel 6 in the 2.4 GHz space is easier to display in a user interface and is easier for humans to remember than representing the channel by its center frequency of 2.437 GHz.

2.4 GHz and 5 GHz channels are within the unlicensed frequency space and governments regulate which channels are legal for use within their boundaries and how much power we can use upon them, meaning there is limited bandwidth for our use. We need to be very careful in our channel planning when designing and deploying WLANs to avoid creating contention problems for ourselves. Enough contention problems will happen on their own, without a designer building them into the WLAN.

Different PHYs take advantage of the space as needed to support the specifications of our use within the PHYs. Earlier PHYs did not use the space as efficiently as newer PHYs. As our usage of Wi-Fi not only grew but also became an expected primary connection method for most enterprise deployments, we needed to focus on improving airtime utilization to accommodate the densely populated networks and congested airspace. Improving the PHYs use of the frequencies has helped, although we are still limited by the frequency space allocated as non-licensed and the channels themselves.

When using the DSSS PHY, the channels are 22 MHz wide. When using an OFDM PHY, ERP PHY, HT PHY, or VHT PHT, the channels are 20 MHz wide, though they can be combined to form 40, 80 and 160 MHz channels depending on the PHY in use. The 2.4 GHz spectrum has only 100 Hz in width. However, there are 14 channels in that space, each 22 MHz wide with DSSS and 20 MHz wide with OFDM. That means when you are using DSSS 308 MHz of space seems to be available, 14x22=308, and when you are using OFDM 280 MHz of space seems to be available, 14x20=280. So, there is obviously overlapping of the channels in 2.4 GHz. Overlapping channel interference is a big problem of radios in this space. The center frequency of the channels used need to be at least 25 MHz apart to ensure there is no overlap. That is why you see a three-channel plan used in 2.4 GHz, mostly 1, 6 and 11 in use.

HT-OFDM uses channel bonding. However, the practical use of channel bonding should be restricted to the 5 GHz space, where more frequency space exists, and the channels do not overlap. When using channel bonding in the 2.4 GHz spectrum, you can bond only

168

two non-overlapping channels. In a deployment this means you could have one bonded channel AP within a physical space, leaving only a single non-overlapping channel for other uses. This is not an efficient model. Novice installers will want to get the highest theoretical speed from an AP. So, without knowing what they should about the channels in 2.4 GHz, they turn on bonding on the APs and created massive problems. Then wonder why they are not getting the speeds promised by the sticker on the box.

When you are diagnosing problems in 2.4 GHz, look for the use of channel bonding, overlapping channel interference, and co-channel interference. They are very commonly found and are easily resolved problems. The number one cause of WLAN problems is bad design (Have we said that before?). It is not the instrument that makes a mistake but rather the musician.

In the 5 GHz spectrum, we have more channels to use. These channels are all OFDM channels, 20 MHz wide. They do not overlap in their usable space. However, we still must be mindful of the proper use of channel bonding and co-channel interference, just as in the 2.4 GHz space.

Additionally, in 5 GHz you will need to be aware that using some channels requires DFS support, U-NII 2 and U-NII 2e channels. Dynamic Frequency Selection (DFS), refers to a mechanism allowing unlicensed devices to share the 5 GHz frequency space which has been allocated to radar systems without causing interference to those radars. Some applications, such as voice, should not be used on these channels. If there is a DFS event that causes a channel change, calls and other connections may be dropped. Look for DFS information in beacon frames. Also, when troubleshooting in 5 GHz, look for DFS channel use in protocol analysis and neighboring radar use in spectrum analysis, if you can catch the radar pulses in your analyzer. Along with knowing the device support for DFS, knowing the applications to be used in the space and whether a DFS event is likely will guide your use of DFS channels. Even in high density deployments, many people do not use DFS, limiting the number of available channels. Before recommending that they be used, you must verify device support, the likelihood of a DFS event, and whether the channels can legally be used in that location.

Based upon the devices abilities, the application requirements and the environment in which they are to be deployed, you should be able to plan channel use and re-use effectively. Just as in 2.4 GHz, the use of channel bonding needs to be carefully done. There are more non-overlapping channels in the 5 GHz space, so bonding should be easier. Stations will benefit more from having fewer radios with which to contend for the medium than they will from having a wider channel to use when they win the contention. The reduced bandwidth of an unbonded channel with less contention will give each station more chances to transmit than a wide channel with greatly increased contention. Is it necessary and if so how wide should the bonded channels be that are used? VHT-OFDM can use channels as wide as 160 MHz. Will the clients support that width or is that just something APs and theory support? If the AP is bonding out to 160 MHz and the clients only support 40 or 80 MHz, you are wasting space. Bonding should not be used in high density deployments, even in 5 GHz. So, where should channel bonding be used? It should be used in 5 GHz within low density deployments where the medium is relatively clean, little to no interference from neighboring WLANs and or noise.

When there are problems, knowing what the client devices need combined with a knowledge of the properties of the channels will help you solve channel related issues quickly.

Noise

Noise, in general, is discussed in chapter 9, Spectrum Analysis. That chapter focuses on Layer 1 noise and how to find and identify it. At Layer 2, the analysis is focused on how that noise impacts transmissions and how you can see that in protocol analysis. This is important because if a computer receives information it cannot interpret to be anything meaningful, it either sees it as noise or corrupted data. Either way, the intended receiver in this case will not acknowledge the transmission, causing the sender to retransmit the frame.

Also, as you learned earlier, the SNR is important. A strong SNR allows stations to use higher data rates and communicate more efficiently. Data rates are impacted by several factors, largely the signal-to-noise ratio (SNR). SNR is the noise floor value in dBm minus the signal strength value in dBm. Being able to calculate the SNR is a useful skill. A channels capacity is dictated by three primary factors: bandwidth, signal strength, and noise or interference. While capturing frames, most analysis applications report traditional RF metrics, like signal strength, noise, and SNR. This information can be of great use. If you see a high noise level in protocol analysis, you can determine that noise is a problem without switching to a spectrum analyzer.

Alternatively, you could use the information detected about noise in protocol analysis to make you want to switch over to a spectrum analyzer to find the noise source. Protocol analyzers will be able to show you that noise exists and at what signal strength but are not able to guide you to the sources like a spectrum analyzer can. If the noise floor is too close to the received signal strength, the signal may be corrupted, or it may not even be detected. Wi-Fi exists at Layers 1 and 2 of the OSI model. Don't forget to analyze both layers in trying to resolve problems.

Figure 3.47 shows you both the signal level and the noise Level detected during a frame capture. Some applications require a stronger signal than others. For example, RTLS likes a -62 dBm signal or higher and voice likes -67 dBm or higher. This is only half of the SNR required to work properly and assumes a standard noise floor of -95 dBm. If the noise level is increased without a corresponding increase in the signal strength, applications can fail. In an RTLS deployment, if the noise level is not the standard -95 dBm but is -80 dBm the signal strength required for RTLS to work would need to be increased as well, to -47 dBm to maintain the 33 dBm SNR required for RTLS to function properly. It might be easier to change channels to avoid the noise or find the extra noise sources and mitigate them. Knowing how the noise level impacts the use of wireless technologies and where to find the detected noise in protocol analysis is a valued skill.

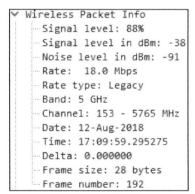

Figure 3.47: Wireless packet information illustrating Signal level and Noise level

Chapter Summary

The functions at the Physical layer or PHY require your understanding to be a successful wireless professional. If you need to know what is happening versus what should be happening in a WLAN, knowing how each PHY functions is required. At their core, they are very similar. As the use of 802.11 technologies has increased and the demand for higher speeds and greater throughput have increased the specifications of the PHYs have changed. Your knowledge of how the PHY is being used will assist you in network validation and troubleshooting. From poor implementations to congestion and backwards compatibility, many things will impact how the devices are required to operate within a given PHY. Reading the PHY information elements in your protocol analysis will tell you how the captured frame was sent. The only thing you may not be able to read in a capture is an encrypted payload. Everything else you need to know about the usage of the PHY in a WLAN is in the capture.

Facts to Remember

- The PLCP and PMD are sublayers of the PHYs defined in 802.11.
- The PLCP places header information before the MPDU that is used by radios during the reception of frames.
- The PMD is responsible for modulating and demodulating bits onto and off the RF medium.
- DSSS and HR/DSSS channels are 22 MHz wide while OFDM, ERP, HT, and VHT channels are 20 MHz wide or some factor thereof.
- The radiotap header shows information passed up from the drivers about the PHY.
- While you can see noise in a protocol capture, it is not always reliable.

Review Questions

1. What is the purpose for the Carrier Sense/Clear Channel Assessment?

    A. To determine the state of the medium

    B. To determine which PHY is in use within the service set

    C. To determine the contention method in use

    D. To determine the association count of the AP

2. The PLCP Protocol Data Unit (PPDU) is comprised of how many parts?

    A. 2

    B. 4

    C. 3

    D. 5

3. Which sub-layer is responsible for transmitting and receiving bits onto and off the medium.

    A. The PLCP

    B. The LLC

    C. The PMD

    D. The MAC

4. What part of a frame transmission contains the Synchronization (Sync) field and Start Frame Delimiter (SFD) field?

    A. The MPDU

    B. The Preamble

    C. The MSDU

    D. The Payload

5. The higher data rates found in OFDM are largely due to the use of which modulation type?

A. DBPSK

B. QAM

C. DQPSK

D. CCK

6. Of the 52 sub-carriers used on a single OFDM channel, how many are available for transmitting data versus being used as pilot sub-carriers?

A. 4

B. 48

C. 51

D. 36

7. Within which portion of an HT/OFDM header can you determine if the Greenfield mode of operation is in use?

A. The A-MPDU Parameters

B. The HT Capabilities Information

C. The Supported MCS Set

D. The Element ID

8. When using VHT/OFDM in a Mixed environment, what do the VHT PPDUs have in common with legacy HT PPDUs?

A. The first field is the same.

B. The first three fields are the same.

C. The MU-VHT SIG-A Format is the same.

D. The SU-MIMO VHT-SIG-B Format is the same.

9. True or False: An MSDU and a PSDU are essentially the same thing.

      A. True

      B. False

10. Why are some Link Layer header types are called pseudo-headers?

      A. They are not actually transmitted with the frame.

      B. They allow additional header information that is not PHY specific.

      C. They allow additional header information that is vendor specific.

      D. They allow for future compatibility as the 802.11 standard evolves.

Review Answers

1. The correct answer is A. The Carrier Sense/Clear Channel Assessment. CS/CCA, is used to determine the state of the medium, BUSY or IDLE. The CS/CCA procedure is executed while the receiver is turned on and the station is not currently receiving or transmitting a packet

2. The correct answer is C. The PPDU has three parts, the Preamble, the Header and the PSDU.

3. The correct answer is C. The Physical Medium Dependent (PMD) sublayer is the service within the PHY responsible for transmitting and receiving bits onto and off of the medium.

4. The correct answer is B. The Preamble contains two important components, the Synchronization (Sync) field and Start Frame Delimiter (SFD) field.

5. The correct answer is B. The higher data rates were available largely due to the use of Quadrature Amplitude Modulation or QAM.

6. The correct answer is B. 48 sub carriers are available for data on a single OFDM channel. The remaining 4 are pilot subcarriers with a carrier separation of 0.3125 MHz (20 MHz/64).

7. The correct answer is B. The HT Capabilities Information Field contains the HT-Greenfield information.

8. The correct answer is B. When using VHT/OFDM in a Mixed environment, the first three fields are the same. MU-MIMO was not part of the HT PHY.

9. The correct answer is A. Both terms refer to Layer 3 and up payloads as they are encapsulated or unencapsulated in transmission or reception. The term you should use to describe the encapsulated payload should reflect the sublayer from which it which the traffic is received, MSDU from the MAC and PSDU from the PLCP.

10. The correct answer is A. Some Link Layer header types are called pseudo-headers because they are not actually transmitted with the frame. They are used to convey information within a single device.

Chapter 4: 802.11 MAC Frames

Objectives Covered:

4.2 Identify and use MAC information in captured data for analysis

4.3 Validate BSS configuration through protocol analysis

4.4 Identify and analyze CRC error frames and retransmitted frames

The name for a unit of data at Layer 2 is referred to as a frame. Contrast that with Layer 3, in which it is referred to as a packet. Most 802.11 captures are in fact "Frame captures" as opposed to "packet captures", though many analysts use the terms interchangeably. Frames, since they are responsible for both information transfer/encapsulation, and the management of the wireless medium, come in a variety of sizes and functions, which will be covered in depth, in this chapter.

802.11 Frame Types

802.11 networks use three primary frame types: management, control, and data frames.

Management Frames

Management frames are exactly what one would expect from the name: they manage the medium itself. There are, in total, 14 Types of management frames, with two values reserved for later use. These can be found in Table 4.1, along with the bit values for each. All management frames are indicated by a "type value" of 00.

Bit Value	Description	Bit Value	Description
0000	Association Request	0001	Association Response
0010	Reassociation Request	0011	Reassociation Response
0100	Probe Request	0101	Probe Response
0110	Timing Advertisement	0111	Reserved
1000	Beacon	1001	ATIM
1010	Disassociation	1011	Authentication
1100	Deauthentication	1101	Action
1110	Action No Ack	1111	Reserved

Table 4.1: Management Frame Subtypes

The Frame subtype and type, together, tell us the function and type of frame. Note that the spot for "15" and "7" have been reserved for future use. The following provides details about each of these management frame subtypes.

0000 - Association Request: After Authentication, this is the next step to joining the BSS. This frame, along with being an integral part of the process of joining a BSS, carries information that allows an AP to sync with a NIC. It contains up to 24 fields, most of which inform the BSS of the capabilities and functions of the NIC itself. A selection of the fields is below.

- Capability Information
- Listen interval
- SSID
- Supported Rates and Extended Rates
- Channels supported
- QoS Capability

 Remember, the Association request should reflect the settings of the BSS. If it doesn't, several things can happen, including a join failure. STAs join BSSs with which they are compatible.

0001 - Association Response: The Association Response frame body is up to 31 sections long, and contains information about the BSS as well. Most Importantly, the Association Response frame will include a status code to indicate if the response is positive or negative, and if negative, to indicate a reason. If positive, it will indicate the Association ID (AID). In open systems, this will be the final step before one may use the AP to pass data into and out of the Distribution System (DS). It also includes:

- RCPI, An measure of the RF power received in the selected channel
- HT Capabilities and Operation when HT is in use
- If used, an EDCA Parameter set
- 20/40 Coexistence settings
- As before, the last element is a vendor specific element

0010 - Reassociation Request: Initiated in case of roaming from one associated access point to the next, this frame facilitates the transfer from one AP to another inside the same BSS. Importantly, it is sent from the Client to the new AP. This will include data to allow the BSS to reroute the data buffered during the time the client is roaming. This will include, similarly to the Association frame, the SSID of the BSS. If fast transition (FT) is enabled, it will be listed here. It consists of a maximum of 29 fields. It also includes:

- Capability information

- Current AP
- Several optional fields that are enabled based on the BSS's settings

0011 - Reassociation Response: The Reassociation response is sent from the AP that the client is attempting to roam to, and bears the same similarities to the Association Response that the Reassociation request bears to its original counterpart. It consists of up to 34 fields, and can be a positive or negative, indication a success or failure to join the BSS. It will include a status code that informs the client if it has been allowed to reassociate, and if not, for what reason it was rejected. It will include a new AID and fresh information about the BSS that the station might have missed.

- Includes information on association
- AID
- Supported data rates

0100 - Probe Request: A Probe Request is sent when a station/client is requesting information from all access points or a specific AP. Either way, all AP's that hear on the channel must respond. A "Hidden SSID" network requires that the client have the SSID in the probe request to connect to a network. Looking for a Probe Requests and Responses that matches the BSSID is one of the primary ways to "find" a hidden network. The Probe Request is the primary tool in Active Scanning. Probe Requests, along with Beacon frames, are some of the richest points for gathering data on the BSS. Probe Requests:

- Are used to begin the association process
- Are used regardless of the SSID being "shown" in the Beacon
- Are sent exclusively by client STA
- Will contain a "Mesh ID" in Mesh networks

0101 - Probe Response: A Probe Response is the reaction of an AP to a Probe Request. It will contain a timestamp, the beacon interval, capability information and the SSID. It primarily exists to allow Clients to begin the association process. It can contain up to 71 elements. It is one of the most descriptive frames to find out information about a BSS. This will nearly always be sent by the AP, and will always be sent by something serving as an AP (such as in a mesh system):

- Sent from an AP to a STA
- Contains nearly all the information you would want to know about the BSS

180

- Key to the Association process

0110 - Timing Advertisement: Primarily a product of 802.11p, the Timing Advertisement frame allows the BSS to sync to a clock, for the use of bursting in transmissions, originally as a way to allow high speed vehicles to transmit when they had the opportunity. The timing advertisement frame is one of the shortest, with only 7 elements: Timestamp, Capability, Country, Power Constraint, the Time advertisement, Extended Capabilities and the final, reserved vendor specific field.

1000 - Beacon: The foundation of how we see our networks, Beacon frames are much like unsolicited Probe Responses. Most of the time you "see" networks on your device, this is what your device has interpreted, especially if you aren't actively searching for networks. Like the Probe Response, this is a potentially very long frame, with 68 possible fields. Beacon frames are sent out each beacon interval and are a way of advertising, via broadcast, the features and presence of the network. Each SSID in each BSS will send out a beacon. Even hidden SSIDs will send out a NULL SSID Beacon. This is part of the danger of having too many SSIDs. It takes time to send a beacon frame and they still must win a TxOP (transmit opportunity) to transmit, like everything else. If you have many SSIDs, you may see your airtime being taken up by many Probe Responses and Beacons. This is referred to as excessive management overhead, as it is not actually stations transmitting data that are taking up the majority of the time on the medium. Beacons:

- Are sent at a certain interval, that is usually configurable
- Must contend for the medium like other frames
- Display a wide range of characteristics of the BSS
- May be the first step in joining a BSS, as it is the only way a "passive" system will see the BSS
- Announce the Channel width and capabilities of the BSS

1001 – ATIM (Announcement Traffic Indication Message): An ATIM tells stations that are engaged in power save operations that the transmitting Ad-Hoc STA has buffered frames for them, to be sent upon waking. This is only present in an IBSS, and as such is not seen as often. IBSS presents serious security concerns and is also inefficient. Be wary of connecting to any IBSS.

1010 - Disassociation and 1100 – Deauthentication: Both Deauthentication and Disassociation frames have much the same result on the recipient of the frame: an end to the authentication or association of the subject from the BSS. Note that a Deauthentication frame will force the target client to renegotiate the entire connection, while a Disassociation frame will nominally only force a reassociation, as the authentication state is still considered valid. A frame of this nature is sent with a reason code, listed in Figures 4.1 and 4.2.

Reason code	Name	Meaning
0		Reserved
1	UNSPECIFIED_REASON	Unspecified reason
2	INVALID_AUTHENTICATION	Previous authentication no longer valid
3	LEAVING_NETWORK_DEAUTH	Deauthenticated because sending STA is leaving (or has left) IBSS or ESS
4	REASON_INACTIVITY	Disassociated due to inactivity
5	NO_MORE_STAS	Disassociated because AP is unable to handle all currently associated STAs
6	INVALID_CLASS2_FRAME	Class 2 frame received from nonauthenticated STA
7	INVALID_CLASS3_FRAME	Class 3 frame received from nonassociated STA
8	LEAVING_NETWORK_DISASSOC	Disassociated because sending STA is leaving (or has left) BSS
9	NOT_AUTHENTICATED	STA requesting (re)association is not authenticated with responding STA
10	UNACCEPTABLE_POWER_CAPABILITY	Disassociated because the information in the Power Capability element is unacceptable
11	UNACCEPTABLE_SUPPORTED_CHANNELS	Disassociated because the information in the Supported Channels element is unacceptable
12	BSS_TRANSITION_DISASSOC	Disassociated due to BSS transition management
13	REASON_INVALID_ELEMENT	Invalid element, i.e., an element defined in this standard for which the content does not meet the specifications in Clause 9
14	MIC_FAILURE	Message integrity code (MIC) failure
15	4WAY_HANDSHAKE_TIMEOUT	4-way handshake timeout
16	GK_HANDSHAKE_TIMEOUT	Group key handshake timeout
17	HANDSHAKE_ELEMENT_MISMATCH	Element in 4-way handshake different from (Re)Association Request/Probe Response/Beacon frame

Figure 4.1: Reason Codes (0-17)

There are more reason codes than listed in Figures 4.1 and 4.2, but for brevity, they shall be omitted here. Consult the IEEE Std 802.11-2016, Table 9-45 for a full reference. Note also, that the Deauth and Deassoc frames have a nearly identical structure, and a quite small body. They can be sent broadcast by an AP, Unicast by an AP, or Unicast by a client, to inform or to force the desired result. This is one of the reasons for protected management frames; to protect against a "Spoofed" BSSID sending a Deauth and forcing the entire Service set to reconnect.

Reason code	Name	Meaning
18	REASON_INVALID_GROUP_CIPHER	Invalid group cipher
19	REASON_INVALID_PAIRWISE_CIPHER	Invalid pairwise cipher
20	REASON_INVALID_AKMP	Invalid AKMP
21	UNSUPPORTED_RSNE_VERSION	Unsupported RSNE version
22	INVALID_RSNE_CAPABILITIES	Invalid RSNE capabilities
23	802_1_X_AUTH_FAILED	IEEE 802.1X authentication failed
24	REASON_CIPHER_OUT_OF_POLICY	Cipher suite rejected because of the security policy
25	TDLS_PEER_UNREACHABLE	TDLS direct-link teardown due to TDLS peer STA unreachable via the TDLS direct link
26	TDLS_UNSPECIFIED_REASON	TDLS direct-link teardown for unspecified reason
27	SSP_REQUESTED_DISASSOC	Disassociated because session terminated by SSP request
28	NO_SSP_ROAMING_AGREEMENT	Disassociated because of lack of SSP roaming agreement
29	BAD_CIPHER_OR_AKM	Requested service rejected because of SSP cipher suite or AKM requirement
30	NOT_AUTHORIZED_THIS_LOCATION	Requested service not authorized in this location
31	SERVICE_CHANGE_PRECLUDES_TS	TS deleted because QoS AP lacks sufficient bandwidth for this QoS STA due to a change in BSS service characteristics or operational mode (e.g., an HT BSS change from 40 MHz channel to 20 MHz channel)
32	UNSPECIFIED_QOS_REASON	Disassociated for unspecified, QoS-related reason
33	NOT_ENOUGH_BANDWIDTH	Disassociated because QoS AP lacks sufficient bandwidth for this QoS STA
34	MISSING_ACKS	Disassociated because excessive number of frames need to be acknowledged, but are not acknowledged due to AP transmissions and/or poor channel conditions
35	EXCEEDED_TXOP	Disassociated because STA is transmitting outside the limits of its TXOPs
36	STA_LEAVING	Requesting STA is leaving the BSS (or resetting)
37	END_TS END_BA END_DLS	Requesting STA is no longer using the stream or session
38	UNKNOWN_TS UNKNOWN_BA	Requesting STA received frames using a mechanism for which a setup has not been completed
39	TIMEOUT	Requested from peer STA due to timeout
45	PEERKEY_MISMATCH	Peer STA does not support the requested cipher suite

Figure 4.2: Reason Codes (18-45)

You might see a Deauth when:

- A station is leaving the BSS
- Unspecified- Kind of a wildcard, or not known
- Inactivity timeout
- Roaming/Transition, the STA is moving AP to AP
- Security handshake fail due to timeout
- 802.1X Failure
- If you can't join, or keep getting dropped, check the status code!

1011 - Authentication: Described in the standard under section 11.3.4, Authentication is the second stage taken to join a BSS. It is initiated by the STA, after the probe request and probe response. The Authentication frame arbitrates the process of the station and AP establishing who they are, whether in an SAE, WEP, PSK or 802.1X Environment. Null authentication is used in all situations except WEP, which is to be considered deprecated, and should not be used. The specifics of the process are part of your CWNA studies. The Authentication process in most cases will be two frames, Authentication frame STA > AP and the second, from AP > STA.

1101 - Action: Action frames prompt the recipient to take a specific action, or more precisely a category of actions. Specifically, it facilitates spectrum management, QoS actions, Block ACK controls, radio measurement, and management of HT operations. Each additional category of actions has its own element tree, to specify the type of action or set of actions to be requested or responded to. Since there is a wide variety of Action frames, we will not detail them here. All information is available in the IEEE standard 802.11-2016, beginning on page 1156, Section 9.6.

- Spectrum Management actions - Measurement request and report, TPC Request and report and channel switch announcement. Notably, channel switch announcements will occur when the BSS is forced to change channels utilized, such as with a DFS event.
- QoS action frames can be used to alter the details of the QoS arrangements between station and AP. Specifically, one of the more useful QoS frames informs the STA of the BSS's QoS Mapping, so it can be configured properly.

- The Block Ack variation is used to configure the process of sending block acks for a more efficient communication, sending an ADDBA Request and receiving a ADDBA Response. This then allows the BSS and STA to only ack at the END of a transmission, instead of ack'ing each frame sent.
- The other action frames are covered in detail within the standard and will be omitted for brevity.

1110 - Action No Ack: An action frame that does not require an acknowledgement. It ONLY consists of the Action field.

Control Frames

According to the 802.11 standard:

> *MAC Control Frames are used to support the delivery of IEEE 802.11 Data, Management, and Extension Frames.*

From this, you can see that Control frames are used to control the delivery of other frames. Unlike Management frames, they do not have a frame body. All Control Frames are designated Type 01. The subtypes are listed in Table 4.2.

0100	0110	0111	1000	1001	1010	1011
Beamforming Report Poll	Control Frame Extension	Control Wrapper	Block Ack Request	Block Ack	Ps-Poll	Request to Send [RTS]
1100	1101	1110	1111			
Clear To Send [CTS]	Ack	CF-END	CF-END + CF-ACK			

Table 4.2: Control Frame Subtypes

The following details the specific of each Control frame subtype.

0100 - Beamforming Report Poll: Part of the beamforming mechanism used by HT and VHT, this is a control frame that solicits the clients to return the explicit information needed to beamform properly. Beamforming is the process of manipulating the phase of the outgoing signals so that at the proper place where the client is, the signals recombine. This is a constructive use of multipath propagation. As a rule, if signals cross and they are inversely phased (for example, the trough of one wave and the peak of another) they will cancel out. Whereas here, in this example, if they are in sync (for example, the peak of one waveform and the peak of another) they will amplify each other. They are still subject to free space path loss and as such the total strength after amplification will be less than the total signal strength was an inch from the AP. This was an improvement over the exclusively destructive multipath of 802.11a/b/g PHYs and was built upon later with 802.11ac.

0110 - Control Frame Extension: The Control Frame Extension type is used to increase the subtype space to allow additional variants by reusing Bits 8-11. Types indicated by this control frame type are usually of the DMG type or a Grant or Grant Ack.

0111 - Control Wrapper: The Control Wrapper subtype is primarily used to allow space for utilization of the more diverse HT functions. An example is the facilitation of transmit beamforming, which has only partially seen adoption as of the time of this writing.

1000 - Block Ack Request: This is how a station requests to use the more efficient system of block acks, and to inform that a block ack is desired, following a series of QoS Data submission. It specifically signals that a block has completed and requests a Block Ack to acknowledge that the full measure of the transmission has been sent and received correctly. As you learned in CWNA, if it does not receive the Block Ack, or if there is a mistake with the Block Ack, it must then retransmit. Note that retransmitting a full block takes much longer than it would otherwise take to retransmit a single frame, and only by maintaining a low retry rate does it maintain its efficiency over Acks every frame. There are limited circumstances where it is either not more efficient, or does not fit the use case, to use block acks.

1001 - Block Ack: The second part of the sequence detailed above, this is the acknowledgement for the aggregated data payload that was sent. It can be sent, like the request, from either an AP or a STA. Note that only later PHYs can take advantage of this frame. 802.11a/b/g are incapable of using it in production chipsets.

1010 - PS-Poll: A Ps-Poll Frame is sent from the STA to the AP when the STA wakes and receives a Beacon frame. The Beacon will list the AIDs of any stations for which it has buffered traffic in the TIM. Seeing this, the STA Sends the PS-Poll frame to the AP to indicate it is awake and ready to receive the buffered data. It continues sending PS-Polls and receiving data until one of the frames has the More Data bit set to 0. At that point it can Ack the last data frame and go back to sleep.

1011 - RTS, Request-To-Send: RTS is a supplement to CSMA/CA. This is the first part of the RTS/CTS sequence, which is used to clear the medium to allow a transmission in an area of high use, or for an abnormally long frame. The RTS is generated by a STA and sent to the AP, which will respond with a CTS, when the medium is clear. Notably, the RTS frame will contain the duration value for the transmission to be used by the following CTS.

1100 - CTS, Clear to Send: The second of the two RTS/CTS exchange, this is the AP recognizing, and to some degree reserving, the medium for the incoming transmission. It does this by the duration value, which will force all the stations listening to set the NAV timer, so that they cannot contend with the medium until the "approved" transmission has completed. It also informs the STA that is may now transmit. Its duration field will include the entirety of the RTS' duration field, minus the time taken to transmit the CTS, and the SIFS prior. At times, APs could send a CTS with no preceding RTS, which is colloquially known as CTS-to-Self.

When one is conducting protocol analysis, even the most basic of engines will show you the Retransmission bit. A few of these is normal in the operation of 802.11, but a large amount can spell trouble. The amount that is dangerous will be slightly different for each given network. Establishing a baseline is crucial.

1101 - Ack/Acknowledgement: In the many 802.11 communications, this frame will follow every frame sent back and forth, excepting ActionNoAck and Acks themselves and frames that can use a Block Ack. This is the receiving STA (which can be a client or AP) certifying that it has successfully received and decoded the last transmission successfully. If it passes the CRC and the frame doesn't have errors in it, the ACK will be transmitted to the sending STA. Otherwise, a retransmit will occur, incrementing the Retry bit to 1, but not changing the Sequence Identifier.

1110 - CF-End: This signals the end of a Contention-Free period in a PCF system. As PCF is not used in production systems, this is somewhat of a rarity, and is not part of the Wi-Fi Alliance Interoperability Certification. This author has yet to encounter a PCF system, and CF frames are usually a sign of CRC errors.

1111 - CF-End+CF-Ack: When a PCF system is used, this signals the end of contention-free operation, and Acks the last frame.

Data Frames

Using the Type value 10, the Data frame types are in general, a combination of data and an extra action, or simply data. We will cover a few of importance below.

0000 - Data: Your basic Data frame. It carries a data payload and that is its primary purpose. Counter-intuitive but true, most frames sent are not data frames but management and control frames.

0100 - Null Data: The Null Data frame is a frame that carries no data. Its primary usage is to be a carrier for the power save bit. It can be used to inform an AP that the STA is ready to receive data, if it had previously indicated that it was in Power save mode. We will discuss it further when we discuss the power save bit later. It can also be used to indicate that it is going off channel to roam or scan. We also have the QoS Null Data frame. The availability of the QoS Null Data frame depends primarily on the STA's support for QoS. Some legacy STAs will not. The QoS Null Data frame is subtype 1100.

1000 - QoS Data: Carries data in a QoS marked frame based on 802.11e Access Categories (ACs) and the Wi-Fi Multimedia (WMM) Wi-Fi Alliance certification. Many data frames traversing 802.11n and 802.11ac networks are QoS Data frames.

MAC Frame Format

The format for a frame differs slightly between frame types: Data, Management, and Control Frames are all different formats, and range from the gigantic jumbo frames some vendors use to the small and simple Ack frame. They follow several patterns, usually by the type of frame, then by the subtype. We will cover them here in-depth.

General Frame Format

Each frame consists generally of a few main components:

- A MAC header that may include the Frame Control, Duration, Addresses, Optional Sequence Control, QoS Control and HT Control fields.
- A variable length frame-body, which may contain information specific to the frame and subtype and may not be included in some frames, like the RTS and CTS frames.

- A FCS, or frame check sequence, which contains a 32-bit CRC [Cyclic Redundancy Check] based on the ITU-T V4.2.

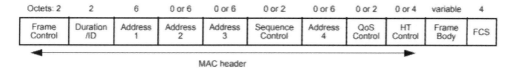

Figure 4.3: 802.11 General Frame Format

In Figure 4.3 above, you see the General Frame Format. The represents the basic format of an 802.11 frame. We'll dive into each of the sections individually to get a better understanding. Frame capture engines decode part of the information with varying degrees of reliability. Sometimes they fail. Having a solid basis in the root knowledge will help you immensely. We will try to include in this section as many graphics and real-world examples as possible to break up the stream of information. It, at times, feels as if one is drinking from a firehose, especially if you have just completed your CWNA studies. Take your time, and if possible, do some captures of your own and prioritize understanding each portion, instead of trying to complete it all at once.

 A word of advice for studying: This can seem like dry reading, second only to reading the 802.11 standard itself, but it is some of the best information for getting acquainted with the standard and the way that it actually works, as well as informing a great deal of troubleshooting that you may do.

There are two main anatomies of a frame control field: What here we will refer to as the "General" and the "Control Frame Extension". As you learned previously, the control frame extension type is used to allow for reuse of the b8-b11 bits.

The Frame Control field, as seen in Figure 4.4, is two octets long, or 16 bits. Here they are numbered from b0 to b15, and this convention in general is held across the Standard. This format is the case in every example that is not the Control Frame Extension designate (remember, Type 1- Subtype 6 from above).

Protocol Version - The first field, the name is also somewhat misleading. This is in place in case of a major revision by the IEEE and should currently always be set to 0. If a new version that is "Incompatible" is released, the IEEE will increment at that juncture. You can find the full text in the 2016 standard, under 9.2.4.1.2.

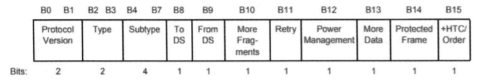

B0 B1	B2 B3	B4 B7	B8	B9	B10	B11	B12	B13	B14	B15
Protocol Version	Type	Subtype	To DS	From DS	More Frag-ments	Retry	Power Management	More Data	Protected Frame	+HTC/ Order
Bits: 2	2	4	1	1	1	1	1	1	1	1

Figure 4.4: Frame Control field details

Type and Subtype - Two different fields, the Type field is two bits in length, and the subtype is four bits in length. We discussed these values a bit before, with the types of frames. It includes four possible values [00-11] for the type, and four bits [0000-1111] for the Subtype.

You must know what kind of frame is going past in your captures. Knowing what should be traveling across the network is half the battle and the other half is what is traveling across the network. Most protocol analyzers will make this easy to tell, as shown in Figure 4.5, but it behooves a good engineer to know the manual decode, especially when multiple parties are decoding, sometimes the analyzer will function improperly, or not at all.

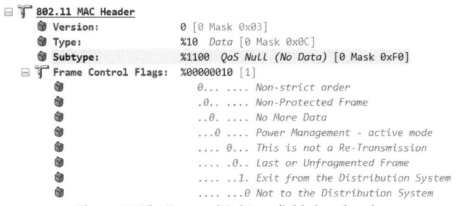

Figure 4.5: The Type and Subtype fields in a decode

190

To/From DS - Two fields of one bit each. These describe the path of the frame and indicate if it is in a mesh system. Think of the bits as True/False instead of a numerical value.

If To DS and From DS both equal 0, the transmission is from station to station within an IBSS, from STA to STA in a BSS, or a non-ap to another non-ap in an infrastructure system. If client isolation is in effect with your system, you shouldn't see frames with these flags and this can serve as a warning. This is the only combination for an IBSS transmission as they do not possess a DS-structure.

If To DS=1 and From DS=0, it is a frame sent from a STA associated to an AP, sent into the DS.

If To DS=0 and From DS=1, it is a frame exiting the DS, or being sent from the AP. Alternately a group addressed mesh Data frame with the Mesh control field present, using the three-address MAC header format. This is the only combination for Frames from an AP and group addressed frames transmitted by a mesh STA.

If To DS=1 and From DS=1, it is a mesh system data frame using the four-address MAC header format. This will always be indicative of a transmission between STAs in a mesh BSS.

When first examining a Frame capture, this is a good indication of the direction of the flow of the frames. Knowing where the conversation is headed, and who is on the DS side can be crucial. Often overlooked is developing an intuitive understanding of what is happening, and small pieces like this can help pull the pieces together. Figure 4.6 shows the To DS and From DS fields.

More Fragments - The More Fragments field is a single bit in length and is set to True (1) in all Data or management frames that have another fragment of the current MSDU following. If there are no more, or it is not fragmented, it is set to False (0). In Control frames of the Extension subtype, this is integrated into the Control frame extension field. Figure 4.7 highlights the More Fragments field. Note that it is set to 1 where the decode reads, "More Fragments to Follow."

```
🎲 Version:              0 [0 Mask 0x03]
🎲 Type:                 %10  Data [0 Mask 0x0C]
🎲 Subtype:              %1000  QoS Data [0 Mask 0xF0]
⊟ 🎵 Frame Control Flags:  %01010001 [1]
   🎲                      0... ....  Non-strict order
   🎲                      .1.. ....  Protected Frame
   🎲                      ..0. ....  No More Data
   🎲                      ...1 ....  Power Management - power save mode
   🎲                      .... 0...  This is not a Re-Transmission
   🎲                      .... .0..  Last or Unfragmented Frame
   🎲                      .... ..0.  Not an Exit from the Distribution System
   🎲                      .... ...1  To the Distribution System
🎲 Duration:             40  Microseconds [2-3]
```

Figure 4.6: To DS and From DS fields

```
🎲 Type:                 %01  Control [0 Mask 0x0C]
🎲 Subtype:              %0110  Reserved [0 Mask 0xF0]
⊟ 🎵 Frame Control Flags:  %00011101 [1]
   🎲                      0... ....  Non-strict order
   🎲                      .0.. ....  Non-Protected Frame
   🎲                      ..0. ....  No More Data
   🎲                      ...1 ....  Power Management - power save mode
   🎲                      .... 1...  This is a Re-Transmission
   🎲                      .... .1..  More Fragments to Follow
   🎲                      .... ..0.  Not an Exit from the Distribution System
   🎲                      .... ...1  To the Distribution System
🎲 Extra bytes (Padding):(28 bytes) [2-29]
```

Figure 4.7: More Fragments field set to 1

Retry Subfield - One bit in length, the Retry subfield is just what one would think. It indicates that this is a retransmission of a previous message that was not ACK'd. Many protocol analyzers use this to determine overall retry rate (Retried/Total Frames = percent Retry). A common issue with retried frames is that they take up the medium, just like any other frame. Generally, the retry rate is also included in the algorithmic determination of the current modulation, since there is no way for a Tx STA to know what the distance from it to the Rx STA is, or the degree of other impediments it might encounter. It will also be compared against the sequence number to make sure that if it resulting in an action at a higher level, or presents information, it is only processed once. Some Voice applications are particularly vulnerable to retries and, depending on what frame exactly is being retried, can present a vulnerability as seen with KRACK attacks.

Beware of underestimating the retry rate when capturing from a single adapter. A good aggregated and synced capture from many points in the BSS is much more desirable, as your adapter can only "listen" on one channel, and only in one place. You might not be able to hear a Tx from the opposite side of the BSS, which will take up airtime and contribute to the over-utilization that may be plaguing your BSS.

Power Management subfield - One bit in length, the Power Management subfield is a key part of mitigating the power expenditure of battery driven devices. The value in this field indicates the mode of the STA on successful completion of the Sequence of transmissions (0 for remaining "awake", 1 for "sleeping"). The Power Management subfield is to be considered reserved in all management frames transmitted to an AP that it is not associated with, such as a Probe Request. The power management subfield is also considered reserved in all AP-originated transmissions. In case of an IBSS, it is valid only in certain exchanges and indicates the same sleep/wake status. Figure 4.8 shows the Power Management bit in a decode.

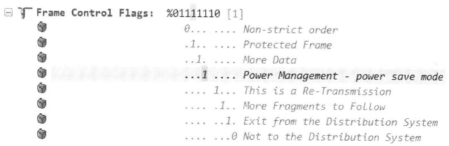

Figure 4.8: Power Management bit set to 1

If response times seem a bit slow, you might check what power save settings are on your client devices. Some devices will in fact disable one or both Tx chains and even a Rx chain when it is in sleep mode. If your RSSI/RCPI is different when your device is in high battery state or plugged in than it is when it is in low battery, this may be a significant issue. Smaller devices may also lose maximum Tx power when battery is low.

More Data subfield - The more Data subfield is one bit in length. A non-DMG STA/AP uses the More data subfield to indicate to a STA in Power-save mode that it has more transmissions/information held in the buffer for the STA, before the STA goes back to sleep. Please see the Figure 4.8 for an example, shown between the "Protected" bit and the Power Management bit. This, combined with the Power Management subfield, can govern power save. If a station is awakened, to receive data following its AID in the TIM from a beacon, it will stay awake for the buffered frames. If transmitting individually, each transmission will indicate to the STA that there is more data incoming for that STA, ensuring the STA does not go back to sleep.

When observing your power save devices, this is a good indication whether they are performing the function they should. If you're on the development side of 802.11, this is a relatively easy test of a driver function.

Protected Frame subfield - The Protected frame subfield is one bit in length. It is set to 1/true if the frame body has been processed by a cryptographic encapsulation algorithm. It will otherwise be set to 0. Figure 4.9 shows the Protected field bit set to 1.

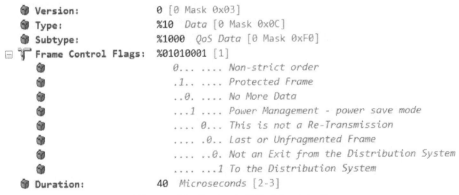

Figure 4.9: Protected field set to 1

Address Fields – Leaving the Frame Control field, in the general frame format, the address fields are all 6 0ctets in length (48 bytes) and represent directly a MAC address, the same as would be used otherwise in 802.11 or 802.3 communications. They directly follow the Duration ID in the format and can be optionally up to four fields. Only one of the four must be present in every frame, but up to four may be present. Notably, as shown in Table 4.3, the entire 48 bits are used, but only 46 bits are used for the address itself. The first and second (LSB's) identify the address type. The First, or the I/G bit, is set to 1 for multicast and broadcast addresses, or "targeted at a group" [Individual/group I/G]. If set to 0, it is targeted at an individual address. The second, The U/L bit, indicates either a Universally administered address, or a Local is in use. A locally administered address is one that has been set or altered by the administrator, as opposed to the "universal" address, which is the BIA or "Burned-In-Address", the address assigned on creation of the device/chipset.

Individual/Group [1 bit]	Universal/Local [1 bit]	46-bit MAC Address

Table 4.3: The Structure of the Address Fields

The four fields are as follows, the SA [source address], the TA [Transmitter address], the RA [Receiver address], and the DA [destination address]. The only field that is always used is the RA. What's the difference? The RA is the immediate recipient of the frame being sent. The DA, by contrast, is the final intended destination of the transmission. The SA is the opposite of the DA and is the source of the data being transmitted. The TA, then, is the STA transmitting the frame in question, but not the one always that "Generated" the frame. Some notable cases:

- In most non-root transmissions on a mesh network, all fields will be used. Please see Figure 4.10.
- CTS frames will only have ADD1, RA
- Management frames will usually have RA, TA and the BSSID in Slot 3
- Data frames will have the RA and TA, and depending on conditions, the SA and DA OR BSSID.
- In general, ADD1 will hold RA.
- ADD2 will hold TA
- ADD3 will hold BSSID or SA or DA
- ADD4 will hold BSSID or SA

To summarize concisely: The DA is the final recipient, The SA the STA that generated the data, The RA the immediate recipient, and the TA the transmitting STA.

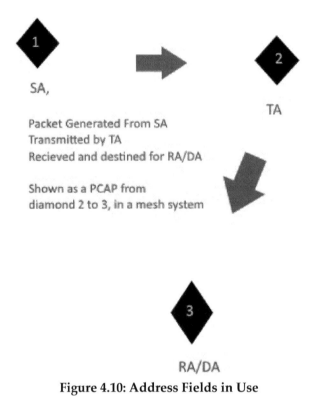

SA,

Packet Generated From SA
Transmitted by TA
Recieved and destined for RA/DA

Shown as a PCAP from
diamond 2 to 3, in a mesh system

TA

RA/DA

Figure 4.10: Address Fields in Use

Frame Check Sequence [FCS] - An error-checking field, the Frame check sequence, or FCS is the product of a mathematical calculation that includes all the fields of the MAC header and Frame body field. These are referred to as "Calculation fields" in the standard. When the Frame is received, the FCS is recalculated and compared, and if they are different, the frame is assumed to be corrupt or damaged, and is discarded. The Exact way it is calculated is outside of the scope of this exam and material, but may be read in the standard directly, located at 9.2.4.8 "FCS Field" in the 802.11-2016 Standard document.

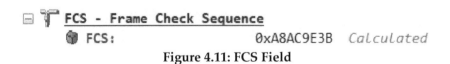

Figure 4.11: FCS Field

Many FCS errors can be a good indication that you have high amounts of interference, or collisions. This could be because of Co-channel Interference (CCI), Adjacent Channel Interference (ACI), frequent and sudden DFS events or even a non-Wi-Fi interferer, such as a leaky microwave. For a more precise troubleshooting session, see if you can correlate absolute time with a period of FCS errors.

 CRC errors in a laptop-based protocol analyzer are not always a sign of problems. You may be far from the AP and the AP may be able to demodulate frames sent to it without issue, but at your location the signal strength is not enough. It is up to the analyst to determine if the CRC errors are because of capture location or because of a problem.

802.11 Management Frame Formats

As discussed previously, the general format of a management frame isn't drastically divergent from the General format. Several frames have the biggest difference, if any at all, in the "Information Elements" in the frame body, included below. These are small bits, or groups of bits that indicate certain characteristics which are different for each individual Frame type. Not all have a body, however, for instance, the ATIM frame is in fact a Null body.

Beacon Frames

The Beacon frame is transmitted by the AP to announce the existence of and capabilities of the BSS. An AP sends a Beacon frame for each SSID that it offers. Beacon frames can be more than 300-400 bytes in size and this is reason enough to limit the number of SSIDs to the recommended 3-5 SSIDs per radio (remembering that an AP may have two or three radios in common implementations for 2.4 GHz and 5 GHz operations).

The Beacon frame information elements are defined in Table 9-27 of the 802.11-2016 standard document. A few key components will be referenced here as they are of utmost importance:

- **Beacon Interval:** The time between Beacon frames, which defaults to 102.4 ms. This means that approximately 10 times per second, each SSID will require an attempt to send a Beacon frame. In reality, the AP must contend for the medium to send this frame just as any other frame. Therefore, in a busy channel, with lots of data traffic as well as multiple SSIDs per AP and multiple APs seen on the channel, it will result in less than per second. The Beacon Interval value can be changed in most enterprise APs, but it is not commonly recommended as it is unknown how some client devices might respond.

- **Capability Information:** This includes things like whether the SSID is part of an ESS or an IBSS, if encryption is in use, if spectrum management is available, if radio measurement is available, and if Block Ack can be used.
- **SSID:** The SSID (network name) of the network announced in the Beacon frame.
- **Supported Rates:** Indicates the data rates supported and which are basic rates versus operational rates. Basic rates must be supported by the client STA to connect. Operational rates are optional.
- **Extended Supported Rates:** Because the Supported Rates section was not large enough to handle all rates (no more than 8) eventually (in the 54 Mbps and slower days) this section was added. The basic rates and operational rates concept still applies.
- **Traffic Indication Map (TIM):** Used to indicate the AIDs of STAs with frames buffered on the AP during power save.
- **Country:** Used to indicate the region in which the AP is operating and, therefore, the regulatory restrictions under which it must function.
- **Robust Security Network Information Element (RSN IE):** Indicates the security used for group communications (multicast or broadcast) and individual communications (unicast).
- **HT Capabilities and HT Information:** Used to indicate the features and capabilities of 802.11n supported by the AP.
- **VHT Capabilities and VHT Operation:** Used to indicate the features and capabilities of 802.11ac supported by the AP.
- **Vendor Specific (WME):** Wireless Multimedia Extensions (WME), which are commonly present to indicate the WMM values in use, such as the AIFSN and ECWmin and ECWmax for each Access Category (AC).

Again, this is a partial listing of what is included in the Beacon frames. For full details, see the 802.11-2016 standard. Figure 4.12 shows a decode of a Beacon frame, partially expanded, from CommView for WiFi.

```
> Wireless Packet Info
> 802.11
∨ Beacon
    ⋯Timestamp: 1561387.417992 sec
    ⋯Beacon Interval: 0x00C8 (200) - 204.800 msec
    ∨ Capability Information: 0x1011 (4113)
        ⋯ESS: 1
        ⋯IBSS: 0
        ⋯CF-Pollable: 0
        ⋯CF-Poll Request: 0
        ⋯Privacy: 1
        ⋯Short Preamble: 0
        ⋯PBCC: 0
        ⋯Channel Agility: 0
        ⋯Spectrum management: 0
        ⋯QoS: 0
        ⋯Short slot: 0
        ⋯APSD: 0
        ⋯Radio Measurement: 1
        ⋯DSSS-OFDM: 0
        ⋯Block Ack: 0
        ⋯Immediate Block Ack: 0
    ⋯SSID: COMCAST5H
> Supported rates
> Traffic indication map (TIM): Bits 0 - 7, Stations with AID = 12, 3, 4
> Country Information
∨ RSN Information Element (802.11i)
    ⋯Version: 0x0001 (1)
    ⋯Group Key Cipher Suite: 00 0F AC 04 - CCMP
    ⋯Pairwise Key Cipher Suite Count: 0x0001 (1)
    > Pairwise Key Cipher Suite List
    ⋯Authenticated Key Management Suite Count: 0x0001 (1)
    > Authenticated Key Management Suite List
    > RSN Capabilities: 0x000C (12)
> QBSS Load Element: 802.11e CCA Version
> HT Capabilities element
> HT Information element
> Extended Capabilities
> VHT Capabilities
∨ VHT Operation
    > VHT Operation Info: 0x9B01
> VHT Tx Power Envelope (IEEE Std 802.11ac/D5.0)
> Vendor specific: MICROSOFT CORP., WPS
> Vendor specific: (221), BROADCOM CORPORATION, Tag not interpreted
> Vendor specific: MICROSOFT CORP., WME
```

Figure 4.12: Beacon frame decode

It is important to know that beacons are sent at a target beacon transmission time (TBTT). That is, they are configured by default to be transmitted every 100 Time Units (TUs) and this default equals 102.4 ms. However, you have now seen that many frames are transmitted on the wireless medium. For this reason, it is likely that occasions will occur when the beacon frame simply cannot be sent every 100 TUs but will be sent as soon as possible after 100 TUs.

Probe Request and Probe Response Frames

The beginning of the association process, the probe request also is a product of active scanning and actively seeks to find a connectable network. It is sent to the broadcast address [FF:…:FF] for active scanning. It then starts a Probe Timer countdown and waits for a response from any available network on that channel. If it hasn't received an answer or even if it has and has not located an AP to which it desired to connect, it changes channels and attempts again, cycling through the channels that it is configured to utilize. Note that if a STA cannot use, say UNII-2e, it should not probe those channels, and if the BSS is exclusively on those channels, you will be unable to connect to the network.

In addition, in the frame body, the Probe Request can specify the SSID it is seeking, or it can send a wildcard/null Probe Request in the SSID element to request that all SSIDs respond. As a rule, this will be sent with Address 1 being a RA/DA of broadcast, the Address 2 (TA) being the probing device, and the Address 3 representing the BSSID as broadcast as well.

Included in the Probe Request, the SSID and the supported rates, as well as 20/40 coexistence are of particular interest when troubleshooting. Paying close attention to the conditions surrounding Probe Requests can be of great utility when testing the more intentionally obscured details of client's RF behavior.

The Probe Response is sent at the lowest common rate that the STA and AP have in common. It can also be seen as a somewhat modified beacon frame, albeit one that is not sent as a result of the Beacon interval. Because of substantive overlap, the full elements list will not be listed here. Some things to keep in mind:

- The probe request Does not contain a TIM or a QoS capability frame.
- It is addressed to a specific station, the one who sent the request
- It is partially tailored to the specific elements that were flagged in the request
- It does include the beacon interval for the BSS

200

Authentication Frames

The Authentication frame body isn't as verbose as the Beacon or Probe Response frames, but is still important and can be a wealth of information. With the deprecation of WEP however, most often only two Authentication frames are sent. Special attention should be paid to Element 3, Status Code. Notably this will have the rejected or not rejected message in message two of the authentication exchange. All elements for the Authentication frame are defined in the 802.11-2016 standard.

An interesting aside here is the inclusion of the SAE (Simultaneous Authentication of Equals). With WPA3 looming at the time of this writing, SAE looks to be a larger factor in at least the enterprise space. The Finite Cyclic group is in service to this end in element 10. This will introduce further salt to passwords and keys that do not meet specific security requirements. While user error will never be eliminated, and people are the largest security hole you will find, any mitigating factor is worth pursuing.

Figure 4.13 shows the four-frame exchange for an iPhone to authenticate with a NETGEAR router. Figure 4.14 shows the Authentication frame of this exchange decoded with a successful Status value of 1. Both images are from CommView for WiFi.

613	MNGT/AUTH	Apple:4C:27:C7	Netgear:07:10:27	54	20:04:33.298747	-44	6	Status=Successful, Trans....
614	CTRL/ACK	N/A	Apple:4C:27:C7	10	20:04:33.298761	-37	6	
615	MNGT/AUTH	Netgear:07:10:27	Apple:4C:27:C7	41	20:04:33.298763	-35	6	Status=Successful, Trans....
616	CTRL/ACK	N/A	Netgear:07:10:27	10	20:04:33.298764	-43	6	

Figure 4.13: Authentication frame exchanges

```
> Wireless Packet Info
> 802.11
∨ Authentication
    Algorithm Number: 0x0000 (0) - Open System
    Transaction Sequence Number: 0x0002 (2)
    Status Code: 0x0000 (0) - Successful
  ∨ Vendor specific: (221), BROADCOM CORPORATION, Tag not interpreted
      Tag: Vendor Specific
      Length: 9
      OUI: BROADCOM CORPORATION
      OUI Type: 2
      Not interpreted
```

Figure 4.14: Authentication response decoded

Deauthentication Frames

One of the shortest frames, a Deauthentication frame (called a Deauth frame for short) only consists of the reason code and optional elements. There is a large amount of possible Deauth reason codes and they are documented in the 802.11-2016 standard.

When troubleshooting, the Deauthentication status code is one of the most useful fields you will find, especially when troubleshooting drops, or when hunting down join errors.

Association Request and Response Frames

The Association Request frame is sent by the STA to the AP in the last stages of an open authentication process and before either 802.1X/EAP authentication or the 4-way handshake if PSK is used. This frame isn't as large as the Authentication frame. Notable features include the SSID, client's supported rates, QoS information and other capabilities. It is important to note that this frame tells you much more about the client STA's capabilities than the AP's. A good way of conceptualizing the exchange in context is "This is what I can do. Will this work for you and the BSS?" as opposed to during authentication, which is better conceptualized as "This is who I am, who are you?" Pay special attention in your captures to which STA sent the Association request/Auth request. The frames are similar, and if the decoder doesn't help, or you don't know which address the STA or AP is, seeing who SENDS the Assoc/Auth request is a dead giveaway. An AP will never ask to associate with a STA.

The respondent frame to the Association Request is the Association Response. This frame reflects the actual settings of the BSS to the client trying to join. It will also carry a status code as Element 2 (positive or negative), the AID for the STA to use as Element 3, and additionally a measurement field if requested. As before, for reference, the 802.11-2016 standard provides details of all the elements. Figure 4.15 shows an association exchange and Figure 4.16 shows the decode of the Association Response frame that was successful.

428	MNGT/ASS. REQ.	Apple:4C:27:C7	Netgear:07:10:27	194	20:18:23.892215	-48	6	SSID=COMCAST5H, Seq=...
429	CTRL/ACK	N/A	Apple:4C:27:C7	10	20:18:23.892224	-36	6	
430	MNGT/ASS. RESP.	Netgear:07:10:27	Apple:4C:27:C7	186	20:18:23.900859	-35	6	Successful, Assoc.ID=2, S...
431	CTRL/ACK	N/A	Netgear:07:10:27	10	20:18:23.900830	-43	6	

Figure 4.15: Association frame exchange

 Remember, there is only one Authentication frame, but there is both an Association Request and Association Response frame. The difference between the to Authentication frames is that one is from the client (the first one – transaction sequence number 1) and the other is from the AP (the second one – transaction sequence number 2). Like other frames, these frames must be acknowledged as seen the frame exchange images for both frame types.

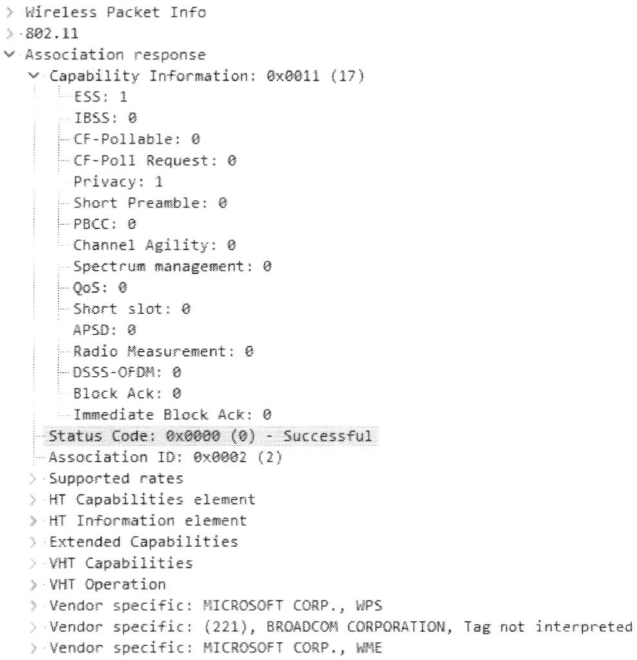

```
> Wireless Packet Info
> 802.11
v Association response
   v Capability Information: 0x0011 (17)
      ESS: 1
      IBSS: 0
      CF-Pollable: 0
      CF-Poll Request: 0
      Privacy: 1
      Short Preamble: 0
      PBCC: 0
      Channel Agility: 0
      Spectrum management: 0
      QoS: 0
      Short slot: 0
      APSD: 0
      Radio Measurement: 0
      DSSS-OFDM: 0
      Block Ack: 0
      Immediate Block Ack: 0
   Status Code: 0x0000 (0) - Successful
   Association ID: 0x0002 (2)
> Supported rates
> HT Capabilities element
> HT Information element
> Extended Capabilities
> VHT Capabilities
> VHT Operation
> Vendor specific: MICROSOFT CORP., WPS
> Vendor specific: (221), BROADCOM CORPORATION, Tag not interpreted
> Vendor specific: MICROSOFT CORP., WME
```

Figure 4.16: Association Response frame

Reassociation Request and Response Frames

Closely related in structure to the Association frame, the Reassociation frame also carries the same information about the client, but also carries information about the current association, such as the current SSID and the current AP's address. This frame is only sent from a STA to an AP when it is already associated to the ESS, and wants to roam, or when the STA left the cell for a short time and wants to rejoin the cell. With the exception of the Roam, this can be directly compared to an Association frame.

Just as the Reassociation Request is similar to the Association Request, the Reassociation Response is similar to the Association Response. After the AP Acks the Reassociation Request, it will respond with a Reassociation Response. This can be positive or negative, and like the Association Response, will bear a status code, with either a success, or a reason code for the failure/refusal. If positive, it will also bear the AID for the new association. Also like the Association Response, it can be leveraged for measurement and even may bear a future channel guidance field.

Seeing how many Reassociation Responses verses Reassociation Requests it can be a good indicator of how often your clients are roaming and roaming successfully. You can also estimate a client's roam threshold and hysteresis with some level of accuracy. Paired in the right lab environment with careful attention and comparative analysis of when Probe Requests are sent, this can be used to roughly determine the scan threshold as well.

Data Frames and QoS Data Frames

Data frames carry data or may be used for control functions related to power management when the null data frame is used. Data frames use the general frame format discussed previously in this chapter. They include the full header for the specific MAC/PHY being used, and include an MSDU with the exception of the Null Data frame. The term null should be understood quite literally as there are 0 bytes in the Frame Body of a Null Data frame. Data frames come in two primary types:

1. Data: standard non-QoS data using standard DCF rules.
2. QoS Data: QoS data using EDCA rules.

When performing analysis, the following are important items to remember related to Data and QoS Data frames:

- The size of the data frames traversing the network tell you about network capacity and performance. If your network has larger Data or QoS Data frames passing through than you expected, you may have to add more APs or change AP configurations to handle the load.
- If you capture in the AP or very close to the AP and see a significant number of CRC error Data and QoS Data frames, STAs may not be backing off with DRS as they should be. Check for firmware updates for the STAs in question.
- If you do not see the Data or QoS Data frames in your capture but see RTS/CTS and Ack or Block Ack frames, it is not necessarily a bad sign. Your capture device may not support the number of streams used for the actual data transfer. Additionally, you may have forgotten that you filtered out data frames as many analysts frequently do. Simply stop the capture, unfilter data frames, and start the capture again.

802.11 Control Frame Formats

Control frames are used to control access to the medium for STAs that are connected to an AP or the WLAN. The following frames are defined as control frames and are used in production WLANs:

- ACK: acknowledgement frame used to signal receipt of a frame.
- RTS: request to send (RTS) frame used to request the target STA to send a CTS frame.
- CTS: clear to send (CTS) frame used to clear the medium for transmission of another frame.
- BlockAckReq: frame used to request block acknowledgement.
- BlockAck: block acknowledgement for multiple frames in a burst.
- Control Wrapper: used to carry other control frames while including an HT Control field.

Control frames have a limited 802.11 header followed by the information needed for the specific control frame. The Frame Control field is the same across control frames and is depicted in Figure 4.17.

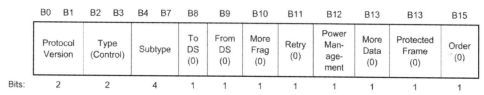

Figure 4.17: Frame Control Field of the Control Frame

RTS/CTS Frames

RTS and CTS frames are used to clear the medium for transmission of larger frames. In environments with many collisions (typically detected with high retry rates), it can improve efficiency to enable RTS/CTS for communications. The RTS frame is transmitted by the STA desiring to send a larger frame. The CTS frame is sent back as a response. Figure 4.18 shows the format of the RTS frame and Figure 4.19 shows the format of the CTS frame.

The Duration field in RTS/CTS frames is very important. In the RTS frame it is a time in microseconds represented by:

```
Data or management frame duration + CTS duration + one ACK
duration + three SIFS
```

This formula allows the medium to be cleared for the entire duration of the data frame transmission. The CTS response frame has a duration in microseconds represented by:

```
Value of the duration field from the preceding RTS frame -
CTS duration - one SIFS
```

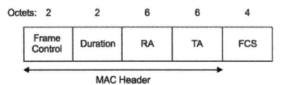

Figure 4.18: RTS Frame

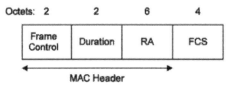

Figure 4.19: CTS Frame

What is sometimes called CTS-to-Self is a CTS frame sent without a preceding RTS frame. It is called CTS-to-Self as the RA field is set to its own address, but all STAs within range will hear the frame and set their NAV timers accordingly from the Duration field of the CTS frame. The Duration field of a CTS-to-Self frame is represented by:

```
Data or management frame duration + two SIFS + one ACK
```

This formula assumes the management frame requires an acknowledgement. If it does not, simply remove the ACK to determine the Duration field value.

Acknowledgement Frames

ACK frames are sent immediately after data and management frames to inform the transmitter that the frame was received. Without an ACK frame, the transmitter assumes the frame was lost due to corruption from interference or some other issue and retransmits the frame. At each retransmission, the random backoff timer length is increased until it reaches a maximum of 1023. This prevents a STA from consuming

206

excessive airtime without doing the right thing—lowering the data rate so that the frame can get through or roaming to another AP. It is better, by far, to send a frame at 54 Mbps and get it through than to send it five times to get it through at 150 Mbps. The inability to get a frame through without excessive retries is a factor in vendor algorithms for deciding on data rate shifting events.

The ACK frame is a simple frame with Frame Control, Duration, RA and FCS subfields. The frame format is identical to a CTS frame in size. It uses the address of the STA that sent the frame being acknowledged in the RA subfield and not the address of the STA sending the ACK frame. Unlike the CTS frame, if the immediately previous frame had the More Fragments bit set to 0, the Duration in the ACK frame is set to 0. CTS frames always have some length value in the Duration field because it is always setting up for transmission of a frame or frames. The ACK frame may be involved in a communication where more fragments are to come. In this scenario, it will set the Duration field value based on the following:

```
Duration value of previous frame + ACK time + SIFS time
```

When calculating Duration field values that include a fraction of a microsecond in the result, the value is always rounded up to the next microsecond.

Block Ack and Related Frames

Another short frame, the Block Ack Request (BAR) holds only the Frame Control, duration, Address 1, Address 2, the BAR Control and BAR Information fields, and the FCS. Figure 4.20 shows the BAR frame format.

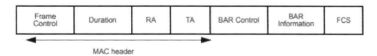

Figure 4.20: Block Ack Request (BAR) frame format

The Block Ack frame has nearly identical format to the BAR request, with the same variant fields as well. This frame is used to ack a large block of transmissions when Block Ack is in use (nearly always 802.11n or 802.11ac operations).

Validating BSS Configuration

Validating settings is one of the most valuable things you will do as a WLAN engineer, regardless of whether you are an architect, analyst, or a security engineer. If you enter the consulting side of the business, you may also be called upon to follow up on another's work, whether your own team or another third-party company. Even working for a single company, validation is essential to change management and with any sort of upgrades. This section will cover a few key sections of validation, with reasoning about the importance of each, as well as a practical portion of a frame capture for you to view. In this writer's opinion, it is vital to look through packet captures for any WLAN engineer, regardless of role. It can seem a bit dry at times, but it will undoubtedly lead you to a greater understanding of your environment and 802.11 overall. You may not need to recall exactly the placing of every bit but knowing what the bits represent and placing them in the greater context of the BSS and your operation gives you an in depth understanding no amount of other tool use or documentation can.

Country Code

The country code was added to the standard officially when 802.11 was young, with the ratification of 802.11d-2001. The purpose of country codes (also known as regulatory domains) is to inform both the engineer and the internal workings of the BSS what rules for transmission it must abide by, including, but not limited to:

- Channelization (what channels are valid, for example, UNII-2e, 2.4GHz ch 14, etc.)
- Hopping patterns (not much use today as FHSS is not used)
- A few new "MIB" values

A few specific domains that have been defined, including but not limited to: Americas/FCC, Europe/ETSI, Japan and China.

From the standard:

> "When a STA with dot11MultiDomainCapabilityActivated true enters a regulatory domain, before transmitting, it shall passively scan to learn at least one valid channel, i.e., a channel upon which it detects IEEE 802.11 frames. The Beacon frame transmitted by non-DMG STAs and the DMG Beacon or Announce frame transmitted by DMG STAs contains information on the country code, the maximum allowable transmit power, and the channels that may be used for the regulatory domain."

As seen in Figure 4.21, the country code for this transmission is "US", and it also gives a number of other informative fields, namely, starting channel, "number of channels" the highest transmit power allowed in this domain, subject to the "Environment field". You may remember from your CWNA studies that the EIRP differs for channel sets in some regulatory domains and also if the environment is interior or exterior. In this particular capture, we can see that this network is using 5 GHz and visible is only UNII-1 channels. Of note is that the "Environment" subfield is set to "ANY". This means that it will use the more restrictive interior regulatory demands in this case, as the BSS does not know that the higher EIRP for higher channels used outside is allowable.

```
⊟ ⊺ Country
      ⊛ Element ID:            7  Country [64]
      ⊛ Length:               78 [65]
      ⊛ Country Code:         US [66-67]
      ⊛ Environment:          0x20  Any [68]
      ⊛ Starting Channel:     36 [69]
      ⊛ Number of Channels:   1 [70]
      ⊛ Max Tx Power (dBm):   24 [71]
      ⊛ Starting Channel:     40 [72]
      ⊛ Number of Channels:   1 [73]
      ⊛ Max Tx Power (dBm):   24 [74]
      ⊛ Starting Channel:     44 [75]
      ⊛ Number of Channels:   1 [76]
      ⊛ Max Tx Power (dBm):   24 [77]
      ⊛ Starting Channel:     48 [78]
```

Figure 4.21: The Country Code element

If you are in the North American Regulatory domain, and see frames tagged as European or Chinese, you should be asking questions. The FCC is an expensive enemy to have and is never worth it. Due diligence pays off.

Minimum Basic Rate and Supported Rates

A Basic Rate is all or a subset of the supported rates that an AP can communicate with. The minimum then, is the lowest rate that the AP will possibly communicate on. You should recall the difference between supported (operational) and supported (basic) rates from your previous studies. If the AP and the STA do not share at least one basic rate, it can be detrimental or fatal to the association.

As seen in Figure 4.22, in the actual capture, the rates that are supported are all listed, with the basic rates being a subset of the supported. They are indicated specifically by a flag bit that says "Basic/Not Basic" (1/0). In this particular capture, the basic rates are 6Mbs, 12 Mbps, 24 Mbps. The rest (9-54) are supported, but not required – they are operational according to the standard, but we tend to call them supported rates. Therefore, the minimum basic rate would be 6 Mbs. Notably, this is the rate at which beacons are delivered, along with a handful of other frames that must be sent with surety of reception, rather than efficient use of the medium's airtime.

```
⊟  🌦  Supported Rates
    🌑  Element ID:              1  Supported Rates [44]
    🌑  Length:                  8 [45]
    🌑  Supported Rate:          6.0  Mbps  (BSS Basic Rate) [46]
    🌑  Supported Rate:          9.0  Mbps  (Not BSS Basic Rate) [47]
    🌑  Supported Rate:          12.0  Mbps  (BSS Basic Rate) [48]
    🌑  Supported Rate:          18.0  Mbps  (Not BSS Basic Rate) [49]
    🌑  Supported Rate:          24.0  Mbps  (BSS Basic Rate) [50]
    🌑  Supported Rate:          36.0  Mbps  (Not BSS Basic Rate) [51]
    🌑  Supported Rate:          48.0  Mbps  (Not BSS Basic Rate) [52]
    🌑  Supported Rate:          54.0  Mbps  (Not BSS Basic Rate) [53]
```

Figure 4.22: Supported Rates element

Supported rates are the set inclusive of all displayed rates in this set. All basic rates must be supported, but not all supported must be basic. A common tactic to deny loss of performance is to raise the minimum basic rate, to "soft screen" out less capable clients, and to virtually reduce the cell size instead of making a power change, especially in VoIP heavy networks, or networks with higher than average cell-overlap. It is essential that you understand disabling low data rates does not reduce the cell size at all, because PHY headers still transmit at the lowest rate of the band (either 1 or 2 Mbps in 2.4 GHz and 6 Mbps in 5 GHz).

Beacon Intervals

The Beacon interval is, simply put, the time interval in which the AP in question sends beacons or, rather, the AP attempts to send beacons. It is more precise that the AP enters contention operations at the expiry of the internal timer to send the beacon frame out. Just like any STA, the AP is half duplex, and therefore must contend with the medium. The beacon interval is technically set in "TUs" or Time Units, which are by definition 1024 microseconds each. Therefore, the most common timer setting, 100 TUs, is more closely represented by 102.4 ms, instead of the 100 ms. Some vendors display this as 100 ms, presumably to be more user friendly. What you are setting then, isn't technically the beacon interval time, but the Target beacon transmission time (TBTT) as noted previously in this chapter.

Notably, if the medium is busy for two full TBTT [about 204 ms, an incredibly long time for 802.11], the beacon will be granted an escalated priority. Earlier in this chapter we covered beacon frames somewhat exhaustively. Also notable is the timestamp, which along with a few other fields, keeps the BSS synchronized. If the BSS could not stay synchronized, contention for the medium would happen staggered instead of in line and would result in unacceptable amounts of collisions and a failure of the CSMA/CA process.

WMM Settings

Wi-fi Multimedia (WMM) is a pseudo-QoS setting that specifically enables probabilistic weighted contention between different classes of frames. It is separated into four ACs (Access Categories), which from "top" to "bottom" are:

- AC_VO, Access Category Voice
- AC_VI, Access Category Video
- AC_BE, Access Category Best Effort
- AC_BK, Access Category Background

WMM is a vital part of the EDCA process, allowing the applications to "weight" different types of traffic so they have priority access to the medium. The specific settings for the BSS are listed in the beacon frame, and will be are shown in Figure 4.23, along with a capture from a WMM tagged frame in Figure 4.24. As you will notice in the capture, the ECWMin and ECWMax varies between categories. The ECW is the size of the "contention window" that will be added to the frame's timer before it can be considered to have "won" the TxOP. Note that the smaller the window, the higher the priority.

If you're on the development side of the field, or work for a company with proprietary products and application, you should get familiar with these values. You may be required to set them manually; Some vendors allow you to tweak the settings for even greater priority for certain categories. Treat these settings with proper deference- in higher density environments this can change the performance of your devices substantially.

```
∨ Vendor specific: MICROSOFT CORP., WME
    ─ Tag: Vendor Specific
    ─ Length: 24
    ─ OUI: MICROSOFT CORP.
    ─ OUI Type: 2
    ─ Type: 0x02 (Unknown value)
    ─ WME Subtype: Parameter Element
    ─ WME Version: 1
  > WME QoS Info: 0x84
    ─ Reserved: Must Be Zero
  ∨ Ac Parameters: ACI 0 (Best Effort), ACM No, AIFSN 3, ECWmin 4, ECWmax 6, TXOP 0
    > ACI / AIFSN Field: 3
    > ECW: 64
    ─ TXOP Limit: 0
  ∨ Ac Parameters: ACI 1 (Background), ACM No, AIFSN 7, ECWmin 4, ECWmax 10, TXOP 0
    > ACI / AIFSN Field: 27
    > ECW: A4
    ─ TXOP Limit: 0
  ∨ Ac Parameters: ACI 2 (Video), ACM No, AIFSN 1, ECWmin 3, ECWmax 4, TXOP 94
    > ACI / AIFSN Field: 41
    > ECW: 43
    ─ TXOP Limit: 94
  ∨ Ac Parameters: ACI 3 (Voice), ACM No, AIFSN 1, ECWmin 2, ECWmax 3, TXOP 47
    > ACI / AIFSN Field: 61
    > ECW: 32
    ─ TXOP Limit: 47
```

Figure 4.23: WMM Parameters

```
⊟ ▼ QoS Control Field:      %0000000000000111 [24-25]
  ⊙                         -------- ........  AP PS Buffer State: 0
  ⊙                         ........ x.......  Reserved
  ⊙                         ........ .00.....  Ack: Normal Acknowledge
  ⊙                         ........ ...0....  EOSP: Not End of Triggered Service
  ⊙                         ........ ....0111  UP: 7 - Voice
```

Figure 4.24: A QoS Tagged 802.11 frame

RSN Settings

The RSN (Robust Security Network) Element is present in:

- Beacon frames
- Probe response frames
- Association/Reassociation Request frames

It carries a description of the security options that the client must support and should most often be carrying the indication 00-0f-ac-04, for CCMP in current networks. This aligns with the WPA2 standard. The RSN IE indicates the cipher suite, while a later part of the frame will indicate the authentication method to be used, such as 802.1X or Pre-shared Key. If auditing the capabilities of clients in your BSS, or the AP in your BSS, this is a good indicator for security compliance. If you administer an 802.1X environment, using MS-CHAPv2, you shouldn't see this element in any of your BSS's frames reading "PSK". Figure 4.25 shows an RSN element decode.

```
RSN Information
    Element ID:          48  RSN Information [206]
    Length:              24 [207]
    Version:             1 [208-209]
    Group Cipher OUI:    00-0F-AC    IEEE 802.11 [210-212]
    Group Cipher Type:   2  TKIP [213]
    Pairwise Cipher Count:2 [214-215]
    PairwiseKey Cipher List
        Pairwise Cipher OUI:  00-0F-AC-04  CCMP - default in an RSN [216-219]
        Pairwise Cipher OUI:  00-0F-AC-02  TKIP [220-223]
    AuthKey Mngmnt Count: 1 [224-225]
    AuthKey Mngmnt Suite List
        AKMP Suite OUI:      00-0F-AC-02  PSK [226-229]
    RSN Capabilities:    %0000000000000000 [230-231]
                         xx...... ........ Reserved
                         ..0..... ........ Extended Key ID for Individually Addressed Frames: PTKSA and STKSA
                         ...0.... ........ PBAC Not supported
                         ....0... ........ SPP A-MSDU Required Not Allowed
                         .....0.. ........ SPP A-MSDU Capable Not supported
                         ......0. ........ PeerKey Handshake Not supported
                         .......x ........ Reserved
                         ........ 0....... Management Frame Protection Capable (MFPC): disabled
                         ........ .0...... Management Frame Protection Required (MFPR): not mandatory
                         ........ ..00.... GTKSA Replay Ctr: 0 - 1 replay counter
                         ........ ....00.. PTKSA Replay Ctr: 0 - 1 replay counter
                         ........ ......0. Does not Support No Pairwise
                         ........ .......0 Does Not Support Pre-Authentication
```

Figure 4.25: RSN IE decoded

HT and VHT Operations

Governing the "higher" functions of the more advanced PHYs, fields detail the capabilities that the BSS offers to 802.11n and 802.11ac operations. If your network is performing in b/g as expected, but you're not getting the extra functionality and rates of higher order PHYs, this is the place to look. Due to space concerns, the full listing cannot be posted here. Figure 4.26 is a sampling of the HT and VHT operations fields from a Beacon frame. Not the individual flags for improvements in HT and VHT that would otherwise not have a place in many frames. This enables the joining STA to understand the capabilities to avoid data loss due to incompatibility. The HT and VHT fields also show the applicable modulation and coding schemes (MCSs) for each.

```
⊟ 🔱 HT Operation Information
    💾 Element ID:              61  HT Operation Information [232]
    💾 Length:                  22  [233]
    💾 Primary Channel:         52  [234]
⊟ 🔱 HT Operation Element 1:%00000000 [235]
    💾                          xxxx.... Reserved
    💾                          ....0... RIFS Mode: Use of RIFS Prohibited
    💾                          .....0.. STA Channel Width: 20 MHz Channel Width
    💾                          ......00 2nd Channel Offset: No Secondary Channel Present
⊟ 🔱 HT Operation Element 2:%0000000000010111 [236-237]
    💾                          xxxxxxxx xxx..... Reserved
    💾                          ........ ...1.... OBSS Non-HT STAs: Use of Protection for Non-HT STAs
    💾                          ........ ....0... Reserved: not set
    💾                          ........ .....1.. Non-Greenfield STAs: One or more HT STAs are Not Greenfield Capable
    💾                          ........ ......11 HT Protection: HT Mixed Mode
⊟ 🔱 HT Operation Element 3:%0000000000000000 [238-239]
    💾                          xxxx.... ........ Reserved
    💾                          ....0... ........ PCO Phase: Switch To/Continue Use 20MHz Phase
    💾                          .....0.. ........ PCO Active: Not Active in the BSS
    💾                          ......0. ........ L-SIG TXOP Protection: Not Full Support
    💾                          .......0 ........ Secondary Beacon: Primary Beacon
    💾                          ........ 0....... Dual CTS Protection: Not Required
    💾                          ........ .0...... Dual Beacon: No Secondary Beacon Transmitted
    💾                          ........ ..xxxxxx Reserved
⊟ 🔱 VHT Capabilities element
    💾 Element ID:              191  VHT Capabilities element [266]
    💾 Length:                  12  [267]
⊟ 🔱 VHT Capabilities Info:%00110011100010100111100110110010 [268-271]
    💾                          xx...... ........ ........ ........ Reserved
    💾                          ..1..... ........ ........ ........ Tx Antenna Pattern Consistency: Tx antenna pattern does not change
    💾                          ...1.... ........ ........ ........ Rx Antenna Pattern Consistency: Rx antenna pattern does not change
    💾                          ....00.. ........ ........ ........ VHT Link Adaptation Capable: No Feedback
    💾                          ......11 1....... ........ ........ Maximum AMPDU Length Exponent: 1048575
    💾                          ........ .0...... ........ ........ +HTC-VHT Capable: Not supported
    💾                          ........ ..0..... ........ ........ VHT TXOP PS: Not supported
    💾                          ........ ...0.... ........ ........ MU Beamformee Capable: Not supported
    💾                          ........ ....1... ........ ........ MU Beamformer Capable: Supported
    💾                          ........ .....010 ........ ........ Number of Sounding Dimensions: 3
    💾                          ........ ........ 011..... ........ Compressed Steering Number of Beamformer Antennas Supported: 4
    💾                          ........ ........ ...1.... ........ SU Beamformee Capable: Supported
    💾                          ........ ........ ....1... ........ SU Beam-former Capable: Supported
    💾                          ........ ........ .....001 ........ Rx STBC: support of one spatial stream
    💾                          ........ ........ ........ 1....... Tx STBC: Supported
    💾                          ........ ........ ........ .0...... Short GI for 160 and 80+80 MHz: Not supported
    💾                          ........ ........ ........ ..1..... Short GI for 80 MHz: Supported
    💾                          ........ ........ ........ ...1.... Rx LDPC: Supported
    💾                          ........ ........ ........ ....00.. Supported Channel Width Set: no support for 160 or 80+80 MHz
    💾                          ........ ........ ........ ......10 Maximum MPDU Length: 11454 octets
```

Figure 4.26: HT and VHT fields

Many of the flags and settings in these fields are difficult to access "Nerd Knobs". Be cautious when setting them manually. Some HT/VHT settings may conflict and cause poor performance. 802.11 vendors in general are very good at making sure the products are easy to use, but if you're an optimization junkie and have full client control of your environment, this may be your favorite set of controls.

Channel Width

Until the advent of 802.11n and 802.11ac, All channel widths on "regular" PHYs was set to 20 MHz or 22 MHz, and wasn't considered an issue. Now, administering aggregated or bonded channels, when validating higher order PHY networks, there must be a way to view the current channel width. This is in the information element sections that we discussed just previously. They are shown in Figure 4.27 in HT, then in VHT.

```
⊟ ⏼ HT Operation Element 1:%00000000 [235]
    🌐                         xxxx.... Reserved
    🌐                         ....0... RIFS Mode: Use of RIFS Prohibited
    🌐                         .....0.. STA Channel Width: 20 MHz Channel Width
    🌐                         ......00 2nd Channel Offset: No Secondary Channel Present
⊟ ⏼ VHT Operation element
    🌐 Element ID:              192  VHT Operation element [280]
    🌐 Length:                  5 [281]
  ⊟ ⏼ VHT Operation Information:
        🌐 Channel Width:           0  20 MHz or 40 MHz [282]
        🌐 Center Frequency Channel for 80 and 160 MHz operation: 0 [283]
        🌐 Center Frequency Channel for 80+80 MHz operation: 0 [284]
```

Figure 4.27: Channel Width in a decode

In enterprise networks, there is almost never a need for 80 MHz or 160 MHz wide channels. In smaller environments, where channel reuse is possible, 40 MHz is permissible and even in common office enterprise networks but should be carefully evaluated as to the needs of not only your organization, but those who neighbor you. Remember, 802.11 is a shared medium, and walls don't mean the end of your cells. Be considerate of your neighbors and use 20 MHz where viable and when you need the extra throughput, carefully implement the HT/VHT exclusive rates. Much like adding more APs is not always the answer, a larger channel is not always the answer.

Primary Channel

In 40Mhz and higher operations, channels are typically bonded, and usually adjacent. There is therefore, a Primary and Secondary channel. These will be listed with an information element (secondary channel offset) that dictates either code [1], which indicates the secondary channel is above the primary, [3] Which indicates the secondary channel is below the primary, or [0] which indicates the lack of a secondary channel.

If bonding channels in the UNII-2e spectrum space, be wary of DFS events. Ideally, in areas where DFS is a large concern, they should be avoided and then used only if the benefit outweighs the concern for interruption of service. Always have a non-UNII-2e channel allowed, so a DFS event does not shut down your WLAN.

Hidden or Non-Broadcast SSIDs

A hidden or non-broadcast SSID is not a security measure. Here we will examine why, though it will be covered much more in depth in the CWSP materials. Though, in the Beacon frame, the SSID will be null, or unlisted, whenever a client wants to connect, it must send a Probe Request frame with the SSID in the clear. The BSS serving the SSID will send a confirmation Probe Response that affirms the SSID and provides the needed information to connect. Some tools have been created to automate the process of gathering hidden SSIDs, though through a frame capture, it is relatively simple to detect. If you see frames that belong to a null SSID, note the BSSID, and compare this with captured Probe Requests. The Probe Request, or even better the Probe Response, will carry the SSID for the hidden network, otherwise, even STAs that knew the SSID couldn't sync appropriately with the AP.

CRC Error Frames and Retransmissions

CRC, or cyclic redundancy checks, confirm the integrity of the packet sent, as any amount of interference or reception errors can break the frame's function. As we have seen through the last section, a great deal of the specifics of the protocols are governed by a single bit, placed in a single field. Take for example, a misplaced bit in the channel field. If we are transmitting on Channel 56 instead of 64, the AP and other stations aren't going to hear our transmissions, leading to rampant retransmissions.

Speaking of retransmissions, I like to think of the retry rate as the "Dipstick" of 802.11. When you pull the oil dipstick out of your car, you assess the level and condition of the oil, but it is somewhat subjective. A modern car on the first oil change is going to look much different than a classic from 1980. So, it is with your WLAN. The amount of retires that may become concerning varies between networks. In a small network, a 20% retry rate might not be concerning to function. In a high-density network, like a sports venue, or a conference, a 20% retry rate can take up the last few percent of airtime you have remaining! It's up to you to determine the amount that is concerning for your network, and establishing a baseline pays dividends. Figure 4.28 shows CRC information that has been calculated for you. Usually, this is done by whatever packet analysis engine that you will be running, and viewable in the statistics section. The image in Figure 4.28 is from OmniPeek Wi-Fi Analyzer.

	Packets	Bytes	Value
Total Bytes		7,336,423	
Total Packets	39,853		
Total Broadcast	6,277	2,379,412	
Total Multicast	464	120,726	
Average Utilization (percent)			0.084
Average Utilization (bits/s)			375,990
Current Utilization (percent)			0.080
Current Utilization (bits/s)			360,064
Max Utilization (percent)			0.190
Max Utilization (bits/s)			852,944
∨ **Errors**	**Packets**	**Bytes**	**Value**
Total	7,008		
CRC	7,008		

Figure 4.28: CRC errors

As you can see, the amount of retries due to CRC errors is 7,008 out of 7,336,423 total captured packets. That amounts to 0.095% of all transmissions bearing CRC errors. An extraordinarily low amount of errors and nothing to be concerned about. This usually translates to a low to acceptable amount of interference on the channel that the AP/STAs are transmitting on. As the chart in Figure 4.28 shows, all retries here were generated by CRC/FCS errors. Remember that a number of things can prompt a retry: a CRC failure, an FCS mismatch, no received Ack, a near-far problem, interference, and collisions. A good guideline is that data networks should maintain <10-15% retry at the absolute most, and voice networks should be <1-2%. Higher minimum basic rates can also cause higher retry, as the MCS cannot scale low enough to allow the transmission to be decoded at the range it is sent. Also of note, is this is from a single capture point. To appropriately measure, it is suggested to aggregate multiple synced captures. And, remember, CRC errors in a laptop-based capture solution can mean nothing more than that they were not intended for you at your location but the actual receiver may have processed the transmissions just fine.

Chapter Summary

In this chapter, you went into depth with the 802.11 standard in relation to MAC frames. This information will prove invaluable as you analyze wireless networks. Again, use a protocol analyzer and spend time digging into the captured frames. There is not better way to learn!

Facts to Remember

- 802.11 frames have a type and subtype that defines what the frame is.
- The three primary types are management, control and data frames.
- The subtype defines which frame, within the type, is actually transmitted.
- The Beacon frame tells the world about the BSS provided by the AP.
- Two data frame subtypes are very commonly seen: Data frames and QoS Data frames.
- The Retry bit determines if the STA has attempted to transmit the frame before.
- The entire General Frame format is not used by every frame, in fact, some Control frames are much smaller.
- The Duration value in the RTS and CTS frames is very important to the exchange process.
- CRC errors in a laptop-based capture do not always indicate a problem; sometimes they simply indicate that the frame was not for you at your location.
- The status code in Authentication frames determines whether the AP has approved the authentication request.

Review Questions

1. What type and subtype designation is applied to a Beacon Frame?

    a) Type 00 and Subtype 0001
    b) Type 00 and Subtype 1000
    c) Type 01 and Subtype 0001
    d) Type 01 and Subtype 1000

2. Communication between two mesh STA use how many Address fields?

    a) One
    b) Two
    c) Three
    d) Four

3. The Duration field describes which of the following

    a) The Time to transmit the frame that carries it
    b) The Time that has elapsed in the current "conversation"
    c) The Time remaining for the Frames to follow this one in a given transmission
    d) The Time remaining for the Frames to follow this one in a given transmission, including spacing.

4. Beacon frames are normally transmitted in what interval?

    a) Every 100 ms
    b) Every 100 Tu
    c) When contention allows
    d) A & C
    e) B & C
    f) None of the above

5. A power management subfield value of 1 indicates which of the below?

    a) A station is asleep, and frames must be buffered until the next waking period
    b) A station is awake and ready to receive frames
    c) A station will be awake after this exchange, and able to receive more frames
    d) A station will be asleep after this exchange and frames must be buffered until the next waking period

6. An FCS has the most in common with which of the following?

    a) A Diffie-Hellmen Exchange
    b) A SHA-256 Hash of a file
    c) A functional control section
    d) A Start Frame Delimiter

7. An 802.11n system is capable of which of the following channel widths

    a) 20Mhz
    b) 40Mhz
    c) 20 and 40Mhz
    d) 20, 40 and 80Mhz

8. You are using MS-CHAPv2 to secure your enterprise network, which of the following should be present in AKMP Suite OUI, in the RSN fields of your beacon frames?

    a) CCMP
    b) RSA
    c) TKIP
    d) 802.1X

9. In an 802.11a network, which of the following should be sent from the AP immediately after your Data frame?

    a) BlockAck
    b) BlockAckRequest
    c) AckRequest
    d) QoS Null Data
    e) None of the above

10. What WMM category should a VOIP phone transmission be under, and what should the values be?

    a) AC_BE, Lowest ECW Max/Min
    b) AC_VI, Highest ECW Max/Min
    c) AC_VO, Lowest ECW Max/Min
    d) AC_VO, Highest ECW Max/Min

Review Answers

1. The correct answer is B: A Beacon frame is a management frame, type 00 and subtype 1000. It carries vital information about the BSS to prospective clients and also contains advisory fields. Type 01 is a Control frame, and subtypes 0001-0011 are reserved. Subtype 1000 is a block ack request. Management subtype 0001 is an association response.

2. The correct answer is D: Conversations between two mesh STA use all four address fields, as they must designate who is transmitting, TA, who is receiving, RA, who the source of the transmission was, SA, and the ultimate destination of the frame, DA. Some of the shortest frames, such as Acks, only use one of the address fields.

3. The correct answer is D: To keep from "stepping on" other frames and maintain the integrity of a CTS medium reservation, the duration field must calculate and display the total remaining time in the transmission, plus the interframe spaces, and the Ack(s). If it did not, the medium would not be reserved, and contention would begin, likely resulting in collisions.

4. The correct answer is B: Beacon frames must contend for use of the medium like any other frame, and are most often by default sent once every 100 TU. While this is similar to 100ms., but not exactly that, it is divergent enough that over time, the proportion of beacons would be much higher or lower than expected. If the Beacon did not contend for the medium, collisions are likely, or best case, the appropriate STAs would not hear the frame. Beacons are not retransmitted under most conditions. Each SSID also must generate its own beacon frame; This is one of the dangers of having too many SSIDs, both beacon frames and probe response frames must be generated by every SSID, adding management overhead to the contention for airtime.

5. The correct answer is D: Similar to the duration value, the power save bit indicates the future position of the radio- If the radio was asleep, it couldn't send a frame at all, nor could it hear an ack. Think of it as "power save [will be] True/False"

6. The correct answer is B: The Frame Check Sequence [FCS] is calculated against the value of all other fields, and then used for the receiving STA to compare it's own FCS/CRC to make sure that nothing has changed. If the value calculated at one end differs from the other, the frame will not be Ack'd, and a retry must occur. The Diffie-Hellman Exchange is used in cryptography. C is not a valid 802.11 Term. A Start Frame delimiter is detailed on the physical layer section of this reference and signals the beginning of transmission.

7. The correct answer is C: 802.11n provides for both 20 and 40 MHz operation in the 2.4 and 5 GHz spaces. 80 and 160 [or 80+80] MHz channel widths are only allowed currently in 802.11ac operations. Unless there is a compelling reason to not, it is suggested that 20Mhz is deployed most often, with 40Mhz used as needed only. 80Mhz and above are not recommended for Enterprise use. In 2.4Ghz operation, use of 40Mhz is strongly discouraged due to already limited channel reuse patterns and limited spectrum.

8. The correct answer is D: The AKMP suite OUI indicated what process of authentication is being used. In this case, MS-CHAPv2 is part of the 802.1X family of port-based authentication protocols. If WPA-2 Personal is being used, the field should display PSK.

9. The correct answer is E: 802.11a is not capable of BlockAcks, and as such, every packet that requires acknowledgement must be replied to with an ACK within a certain time period or is retried. BlockAcks May be present in higher order PHY.

10. The correct answer is C: AC_VO is the highest priority, and therefore the "window" that it sets for contention should also be both the most restrictive and "smallest", to make sure the relevant timer has the best chance of winning contention in the smallest amount of time. VOIP, being a voip protocol, should be tagged uner AC_VO. Video is AC_VI, most other traffic either AC_BE or AC_BK.

Chapter 5: BSS Association, Transition, and Security Exchanges

Objectives Covered:

6.1 Capture, understand, and analyze BSS discovery and joining frame exchanges

6.2 Analyze roaming behavior and resolve problems related to roaming

The fundamental basics of Wi-Fi connectivity begin with finding and associating to a basic service set (BSS). There are a series of frames involved when it comes to a successful Wi-Fi connection. APs are constantly communicating their available SSIDs out to any device that will listen. Actually, it's done so at a regular interval.

Wi-Fi devices are always listening and looking for networks to join, even if the network is not available, as you learned about with Probe Request frames in the preceding chapter. With everyone being mobile in the workplace, the Wi-Fi network infrastructure needs to be robust to handle the transitions from AP-to-AP while maintaining little downtime and latency.

In a highly insecure world, security cannot be ignored. Wi-Fi communications, transmitting in the open for anyone to hear, must be secured starting from when a station connects to an AP. User authentication must be encrypted properly and analyzing a secure frame exchange will help an engineer validate the security of their Wi-Fi network.

This chapter covers all of these exchanges as they occur in 802.11 networks. Some review information from preceding chapters will be presented, though in a different way, and much new and important information will be provided as well.

Beacon Frames and BSS Announcement

When stations (STAs) begin searching for a Wi-Fi network to join, they either do so by passively scanning for available networks or actively scanning by probing for Wi-Fi networks they know about. An access point may not be visible and hidden away in the ceiling, in the wall, under a table, on a different floor, or in another room. A STA must discover a network to join and it does it in one of two methods.

The first method is by passively scanning for a BSS to join. For the STA to become a member of a particular BSS, it must scan for a Beacon containing that BSS's SSID and return a frame matching the SSID's parameters. The second method is active scanning, probing for a specific network the STA knows about. It waits for a response from an access point that is responsible for that network.

A Beacon frame is transmitted by access points to communicate information, to passive and active scanning STAs, about the Wi-Fi networks in the access point's serviceable area.

The access point broadcasts Beacon frames periodically using a time interval called target beacon transmission time (TBTT) or Beacon Interval. This is measured using time units (TU). The IEEE 802.11 standard defines a TU as measurement of time equal to 1024 microseconds. Most vendors allow the modification of the default Beacon Interval on some access points.

As any other STA, the access point must contend for airtime to transmit a Beacon frame if the medium is busy. The access point will attempt to transmit the Beacon frame when it gains access to the shared medium. It is possible to have too many SSIDs configured on an access point. Each SSID will have a Beacon frame transmitted. Excess Beacon frame transmissions may create airtime starvation.

The way an access point transmits a Beacon frame for each SSID is by assigning a unique address to each using a BSSID. The BSSID is how a station knows which basic service set and AP combination it is associating to as opposed to others it may see in the area with the same SSID.

To capture a Beacon frame, use an appropriate capture tool to place the adapter in monitor mode. Capture near the access point which is the source of Beacon frames. Start capturing frames on a specific channel and channel width, then analyze in a protocol analyzer such as Wireshark.

Hidden SSIDs, although sometimes errantly used as a security measure, broadcast their own Beacon frames. In a frame capture, the Beacon will list the SSID field as blank or as a Wildcard SSID. The SSID name can be found in an active Probe Request frame by a preconfigured station set to use the hidden SSID.

Figure 5.1 shows a Beacon frame capture example. As discussed, the Beacon Interval is identified within the frame along with many other fields containing mandatory and optional elements. These elements list the compatibility requirements for STAs joining a BSS.

Upon successfully joining a BSS, the STA will assume the timing synchronization function (TSF) timer value from the Beacon frame's parameters. The purpose of the TSF timer is to keep the timers of all STAs in the same BSS synchronized.

```
▶ Radiotap Header v0, Length 25
▶ 802.11 radio information
▶ IEEE 802.11 Beacon frame, Flags: ........C
▼ IEEE 802.11 wireless LAN
   ▼ Fixed parameters (12 bytes)
        Timestamp: 0x000003ff77850039
        Beacon Interval: 0.102400 [Seconds]
      ▶ Capabilities Information: 0x1511
   ▼ Tagged parameters (351 bytes)
      ▶ Tag: SSID parameter set: CWAP
      ▶ Tag: Supported Rates 24(B), 36, 48, 54, [Mbit/sec]
      ▶ Tag: DS Parameter set: Current Channel: 60
      ▶ Tag: Traffic Indication Map (TIM): DTIM 0 of 0 bitmap
      ▶ Tag: Country Information: Country Code US, Environment Any
      ▶ Tag: Power Constraint: 3
      ▶ Tag: QBSS Load Element 802.11e CCA Version
      ▶ Tag: AP Channel Report: Operating Class 5, Channel List : 36, 44, 48, 132, 153, 157, 161, 165,
      ▶ Tag: RM Enabled Capabilities (5 octets)
      ▶ Tag: Mobility Domain
      ▶ Tag: HT Capabilities (802.11n D1.10)
      ▶ Tag: RSN Information
      ▶ Tag: HT Information (802.11n D1.10)
      ▶ Tag: Extended Capabilities (8 octets)
      ▶ Tag: VHT Capabilities
      ▶ Tag: VHT Operation
      ▶ Tag: VHT Tx Power Envelope
      ▶ Tag: Vendor Specific: Microsoft Corp.: WMM/WME: Parameter Element
      ▶ Tag: Vendor Specific: Atheros Communications, Inc.: Advanced Capability
      ▶ Tag: Vendor Specific: Cisco Meraki
      ▶ Tag: Vendor Specific:        Cisco Systems, Inc.: Aironet CCX version = 5
      ▶ Tag: Vendor Specific:        Cisco Systems, Inc.: Aironet Client MFP Disabled
```

Figure 5.1: Beacon frame capture

802.11 State Machine

Beacons are transmitted at an interval to allow STAs to join a particular BSS. Once a BSS has been selected, a series of frames are exchanged between the STA and AP. The process of joining a BSS is called the 802.11 State Machine.

The sequence of frames is:

1. Probe Request
2. Probe Response
3. 802.11 Authentication from station
4. 802.11 Authentication from access point
5. Association Request
6. Association Response

The STA transmits a Probe Request to the BSSID listed in a Beacon frame the STA received. The AP responds with a Probe Response frame. Next, the STA transmits an open system Authentication frame to the AP. The AP responds with an open system Authentication frame, indicating a successful transaction. Moving forward, the STA sends an Association Request frame and the AP responds with an Association Response frame. Any further security such as 802.1X or PSK is performed after the 802.11 State Machine. Figure 5.2 visualizes the exchange of frames.

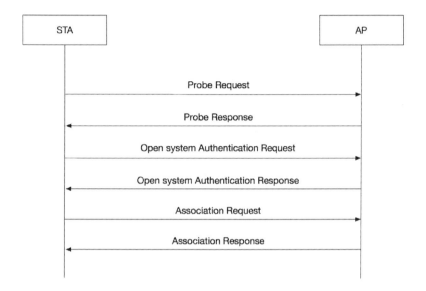

Figure 5.2: 802.11 State Machine

802.11 Authentication is not a security method of authenticating to the AP. Open System authentication simply allows any STA to join the distributed system.

Probe Request Frame

The Probe Request frame originates from a station wanting to join a particular BSS. It is done in one of two methods. First, a station preconfigured with previously connected SSIDs will actively probe for those networks it remembers. In the second method, a station receives a Beacon frame from an access point and requests to join the BSS by sending a Probe Request with the indicated SSID listed in the frame.

A Probe Request frame is a subtype of a Management frame, as indicated in the Frame Control field. It is a broadcast frame originating from a station. The source address (SA) and transmitter address (TA) is set to the station transmitting the Probe Request. The destination address (DA) and receiver address (RA) are set to the broadcast address.

The elements within the Probe Request frame help to identify the type of station attempting to join a particular SSID. If the HT Capabilities element is present, a station is advertising 802.11n capabilities. Similarly, if a VHT Capabilities element is advertised, then the station is 802.11ac capable.

By analyzing a Probe Request frame, the capabilities of a station can be revealed. This can be incredibly useful during troubleshooting. For example, the VHT Information field, within the VHT Capabilities element, can indicate potential compatibility issues with the BSS.

Figure 5.3 shows the VHT Capabilities Info field of an iPhone 7 Plus. The advertisement of a VHT element shows it supports 802.11ac. Beneath the VHT Capabilities field are subfields indicating the supported channel widths, such as up to 80 MHz channel widths but not 160 MHz or 80+80 MHz.

```
▽ Tag: VHT Capabilities
    Tag Number: VHT Capabilities (191)
    Tag length: 12
  ▽ VHT Capabilities Info: 0x0f805032
      .... .... .... .... .... .... ..10 = Maximum MPDU Length: 11 454 (0x2)
      .... .... .... .... .... .... 00.. = Supported Channel Width Set: Neither 160MHz nor 80+80 supported (0x0)
      .... .... .... .... .... ...1 .... = Rx LDPC: Supported
      .... .... .... .... .... ..1. .... = Short GI for 80MHz/TVHT_MODE_4C: Supported
      .... .... .... .... .... .0.. .... = Short GI for 160MHz and 80+80MHz: Not supported
      .... .... .... .... .... 0... .... = Tx STBC: Not supported
      .... .... .... .... .000 .... .... = Rx STBC: None (0x0)
      .... .... .... .... 0... .... .... = SU Beamformer Capable: Not supported
      .... .... .... ...1 .... .... .... = SU Beamformee Capable: Supported
      .... .... .... 010. .... .... .... = Beamformee STS Capability: 3 (0x2)
      .... .... .000 .... .... .... .... = Number of Sounding Dimensions: 1 (0x0)
      .... .... 0... .... .... .... .... = MU Beamformer Capable: Not supported
      .... ...0 .... .... .... .... .... = MU Beamformee Capable: Not supported
      .... ..0. .... .... .... .... .... = TXOP PS: Not supported
      .... .0.. .... .... .... .... .... = +HTC-VHT Capable: Not supported
      ..11 1... .... .... .... .... .... = Max A-MPDU Length Exponent: 1 048 575 (0x7)
      11.. .... .... .... .... .... .... = VHT Link Adaptation: Both (can provide unsolicited feedback and respond to VHT MRQ) (0x3)
    ..0 .... .... .... .... .... .... .... = Rx Antenna Pattern Consistency: Not supported
    ..0. .... .... .... .... .... .... .... = Tx Antenna Pattern Consistency: Not supported
    00.. .... .... .... .... .... .... .... = Extended NSS BW Support: 0x0
```

Figure 5.3: VHT Capabilities Information Field

Other capabilities such as the number of spatial streams and MCS rates supported by a station can be found under the Rx and Tx VHT-MCS map subfield. The purpose for these fields is to determine the rates a station can achieve.

In Figure 5.4, a single VHT spatial stream is supported with MCS rates of 0–9. When referenced at http://mcsindex.com, the max data rate that can be achieved at MCS 9 with an 80 MHz channel width using short guard interval is 433.3 Mbps.

```
▼ Tag: VHT Capabilities
    Tag Number: VHT Capabilities (191)
    Tag length: 12
  ▶ VHT Capabilities Info: 0x0f805032
  ▶ VHT Supported MCS Set
  ▼ Rx MCS Map: 0xfffe
        .... .... .... ..10 = Rx 1 SS: MCS 0-9 (0x2)
        .... .... .... 11.. = Rx 2 SS: Not Supported (0x3)
        .... .... ..11 .... = Rx 3 SS: Not Supported (0x3)
        .... .... 11.. .... = Rx 4 SS: Not Supported (0x3)
        .... ..11 .... .... = Rx 5 SS: Not Supported (0x3)
        .... 11.. .... .... = Rx 6 SS: Not Supported (0x3)
        ..11 .... .... .... = Rx 7 SS: Not Supported (0x3)
        11.. .... .... .... = Rx 8 SS: Not Supported (0x3)
  ▼ Tx MCS Map: 0xfffe
        .... .... .... ..10 = Tx 1 SS: MCS 0-9 (0x2)
        .... .... .... 11.. = Tx 2 SS: Not Supported (0x3)
        .... .... ..11 .... = Tx 3 SS: Not Supported (0x3)
        .... .... 11.. .... = Tx 4 SS: Not Supported (0x3)
        .... ..11 .... .... = Tx 5 SS: Not Supported (0x3)
        .... 11.. .... .... = Tx 6 SS: Not Supported (0x3)
        ..11 .... .... .... = Tx 7 SS: Not Supported (0x3)
        11.. .... .... .... = Tx 8 SS: Not Supported (0x3)
```

Figure 5.4: Rx and Tx VHT-MCS Map subfield

Probe Response

Upon receiving a Probe Request initiated by a station, an access point will contend for the medium and send a Probe Response frame containing information about the BSS a station must be able to support. A Probe Response is a unicast frame sent to the destination address (DA) of the station which the Probe Request originated from.

Looking at the contents of the Probe Response frame in Figure 5.5, you'll notice it contains many of the same fields and information elements as a Beacon frame. It may be hard to point out because of the number of fields present but there are differences.

The Probe Response frame doesn't contain the Traffic indication map (TIM) field, QoS Capability element, AP Channel Report element, FMS Descriptor element, and the HCCA TXOP Update Count element.

The Probe Response frame will contain a Requested element if it has been requested by the probing station.

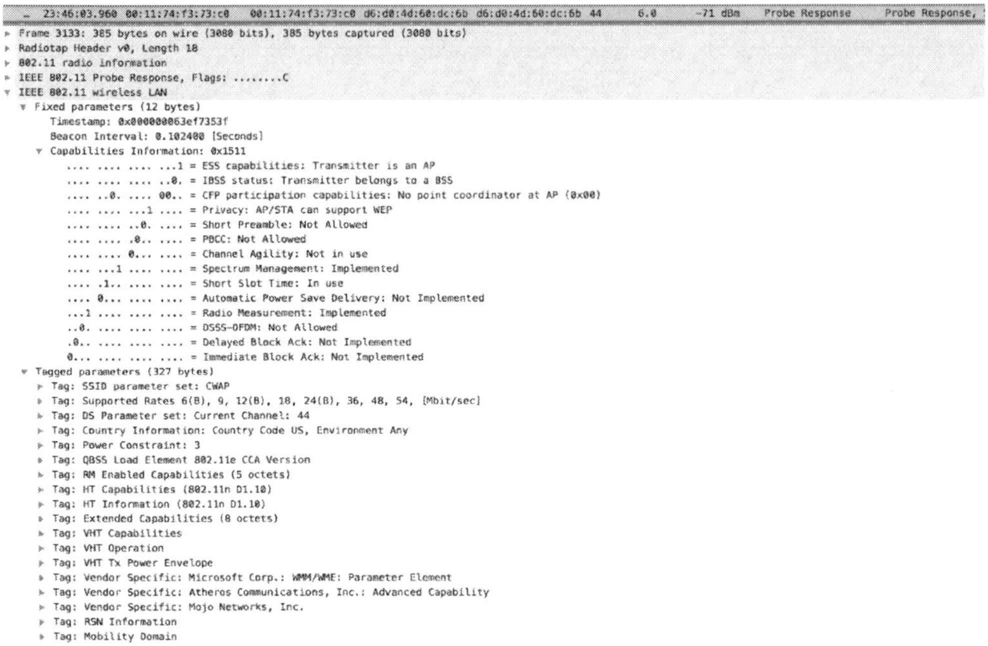

Figure 5.5: Probe Response frame capture

Authentication Frame

The Authentication frame can get confused with a type of user authentication. The Authentication frame is part of the Open System authentication method which operates at the link level between stations. There are two authentication messages exchanged in this transaction as you learned in the preceding chapter.

In the initial state, the station is neither authenticated or associated yet to the BSS.

The station generates the first of two authentication frames. A station will have its MAC address as the SA and TA fields. The DA and RA will be the target BSSID. This first message requests authentication to the access point.

The receiving access point will respond with its own unicast authentication frame setting the originating station's MAC address in the DA and RA field. The TA and SA field is the

MAC address of the BSSID. This second message contains the authentication result. If the result is "successful," then the station is authenticated with the access point. If the result is not "successful," then the station must reattempt authentication or attempt with another AP.

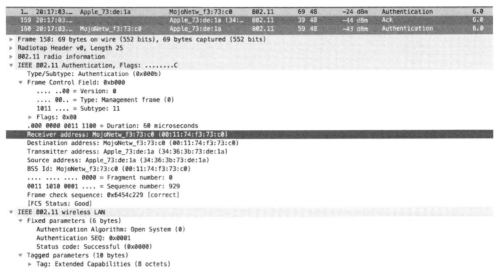

Figure 5.6: Authentication Request Frame

Figure 5.7: Authentication Response frame

Order	Information	Notes
1	Authentication algorithm number	
2	Authentication transaction sequence number	
3	Status code	
4	Challenge text	Present only in certain Authentication frames.
5	RSN	RSNE present in certain Authentication frames.
6	Mobility domain	Present in certain Authentication frames.
7	Fast BSS Transition	Present only in certain Authentication frames.
8	Timeout interval	
9	RIC	Resource information container.
10	Finite Cyclic Group	Present in certain Authentication frames. Used with SAE.
11	Anti-Clogging Token	Present in certain Authentication frames. Used with SAE.
12	Send-Confirm	Used for anti-replay purposes. Present in certain Authentication frames. Used with SAE.
13	Scalar	Present in certain Authentication frames. Used with SAE.
14	Finite field element	Used with SAE.
15	Confirm	Used with SAE.
16	Multi-band	Optionally present.
17	Neighbor Report	Used with 802.11k.
Last	Vendor Specific	Optionally present.

Table 5.1 Authentication Frame body

Association Frame

After the station successfully passes authentication to the access point, it moves on by sending a unicast Association Request frame destined to the access point. This management frame is transmitted at the highest minimum data rate supported. The DA and RA is set to the BSSID. The SA and TA are set to the station's MAC address.

Capture location is important when troubleshooting. If an access point does not receive an Association Request frame, move the capture location to the transmitting station to verify the Association Request is being sent out.

The receiving access point responds to an Association Request frame with an Acknowledgement frame. Then it transmits an Association Response frame with a status code for the station. If successful, the station receives an Association ID for the BSS.

An HT or VHT station declares it is an HT or VHT station by transmitting the respective HT/VHT Capabilities element within the Association Request/Response frame. This is also present in the Beacon and Reassociation frames.

Table 5.5 Association Request frame body

Order	Information	Notes
1	Capability information	
2	Listen interval	
3	SSID	
4	Supported Rates and BSS Membership Selectors	
5	Extended Supported Rates and BSS Membership Selectors	Used when there are more than eight supported rates, otherwise optional.
6	Power Capability	Present when Radio Management is true.
7	Supported Channels	Present when Spectrum Management Required is true.
8	RSN	Used with 802.11i.
9	QoS Capability	Used with 802.11e.
10	RM Enabled Capabilities	Used with 802.11k.
11	Mobility Domain	Used with 802.11r.
12	Supported Operating Classes	Used with 802.11k.
13	HT Capabilities	Advertises capabilities of a HT STA.
14	20/40 BSS Coexistence	Indicates support for the 20/40 BSS Coexistence Management frame and its use.

15	Extended capabilities	Carries information about the capabilities of an 802.11 STA.
16	QoS Traffic Capability	Provides information about types of traffic generated by a non-AP QoS STA and is used by a QoS AP.
17	TIM Broadcast Request	STA requesting information about periodic TIM broadcast.
18	Interworking	Contains information about the interworking service capabilities of a STA.
19	Multi-band	
20	DMG Capabilities	Used with 802.11ad.
21	Multiple MAC sublayers	
22	VHT Capabilities	Used with 802.11ac.
23	Operating Mode Notification	
Last	Vendor Specific	Optionally present.

Table 5.6 Association Response frame body

Order	Information	Notes
1	Capability Information	
2	Status code	
3	AID	
4	Supported Rates and BSS Membership Selectors	
5	Extended Supported Rates and BSS Membership Selectors	Used when there are more than eight supported rates, otherwise optional.
6	EDCA Parameter Set	Used with 802.11e.
7	RCPI	Used with 802.11k.
8	RSNI	Used with 802.11k.
9	RM Enabled Capabilities	Used with 802.11k.
10	Mobility Domain	Used with 802.11r.
11	Fast BSS Transition	Used with 802.11r.
12	DSE registered location	Used with 802.11y.

13	Timeout Interval (Association Comeback time)	
14	HT Capabilities	Advertises capabilities of an HT.
15	HT Operation	Used with 802.11n.
16	20/40 BSS Coexistence	Indicates support for the 20/40 BSS Coexistence Management frame and its use.
17	Overlapping BSS Scan Parameters	Used by an AP to indicate values used by BSS members when performing OBSS scan operations.
18	Extended Capabilities	Carries information about the capabilities of an 802.11 STA.
19	BSS Max Idle Period	Used with 802.11v.
20	TIM Broadcast Response	STA requesting information about periodic TIM broadcast.
21	QoS Map	Used with 802.11e.
22	QMF Policy	Used with 802.11ae.
23	Multi-band	
24	DMG Capabilities	Used with 802.11ad.
25	DMG Operation	Used with 802.11ad.
26	Multiple MAC Sublayers	
27	Neighbor Report	Used with 802.11k.
27	VHT Capabilities	Used with 802.11ac.
28	VHT Capabilities	Used with 802.11ac.
29	Operating Mode Notification	
30	Future Channel Guidance	
Last	Vendor Specific	Optionally present.

The Association Response frame is very similar to the Association Request frame. The main difference is the Association Response frame will contain a Status Code field and Association ID (AID) element. The AID is assigned by an AP to a station.

The Status Code field is used in the Association Response frame to indicate whether the association was successful or not. If the status was a failure, the field would include a failure cause code which can be due to an incompatibility.

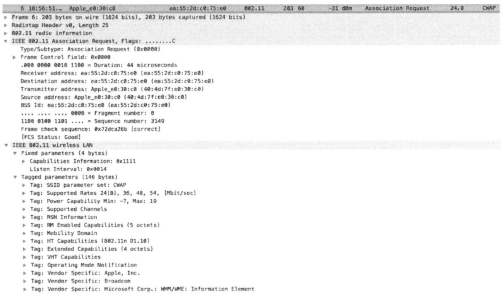

Figure 5.8: Association Request Frame

802.11 Security

We've discussed a station joining a BSS with an unsecured connection. The authentication and association frame exchanges all occur before any security frames are exchanged between AP and station.

The 802.11 standard defines security under a robust security network (RSN). Within an RSN are many other components bringing together a robust security network association (RSNA).

In the next few sections, we'll go through pre-shared key (PSK) authentication, the 4-way handshake, and 802.1X/EAP frame exchanges.

236

```
    8 10:56:51...   ea:55:2d:c0:75:e0         Apple_e0:30:c0      802.11    333 60    -34 dBm   Other Management Frame   24.0
▶ Frame 8: 333 bytes on wire (2664 bits), 333 bytes captured (2664 bits)
▶ Radiotap Header v0, Length 25
▶ 802.11 radio information
▼ IEEE 802.11 Association Response, Flags: ........C
    Type/Subtype: Association Response (0x0001)
  ▶ Frame Control Field: 0x1000
    .000 0000 0010 1100 = Duration: 44 microseconds
    Receiver address: Apple_e0:30:c0 (40:4d:7f:e0:30:c0)
    Destination address: Apple_e0:30:c0 (40:4d:7f:e0:30:c0)
    Transmitter address: ea:55:2d:c0:75:e0 (ea:55:2d:c0:75:e0)
    Source address: ea:55:2d:c0:75:e0 (ea:55:2d:c0:75:e0)
    BSS Id: ea:55:2d:c0:75:e0 (ea:55:2d:c0:75:e0)
    .... .... .... 0000 = Fragment number: 0
    0010 0100 1010 .... = Sequence number: 586
    Frame check sequence: 0x4f0cd160 [correct]
    [FCS Status: Good]
▼ IEEE 802.11 wireless LAN
  ▼ Fixed parameters (6 bytes)
    ▶ Capabilities Information: 0x1411
      Status code: Successful (0x0000)
      ..00 0000 0000 0001 = Association ID: 0x0001
  ▼ Tagged parameters (274 bytes)
    ▶ Tag: Supported Rates 24(B), 36, 48, 54, [Mbit/sec]
    ▶ Tag: RM Enabled Capabilities (5 octets)
    ▶ Tag: Mobility Domain
    ▶ Tag: Fast BSS Transition
    ▶ Tag: HT Capabilities (802.11n D1.10)
    ▶ Tag: HT Information (802.11n D1.10)
    ▶ Tag: Extended Capabilities (8 octets)
    ▶ Tag: BSS Max Idle Period
    ▶ Tag: VHT Capabilities
    ▶ Tag: VHT Operation
    ▶ Tag: Vendor Specific: Microsoft Corp.: WMM/WME: Parameter Element
```

Figure 5.9: Association Response Frame

Pre-shared Key Authentication (PSK)

A station attempting to set up a security association with an access point may not know the security policy required. The station sends a Probe Request frame to the AP to find out what its security policy is before setting up a security association. The most common 802.11 security method used, because of home networks, is with a password: pre-shared key (PSK). But it is more common in enterprise deployments to use 802.1X/EAP authentication

An access point advertises its security capabilities in the following frame types:

- Beacon
- Announce
- Information Response
- Probe Response

Included, will be the authentication and cipher suites enabled. A station may not be able to associate to the AP if it does not support the authorized authentication and cipher suites. This process occurs after the station performs 802.11 authentication and association to those chosen AP.

Once the station discovers the AP's security policy, through the Beacon frame, and completes authentication and association, the station and AP will negotiate a security policy. In Pre-Shared Key (PSK), the Pairwise Master Key (PMK) is the PSK. From the PMK a Pairwise Transient Key (PTK) is derived. In this scenario, the AP will hold an Authenticator role and the station will be the Supplicant.

Next, a 4-way handshake is initiated with EAPOL-Key frames being used. Upon successfully completing the 4-way handshake, which is described in a later section, the station is now joined to the BSS using a PSK.

4-Way Handshake

The RSNA process uses EAPOL-Key frames to form the 4-Way Handshake. It is used with PSK and 802.1X authentication. The frames are exchanged between the station and AP; used to secure communications between the Supplicant and Authenticator. For 802.1X authentication, the 4-way handshake occurs after EAP authentication.

During the 4-way handshake frame exchange, the Supplicant and Authenticator derive a PTK from their own PMK. From the PTK is derived the SNonce for the Supplicant and the ANonce for the Authenticator.

The Authenticator holds the GMK which is used to derive the GTK. The GTK, used to encrypt broadcast and multicast messages for stations joined to a BSS, is delivered to a station in message 3 of the 4-way handshake. Transfer of the GTK is called the Group Key handshake. Figure 5.10 shows the 4-Way Handshake sequence between a Supplicant and Authenticator.

It is called the 4-way handshake because of four messages which are exchanged between the Supplicant and the Authenticator. The flow of the 4-way handshake is as follows:

Message 1: The Authenticator sends an EAPOL-Key frame to the Supplicant containing an ANonce for PTK generation. Within the frame contains fields describing what type of encryption is being used, for example, AES Cipher or AES-128-CMAC. The Supplicant will use the message to generate an SNonce and derive a PTK.

Message 2: The Supplicant sends an EAPOL-Key frame to the Authenticator containing an SNonce, RSNE, and MIC. A PTK is derived from the SNonce and ANonce. The

Authenticator will confirm the key replay counter corresponds to Message 1 and will then verify the MIC for message 2.

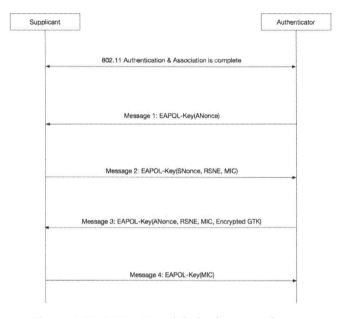

Figure 5.10: 4-Way Handshake frame exchange

```
  5 22:24:49._  Mist_01:e6:d3              Apple_e0:30:c0      EAPOL      162 48    -56 dBm  EAPOL                    6.0
▶ Frame 5: 162 bytes on wire (1296 bits), 162 bytes captured (1296 bits)
▶ Radiotap Header v0, Length 25
▶ 802.11 radio information
▶ IEEE 802.11 QoS Data, Flags: ......F.C
▶ Logical-Link Control
▼ 802.1X Authentication
    Version: 802.1X-2004 (2)
    Type: Key (3)
    Length: 95
    Key Descriptor Type: EAPOL RSN Key (2)
    [Message number: 1]
  ▼ Key Information: 0x008a
        .... .... .... .010 = Key Descriptor Version: AES Cipher, HMAC-SHA1 MIC (2)
        .... .... .... 1... = Key Type: Pairwise Key
        .... .... ..00 .... = Key Index: 0
        .... .... .0.. .... = Install: Not set
        .... .... 1... .... = Key ACK: Set
        .... ...0 .... .... = Key MIC: Not set
        .... ..0. .... .... = Secure: Not set
        .... .0.. .... .... = Error: Not set
        .... 0... .... .... = Request: Not set
        ...0 .... .... .... = Encrypted Key Data: Not set
        ..0. .... .... .... = SMK Message: Not set
    Key Length: 16
    Replay Counter: 1
    WPA Key Nonce: 17f723a6956dc292bb19807e65530d958466f0c4ee8a4275...
    Key IV: 00000000000000000000000000000000
    WPA Key RSC: 0000000000000000
    WPA Key ID: 0000000000000000
    WPA Key MIC: 00000000000000000000000000000000
    WPA Key Data Length: 0
```

Figure 5.11: Message 1 of 4-way handshake

```
7  22:24:49..  Apple_e0:30:c0              Mist_01:e6:d3        EAPOL      184 48      -37 dBm  EAPOL                    6.0
    Version: 802.1X-2004 (2)
    Type: Key (3)
    Length: 117
    Key Descriptor Type: EAPOL RSN Key (2)
    [Message number: 2]
  ▼ Key Information: 0x010a
        .... .... .... .010 = Key Descriptor Version: AES Cipher, HMAC-SHA1 MIC (2)
        .... .... .... 1... = Key Type: Pairwise Key
        .... .... ..00 .... = Key Index: 0
        .... .... .0.. .... = Install: Not set
        .... .... 0... .... = Key ACK: Not set
        .... ...1 .... .... = Key MIC: Set
        .... ..0. .... .... = Secure: Not set
        .... .0.. .... .... = Error: Not set
        .... 0... .... .... = Request: Not set
        ...0 .... .... .... = Encrypted Key Data: Not set
        ..0. .... .... .... = SMK Message: Not set
    Key Length: 16
    Replay Counter: 1
    WPA Key Nonce: 3cd8193a64e893a04e818bf62fd9409804c3ecf1b3c661cf...
    Key IV: 00000000000000000000000000000000
    WPA Key RSC: 0000000000000000
    WPA Key ID: 0000000000000000
    WPA Key MIC: b9b69086f00bfeb945c2cbea4d24df83
    WPA Key Data Length: 22
  ▼ WPA Key Data: 30140100000fac040100000fac040100000fac020c00
    ▼ Tag: RSN Information
        Tag Number: RSN Information (48)
        Tag length: 20
        RSN Version: 1
      ▶ Group Cipher Suite: 00:0f:ac (IEEE 802.11) AES (CCM)
        Pairwise Cipher Suite Count: 1
      ▶ Pairwise Cipher Suite List 00:0f:ac (IEEE 802.11) AES (CCM)
        Auth Key Management (AKM) Suite Count: 1
      ▶ Auth Key Management (AKM) List 00:0f:ac (IEEE 802.11) PSK
      ▶ RSN Capabilities: 0x000c
```

Figure 5.12: Message 2 of the 4-way handshake

Message 3: Authenticator derives a PTK from the ANonce and SNonce. The MIC is also verified from the supplicant. The authenticator will send message 3 with an ANonce, RSNE from the Beacon or Probe Response frames, MIC, and GTK.

Message 4: Supplicant sends the fourth EAPOL-Key frame to the authenticator. This last message notifies the authenticator whether the temporal keys were installed.

In a PSK installation, communications between station and access point are protected following message 4 of the 4-way handshake. In an 802.1X deployment, the 4-way handshake follows the EAP authentication frames.

```
   8  22:24:49._  Mist_01:e6:d3              Apple_e0:30:c0      EAPOL      218 48      -57 dBm    EAPOL                                6.0
```
▸ Frame 8: 218 bytes on wire (1744 bits), 218 bytes captured (1744 bits)
▸ Radiotap Header v0, Length 25
▸ 802.11 radio information
▸ IEEE 802.11 QoS Data, Flags: ......F.C
▸ Logical-Link Control
▾ 802.1X Authentication
    Version: 802.1X-2004 (2)
    Type: Key (3)
    Length: 151
    Key Descriptor Type: EAPOL RSN Key (2)
    [Message number: 3]
  ▾ Key Information: 0x13ca
      .... .010 = Key Descriptor Version: AES Cipher, HMAC-SHA1 MIC (2)
      .... 1... = Key Type: Pairwise Key
      ....00 .... = Key Index: 0
      .... .1.. .... = Install: Set
      .... 1... .... = Key ACK: Set
      ....1 .... = Key MIC: Set
      .... ..1. .... = Secure: Set
      .... .0.. .... = Error: Not set
      .... 0... .... = Request: Not set
      ...1 .... = Encrypted Key Data: Set
      ..0. .... = SMK Message: Not set
    Key Length: 16
    Replay Counter: 2
    WPA Key Nonce: 17f723a6956dc292bb19807e65530d958466f0c4ee8a4275...
    Key IV: 00000000000000000000000000000000
    WPA Key RSC: 0000000000000000
    WPA Key ID: 0000000000000000
    WPA Key MIC: 4a5d296efee1ebbaeec5f166c747438f
    WPA Key Data Length: 56
    WPA Key Data: 9ab8b6d0271b6dfa5a3aa11a12420f1c2dac2b138efdd297...

Figure 5.13: Message 3 of the 4-way handshake

```
  10  22:24:49._  Apple_e0:30:c0              Mist_01:e6:d3      EAPOL      162 48      -37 dBm    EAPOL
```
▸ Frame 10: 162 bytes on wire (1296 bits), 162 bytes captured (1296 bits)
▸ Radiotap Header v0, Length 25
▸ 802.11 radio information
▸ IEEE 802.11 QoS Data, Flags: ....TC
▸ Logical-Link Control
▾ 802.1X Authentication
    Version: 802.1X-2004 (2)
    Type: Key (3)
    Length: 95
    Key Descriptor Type: EAPOL RSN Key (2)
    [Message number: 4]
  ▾ Key Information: 0x030a
      .... .010 = Key Descriptor Version: AES Cipher, HMAC-SHA1 MIC (2)
      .... 1... = Key Type: Pairwise Key
      ....00 .... = Key Index: 0
      .... .0.. .... = Install: Not set
      .... 0... .... = Key ACK: Not set
      ....1 .... = Key MIC: Set
      .... ..1. .... = Secure: Set
      .... .0.. .... = Error: Not set
      .... 0... .... = Request: Not set
      ...0 .... = Encrypted Key Data: Not set
      ..0. .... = SMK Message: Not set
    Key Length: 16
    Replay Counter: 2
    WPA Key Nonce: 0000000000000000000000000000000000000000000000000000000000000000...
    Key IV: 00000000000000000000000000000000
    WPA Key RSC: 0000000000000000
    WPA Key ID: 0000000000000000
    WPA Key MIC: ccebb2422263063a4b30616a1dd57d67
    WPA Key Data Length: 0

Figure 5.14: Message 4 of the 4-way handshake

802.1X EAP Exchanges

In an 802.1X RSNA, there are three roles involved:

- Supplicant
- Authenticator
- Authentication Server

The Supplicant needs access to the Wi-Fi network. It requests access through the Authenticator, or access point, which carries a port access entity component. And then there's the Authentication Server which authenticates elements of the RSNA provided by the Supplicant.

Capture location of 802.1X EAP frames is important. With three different roles involved, there are two capture points. The first is between the Supplicant and the Authenticator. The second is between the Authenticator and the Authentication Server, which, instead of 802.11 frames, are RADIUS frames. The first location is captured using a wireless protocol analyzer and the second is captured using a wired protocol analyzer.

In a BSS, a station associates to an AP but has all non-802.1X MSDUs blocked from being sent or received through the controlled port. The controlled port remains blocked until the 802.1X state returns true for the station.

The frame exchange with 802.1X authentication begins after the 802.11 State Machine. Following the successful Association Response frame from the AP, the 802.1X process begins with a blocked controlled port.

The EAP authentication process begins with the Authenticator (access point) sending an EAP-Request or the Supplicant sends an EAPOL-Start frame. View Figure 5.15 for the EAP frame exchange sequence.

The Supplicant receives the EAP-Request frame requesting an identity. In response, an identity is provided by the Supplicant within an EAP-Response frame. The Authenticator forwards the EAP-Response frame to the Authentication server as a RADIUS Access Request.

EAP messages will be exchanged between the Supplicant and Authentication Server through the Authenticators Uncontrolled Ports, allowing only EAP messages to pass through. At this point, to see the full conversation, a capture needs to occur in two locations. One between the Supplicant and the Authenticator and another between the

Authenticator and the Authentication Server.

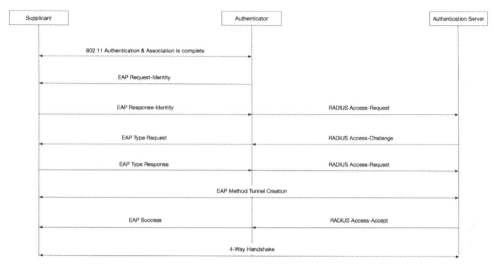

Figure 5.15: 802.1X EAP frame exchange

802.1X EAP messages are sent as Data frames over the 802.11 medium. The Supplicant and Authentication Server must be configured to use the same EAP type. There are various EAP types available to use, below are just a few:

- EAP-MD5
- EAP-TLS
- EAP-TTLS
- EAP-PEAP
- EAP-GTC
- EAP-SIM
- PEAP

A series of EAP messages are exchanged between the Supplicant and Authentication Server, through the Authenticator, to authenticate each other and generate a PMK.

This outer authentication EAP method is either proposed by the authentication server or the station will propose a method. After an EAP method is selected, the authentication server presents a certificate to the station.

The server certificate is used to build a secure TLS tunnel. The traffic will be encrypted. The station and authentication server use an inner authentication method to encrypt exchanged data.

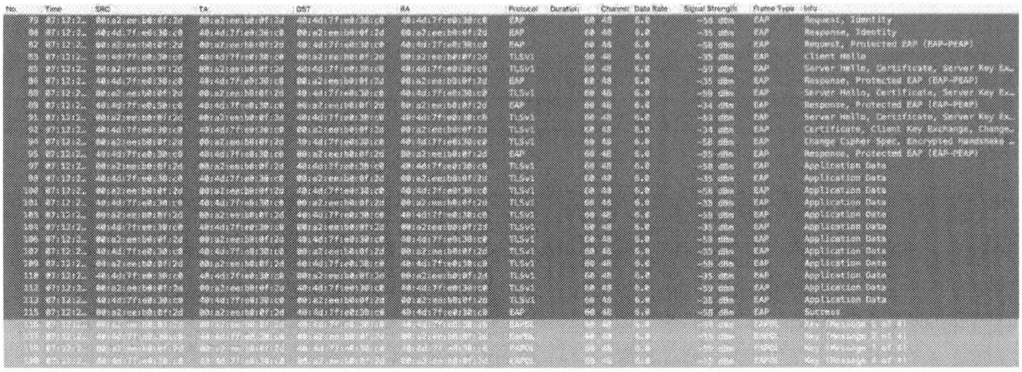

Figure 5.16: 802.1X EAP exchanges and 4-way handshake

The type of method used can be EAP-PEAP, for example. Another, more secure method can be EAP-TLS.

After providing identities, sending certificates, selecting an outer and inner authentication EAP method, and authenticating the user, the last EAP frame will either be a Success or Failure.

If the Authentication Server sends an EAP frame with the Success code, the station and Authenticator move onto the 4-way handshake.

Identifying the type of EAP methods used within 802.1X frame exchanges will be shown in the third EAP frame exchange (Figure 5.17). This EAP frame is transmitted by the Authenticator and destined to the station. The type of frame is an 802.1X EAP request. The Authentication Server will request the type of EAP method to encrypt communications.

802.11 Roaming

Initially, a station will associate to the access point that responds to a Probe Request. As stations move into another area, the signal will degrade, and the station starts probing for a new access point to associate to.

244

An access point that is part of an extended service set will allow a previously connected station to reassociate to a new access point. This is a basic roam from one access point to another. The station will decide what metrics would be considered for a roaming decision, such as RSSI and SNR, and others.

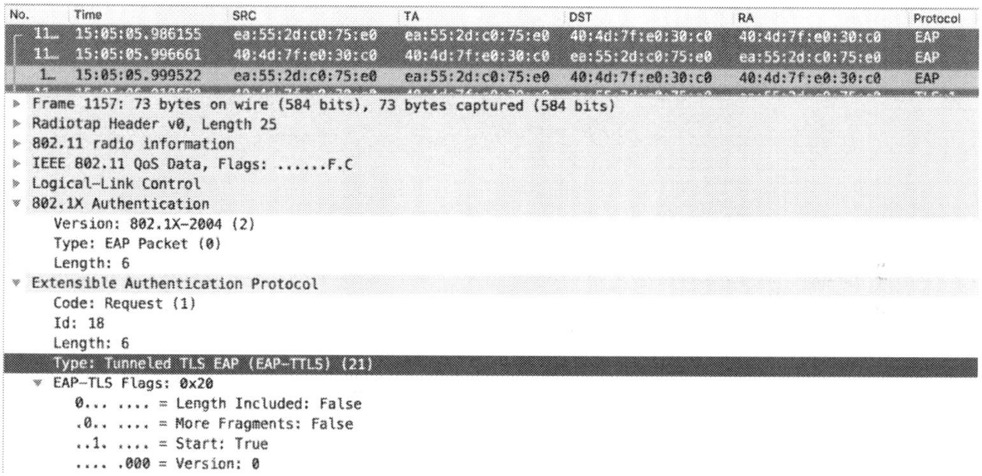

Figure 5.17: EAP Method Request Type

In an 802.1X BSS, a station goes through the 802.11 Open System authentication and association frame exchange, followed by EAP frame exchanges, and then the 4-way handshake. As a station moves closer to a new access point, it will begin with the 802.11 Open System authentication & association frame exchange but instead of an association frame, the station will send a unicast Reassociation Frame destined to the target access point it desires to roam to.

Within a Reassociation Frame, the station will populate the Current AP Address field with the MAC address of the AP in which the station is currently associated. If the station was already on the network with a security association, the PMKID field would be populated under the RSN Element, which is not the case in Figure 5.18.

Non-Fast Transition roaming takes additional time for a station to transition to a new access point. Certain applications do not handle very well to the latency and jitter caused by this transition time.

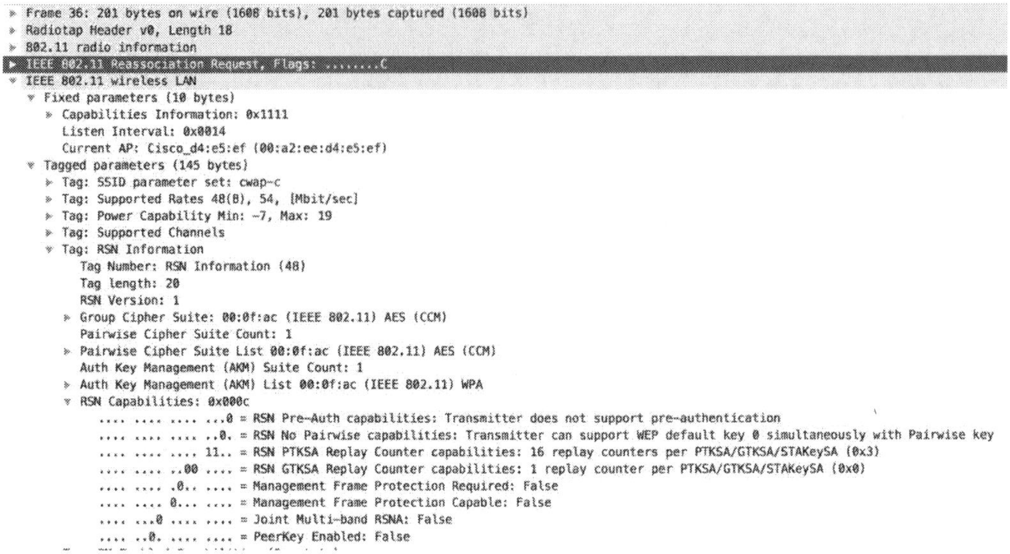

```
▸ Frame 36: 201 bytes on wire (1608 bits), 201 bytes captured (1608 bits)
▸ Radiotap Header v0, Length 18
▸ 802.11 radio information
▸ IEEE 802.11 Reassociation Request, Flags: ........C
▾ IEEE 802.11 wireless LAN
   ▾ Fixed parameters (10 bytes)
      ▸ Capabilities Information: 0x1111
         Listen Interval: 0x0014
         Current AP: Cisco_d4:e5:ef (00:a2:ee:d4:e5:ef)
   ▾ Tagged parameters (145 bytes)
      ▸ Tag: SSID parameter set: cwap-c
      ▸ Tag: Supported Rates 48(B), 54, [Mbit/sec]
      ▸ Tag: Power Capability Min: -7, Max: 19
      ▸ Tag: Supported Channels
      ▾ Tag: RSN Information
           Tag Number: RSN Information (48)
           Tag length: 20
           RSN Version: 1
         ▸ Group Cipher Suite: 00:0f:ac (IEEE 802.11) AES (CCM)
           Pairwise Cipher Suite Count: 1
         ▸ Pairwise Cipher Suite List 00:0f:ac (IEEE 802.11) AES (CCM)
           Auth Key Management (AKM) Suite Count: 1
         ▸ Auth Key Management (AKM) List 00:0f:ac (IEEE 802.11) WPA
         ▾ RSN Capabilities: 0x000c
              .... .... ...0 = RSN Pre-Auth capabilities: Transmitter does not support pre-authentication
              .... .... ..0. = RSN No Pairwise capabilities: Transmitter can support WEP default key 0 simultaneously with Pairwise key
              .... .... 11.. = RSN PTKSA Replay Counter capabilities: 16 replay counters per PTKSA/GTKSA/STAKeySA (0x3)
              .... ...00 .... = RSN GTKSA Replay Counter capabilities: 1 replay counter per PTKSA/GTKSA/STAKeySA (0x0)
              .... .... .0.. .... = Management Frame Protection Required: False
              .... .... 0... .... = Management Frame Protection Capable: False
              .... ..0 .... .... = Joint Multi-band RSNA: False
              .... ..0. .... .... = PeerKey Enabled: False
```

Figure 5.18: Reassociation Request frame

As you can see in Figure 5.19, from frame 33 through 61, it took this particular station 227ms to fully roam to its target AP. It started with 802.11 Authentication, went through 802.1X authentication, and completed with the 4-way handshake.

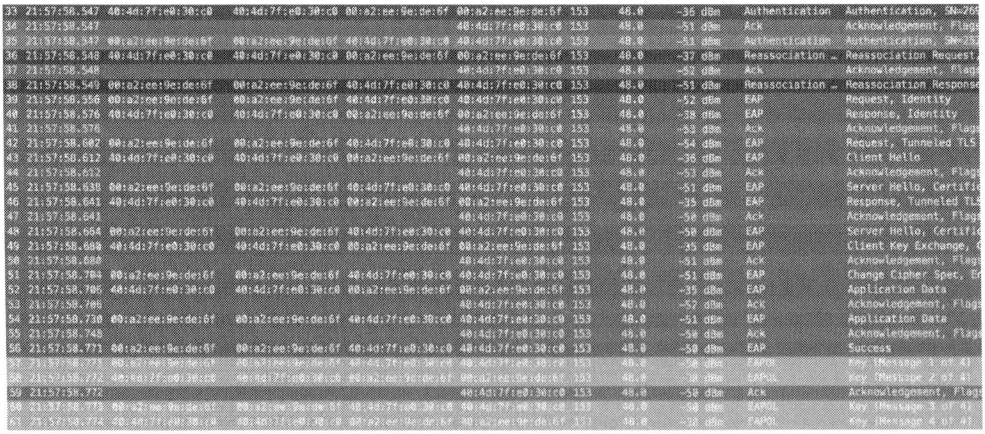

Figure 5.19: Frames during roaming

In the next section we'll discuss how to minimize the amount of time it takes a station to roam between BSSs.

In an open SSID, a station would go through the 802.11 State Machine when roaming to another AP. With no security in place, EAP and 4-way handshake frames are not exchanged.

Pre-FT (802.11r) Fast Secure Roaming Mechanisms

Prior to 802.11r being amended in 2009, there were methods in which assisted stations in roaming securely. These methods helped reduce the time it took for a station spent doing 802.1X EAP exchanges.

Those Pre-Fast Transition methods are:

- Preauthentication
- PMK Caching

Preauthentication

Preauthentication is a method used where a station may authenticate with multiple APs at a time. The APs must be in the same ESS and advertise Preauthentication in their Beacon frame.

Under the RSN Information Element, the subfield RSN Pre-Authentication Capabilities will have its bit set to 1. It is located under the RSN Capabilities field, as seen in Figure 5.20.

```
▽ Tag: RSN Information
      Tag Number: RSN Information (48)
      Tag length: 20
      RSN Version: 1
    ▷ Group Cipher Suite: 00:0f:ac (IEEE 802.11) AES (CCM)
      Pairwise Cipher Suite Count: 1
    ▷ Pairwise Cipher Suite List 00:0f:ac (IEEE 802.11) AES (CCM)
      Auth Key Management (AKM) Suite Count: 1
    ▷ Auth Key Management (AKM) List 00:0f:ac (IEEE 802.11) WPA
    ▽ RSN Capabilities: 0x0001
         .... .... .... ...1 = RSN Pre-Auth capabilities: Transmitter supports pre-authentication
         .... .... .... ..0. = RSN No Pairwise capabilities: Transmitter can support WEP default key 0 simultaneously with Pairwise key
         .... .... .... 00.. = RSN PTKSA Replay Counter capabilities: 1 replay counter per PTKSA/GTKSA/STAKeySA (0x0)
         .... .... ..00 .... = RSN GTKSA Replay Counter capabilities: 1 replay counter per PTKSA/GTKSA/STAKeySA (0x0)
         .... .... .0.. .... = Management Frame Protection Required: False
         .... .... 0... .... = Management Frame Protection Capable: False
         .... ...0 .... .... = Joint Multi-band RSNA: False
         .... ..0. .... .... = PeerKey Enabled: False
```

Figure 5.20: RSN Information

Preauthentication works is by allowing a station to have an RSNA with an access point prior to attempting reassociation with it. When the 802.1X authentication completes successfully, the result is a PMKSA that is used with other APs. When the station associates with a preauthenticated AP, the supplicant uses the PMKSA and the 4-way handshake. The 802.1X authentication EAP exchanges are skipped altogether because of the PMKSA.

Figure 5.21 shows the frame exchanges of a station roaming to a target AP. It begins the 802.11 authentication and (re)association process. With this BSS supporting 802.1X authentication, notice the station skips those EAP frame exchanges and goes straight to the 4-way handshake. After completing the 4-way handshake, it is deauthenticated from its current AP to roam to the target AP.

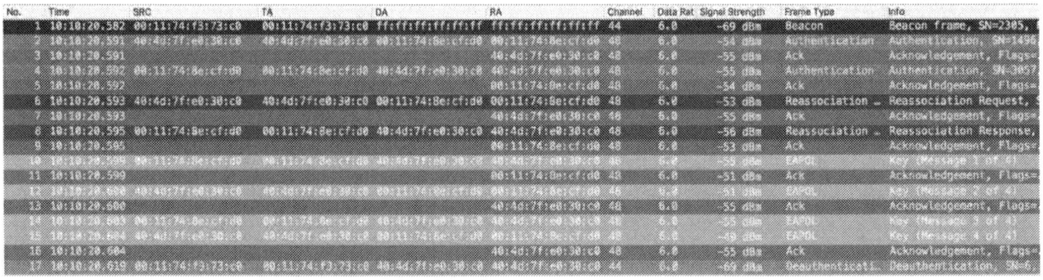

No.	Time	SRC	TA	DA	RA	Channel	Data Rat	Signal Strength	Frame Type	Info
1	10:10:20.582	00:11:74:f3:73:c0	00:11:74:f3:73:c0	ff:ff:ff:ff:ff:ff	ff:ff:ff:ff:ff:ff	44	6.0	-69 dBm	Beacon	Beacon frame, SN=2305,
2	10:10:20.591	40:4d:7f:e0:30:c0	40:4d:7f:e0:30:c0	00:11:74:8e:cf:d0	00:11:74:8e:cf:d0	48	6.0	-54 dBm	Authentication	Authentication, SN=1496
3	10:10:20.591				40:4d:7f:e0:30:c0	48	6.0	-55 dBm	Ack	Acknowledgement, Flags=
4	10:10:20.592	00:11:74:8e:cf:d0	00:11:74:8e:cf:d0	40:4d:7f:e0:30:c0	40:4d:7f:e0:30:c0	48	6.0	-55 dBm	Authentication	Authentication, SN=3057
5	10:10:20.592				00:11:74:8e:cf:d0	48	6.0	-54 dBm	Ack	Acknowledgement, Flags=
6	10:10:20.593	40:4d:7f:e0:30:c0	40:4d:7f:e0:30:c0	00:11:74:8e:cf:d0	00:11:74:8e:cf:d0	48	6.0	-53 dBm	Reassociation …	Reassociation Request,
7	10:10:20.593				40:4d:7f:e0:30:c0	48	6.0	-55 dBm	Ack	Acknowledgement, Flags=
8	10:10:20.595	00:11:74:8e:cf:d0	00:11:74:8e:cf:d0	40:4d:7f:e0:30:c0	40:4d:7f:e0:30:c0	48	6.0	-56 dBm	Reassociation …	Reassociation Response,
9	10:10:20.595				00:11:74:8e:cf:d0	48	6.0	-53 dBm	Ack	Acknowledgement, Flags=
10	10:10:20.599	00:11:74:8e:cf:d0	00:11:74:8e:cf:d0	40:4d:7f:e0:30:c0	40:4d:7f:e0:30:c0	48	6.0	-55 dBm	EAPOL	Key (Message 1 of 4)
11	10:10:20.599				00:11:74:8e:cf:d0	48	6.0	-51 dBm	Ack	Acknowledgement, Flags=
12	10:10:20.600	40:4d:7f:e0:30:c0	40:4d:7f:e0:30:c0	00:11:74:8e:cf:d0	00:11:74:8e:cf:d0	48	6.0	-51 dBm	EAPOL	Key (Message 2 of 4)
13	10:10:20.600				40:4d:7f:e0:30:c0	48	6.0	-55 dBm	Ack	Acknowledgement, Flags=
14	10:10:20.603	00:11:74:8e:cf:d0	00:11:74:8e:cf:d0	40:4d:7f:e0:30:c0	40:4d:7f:e0:30:c0	48	6.0	-55 dBm	EAPOL	Key (Message 3 of 4)
15	10:10:20.604	40:4d:7f:e0:30:c0	40:4d:7f:e0:30:c0	00:11:74:8e:cf:d0	00:11:74:8e:cf:d0	48	6.0	-49 dBm	EAPOL	Key (Message 4 of 4)
16	10:10:20.604				40:4d:7f:e0:30:c0	48	6.0	-55 dBm	Ack	Acknowledgement, Flags=
17	10:10:20.619	00:11:74:f3:73:c0	00:11:74:f3:73:c0	40:4d:7f:e0:30:c0	40:4d:7f:e0:30:c0	44	6.0	-69 dBm	Deauthenticati…	Deauthentication, SN=6,

Figure 5.21: Preauthentication frame exchange

Within the station's reassociation frame is a PMKID Count subfield of the RSN Information field containing a count of 1. The frame also lists that PMKID. The station will use the PMKSA from its association with its first AP.

Preauthentication may not work if the AP has expired the PMKSA. The station would need to undergo a full 802.1X authentication when roaming to another AP.

PMK Caching

PMK caching is a method of speeding up the roaming process when a station roams back to an AP in which it has associated to before. The station and original AP will maintain a PMKSA for some time before expiring. During this time, the station can associate to a target AP and will establish a new PMKSA.

The station then roams back to its original AP and if the cached PMKSA is still valid the station will reassociate, performing Open System authentication with its included PMKID for the PMKSA within the Reassociation Request. The AP verifies it has a cached PMKSA for the station and if so, it will begin the 4-way handshake.

What is the difference between Preauthentication and PMK Caching? With PMK Caching, the PMKID is cached on the AP after the station associates to it. Then upon roaming back to the AP it can skip the 802.1X EAP exchange and move to the 4-way handshake.

Preauthentication creates a PMK that will be stored on a target AP. When a station roams to the target AP it will be able to skip the 802.1X EAP exchange and start the 4-way handshake after 802.11 Open System Authentication and (Re)association.

PMK Caching and Preauthentication do not scale well in a large Wi-Fi deployment. It requires all APs to have a PMKSA with all the stations associated.

Fast Secure Roaming Transition

When a station begins moving across an area, or basic service set (BSS), it will change associations from one BSS to another. The whole 802.11 State Machine process would be repeated with the 4-way handshake. To help with minimizing the station's amount of lost connectivity time, fast basic service set transition could be implemented. The station and APs taking part in this roaming process must be part of the same mobility domain.

Support of the mobility domain is done through the first association of the station. Within Probe Response and Reassociation frames is the Mobility Domain element.

Figure 5.22: Mobility Domain in Probe Response frame

Frame capture of a station using Fast Transition from its current AP to a target AP is performed using multiple adapters. One adapter is listening on the current AP's operating channel while the second adapter is listening to the target AP's channel.

A station moving from its current AP to another AP may use a Fast Transition protocol. It can do so using one of two message exchange methods:

- Over-the-Air
- Over-the-DS

Over-the-Air Fast Transition method is used when a station wants to transition to a new AP by directly communicating with it. It must go through 802.11 authentication with Fast Transition authentication. With Over-the-DS, the transitioning station communicates with the destination AP through its current AP using Fast Transition Action frames and Reassociation Frames.

Over-the-Air Fast Transition

In a secure Wi-Fi network, the station and AP may use Fast Transition authentication. With an RSN in use a new PTK will be derived within the frame exchange, prior to completing reassociation. The station initiating the over-the-air Fast Transition to a target AP goes through four frame exchanges.

Message 1: Originating station transmits an Authentication Request frame to the target AP.

Message 2: The target AP transmits an Authentication Response frame to the originating station.

Message 3: The originating station transmits a Reassociation Frame to the target AP. Within the frame contains a Fast BSS Transition element.

Message 4: The target AP transmits a Reassociation Response frame containing a status code and if Successful the originating station's association has transitioned to the target AP.

Figure 5.3 illustrates these frame exchanges used. Notice that it begins, with the Target AP, with a typical Authentication request frame. This is Open System authentication and is a creative way to quickly see if the target AP has room for any more clients, for it could simply reject the authentication request immediately preventing the client STA from wasting further time.

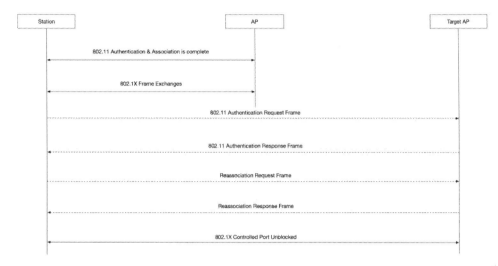

Figure 5.23: FT Over-the-Air frame exchanges

When Fast Transition uses Over-the-Air as its method of roaming, the destination and receiver MAC address is set to the BSSID of the target AP.

The Mobility Domain element will be present in the Beacon, Probe Response, Authentication, and Reassociation frames, as shown in Figure 5.24. If the contents of the Mobility Domain element received by the AP do not match from what is advertised in the Beacon and Probe Response frames, then the AP will reject the Authentication Request indicated with a status code.

```
▼ IEEE 802.11 wireless LAN
  ▼ Fixed parameters (12 bytes)
      Timestamp: 0x000000002b6cc526
      Beacon Interval: 0.102400 [Seconds]
    ▶ Capabilities Information: 0x1111
  ▼ Tagged parameters (290 bytes)
    ▶ Tag: SSID parameter set: cwap-c
    ▶ Tag: Supported Rates 24(B), 36, 48, 54, [Mbit/sec]
    ▶ Tag: DS Parameter set: Current Channel: 153
    ▶ Tag: Country Information: Country Code US, Environment Unknown (0x00)
    ▶ Tag: RSN Information
    ▶ Tag: QBSS Load Element 802.11e CCA Version
    ▶ Tag: RM Enabled Capabilities (5 octets)
    ▼ Tag: Mobility Domain
        Tag Number: Mobility Domain (54)
        Tag length: 3
        Mobility Domain Identifier: 0xe10e
        FT Capability and Policy: 0x00
        .... ...0 = Fast BSS Transition over DS: 0x0
        .... ..0. = Resource Request Protocol Capability: 0x0
```

Figure 5.24: Mobility Domain

Identifying whether Fast Transition is done Over-the-Air is through the Mobility Domain element. Under the FT Capability and Policy field, the Fast BSS Transition over DS subfield is set to a bit 0, as seen in figure 5.24.

When the station receives a Reassociation Response frame with a status code of Successful, the station and target AP can begin transmitting encrypted data.

Over-the-DS Fast Transition

Using Over-the-DS Fast Transition looks similar to Over-the-Air. The main difference between the methods is a station using Fast Transition communicates with the target AP through its current associated AP.

Just as in Over-the-Air Fast Transition, the PTK is derived for the RSN through the frame exchange prior to completing reassociation.

If the target AP has a Mobility Domain element containing the Fast BSS Transition over DS set to 1, the station will initiate over-the-DS FT through the current AP with the following frame exchanges:

Message 1: Originating station sends a FT Request frame to the current AP with the Target AP Address field set to the target AP's BSSID.

Message 2: The target AP sends a FT Response frame to the originating station.

Message 3: The originating station sends a Reassociation frame destined to the target AP.

Message 4: The target AP responds with a Reassociation Response frame to the originating station. If the frame contains a Status code of Successful, the station has transitioned to its target AP.

The main difference compared to Over-the-Air FT is in Over-the-DS, the station initiates FT with a Fast BSS Transition Action Request frame. This Action frame has a destination address of the current associated AP. Within the FT Action Request frame, the source address is that of the originating station and the destination is of the target AP's BSSID.

The process is illustrated in Figure 5.25.

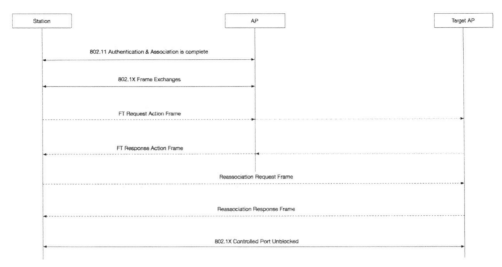

Figure 5.25: FT Over-the-DS frame exchanges

The FT Action Request frame will be destined to the target AP through the current AP. Figure 5.26 shows the details of the FT Action Request frame.

Figure 5.26: FT Action Request frame

When using Over-the-Air FT, this frame is an Authentication Request frame with a destination address of the target AP. In other words, the station communicates with the target AP directly.

Following the FT Action frames, the station will perform reassociation directly with the target AP. Message 3, the Reassociation Request frame, will have a destination address set to the target AP's BSSID. The source address will be set to the station's MAC address.

The target AP validates the MIC and verifies the Mobility Domain element matches. The target AP then sends a Reassociation Response frame with the source address set to the target AP's BSSID and the destination address set to the originating station.

Once the reassociation has been deemed successful, the PTKSA is fresh and the 802.1X uncontrolled port will be opened.

Roaming Analysis

Validating and troubleshooting roaming can be a challenge. It's critical to capture frames closer to the roaming station to understand how the roaming process is affecting the station. To capture frames pertaining to roaming, multiple adapters must be used. Additionally, the software used to analyze the frames must support channel aggregation. The purpose of using channel aggregation is to have the software combine the captured frames into one capture file.

Each adapter is configured to monitor on channels which a station is going to roam to. This allows the capture of necessary reassociation frames, 4-way handshakes, beacon frames, and 802.1X authentication frames. When a station roams, the troubleshooting tools must follow physically with the STA for accurate capture.

Improvements in Fast Transition

Radio measurements allow a station to better understand their radio environment. A station can request this measurement from its associated AP, take the measurement locally, or be requested of the measurement by another station or AP. These measurements extend the capability of a station to improve reliability and roaming.

One such measurement is the Neighbor Report, sent to an AP from a station. The AP returns a report with information about known neighbor APs. The station uses this list of neighboring APs as potential roaming candidates.

Figure 5.27: Neighbor Report Request frame

254

Taken from 802.11k, Radio Resource Management, two frames are exchanged between a station and its associated AP. A station will send a unicast Action Management Frame to its associated AP, requesting a Neighbor Report of the indicated SSID.

The AP responds to the station with a unicast Action Management Frame with a Neighbor Report Response containing a list of neighboring APs, their BSSID, and operating channels.

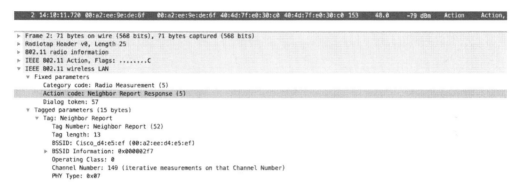

Figure 5.28: Neighbor Report Response frame

Information pertaining to a specific BSSID will be reported in the BSSID Information subfield. These subfields help determine if the BSSID is considered as a candidate for roaming by the station.

Specifically, the AP Reachability field indicates whether the BSSID is reachable by the station. The bits set within this field determine the reachability as indicated in the Table 5.7.

Value	Reachability	Usage
0	Reserved	Not used.
1	Not Reachable	Station will not receive a response from AP for roaming or preauthentication.
2	Unknown	AP is unable to determine if the value Reachable or Not Reachable is to be returned.
3	Reachable	Station sending a preauthentication frame to BSSID can receive a response from an AP that is capable.

Table 5.7 AP Reachability field values

Interoperability with External Networks

Many organizations are looking at unlicensed frequency as a way to address connectivity needs. The 802.11u amendment and Hotspot 2.0 were created to address interworking with external networks in a seamless and secure fashion.

802.11u and Hotspot 2.0 help stations, on a cellular network, discover a Wi-Fi network before joining it. Parameters that can be discovered include:

- Roaming partners
- Venue name
- Venue type
- EAP methods
- Free or paid
- And more…

Stations and APs advertise their support through the Interworking Element. When enabled on an infrastructure BSS, a station can transmit an Access Network Query Protocol (ANQP) Request.

An access point advertises support of 802.11u and Hotspot 2.0 in a Beacon and Probe Response frame, as seen in Figure 5.29.

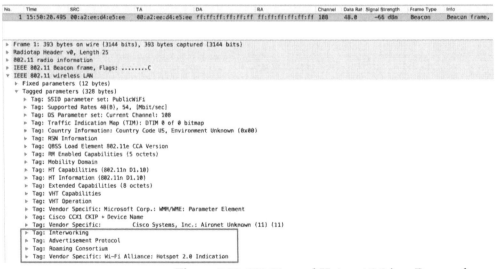

Figure 5.29: 802.11u and Hotspot 2.0 in a Beacon frame

An ANQP Request consists of ANQP elements, including:

- Query List
- Vendor Specific
- TDLS Capability

The ANQP Request is then transported within an ANQP Query Request field of a Generic Advertisement Service (GAS). The GAS provides a framework to transport ANQP services.

The basic message exchange concept, through 802.11u and Hotspot 2.0, between the AP and station is as follows:

1. AP transmits Beacon frame containing advertisement of Interworking and Hotspot 2.0
2. Station, through active or passive scanning, identifies AP and sends a Probe Request to target AP.
3. Station and AP perform 802.11 Open System authentication and association.
4. Station transmits an ANQP request.
5. Access point transmits an ANQP response back to the querying station.
6. Station selects its service provider, if listed in the ANQP response.
7. Station proceeds authenticating with the authentication server of the service provider.

Analyzing and Troubleshooting Roaming Issues

Stations have full control over whether they decide to roam to another access point. Sometimes stations exhibit unexpected behavior by sticking to their original access point or excessively roam between multiple access points. Further frame analysis can help identify the root cause to these specific issues after station-related problems have been ruled out.

Sticky Clients

Ideally, you want a client to select an AP with the best signal, so it can transmit and receive frames at the highest data rate. As clients begin moving away from their associated AP they dynamically shift their data rates to lower values.

Capturing frames near the sticky client is the best location for troubleshooting.

Gather information about the client to understand why the client may not be roaming properly:

- Operating channel
- Band support
- Channel support
- PHY support

Many factors can prevent a client from roaming to a better AP. Identify what data rate the client is associating to its current AP while moving towards a more ideal AP. If it maintains connectivity with low data rates, then this setting on the BSS may need to be reconfigured.

With a frame capture set to the client's current associated channel and the ideal channel, identify whether the Beacon frames are heard at a stronger signal strength. Clients have their own algorithms to determine when they should roam, and RSSI is a contributing metric.

Lastly, ensure the client supports the target AP's channel and PHY. Look for Authentication and Association frames with success codes.

Other ways to help encourage a client to roam efficiently include support for 802.11k and 802.11v. The 802.11k amendment is Radio Resource Management. It provides a Neighbor Report to the client with a list of APs it can use to make a roaming decision. 802.11v is another amendment called Wireless Network Management and can provide BSS Transition Management to help improve client roaming.

Be aware of client support for each of the features and amendments listed and always validate for each capacity and coverage area.

Excessive Roaming

On the other side of Sticky Clients are clients that roam unnecessarily. This occurs with suboptimal design and configuration. As stated earlier, clients make their own roaming decisions based on proprietary manufacturer algorithms. Troubleshooting close to the client will help provide the answers for excessive roaming.

The troubleshooting info described under Sticky Clients can be used to help resolve excessive roaming. Identifying the root cause may be found in the frame exchanges between the roaming client and APs.

Analyze Beacon frames from the APs the client is roaming to. Are coverage areas showing a disproportionate overlap? A proper design and validation survey will indicate placement for improved coverage and overlap for roaming.

Confirm default settings such as client load balancing which may disassociate clients from an AP which encourage roaming. Verify other configuration details have not been altered from the design, such as data rates set too high of a value.

Chapter Summary

In this chapter, we explored the methods in which a station discovers a BSS and what frame exchanges occur when joining a BSS. You learned about EAP frame exchanges for 802.1X authentication and the 4-way handshake which is also used with PSK protected networks. Then we touched upon Pre-Fast Transition frames and Fast Transition frames for secure roaming. We ended with analyzing and troubleshooting sticky client and excessive roaming clients.

Facts to Remember

- STAs can use Beacons and Probe Requests to locate target BSSs for connectivity.
- Hiding the SSID in Beacon frames provides no real security.
- The Open System connection includes Authentication and Association but offers to real security.
- All RSNs use the 4-way handshake.
- Fast Transition (FT) can be over-the-air or over-the-DS.
- PMK caching is more of a roam back solution.
- Preauthentication and PMC caching do not scale well in large networks

Review Questions

1. After which frame exchange sequence does the 4-way handshake occur?
   a. After Authentication frame exchange
   b. Before Association frame exchange
   c. Before EAP frame exchange
   d. After EAP frame exchange

2. An AP's Association Response frame, with a successful status code, will include which field for the station?
   a. MCS rate to use
   b. Association ID
   c. Identity Request
   d. Access-Request

3. The Group Temporal Key (GTK) is delivered in which message of the 4-way handshake?
   a. Message 1
   b. Message 2
   c. Message 3
   d. Message 4

4. Which method is used to tell a station when to roam?
   a. 802.11k
   b. 802.11v
   c. Fast Transition
   d. None, the station decides when to roam

5. What type of frame is displayed below?

```
7  22:24:49...   Apple_e0:30:c0           Mist_01:e6:d3     EAPOL    184 48    -37 dBm   EAPOL              6.0
  Version: 802.1X-2004 (2)
  Type: Key (3)
  Length: 117
  Key Descriptor Type: EAPOL RSN Key (2)
  [Message number: 2]
▼ Key Information: 0x010a
    .... .... .... .010 = Key Descriptor Version: AES Cipher, HMAC-SHA1 MIC (2)
    .... .... .... 1... = Key Type: Pairwise Key
    .... .... ..00 .... = Key Index: 0
    .... .... .0.. .... = Install: Not set
    .... ...0 0... .... = Key ACK: Not set
    .... ...1 .... .... = Key MIC: Set
    .... ..0. .... .... = Secure: Not set
    .... .0.. .... .... = Error: Not set
    .... 0... .... .... = Request: Not set
    ...0 .... .... .... = Encrypted Key Data: Not set
    ..0. .... .... .... = SMK Message: Not set
  Key Length: 16
  Replay Counter: 1
  WPA Key Nonce: 3cd8193a64e893a04e818bf62fd9409804c3ecf1b3c661cf...
  Key IV: 00000000000000000000000000000000
  WPA Key RSC: 0000000000000000
  WPA Key ID: 0000000000000000
  WPA Key MIC: b9b69086f00bfeb945c2cbea4d24df83
  WPA Key Data Length: 22
▼ WPA Key Data: 30140100000fac040100000fac040100000fac020c00
  ▼ Tag: RSN Information
      Tag Number: RSN Information (48)
      Tag length: 20
      RSN Version: 1
    ▶ Group Cipher Suite: 00:0f:ac (IEEE 802.11) AES (CCM)
      Pairwise Cipher Suite Count: 1
    ▶ Pairwise Cipher Suite List 00:0f:ac (IEEE 802.11) AES (CCM)
      Auth Key Management (AKM) Suite Count: 1
    ▶ Auth Key Management (AKM) List 00:0f:ac (IEEE 802.11) PSK
    ▶ RSN Capabilities: 0x000c
```

    a.   RADIUS Frame

    b.   Message 4 of the 4-way handshake

    c.   Association request frame

    d.   Message 3 of the 4-way handshake

6. Which of the following describes OTA Fast Transition?

    a.   Station sends a reassociation frame directly to the target AP

    b.   Station sends an association frame to target AP through current AP

    c.   Station sends an association frame directly to the target AP

    d.   Station sends reassociation frame to target AP through current AP

7. Which of the following is true about OTA Fast Transition sourced from a station?
    a. The destination and receiver MAC address fields are set to the BSSID of the current AP
    b. The receiver and transmitter MAC address fields are set to the BSSID of the current AP
    c. The destination and receiver MAC address fields are set to the MAC address of the station
    d. The destination and receiver MAC address fields are set to the BSSID of the target AP

8. Describe the frame type

```
▶ IEEE 802.11 Reassociation Request, Flags: ........C
▼ IEEE 802.11 wireless LAN
  ▶ Fixed parameters (10 bytes)
  ▼ Tagged parameters (280 bytes)
    ▶ Tag: SSID parameter set: CWAP
    ▶ Tag: Supported Rates 6(B), 9, 12(B), 18, 24(B), 36, 48, 54, [Mbit/sec]
    ▶ Tag: Power Capability Min: −7, Max: 19
    ▶ Tag: Supported Channels
    ▶ Tag: RSN Information
    ▶ Tag: RM Enabled Capabilities (5 octets)
    ▼ Tag: Mobility Domain
        Tag Number: Mobility Domain (54)
        Tag length: 3
        Mobility Domain Identifier: 0x0900
        FT Capability and Policy: 0x01
        .... ...1 = Fast BSS Transition over DS: 0x1
        .... ..0. = Resource Request Protocol Capability: 0x0
    ▶ Tag: Fast BSS Transition
    ▶ Tag: HT Capabilities (802.11n D1.10)
    ▶ Tag: Extended Capabilities (3 octets)
    ▶ Tag: VHT Capabilities
    ▶ Tag: Operating Mode Notification
    ▶ Tag: Vendor Specific: Apple, Inc.
    ▶ Tag: Vendor Specific: Broadcom
    ▶ Tag: Vendor Specific: Microsoft Corp.: WMM/WME: Information Element
```

    a. 802.11r FT Over-the-Air Association Request
    b. 802.11r FT Over-the-Air Reassociation Request
    c. 802.11r FT Over-the-DS Association Request
    d. 802.11r FT Over-the-DS Reassociation Request

9. A station sending a unicast Action Management Frame to its associated AP, requesting a Neighbor Report of the indicated SSID is part of which amendment?
    a. 802.11r
    b. 802.11k
    c. 802.11v
    d. 802.11h

10. Which of the following describes PMK Caching?
    a. Station roams back to a previously associated AP and skips EAP frame exchanges
    b. Station roams to a target AP, already preauthenticated, skips EAP frame exchanges
    c. Station is preauthenticated to all neighboring APs
    d. Station roams to a taret AP, already preauthenticated, skips the 4-way handshake

Review Answers

1. The correct answer is D. The four-way handshake occurs after EAP authentication, when it is used.
2. The correct answer is B. The Association Response frame, when successful, will include the STA's AID (Association ID).
3. The correct answer is C. The GTK is delivered in message 3 and message 4 tells the AP/controller that the STA is configured and ready to go.
4. The correct answer is D. The decision to roam is left in the hands of the STA with current 802.11 operations.
5. The correct answer is A. This is a RADIUS frame as indicated by the text, "802.1X-2004."
6. The correct answer is A. With OTA FT, the STA sends an authentication frame and then a reassociation frame to the target AP directly over the RF medium.
7. The correct answer is D. The address fields are set in this way.
8. The correct answer is D. This is an over-the-DS (ODS) FT reassociation request frame as the frame subtype is a Reassociation Request, but the FT BSS over DS transition is set to 1.
9. The correct answer is B. 802.11k specified these radio measurement requests.
10. The correct answer is A. PMK caching is a roam-back solution.

Chapter 6: Medium Access Methods and QoS Frame Exchanges

Objectives Covered:

5.1 Understand 802.11 contention algorithms in-depth and know how they impact WLANs

5.2 Analyze QoS configuration and operations

The contention algorithms used in 802.11 networks are essential knowledge for the wireless analysis professional. This chapter explains both Distributed Coordination Function and Enhanced Distributed Channel Access, the two primary methods used in 802.11 networks. Because Enhanced Distributed Channel Access uses QoS in operation, both Wi-Fi Multimedia (WMM) and general QoS concepts are addressed as well.

Contention Algorithms

The first step required to communicate on an 802.11 WLAN is BSS location. The STA must locate an AP to which it desires to connect. This can be performed with active or passive scanning. The 802.11 MAC layer provides the following functions:

- *Scanning*—Before a station can participate in a Basic Service Set, it must be able to find the APs that provide access to that service set. Scanning is the process used to discover Basic Service Sets or to discover APs within a known Basic Service Set. It can be either passive (Beacon management frames) or active (Probe Request and Probe Response frames).
- *Synchronization*—Some 802.11 features require all stations to have the same time. Stations can update their clocks based on the timestamp value in Beacon frames.
- *Frame Transmission*—Stations must abide by the frame transmission rules of the Basic Service Set to which they are associated. These rules are the Distributed Coordination Function (DCF) and Enhanced Distributed Channel Access (EDCA).
- *Authentication*—Open System authentication is performed before a station can be associated with a Basic Service Set.
- *Association*—Once authentication is complete, the station can become associated with the Basic Service Set. This includes discovery of capability information in both directions—from the station to the AP, and from the AP to the station.
- *Reassociation*—When users roam throughout a service area, they may reach a point where one AP within an Extended Service Set will provide a stronger signal than the currently associated AP. When this occurs, the station will reassociate with the new AP.
- *Data Protection*—Data encryption may be employed to assist in preventing crackers from accessing the data that is transmitted on the wireless medium (WM).
- *Power Management*—Since the transmitters/receivers (transceivers) in wireless client devices consume a noteworthy amount of power, power management

features are provided that assist in extending battery life by causing the transceiver to sleep for discreet specified intervals.

- *Fragmentation*—In certain scenarios it is beneficial to fragment frames before they are transmitted onto the WM. This type of scenario most often occurs due to intermittent interference. F
- *RTS/CTS*—Request to Send/Clear-to-Send is a feature of IEEE 802.11 that will help prevent hidden node problems and allow for more centralized control of access to the WM.

The following section provide the specifics of DCF, EDCA, and WMM.

Distributed Coordination Function (DCF)

After being authenticated and associated, a STA may contend for access to the medium. All STAs, including APs, must contend for the medium or for channel access before they can transmit a frame. The Distributed Coordination Function (DCF) is the CSMA/CA method implemented in the 802.11 standard when EDCA is not used. All 802.11 devices support DCF and QoS STAs also support EDCA.

On a shared medium, collisions may occur. These collisions must be handled in some fashion and wireless networks introduced new challenges to collision management. This section explains how collisions are handled, or more accurately, avoided as much as possible, in 802.11 networks.

Ethernet networks (IEEE 802.3) use a form of collision management known as collision detection (CD). Wireless networks use a different form of collision management known as collision avoidance (CA). The full name of the physical media access management used in wireless networks is carrier-sense multiple access/collision avoidance or CSMA/CA.

The essence of CSMA/CA is that collisions can happen at any receiver on the medium at any time during a transmission, and likely cannot be detected by the transmitter at its location. Listening for evidence of a collision while transmitting is thus worthless and not a part of the protocol. Transmissions cannot be aborted early. Collisions are only inferred as one possible explanation for failure to receive an immediate ACK after transmitting a frame in its entirety. The frame must be retransmitted completely. Under these circumstances there is much value in collision avoidance, and therefore is much of it used in the 802.11 protocols.

If you have ever had a conversation with another person on the telephone you have probably experienced a communications collision. When you both started speaking at the same time, neither of you could hear the other effectively. Usually, you will both stop speaking for some random amount of time, and then one of you will start speaking again. Since the time that both of you choose to wait is slightly different, there is a good chance that one of you will be able to communicate the next time. This example would be like collision detection as opposed to collision avoidance.

The "carrier sense" in CSMA means that the devices attempt to sense whether the physical medium is available before communicating. The "multiple access" indicates that more than one device is accessing the physical medium. In a CD implementation of CSMA, when a collision is detected both devices go silent for a random period. Since the time period is different for each device, they are not likely to try communicating at the same time again. This process helps recover from collisions and to avoid another collision. In a CSMA/CD implementation, collisions occur because devices can begin communicating at the same time even though they both listened for "silence" on the physical medium. Silence was indeed detected, but both devices broke the silence at the same moment. On modern Ethernet networks, with switches, collisions are not as much of a concern because devices have dedicated physical wires between them and the switch.

CSMA/CA is used in wireless networks, and it was also used in early Apple LocalTalk networks that were wired networks common to Apple devices. Collision avoidance is achieved by signaling to the other devices that one device is about to communicate. This functionality would be like saying, "Be quiet, for the next few minutes, because I will be talking." in a telephone conversation. You are avoiding the collision by announcing that you are going to be communicating for some time interval. CSMA/CA is not perfect due to hidden node problems, but it provides a more efficient usage of a medium like RF than would CSMA/CD.

To be clear, the transmitting wireless STA starts talking (transmitting) and an early part of the transmission indicates how long the STA will be talking. So, of course, there are other methods used in carrier sense to avoid stepping on another conversation, such as energy detect (ED), which is addressed later in this chapter.

Carrier Sense and Energy Detect (ED)

Carrier sense is the process of checking to see if the medium is in use or busy. If you have multiple telephones in your house and a single line that is shared by all these telephones, you use a manual form of carrier sense every time you use one of the phones to make a call. When you pick up the phone, you listen to see if someone else is already using the phone. If someone is on the line, you may choose to hang up the phone and wait until it becomes available. If you have ever been on the phone when someone else begins dialing without first checking to see if anyone is using the line, you have experienced a form of collision as the tones penetrated your ears and overcame your conversation with noise.

In 802.11 WLANs two kinds of carrier sense are performed: virtual carrier sense and physical carrier sense.

Physical carrier sense uses clear channel assessment (CCA) to determine if the physical medium is in use and is provided by the PHY and not the MAC, though it reports to the MAC. CCA is accomplished by monitoring the medium to determine if the amount of RF energy detected exceeds a particular threshold (energy detect) or if a Wi-Fi signal is being transmitted (carrier sense). Due to the nature of WLAN architectures, there is no requirement for all stations to be able to hear all other stations existing in the same BSS. This is because the wireless AP forms a kind of hub for the BSS. A station may be able to hear the AP and the AP may be able to hear another station, but the two stations may not be able to hear each other. This results in what is commonly known as the hidden node problem, as you likely remember from CWNA studies. For this reason, wireless networks must use other forms of carrier sense in addition to CCA to deal with medium access control.

The other form is virtual carrier sense, which uses a network allocation vector (NAV), and is provided by the MAC and not the PHY. The NAV is a timer in each station that is used to determine if the station can utilize the medium. If the NAV has a value of 0, the station may contend for the medium. If the NAV has a value greater than 0, the station must wait until the timer counts down to 0 to contend for the medium. Stations configure their NAV timers based on Duration fields in other frames using the medium. For example, if a station detects a frame with a specific duration set in the Duration field, it will set the NAV timer to this duration and will wait until that time has expired before contending for access.

Both the physical carrier sense and the virtual carrier sense must show that the medium is available before the station can contend for access. If the NAV timer reaches 0 and the station uses CCA to detect activity on the medium only to find there is such activity, the station still cannot transmit. In this case, another frame may be pulled from the medium and used to set a new NAV timer value for countdown. While it may seem that this would prevent a station from ever communicating, the rate of frame transfer is so high that all these actions usually take place in far less than one second.

 An additional form of carrier sense that is not often written about is what you might call *phantom frame sensing*. In this scenario, the PHY reads an incoming PLCP header length value and loses the incoming signal completely. However, since the header length was read, the device can still defer to the rest of the phantom frame.

Interframe Spacing

After the station has determined that the medium is available using carrier sensing techniques, it still cannot communicate immediately. Instead, it must observe interframe space (IFS) policies. IFS is a time interval in which frames cannot be transmitted by stations within a BSS. This space between frames ensures that frames do not overlap each other. The time interval differs depending on the frame type and the applicable IFS type for that frame.

While the IFS implementation in IEEE 802.11 systems can result in the appearance of Quality of Service (QoS), it should not be confused with 802.11e or any Layer 3 or higher QoS solution. IFS is an 802.11 feature that allows for dependent frames to be processed in a timely manner. For example, a standard 802.11 data frame is transmitted using the DIFS interval, and the ACK to this data frame is sent back using the SIFS interval. Because the ACK uses a SIFS interval, which is shorter in time than DIFS, the ACK frame will take priority over any other standard data frames that are waiting to be transmitted. This way, the original station that transmitted the data frame will receive the ACK frame and not attempt to resend the data frame. The frame to IFS interval relationships that are specified in the 802.11 standard increase the probability that frames will be processed in their proper sequence.

We have mentioned some of the IFS types defined by the 802.11 standard already in earlier chapters. These IFS types include the following types and will now be covered in more detail:

- SIFS and RIFS
- PIFS
- DIFS
- EIFS
- AIFS

The Short Interframe Space (SIFS) is the shortest of the available IFS parameters in 802.11 devices preceding 802.11n. The new RIFS (reduced IFS) IFS is even shorter still, and it was introduced in 802.11n but it was deprecated in 802.11ac for 5 GHz PHYs; however, it is still in use with the Directional Multi Gigabit (DMG) PHY of 802.11ad (though the standard indicates that it may be removed from there as well in a future revision). Frames that are specified to use SIFS will take priority over frames that are specified to use PIFS, AIFS, DIFS, or EIFS. This priority function is simply a result of the IFS length. Since the SIFS is shorter than AIFS, PIFS, and DIFS, stations that are waiting to send a frame that is specified to use a SIFS interval will have a shorter wait time and will therefore have access to the WM before other stations with frames specified for longer IFS types.

- SIFS is used for many different frames including:
- ACK frames immediately following the receipt of a data frame
- CTS frames sent as a response to RTS frames
- Data frames that immediately follow CTS frames
- With the exception of first exchange and error conditions, all frame exchanges made in PCF mode, which is not implemented
- With the exception of the first fragment, all fragment frames that are part of a fragment burst

As technically defined by the IEEE 802.11 standard as amended, the SIFS time interval is to be the time from the end of the last symbol of the previous frame to the beginning of the first symbol of the preamble of the subsequent frame as seen at the air interface. The accuracy level required is +/-10% of the slot time for the PHY in use. For example, the actual SIFS time interval must be within 2 μs of the specified time interval for the DSSS PHY. Slot times for the various PHYs are listed on the next page.

The SIFS times for the various PHYs are listed here:

- FHSS – 28 µs
- DSSS – 10 µs
- OFDM (including HT and VHT) – 16 µs
- HR/DSSS – 10 µs
- ERP – 10 µs

The Reduced IFS (RIFS) is only 2 µs in length and can be used in place of the SIFS in 802.11n networks that do not allow legacy devices (Greenfield mode). If the 802.11n HT PHY is operating in Greenfield mode, which is very uncommon, the RIFS may be used. Since this greatly reduces the time between burst frames as well as between data frames and acknowledgement frames, the overall throughput of the network is improved. However, practically no Greenfield mode HT networks have been implemented because either another nearby network or a single non-HT client in the range of the cell makes it impossible. 802.11ac does not use the RIFS, and it is likely to be completely removed in a later update to the standard.

The Point (Coordination Function) Interframe Space (PIFS) is neither the shortest nor longest interval, resulting in a priority greater than DIFS, but less than SIFS. When an AP needs to switch the network from DCF mode to PCF mode, it will use PIFS frames. PCF is an optional part of IEEE 802.11 and has not been implemented in any market devices. The PIFS duration interval is equal to the SIFS interval for the PHY and one slot time duration for the PHY. For example, DSSS has a 20 µs slot time and a 10 µs SIFS interval resulting in a PIFS interval in a DSSS PHY of 30 µs. For another example, the OFDM PHY has a 9 µs slot time and a 16 µs SIFS interval, resulting in a PIFS interval in an OFDM PHY of 25 µs.

The following are the slot times for the 802.11 PHYs operating in 2.4 and 5 GHz:

- DSSS – 20 µs
- HR/DSSS – 20 µs
- ERP – 20 µs (long); 9 µs (short)
- OFDM – 9 µs
- HT – 20 µs (Long in 2.4 GHz); 9 µs (short in 2.4 GHz and always used in 5 GHz)
- VHT – 9 µs

The Distributed (Coordination Function) Interframe Space (DIFS) is the longest of the three IFS types covered so far. It is used by standard data frames. The greater delay interval ensures that frames specified for SIFS and PIFS intervals can transmit before DIFS data frames. The DIFS interval is calculated as the PHYs SIFS interval plus two times the PHYs slot time. Based on the same numbers used in the previous paragraphs for the PIFS interval calculations and this new algorithm for calculating the DIFS interval, the DSSS PHY has a DIFS interval of 50 μs and the OFDM PHY has a DIFS interval of 34 μs.

The Arbitration IFS (AIFS) is used in quality of service (QoS) stations (those implementing EDCA). AIFS is used for the transmission of all data frames, management frames, and select control frames by a QoS station. The control frames using AIFS include:

- PS-POLL
- RTS
- CTS (when not responding to an RTS)
- BlockAckReq
- BlockAck

The Extended Interframe Space (EIFS) is used when a frame reception begins, but the received frame is incomplete or is corrupted based on the Frame Check Sequence (FCS) value. When the last frame the station received was corrupted, the station uses EIFS for the next frame that it transmits. The EIFS interval is the longest of the IFS intervals, and is calculated based on the following more complex algorithm:

```
EIFS = SIFS + (8 X ACKsize) + Preamble Length + PLCP Header Length + DIFS
```

The time calculation is the amount of time in microseconds that it takes to transfer the 8 ACKs, preamble, and PLCP header. As you can see, the EIFS is more than the DIFS and SIFS combined.

Contention Window (CW)
The IFS delay interval is not the end of the wait for devices that are seeking time on the wireless medium. After the IFS delay interval has passed, the device must then initiate a random backoff algorithm and then contend for the medium. This random backoff algorithm is processed and applied using the contention window.

The phrase *contention window* has caused much confusion, but it is the phrase in use in the 802.11 standard. This "window" is a range of integers from which one is chosen at random to become the backoff timer for the immediate frame queued for transmission. Think of it like a contention range instead of a contention window and it will be a little easier for you.

All stations having a frame to transmit choose a random integer within the range specified as the contention window. Next the predefined algorithm multiplies the randomly-chosen integer by a slot time. The slot time is a fixed-length time interval that is defined for each PHY such as DSSS, FHSS, or OFDM. For example, FHSS used a slot time of 50 μs and DSSS uses a slot time of 20 μs.

As you can see, there are definite variations among the different PHYs supported in the IEEE 802.11 standard as amended. The 802.11n amendment used the standard 9 μs slot time used in existing PHYs that support OFDM.

Now that you have most of the pieces to the media contention puzzle, you can begin to put them together to understand how a wireless station decides when it should try to communicate on the medium. To understand this, imagine that a station has a data frame that it needs to transmit on the medium. This data frame will be required to use the DIFS IFS since it is a standard data frame. Furthermore, imagine that the station uses carrier sense to determine that a frame is currently being transmitted. For discussion's sake, let us assume that the station detected that the frame being transmitted had a Duration/ID field value of 20 μs. The station sets its NAV to count down the 20 μs and waits. The NAV reaches 0, and the station uses carrier sense and detects that the medium is silent. At this time the station must wait for the DIFS interval to expire, and since the station is using the DSSS PHY, it waits for 50 μs. Next, the station waits for the random backoff time period to expire, and when it does the station uses carrier sense and detects that the medium is silent. The station begins transmitting the data frame. All of this assumes the network is using the DCF, otherwise the AIFS would be used before a QoS Data frame is transmitted.

Ultimately, the carrier sense, IFS, and random backoff times are used to decrease the likelihood that any two stations will try to transmit at the same time on the medium. The IFS parameters are also used to provide priority to the more time-sensitive frames such as ACK and CTS frames. The CCA (PHY and MAC), IFS, variable contention window, and random backoff times, together, form the core of DCF.

Even with all these efforts, a collision can still occur. To deal with these scenarios, acknowledgement frames or ACK frames are used. An ACK frame is a short frame that uses the SIFS IFS to let the sending device know that the receiving device has indeed received the frame. If the sending device does not receive an ACK frame, it will attempt to retransmit the frame. Since the retransmitted frame will be transmitted using the rules and guidelines we have talked about so far, chances are the next frame—or one of the next few—will make it through without collisions.

Figure 6.1 illustrates the various components of DCF working together is from the 802.11-2016 standard.

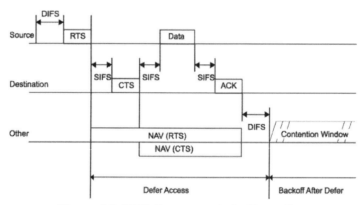

Figure 6.1: DCF Components in Operation

Enhanced Distributed Channel Access (EDCA)

802.11e introduced QoS to the 802.11 family. It implemented a Layer 2 QoS solution for the wireless link. It is the responsibility of the Ethernet-connected devices (APs or controllers) to convert the 802.11 QoS markings to 802.1p and/or DSCP markings for communications on the wired side.

802.11e introduced the Enhanced Distributed Channel Access (EDCA) and the EDCA Function (EDCAF). Today's QoS stations have four queues (though the standard now defines six) and each queue has its own EDCAF. So EDCA is the architectural algorithm and an EDCAF is a specific implementation of EDCA for a queue.

The basic enhancement provided by EDCA is that 802.11 frames are assigned an access category (AC) in one of four values:

- AC_BK – Background—lowest priority
- AC_BE – Best Effort—lowest priority
- AC_VI – Video—middle priority
- AC_VO – Voice—highest priority

Higher-priority categories use smaller contention windows. For example, AC_VO begins with a minimum value of 3 and a maximum value of 7, whereas AC_BK and AC_BE begin with a minimum value of 15 and a maximum value of 1023. As you can see, AC_BK and AC_BE frames (standard data) begin their CW at roughly twice the value of the maximum that a voice frame (AC_VO) would have. Therefore, higher-priority traffic tends to gain access to the medium more frequently than lower priority traffic because they select shorter random backoff times. This variation in random backoff times based on frame priority as a key differentiation between DCF and EDCA.

Additionally, the IFS used is the AIFS, which has a variable duration depending on the AIFS number (AIFSN) associated with the AC. Higher priority ACs have lower AIFSNs and lower priority ACs have higher AIFSNs. The result is that even the IFS is variable depending on the priority of the frame and this is yet another key differentiation between DCF and EDCA.

Now, the time will come when data traffic has counted down the backoff timer such that it will beat voice traffic to the medium, but the best it could hope for is gaining access to the medium once for every two times that voice does in most cases. The real odds are far worse for data traffic, but remember, this is all measured in milliseconds and data traffic will still get through, but latency problems for voice traffic is removed.

The Wi-Fi Alliance created the Wireless Multimedia (WMM) certification to validate that equipment properly implements EDCA as defined in 802.11e (and now 802.11-2016). Devices that are WMM certified should be selected for the Bill of Materials when QoS is essential. In reality, very few 802.11n or 802.11ac devices are sold today that do not implement a QoS STA.

Wi-Fi Multimedia

As stated previously, WMM is the Wi-Fi Alliance certification that indicates a device implements an effective subset of EDCA as introduced in 802.11e. In addition to WMM parameters for the ACs and AIFSNs, they introduce WMM Power Save and WMM Admission Control, also based on capabilities specified in 802.11. WMM specifies the default parameters for the 802.11 ACs as defined in Table 6.1. Note that aCWmin is a variable defined for each PHY in the 802.11 standard. The variables are defined as:

- DSSS – 31
- HR/DSSS – 31
- OFDM – 15
- ERP – 31 or 15 (depending on the need for backward compatibility)
- HT – 15
- VHT – 15

AC	CW(min)	CW(max)	AIFSN
AC_BK	aCWmin	aCWmax	7
AC_BE	aCWmin	aCWmax	3
AC_VI	(aCWmin + 1) / 2 – 1	aCWmin	2
AC_VO	(aCWmin + 1) / 4 – 1	(aCWmin + 1) / 2 - 1	2

Table 6.1: WMM Default Settings

With the values provided for the various PHYs above and the table from WMM (Table 6.1) you can determine that the CWmin for AC_VO would be 3 for VHT ((15 + 1) / 4 – 1 = 3). This would also be the default value for HT, OFDM, and ERP if not protection is required. Other values can be calculated manually, but the following list gives you the results for HT, VHT and OFDM:

- AC_BK – CWmin (15)
- AC_BE – CWmin (15)
- AC_VI – CWmin (7)
- AC_VO – CWmin (3)

Remember that the CWmin value is the starting upper boundary of the contention window, meaning that a STA will choose an integer between 0 and CWmin for the first transmission attempt. If a retry is required, it will double the CWmin and add one on each retry until CWmax is reached. Therefore, based on Table 6.1, the default for an AC_VO frame is that it would never have a CWmax above 7 or a current upper boundary of the contention window beyond that.

Additionally, Figure 6.2 shows the recommended 802.D priorities mapped to the four implemented ACs in 802.11 with their WMM names provided: Background, Best Effort, Video, and Voice.

Priority	802.1D Priority (= UP)	802.1D Designation	Access Category	WMM Designation
lowest	1	BK	AC_BK	Background
	2	-		
	0	BE	AC_BE	Best Effort
	3	EE		
	4	CL	AC_VI	Video
	5	VI		
	6	VO	AC_VO	Voice
highest	7	NC		

Figure 6.2: WMM Mapping of 802.1D User Priority (UP) to 802.11 ACs

QoS Configuration and Operations

EDCA or WMM parameters can be configured in most enterprise APs, controllers, and management systems; however, just because they can be does not mean they should be. Most enterprise environments function well using the WMM default parameters. If they need to be adjusted, ensure you monitor the results and be prepared to reconfigure them back to the defaults if a positive impact is not achieved. Figure 6.3 shows the EDCA/WMM parameters configuration interface in a wireless system.

WMM parameters are included in the Beacon frame from the AP. A WMM-compliant STA is expected to update its WMM parameters to match those of the AP to which it is associated. This behavior results in shared parameters throughout the BSS. Before associating with an AP, the STA must set its WMM parameters to the default values specified in the WMM specification by the Wi-Fi Alliance. These parameters may also be in Probe Response and Association Response frames and a STA must update its parameters to match those provided if the frames are targeted to the STA.

Figure 6.3: Configuring EDCA/WMM Parameters

The TxOP is the transmit opportunity and it defines the maximum amount of time a QoS STA that wins the TxOP may use the medium in bursts. This parameter can also be defined for each AC queue. A TxOP of 0 means that the STA can send only one frame and must then enter contention procedures again. Note that the default WMM values are in Figure 6.3 and that both AC_BK and AC_BE use a TxOP of 0. Also note that, with allowance by WMM, the AP may use different parameters than it advertises for the clients to use. This allows the AP to grant itself greater priority given that the greatest volume of frames on the medium are AP-to-client and not client-to-AP. Again, this is allowed in the WMM specification.

Verifying QoS Parameters

You can verify QoS parameters in two ways: look at the AP configuration or capture frames to view the WMM parameters. Remember, the frames will only tell you what the AP expects the clients to use for their WMM parameter set. The AP may use a different parameter set for itself, which is not announced and must be viewed in the configuration.

The WMM parameter set can be viewed in the following frames:

- Beacon
- Probe Response
- Association Response

Figure 6.4 shows the WMM parameter set in the Beacon frame from a NETGEAR AP. You can see that the contention window, AIFSN, and TxOP are all configured in the parameter set. The Probe Response frame would contain the identical information when transmitted from this same AP. Additionally, the Association Response frame will have matching information.

```
∨ Vendor specific: MICROSOFT CORP., WME
    Tag: Vendor Specific
    Length: 24
    OUI: MICROSOFT CORP.
    OUI Type: 2
    Type: 0x02 (Unknown value)
    WME Subtype: Parameter Element
    WME Version: 1
  > WME QoS Info: 0x84
    Reserved: Must Be Zero
  ∨ Ac Parameters: ACI 0 (Best Effort), ACM No, AIFSN 3, ECWmin 4, ECWmax 6, TXOP 0
    > ACI / AIFSN Field: 3
    > ECW: 64
      TXOP Limit: 0
  ∨ Ac Parameters: ACI 1 (Background), ACM No, AIFSN 7, ECWmin 4, ECWmax 10, TXOP 0
    > ACI / AIFSN Field: 27
    > ECW: A4
      TXOP Limit: 0
  ∨ Ac Parameters: ACI 2 (Video), ACM No, AIFSN 1, ECWmin 3, ECWmax 4, TXOP 94
    > ACI / AIFSN Field: 41
    > ECW: 43
      TXOP Limit: 94
  ∨ Ac Parameters: ACI 3 (Voice), ACM No, AIFSN 1, ECWmin 2, ECWmax 3, TXOP 47
    > ACI / AIFSN Field: 61
    > ECW: 32
      TXOP Limit: 47
```

Figure 6.4: WMM Parameter Set in a Beacon Frame

Consider this, the STA could use the Beacon or Probe Response frame to decide if it wants to connect to the BSS based on WMM parameters. We are not suggesting many if any clients do this, but they could. However, the client is required by WMM certification (assuming it is WMM certified) to apply the WMM parameter set in the Association Response frame when connecting and it is further required to apply any changes that might occur in the Beacon frame during the session. This is the behavior defined in the WMM specification upon which WMM certification is based.

Ensuring End-to-End QoS

Quality of Service (QoS), in the domain of computer networking, can be defined as "the tools and technologies that manage network traffic in order to provide the performance demanded by the users of the network." When implementing QoS, the accuracy of your requirements determines the benefits of your efforts. If the quality requirements are not accurate, the QoS solutions that you implement are not likely to get the results you require. In fact, a poorly designed QoS solution can cause more problems than it solves because it is not properly tuned. Therefore, successful QoS implementation begins with quality requirements development and this usually begins with application review.

Once you have a clear picture of the quality requirements in your network, you can begin to consider the different QoS tools that may assist you in meeting those requirements. These tools will be targeted at reducing latency, jitter, and delay, and they may accomplish these tasks using prioritization, queuing, and even dedicated connections. You can think of QoS tools as a collection of technologies that allow you to use any physical network more efficiently. QoS tools cannot make your network faster, but they can enforce or suggest better use of your network.

The most common driver of QoS on WLANs is VoIP. VoIP packets are different in their demands from standard data packets such as e-mail, FTP, or network printing. VoIP packets demand the following:

- Fast delivery
- Sequential ordering
- Accuracy of data

VoIP packets have demands that are like those of traditional data packets, and they have demands that are very different. The first demand is not usually a requirement of traditional data, and that demand is fast delivery. That statement might seem odd, but traditional data can still get through if there are delays in delivery, VoIP data delivery failures cause calls to drop or quality of audio to suffer. The ultimate reasons for fast delivery are human involvement and the demands of the concept. By human involvement, we mean that humans are listening to the telephone conversation and they must be able to perceive what the other party is saying. If the humans using the system cannot get the results they need, they will discontinue their use of the system. When we speak of the demands of the concept, we're referring to the reality that sound is a stream and if the stream is broken or delayed, its characteristics change.

For example, if you are listening to a VoIP conversation and there are gaps between the sounds (assuming the connection isn't broken completely), you will have a very difficult time listening to that conversation. You may not even be able to recognize what is being said. This reality is the reason that most VoIP systems will drop a phone call if too many packets are lost or if the delay is too great. Fast delivery is important in VoIP systems.

All data must be sequential when it is passed up to the upper layers of the OSI, and many applications accommodate this using the TCP protocol. TCP will resequence the packets if they arrive out of sequence. A UDP solution, such as VoIP, does not receive the benefit of sequencing at the Transport layer. Therefore, the application must take responsibility for resequencing the data. A VoIP processor can certainly do this task, but the problem is that this resequencing adds extra processing delay and can be the factor that leads to dropped calls or poor quality. In a standard IP network, there are few ways to guarantee that all packets will travel the same route and arrive in sequence at the destination; however, QoS can be used to ensure that the packets arrive quickly enough so that there is time remaining for resequencing, if it is needed.

The final requirement is that the data must be accurate. There is no time to retransmit data in a VoIP system. This requirement means that the links must be stable and error rates must be very low. QoS can only help with this insomuch that a less congested network is less likely to generate errors.

Why are you learning all of this? The answer is simple: the QoS we learned about earlier in this chapter is only on the wireless link. For QoS to work properly with your VoIP and other demanding applications, it must be implemented end-to-end. If it's only on the wireless link, it will break while traveling the wired network. If it's only on the wired network, it may break when traveling the wireless network. It must be implemented end-to-end.

The phrase *end-to-end QoS* indicates that all devices in the communication chain (clients, APs, controllers, switches, routers, gateways, etc.) understand and implement the QoS required within their internal frame and packet processing algorithms. If one router in the chain is stripping of QoS tags, from that point forward in the transmission, QoS will not be implemented. If that router is close to either end of the VoIP conversation, it can cause severe call problems.

To validate end-to-end QoS, you can capture frames just before the are sent to a VoIP phone to see if they are properly tagged at the end of the transfer link chain. This capture can be done using a Wi-Fi analyzer on the wireless link at both ends. Do the frames have the proper QoS markings leaving the AP and going to the VoWLAN client? If not, you could capture on the wired side just before the frames enter the AP to ensure the AP is not the problem. If it is not the problem, continue stepping back in the link chain until you find the device that is killing your QoS. It is not always an easy task without advanced configuration tools, but it can be achieved manually.

Chapter Summary

In this chapter, you learned about contention algorithms used in 802.11 WLANs. These included DCF and EDCA. You also learned about WMM parameters used by QoS stations and how to determine the parameters in use for a BSS. Finally, you learned of the important of QoS in the network and how to validate its end-to-end implementation.

Facts to Remember

- DCF is used for standard data frames.
- EDCA is used for QoS data frames.
- WMM specified default parameters for EDCA operations.
- WMM parameters are advertised in Beacon, Probe Response, and Association Response frames.
- The AP may use different WMM parameters than it advertises for the clients to use.
- The AIFS is calculated for each AC and is not a fixed value.
- WMM implements four ACs mapped to 8 UPs.
- End-to-end QoS is essential to effective QoS operations.

Review Questions

1. What is the shortest IFS used on all PHYs?
   a. SIFS
   b. DIFS
   c. EIFS
   d. AIFS

2. What is defined as a range of integers from which a single integer is chosen for the random backoff timer?
   a. NAV
   b. Contention Window
   c. PIFS
   d. Access Category

3. Which AC has the highest priority with default WMM parameters?
   a. AC_VI
   b. AC_VO
   c. AC_BK
   d. AC_BE

4. What is the default parameter for CWmin in the AC_VI AC using WMM parameters?
   a. 3
   b. 15
   c. 31
   d. 7

5. You see two WMM parameter sets in an AP configuration and they differ. What does this usually indicate?
   a. The AP uses the same parameters as the clients
   b. The AP uses different parameters than the clients
   c. The vendor has implemented a non-standard method
   d. You have blurry vision

6. What frame does not contain the WMM parameter settings?
    a. Probe Request
    b. Probe Response
    c. Beacon
    d. Association Response

7. A client STA must do what when it detects a change in the WMM parameter settings in a Beacon frame when it is associated with the transmitting AP?
    a. Nothing
    b. Disconnect
    c. Change its WMM parameters to match every time
    d. Change its WMM parameters to match if not using VoIP

8. What is the purpose of the Duration field in relation to the DCF and EDCA procedures?
    a. Configure the NAV timer in the hearing STAs
    b. Configure the random backoff timer in the hearing STAs
    c. Hearing STAs can select the appropriate IFS based on the value
    d. Nothing, it does not play a role in either procedure

9. What is a key differentiator between DCF and EDCA?
    a. EDCA requires the use of SIFS and DCF does not
    b. EDCA requires the use of a random backoff timer and DCF does not
    c. EDCA allows for variable contention window ranges and DCF does not
    d. EDCA can use shorter slot times than DCF

10. How are the slot times defined in the 802.11 standard?
    a. They are not defined; hardware manufacturers can define them as they will
    b. They are defined for each PHY
    c. They are defined universally with all PHYs using the same value
    d. They are defined variably for each data rate

Review Answers

1. The correct answer is A. The Short Interframe Space (SIFS) is the shortest IFS and is used to prioritize frames that should be delivered in a quick sequence.

2. The correct answer is B. The contention window is the range from which a STA will choose an integer to multiple by the slot time and determine the random backoff time.

3. The correct answer is B. AC_VO (voice) has the highest priority followed by AC_VI (video).

4. The correct answer is D. The default value for CWmin in AC_VI is 7 and the default value for AC_VO is 3.

5. The correct answer is B. The WMM specification states that an AP may use a different WMM parameter set internally than it advertises to the client STAs.

6. The correct answer is A. The Probe Request frame does not include WMM parameters as it would not be essential there. The STA must set its parameters according to the AP's announcement. Therefore, the parameters are in Beacon, Probe Response, and Association frames.

7. The correct answer is C. To be compliant with WMM certification, a client must implement the WMM parameters every time it detects a change in the Beacon frame.

8. The correct answer is A. The Duration field is used to configure the NAV countdown timer in the STA.

9. The correct answer is C. The three major differentiators between DCF and EDCA are: transmit queues, varying AIFS durations, and varying contention windows for different priority frames.

10. The correct answer is B. Slot times are defined for each PHY in the standard. The random backoff integer selected from the contention window range is multiplied by the slot time to determine the duration of the random backoff.

Chapter 7: MAC Operations

Objectives Covered:

6.3 Analyze data frame exchanges

6.5 Analyze behavior and resolve problems related to MAC layer operations

When it comes to MAC Layer operations, the most important things to understand is how the 802.11 MAC works. You've been learning about this all throughout this book. In this chapter, you will see how to capture specific frame exchanges and analyze them, and you will explore some specific MAC Layer operations in addition to data exchanges that are important to understand and analyze. You will begin by learning how to analyze data frame exchanged. This chapter will be mostly demonstration of the process.

For reference purposes, all captures shown in this chapter were created using Wireshark on a MacBook Pro with a 3x3:3 802.11ac internal adapter. Wireshark is chosen because, if you have a MacBook, you can use it with not extra licensing costs. The same captures could be created using CommView for Wi-Fi, OmniPeek, Wi-Fi Analyzer Pro, or any other capture tool that supports 802.11ac and earlier operations. In addition to Wireshark, Airtool, a mac OS add-on is used to simplify the capturing process.

Analyzing Data Frame Exchanges

Data frame exchanges are the actions that drive your users to use the WLAN. They are not concerned with Beacon frames, Probe Request frames, and other such frames as much as data frames. Don't misunderstand, they don't know that the data frames are their biggest concern, but they are. Of course, we know that the data frames couldn't do what they needed to do if all the other control and management frames weren't working as we need them to, but we'll keep that secret to ourselves.

In this section, you will learn to capture data frames, QoS data frames, acknowledgement frames, RTS and CTS frames, and Block Acknowledgement frames.

Capturing Data Frames

Data frames will have a Type of 10 and the Subtype of 0000. The protocol analyzer will typically decode this and indicate that it is a Data frame. Because Data frames are often sent at much higher data rates than Beacon, Ack and other management and control frames, it is important to capture near the device transmitting and receiving the Data frames you wish to capture.

For example, if you attempt to capture data frames from a client that is on the opposite side of the AP from you, you may not be able to properly demodulate the data frames because they are sent at a data rate at which you lack the SNR to demodulate them properly. You may see data frames from the AP to the remote client, but not properly demodulate the data frames from the remote client to the AP.

Figure 7.1 shows a typical Data frame revealing the Type and Subtype fields.

```
▼ Frame Control Field: 0x0862
        .... ..00 = Version: 0
        .... 10.. = Type: Data frame (2)
        0000 .... = Subtype: 0
```

Figure 7.1: A Typical Data frame

As a side note that will not be essential for the CWAP exam, the Airtool utility makes capturing frames simple on a Macbook. Install the Airtool utility (at the time of writing, it is on version 1.7) and Wireshark and you have everything you need to capture frames. Figure 7.2 shows the basic interface of Airtool.

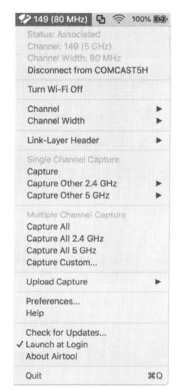

Figure 7.2: Airtool Interface

With this simple and free tool, having a lot of powerful complexity behind the scenes, you can quickly launch a capture that will be saved to a Wireshark capture file at the location of your choosing (the default is the desktop). Then you simply open the capture file and look at your results. If you prefer to analyze the capture in more advanced Wi-Fi analysis tools that Wireshark, simply open the PCAP file in those tools. To download and install this tool on your MacBook (sorry, Windows users), visit cwnp.link/airtool.

Capturing QoS Data Frames

QoS Data frames will have the Type of 10 and the Subtype of 1000. Most protocol analyzers will decode and label the frame as a QoS Data frame in addition to showing the values of the Type/Subtype fields. The QoS Control element will indicate the priority of the frame. Figure 7.3 shows a Best Effort QoS Data frame and Figure 7.4 shows a Voice QoS Data frame.

```
▼ Qos Control: 0x0000
    .... .... .... 0000 = TID: 0
    [.... .... .... .000 = Priority: Best Effort (Best Effort) (0)]
    .... .... ...0 .... = QoS bit 4: Bits 8-15 of QoS Control field are TXOP Duration Requested
    .... .... .00. .... = Ack Policy: Normal Ack (0x0)
    .... .... 0... .... = Payload Type: MSDU
    0000 0000 .... .... = TXOP Duration Requested: 0 (no TXOP requested)
```

Figure 7.3: Best Effort QoS Data frame

```
▼ Qos Control: 0x0006
    .... .... .... 0110 = TID: 6
    [.... .... .... .110 = Priority: Voice (Voice) (6)]
    .... .... ...0 .... = QoS bit 4: Bits 8-15 of QoS Control field are TXOP Duration Requested
    .... .... .00. .... = Ack Policy: Normal Ack (0x0)
    .... .... 0... .... = Payload Type: MSDU
    0000 0000 .... .... = TXOP Duration Requested: 0 (no TXOP requested)
```

Figure 7.4 Voice QoS Data frame

Capturing QoS Data frames is no different from capturing standard Data frames. Capture near the device for which you wish to capture transmitted and received data frames.

Capturing Acknowledgements and Block Acknowledgements

Standard Acknowledgements are simply short frames used to say, "I received your communication." It's like nodding your head while you have a conversation with someone. Acks mean the frame was received. No Ack indicates to the transmitter that a frame expecting an Ack was not received and, therefore, a retransmission attempt occurs.

Interestingly, as you can see in Figure 7.5, Acks are used while setting up a Block Ack agreement.

A STA should send an Ack frame immediately after receiving any non-CRC-error frame requiring an Ack frame. If it does not, the sending of the original frame will retransmit. Retransmitted frames can be identified because the Retry bit in the Frame Control fields will be set to 1.

Block Acknowledgments may include a Add Black Ack Request and Response preceding the data exchange followed by the Add Block Ack Request and Add Block Ack Response. To capture such an exchange, setup your capture device near the AP or near the client that will perform the exchange with the AP. From either location, you should be able to capture the exchange because both the AP and client in question need to be able to transmit and receive all frames in the exchange. The Add Block Ack Request and Add Block Ack Response will be Action frames in your capture. Figure 7.5 shows this exchange process as a concept.

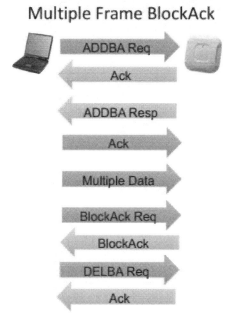

Figure 7.5: Add Block Ack Request and Response and Data Exchange

In Figure 7.6 you see the Add Block Ack Request frame. Note that it is from a client to the NETGEAR AP in this case.

```
3253 23.921724    b8:63:4d:4c:27:c7    Netgear_07:10:27       802.11  6.0   -45 dBm    62 Action, SN=803, FN=0, Flags=........C
3254 23.921798                         b8:63:4d:4c:27:c7 (b... 802.11  6.0   -38 dBm    39 Acknowledgement, Flags=........C
3255 23.921917    Netgear_07:10:27     b8:63:4d:4c:27:c7       802.11  6.0   -37 dBm    62 Action, SN=252, FN=0, Flags=........C
3256 23.921991                         Netgear_07:10:27 (9c... 802.11  6.0   -45 dBm    39 Acknowledgement, Flags=........C
3257 23.922064    b8:63:4d:4c:27:c7    Broadcast              802.11        -47 dBm    438 QoS Data, SN=2, FN=0, Flags=.p.....TC
3258 23.922640    b8:63:4d:4c:27:c7    Broadcast              802.11        -47 dBm    438 QoS Data, SN=2, FN=0, Flags=.p..R..TC
3259 23.923230    b8:63:4d:4c:27:c7    Broadcast              802.11        -47 dBm    438 QoS Data, SN=2, FN=0, Flags=.p..R..TC
3260 23.923382    b8:63:4d:4c:27:c7    Broadcast              802.11        -47 dBm    438 QoS Data, SN=2, FN=0, Flags=.p..R..TC
3261 23.923457                         b8:63:4d:4c:27:c7 (b... 802.11 24.0   -41 dBm    39 Acknowledgement, Flags=........C
    .000 0000 0011 1100 = Duration: 60 microseconds
    Receiver address: Netgear_07:10:27 (9c:3d:cf:07:10:27)
    Destination address: Netgear_07:10:27 (9c:3d:cf:07:10:27)
    Transmitter address: b8:63:4d:4c:27:c7 (b8:63:4d:4c:27:c7)
    Source address: b8:63:4d:4c:27:c7 (b8:63:4d:4c:27:c7)
    BSS Id: Netgear_07:10:27 (9c:3d:cf:07:10:27)
    .... .... .... 0000 = Fragment number: 0
    0011 0010 0011 .... = Sequence number: 803
    Frame check sequence: 0x0d00b6b3 [correct]
    [FCS Status: Good]
▼ IEEE 802.11 wireless LAN management frame
  ▼ Fixed parameters
      Category code: Block Ack (3)
      Action code: Add Block Ack Request (0x00)
      Dialog token: 0x5a
    ▶ Block Ack Parameters: 0x1003, A-MSDUs, Block Ack Policy
      Block Ack Timeout: 0x0000
    ▶ Block Ack Starting Sequence Control (SSC): 0x0020
```

Figure 7.6: Add Block Ack Request Action frame

In Figure 7.7 you see the Add Block Ack Response frame. This frame is transmitted from the NETGEAR AP to the requesting client. Between the Request and Response and after the response is the standard ACK frame.

```
3255 23.921917    Netgear_07:10:27     b8:63:4d:4c:27:c7       802.11  6.0   -37 dBm    62 Action, SN=252, FN=0, Flags=........C
3256 23.921991                         Netgear_07:10:27 (9c... 802.11  6.0   -45 dBm    39 Acknowledgement, Flags=........C
3257 23.922064    b8:63:4d:4c:27:c7    Broadcast              802.11        -47 dBm    438 QoS Data, SN=2, FN=0, Flags=.p.....TC
3258 23.922640    b8:63:4d:4c:27:c7    Broadcast              802.11        -47 dBm    438 QoS Data, SN=2, FN=0, Flags=.p..R..TC
3259 23.923230    b8:63:4d:4c:27:c7    Broadcast              802.11        -47 dBm    438 QoS Data, SN=2, FN=0, Flags=.p..R..TC
3260 23.923382    b8:63:4d:4c:27:c7    Broadcast              802.11        -47 dBm    438 QoS Data, SN=2, FN=0, Flags=.p..R..TC
3261 23.923457                         b8:63:4d:4c:27:c7 (b... 802.11 24.0   -41 dBm    39 Acknowledgement, Flags=........C
    .000 0000 0011 1100 = Duration: 60 microseconds
    Receiver address: b8:63:4d:4c:27:c7 (b8:63:4d:4c:27:c7)
    Destination address: b8:63:4d:4c:27:c7 (b8:63:4d:4c:27:c7)
    Transmitter address: Netgear_07:10:27 (9c:3d:cf:07:10:27)
    Source address: Netgear_07:10:27 (9c:3d:cf:07:10:27)
    BSS Id: Netgear_07:10:27 (9c:3d:cf:07:10:27)
    .... .... .... 0000 = Fragment number: 0
    0000 1111 1100 .... = Sequence number: 252
    Frame check sequence: 0x89fd497d [correct]
    [FCS Status: Good]
▼ IEEE 802.11 wireless LAN management frame
  ▼ Fixed parameters
      Category code: Block Ack (3)
      Action code: Add Block Ack Response (0x01)
      Dialog token: 0x5a
      Status code: Successful (0x0000)
    ▶ Block Ack Parameters: 0x1003, A-MSDUs, Block Ack Policy
      Block Ack Timeout: 0x0000
```

Figure 7.7: Add Block Ack Response Action frame

The preceding exchange establishes the ability to perform Block Ack operations for these two STAs (the client and AP). The Add Block Ack Response will include a Block Ack Policy that indicates either immediate or delayed Block Ack. Immediate Block Ack is the most common policy. Additionally, the Block Ack Timeout Value field will specify the duration, in Time Units (TUs), within which frames must be transmitted or the Block Ack agreement it terminated.

Both Ack and Block Ack captures can be performed near the AP or near the target client. At either location, the protocol analyzer (and adapter/radio) should be able to properly capture and demodulate the frames desired.

Capturing RTS/CTS Exchanges

The final data transfer-related exchange we will explore with captures is the RTS/CTS exchange. This exchange is used as a protection mechanism when less-capable STAs are in the BSS and also to address such problems as the hidden node problem where two clients can see the AP, but the clients can't see each other.

To capture RTS/CTS exchanges, use the same guidelines for capturing data and QoS data frames. Capture near the device you want to monitor.

Figure 7.8 shows an RTS frame captured in transmission from a client (in this case, an Apple iPhone) to the AP (in this case, a NETGEAR AP). Notice that the Duration value is set to 154 microseconds. This observation is important because we will see this value decrement as we look at the CTS and Data frames. Elsewhere in this book, you learned about the RTS/CTS frames and how they are used. The purpose here is to capture them and see their contents.

```
    Type/Subtype: Request-to-send (0x001b)
▼ Frame Control Field: 0xb400
    .... ..00 = Version: 0
    .... 01.. = Type: Control frame (1)
    1011 .... = Subtype: 11
  ▼ Flags: 0x00
      .... ..00 = DS status: Not leaving DS or network is operating in AD-HOC mode (To DS: 0 From DS: 0) (0x0)
      .... .0.. = More Fragments: This is the last fragment
      .... 0... = Retry: Frame is not being retransmitted
      ...0 .... = PWR MGT: STA will stay up
      ..0. .... = More Data: No data buffered
      .0.. .... = Protected flag: Data is not protected
      0... .... = Order flag: Not strictly ordered
    .000 0000 1001 1010 = Duration: 154 microseconds
    Receiver address: Netgear_07:10:27 (9c:3d:cf:07:10:27)
    Transmitter address: b8:63:4d:4c:27:c7 (b8:63:4d:4c:27:c7)
    Frame check sequence: 0x54f6ec3d [correct]
    [FCS Status: Good]
```

Figure 7.8: RTS frame with duration value shown

The next frame of interest will be the CTS frame. It is shown in Figure 7.9. Notice that the duration has decreased by 44 microseconds down to a value of 110 microseconds. Not shown in the portion of the capture in Figure 7.9 is the fact that the 802.11 radio information section shows that the CTS frame itself took 28 microseconds of airtime. Interestingly, the SIFS duration for HT and VHT (which are the devices in use in this case) in the 5 GHz band is 16 microseconds. What is 28 plus 16? That's right! It's 44. Exactly the amount less than the duration value in the RTS frame in Figure 7.8.

```
▼ IEEE 802.11 Clear-to-send, Flags: ........C
    Type/Subtype: Clear-to-send (0x001c)
  ▼ Frame Control Field: 0xc400
      .... ..00 = Version: 0
      .... 01.. = Type: Control frame (1)
      1100 .... = Subtype: 12
    ▼ Flags: 0x00
        .... ..00 = DS status: Not leaving DS or network is operating in AD-HOC mode (To DS: 0 From DS: 0) (0x0)
        .... .0.. = More Fragments: This is the last fragment
        .... 0... = Retry: Frame is not being retransmitted
        ...0 .... = PWR MGT: STA will stay up
        ..0. .... = More Data: No data buffered
        .0.. .... = Protected flag: Data is not protected
        0... .... = Order flag: Not strictly ordered
    .000 0000 0110 1110 = Duration: 110 microseconds
    Receiver address: b8:63:4d:4c:27:c7 (b8:63:4d:4c:27:c7)
    Frame check sequence: 0xb08ff993 [correct]
    [FCS Status: Good]
```

Figure 7.9: CTS frame with duration value shown

The next frame in this exchange is a QoS Data frame which is 182 bytes in size. Now, the RTS and CTS frames were sent at 24 Mbps so that all other STAs in the BSS could hear them and decode their duration values. The QoS Data frame was sent at a much higher data rate with a duration value of 48 microseconds (not shown here), simply meaning that 48 microseconds would be required after the QoS Data frame to complete the transmission.

Here is the final question. What came after the data frame? The answer was a Block Acknowledgement in this case. It was sent at 24 Mbps. Can you guess how long it too to transmit the Block Acknowledgment frame on the medium? You know the answer (assuming everything is working great and there are no driver bugs or other odd problems). Well, after the QoS Data frame, one SIFS would be used (that's 16 microseconds). When you subtract 16 microseconds from 48 microseconds from the QoS Data frame duration value, you get 32 microseconds. That's how long it took to transfer the Block Acknowledgement.

It is useful to know that Wireshark actually calculates the duration. It is not measured somehow from the radio, but it calculated based on known factors. For example, Wireshark can know the following:

- PHY in use
- Preamble structure (length and rate it is sent at)
- PLCP header structure (length and rate it is sent at – at least it can get close)
- MPDU size and data rate it was sent at

Using this information, Wireshark performs the following or a similar calculation:

```
preamble time + frame length * 8 / data rate
```

For this reason, you will notice something important: when Wireshark does not know and report to you the data rate at which the frame was received it will also not report to you the duration required to receive the frame. Without the data rate it cannot calculate this and when you introduce multiple spatial streams it becomes even more complex for the tool.

Resolving Problems with MAC Layer Operations

MAC Layer operations can experience problems in any area of functionality. Other chapters in this study guide have provided you with detailed information on frame formats and normal operations. Earlier in this chapter, you looked specifically at capturing and analyzing data frame exchanges of varying kinds. In this section of the chapter, you will explore specific WLAN operations commonly used, problems that may be introduced, and steps you can take to solve them. The WLAN operations explored in this section include:

- Power Save Operations
- Protection Mechanisms
- Load Balancing
- Band Steering

Power Save Operations

802.11 networks can perform power save for client stations in several ways. There is a method defined in 802.11 that is what you might call traditional power save. Then there is how stations usually used it. Then there is WMM Power save. These three will be briefly addressed in this chapter.

802.11 power save, as it's usually called (it's also called legacy power save), was defined to use PS-Poll (Power Save Polling) frames. This method defined intervals at which client stations should wake up and look at a Beacon frame to see if the Traffic Indication Map (TIM) lists their AIDs as having buffered frames on the AP. Any station having buffered frames would send a PS-Poll frame to the AP, which would respond with an Ack and then begin sending data to the client station. For each Data frame sent to the client station, the More Data bit would be set to 1 as long as more frames were in the buffer. As long as the More Data bit was set to 1, the client station would respond with a PS-Poll frame to keep getting data. When the buffer is empty, the AP sets the More Data bit to 0 in the frame that emptied the buffer and sends it to the station. The station can now either stay awake or go back to sleep until the next listening time (the DTIM window).

The TIM is in the Beacon frame and indicates the AIDs of STAs with traffic buffered for them. Figure 7.10 shows the TIM in a Beacon frame with traffic buffered.

```
∨ Tag: Traffic Indication Map (TIM): DTIM 0 of 1 bitmap
    Tag Number: Traffic Indication Map (TIM) (5)
    Tag length: 4
    DTIM count: 0
    DTIM period: 2
  ∨ Bitmap control: 0x01
      .... ...1 = Multicast: True
      0000 000. = Bitmap Offset: 0x00
    Partial Virtual Bitmap: 08
    Association ID: 0x03
```
Figure 7.10: Beacon frame with TIM

Each Beacon frame includes the TIM and lists STAs with unicast frames buffered. The DTIM Beacon frame, which in the case of Figure 7.10 is every other Beacon because the period is set to 2, includes information about broadcast/multicast buffered frames as well. Note that the DTIM count is 0 (this is a DTIM version of the TIM) and multicast is set to 1 (True) indicated buffered multicast frames on the AP.

That's how 802.11 originally defined power management. It wasn't very efficient and, because of the way it worked, client vendors quickly realized they could "do power management their own way."

In the real-world, stations typically perform the following process today:

1. "Hey AP, I'm going to sleep!"
2. "Hey station, I hear you."
3. "Hey AP, I'm awake!"
4. "Hey station, I've got frames for you. Here's the first and there's more to come."
5. "Got it!"
6. "Here's the next one and there's more to come."
7. "Got it!"
8. "This is the last one I have for you."
9. "Excellent, good night!"

OK, that wasn't very technical. Let's make it more technical.

1. Null frame with PM bit set to 1
2. Ack frame
3. Null frame with PM bit set to 0
4. Ack, data frame with More Data set to 1
5. Ack frame
6. Data frame with More Data set to 1
7. Ack frame
8. Data frame with More Data set to 0
9. Ack frame, Null frame with PM bit set to 1

What is the difference between these? This creative solution works perfectly with 802.11 APs and it only requires two Null frames for every wake sleep scenario regardless of the number of frames buffered on the AP. For example, if there were 10 frames buffered on the AP for the STA, just as an example, 10 PS-Poll frames, in addition to all the data frames and Acks would have to be sent. With the creative method, two Null frames are sent. That's a savings of eight frames in this case. You can probably see why many chose to implement something other than the PS-Poll frame.

This model just presented is effectively WMM-Power Save or WMM-PS. The only significant difference is that WMM-PS provides a mechanism so that the client STA can request only buffered frames from a particular AC. This can be used, for example, to request VoIP frames, but delay receiving that frame that's part of an email message.

Protection Mechanisms

802.11, through the years, has had to implement protection mechanisms. For example, when ERP was added in 2.4 GHz, a method was required to see if any 802.11 DSSS or HR/DSSS stations were present. The ERP element includes a Non-ERP Present bit that is set to 1 if the AP has accepted a Non-ERP STA in to the BSS. It also has a User Protection bit to force members of the BSS to use RTS/CTS. When Non-ERP Present is set to 1 in the Beacon frame, Use Protection is always set to 1 as well. When the Non-ERP Present bit is set to 0, the Use Protection bit can still be set to 1 if the AP sees the Non-ERP Present bit set to 1 in a neighbor BSS. Figure 7.11 shows the ERP element of a Beacon frame.

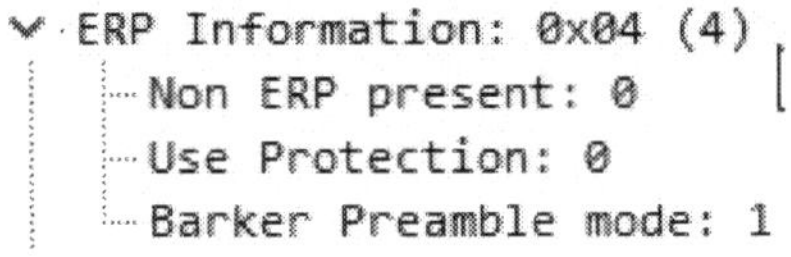

```
∨ ERP Information: 0x04 (4)
   --- Non ERP present: 0              [
   --- Use Protection: 0
   --- Barker Preamble mode: 1
```

Figure 7.11: ERP Element

Here's a catch: how to you capture the ERP element? It's a trick question because it's not about location; it's about the band. The ERP element is only seen in 2.4 GHz Beacon frames because that's where ERP operates. So, capture on 2.4 GHz and you should be able to see this information.

In addition to ERP protection, HT and VHT must have protection mechanisms. Of course, they can also use RTS/CTS and indeed they do. HT offers four modes of operation:

- Modes 0: Greenfield Mode. All APs and STAs are 802.11n and operate with the same channel bandwidth capabilities.
- Mode 1: All members of the BSS are HT STAs, but another BSS is running on the same channel or one of the two channels when 40 MHz is used. This is HT non-Member Protection Mode.
- Mode 2: HT 20 MHz Protection mode, this mode is used if only HT STAs are associated to the BSS but at least one of the STAs can only use a 20 MHz channel while the BSS is configured to use 20/40 MHz.
- Mode 3: HT Mixed Mode, this mode is used if any STAs that are not HT-capable are connected to the BSS.

You can determine the mode of operation for HT communications in the AP Beacon frame. The HT Information element includes the HT Protection mode listed as in Figure 7.12.

```
∨ HT Information element
    ┈Primary Channel: 11 - 2462 MHz
    ┈Secondary Channel Offset: 0x00 (0) - no secondary channel is present
    ┈STA Channel Width: 0 - 20 MHz channel width
    ┈RIFS Mode: 1 - use of RIFS is permitted
    ┈PSMP STAs Only: 0 - Association requests are accepted regardless of PSMP capability
    ┈Service Interval Granularity: 0x00 (0) - 5 ms
    ┈Operating Mode of BSS: All STAs are - 20/40 MHz HT or in a 20/40 MHz BSS or are 20 MHz HT in a 20 MHz BSS (0x0)
    ┈Non-greenfield STAs Present: 1 - one or more associated HT STAs are not greenfield capable
    ┈Transmit Burst Limit: No limit
    ┈OBSS Non-HT STAs Present: Use of protection for non-HT STAs by overlapping BSSs is not needed
    ┈Dual Beacon: No second beacon is transmitted
    ┈Dual CTS Protection: Not required
    ┈Secondary Beacon: 0 - primary beacon
    ┈L-SIG TXOP Protection Full Support: 0 - one or more HT STA in the BSS do not support L-SIG TXOP Protection
    ┈PCO Active: Inactive
    ┈PCO Phase: 0 - switch to or continue 20 MHz phase
```

Figure 7.12: HT Operations in Mode 0

Load Balancing

Load balancing is implemented in different ways by different vendors. It is not specified in the 802.11 standard specifically, but using the behaviors of the 802.11 protocols, vendors have been able to direct clients from busy APs and toward less busy APs.

This is often accomplished by ignoring Probe Request frames on busy APs and acknowledging them on less busy APs. If the client STA is attempting to connect by first probing for an AP with an SSID, this can work well. In addition, APs can reject Authentication frames to prevent from overloading and this will also force the client to find another AP with which to connect.

There is not much to see in protocol captures except the Probe Requests that lack a Probe Response. This is a sign that load balancing or Association limits are in place on the APs. Load balancing is not recommended for voice WLANs.

Band Steering

Like load balancing, band steering can ignore Probe Requests and even reject Authentication or Association requests, but for a different reason. Here, the goal is not simply to move the station to another AP, but possible just to another radio in the same AP. Band steering has a goal, usually, of moving more stations over to the less-crowded 5 GHz band.

More advanced capabilities are often used with band steering. For example, an AP or controller may keep a list of MAC addresses that have been known to connect on 5 GHz. If that MAC address attempts to connect on 2.4 GHz, the infrastructure knows it has dual-band capabilities and it can hard reject it until it connects to the 5 GHz radio.

In both load balancing and band steering, "safe" algorithms consider persistent clients and have a threshold of rejection. For example, they may ignore the first 5 or 10 requests, but then allow the station to connect on the next attempt. This prevents orphaned clients that, for some reason in their driver code, will not move onto another AP.

Both load balancing and band steering require careful design beyond the scope of CWAP preparation. For more information on that, see the CWDP materials.

Chapter Summary

In this chapter, you had the opportunity to see how to capture various frame types and view them in a protocol analyzer based on MAC operations and special features. In the next chapter, you will explore the very technical details of HT and VHT operations.

Facts to Remember

- Data frames and QoS Data frames are best captured near the AP or near the client station being analyzed.
- Acknowledgement and Block Acknowledgement frames are a required part of 802.11 communications.
- It is important to understand the use of the Duration field, particularly in RTS/CTS exchanges.
- The Beacon frame contains much information about protection modes used in the WLAN.
- Power save can work in several different ways including legacy power save and WMM-PS (U-APSD).

Review Questions

1. The WMM-PS power save solution is roughly equivalent to what?

   a. U-APSD

   b. S-APSD

   c. Legacy Power Save

   d. Dozing mode

2. What field reveals the priority of an 802.11 frame using QoS?

   a. HT Information

   b. HT Capability

   c. ERP Element

   d. QoS Control

3. What happens to the Duration field duration value as you move through the RTS, CTS, Data, Ack process?

   a. It increments

   b. It decrements

   c. It stays the same

   d. It is not used

4. How long is a SIFS in HT and VHT 5 GHz operations?

   a. 10 microseconds

   b. 9 microseconds

   c. 16 microseconds

   d. 20 microseconds

5. If used at all, when is a PS-Poll frame used?

   a. When a station needs to setup a Block Ack agreement

   b. When a station requires the use of EDCA

   c. When a station wants to use RTS/CTS

   d. When a station wakes from sleep

6. What kind of frame is an Add Block Request frame?
    a. Data
    b. QoS Data
    c. Action
    d. Beacon

7. What defines the immediate versus delayed Block Ack in a Block Ack Agreement?
    a. It is set automatically based on the PHY
    b. The Block Ack Policy
    c. It is set automatically based on the data rate
    d. Immediate is never used and delayed is always used

8. What does it mean when a station sends a frame to the AP with the Power Management bit set to 1?
    a. The station is awake now
    b. The station is going to sleep
    c. The station wants the AP to wake up
    d. The station wants the AP to go to sleep

9. Non-ERP Present is set to 1. What is Use Protection set to?
    a. 0
    b. 1
    c. 2
    d. 3

10. The Duration value of a frame is set to 0. Most likely, what kind of frame is this?
    a. QoS Data
    b. Data
    c. CTS
    d. Ack

Review Answers

1. The correct answer is A. Unscheduled-Automatic Power Save Delivery is roughly the same as WMM-PS.

2. The correct answer is D. The QoS Control field includes the priority of the frame.

3. The correct answer is B. The Duration field value will decrement as it goes through the RTS/CTS/DATA/ACK exchange.

4. The correct answer is C. The SIFS is 16 microseconds in all 5 GHz PHYs.

5. The correct answer is D. The PS-Poll frame, if used today, would be used to indicate to an AP that a STA is awake and ready to receive a frame from the buffer.

6. The correct answer is C. The Add Block Request and Add Block Response frames are Action frames.

7. The correct answer is B. The Block Ack Policy, which is usually set to Immediate, is responsible for either using immediate or delayed Block Acks.

8. The correct answer is B. When the Power Management bit is set to 1, the station is going into sleep mode and the AP needs to buffer frames for the station.

9. The correct answer is B. The Use Protection but is always set to 1 if the Non-ERP Present bit is set to 1.

10. The correct answer is D. An Ack or Block Ack or any frame not requiring a response will have a Duration value of 0.

Chapter 8: HT and VHT Operations

Objectives Covered:

6.4 Analyze HT/VHT-specific transmission methods

The structures of HT/OFDM and VHT/OFDM, HT and VHT, were discussed in chapter 3, The PHY. Within this chapter we will examine specific operations of HT and VHT beyond their basic structures. You will see that VHT builds upon the use of certain technologies introduced by HT in such a way as to dramatically increase the data rates available.

MIMO

MIMO is used in both HT and VHT communications. The basics of MIMO are covered in the CWNA course. Here, we will examine its use within both PHYs, beginning with the use of MIMO in HT communications, so that you can more clearly see the different implementations.

MIMO uses multiple transmit and receive antennas and spatial streams as opposed to the single antenna and single stream communications found in SISO communications. Multiple antenna use introduces signaling degrees of freedom that were not available in SISO communications. This use of multiple antennas and signals is referred to as the spatial degree of freedom. The spatial degrees of freedom can either be used for antenna diversity, as in SISO, or for multiplexing, as in MIMO, or used in a combination.

One of the most notable improvements in Wi-Fi communications found when moving from SISO to MIMO is the impact of multipath versus the use of multipath. Multipath is a detriment to SISO communications but is used to improve communications when using MIMO. Multipath occurs when radio signals reach the receiving antenna by two or more paths. This can be caused by reflection. In SISO communications, the receiving radio would read the first signal normally but the second instance and beyond of the same signal would cause problems in how the receiver dealt with the frames. To mitigate the problem, APs used two antennas connected to the same radio. The antenna receiving the signal first would have the signal the radio used. The second antennas reception of the frame and beyond would be discarded.

Imagine you are talking to someone but hearing echoes. That is multipath for sound versus RF. The echoes impede your conversation. So, to combat the echoes your body has two ears. When you hear the other person better in one ear than the other, you listen more using that ear and ignore the same speech entering the other ear. This works as a mitigation for sound in the same way antenna diversity works for SISO radios. It doesn't solve the problem but makes communications usable.

When the receiving radio needs to send its ACK for the frame, it transmits using a single antenna, usually the same antenna that was better able to receive the initial transmission.

Rather than trying to compensate for the effects of multipath like SISO radios do, MIMO radios use the effects to improve communications. MIMO requires the use of multiple radios and antennas, called *radio chains*.

MIMO, as used in Wi-Fi, specifically refers to a practical technique for sending and receiving more than one data signal simultaneously over the same channel. This is accomplished in part by exploiting multipath propagation. Since multipath is normally caused by reflection of the signal, MIMO tends to add more of a performance boost indoors than it does outdoors. In a typical indoor environment, multiple RF signals sent by a MIMO radio will take multiple paths to reach the MIMO receivers. For example, multiple copies of three original signals will be received my multiple antennas. The MIMO receiver will then use advanced digital signal processing (DSP) techniques to sort the originally transmitted signals. A high multipath environment actually helps a MIMO receiver differentiate between the unique data streams carried by multiple RF signals. If multiple signals that are sent by a MIMO transmitter all arrive simultaneously at the receiver, the signals will cancel each other, a phenomenon called nulling, and the performance is basically the same as a SISO system.

MIMO improves communications at the Physical layer through more effective use of received signals and more intelligent transmissions. In addition to the benefits of using more than one antenna for transmission and reception, MIMO uses Spatial Multiplexing. This enables a MIMO transmitter/receiver pair to increase its throughput in such a way that there is no increase in bandwidth usage or even in transmit power. Spatial Multiplexing increases the throughput linearly. When using MIMO, the transmitter sends multiple signals carrying different bit streams from each of its antennas. Each of the receiver's antennas receives a linear combination of the transmitted signals.

The wireless channel is a matrix that is a function of transmit/receive antenna array geometry and the reflections, which were a problem for SISO, in the environment. When using MIMO in an environment with a lot of scattering, many reflections of a single transmission, the channel matrix can be inverted. This enables the receiver to decode all the different signals from the various transmit antennas. This produces a multiplexing gain.

Simply put, the multiple signals that confused a SISO receiver can be decoded by a MIMO receiver and combined into a single use that increases the amplitude of the received signal.

It is notable that there is a tradeoff between the amount of diversity and multiplexing gain providable by using MIMO. The devices communicating using MIMO will automatically find a point on the diversity-multiplexing trade off curve based upon the channel conditions.

MIMO has many variants. An HT MIMO radio can transmit up to four unique data streams within the multiple RF signals Each data stream is capable of sending up to 72.2 Mbps of raw data. A MIMO radio will transmit multiple signals with different modulated data via each transmit antenna. This is due to the number of transmit, receive and spatial chains used.

You will find STAs supporting 1X1:1 MIMO up to 4X4:4 MIMO in HT communications. The first number represents, transmit, the second receive and the third the number of spatial streams supported. You may see some early HT APs supporting uneven numbers such as 3X3:2. It is important that you do not confuse the number of radios or antennas used with the number of spatial streams supported. The 3X3:2 radios support three transmitters and three receivers but only support two spatial streams. This was not uncommon to see in earlier HT access points as vendors began to explore the benefits of HT transmissions. Today it is more common to find APs using 3X3:3 or some other variant where the transmit, receive and spatial stream use are all the same, 2X2:2 or 3X3:3 for example.

The support for MIMO the device has is communicated in the Control field of the frames. This is still better than most client devices which usually support 1X1:1 or 2X2:2, with the exception of laptops which may support 3X3:3. The reduced MIMO support in clients as compared to APs is to conserve battery life and reduce the cost of building the devices while also keeping their size in line with user expectations. No one wants a phone the size of a laptop, for example. When the client stations and the AP are using different versions of MIMO, usually the AP supporting more radio chains and spatial streams as in Figure 8.1, the benefits of MIMO are reduced but still provide vastly improved signaling compared to SISO.

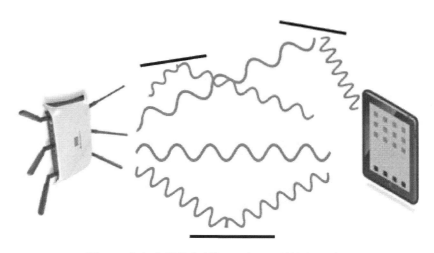

Figure 8.1: A 3X3:3 AP serving a 1X1:1 station

To allow these improvements to truly bolster the use of Wi-Fi, both the transmitter and receiver must understand the communications. To that end, there are information elements in the control field of MIMO transmissions to help the involved stations work together. The MIMO Control field in HT is used to manage the exchange of MIMO channel state or transmit beamforming feedback information used in defining how the involved stations will coordinate their communications. Remember that MIMO systems benefit from a multipath-rich RF environment, where the received signal is primarily derived from reflected signal components. Combining MIMO and OFDM, as used in HT, increases the spectrum efficiency by reducing the transmission energy per bit. The MIMO Control field is 6 octets in length and cam be seen in Figure 8.2.

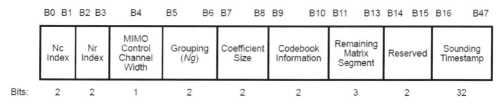

Figure 8.2: MIMO Control Field format

The MIMO Control field defines specific parameters as below:

- The **Nc index** indicates the number of columns in a matrix minus one.

313

- The **Nr Index** indicates the number of rows in a matrix minus one.
- The **MIMO Control Channel Width** indicates the width of the channel, either 20 MHz or 40 MHz, in which a measurement was made.
- The **Grouping Ng** field indicates the number of carriers grouped into one.
- The **Coefficient Size** indicates the number of bits in the representation of the real and imaginary parts of each element in the matrix.
- The **Codebook Information** indicates the size of codebook entries.
- The **Remaining Matrix Segment** contains the remaining segment number for the associated measurement report with values in a rage of 0 to 7.
- The **Reserved** field is not defined.
- The **Sounding Timestamp Contains** the lower 4 octets of the TSF timer value sampled at the instant that the MAC received the PHY-CCA indication (IDLE) primitive that corresponds to the end of the reception of the sounding packet that was used to generate feedback information contained in the frame.

By reading the information in these fields, the receiving station knows how to work with the transmitter.

However, the environment and client capabilities demand that the receiver also provide information for the original transmitter to use in communication. The effectiveness of this is largely determined by the Channel State Information (CSI) estimation method used. CSI refers to the known channel properties. This information describes how a signal propagates from the transmitter to the receiver. It also represents the combined effect of environmental impacts such as scattering, fading, and power decay with distance. The method used to calculate these influences is called channel estimation. The use of CSI makes it possible for radios to adapt their transmissions to current channel conditions. The ability to adapt like this is a critical part of achieving reliable communications using high data rates in HT communications.

CSI must be estimated at the receiver. It is usually quantized and fed back to the transmitter, so that the transmitter can make any needed adjustments to improve communications with the receiver. The transmitter and receiver can have different CSI based upon their perspective of the environmental variables. The CSI at the transmitter and the CSI at the receiver are sometimes referred to as CSIT (transmitter) and CSIR (receiver), to denote where the CSI was calculated.

The overhead of training frame transmission and CSI feedback can decrease efficiency and increase the estimated CSI cost at a given STA. To help, the Action field provides a mechanism for specifying extended management actions. There are different types of these Action/No Action frames, each with their own use and format. Some are compressed, and others are not. A CSI frame is an Action or an Action No Ack frame of category HT. Figure 8.3 shows you its elements.

Order	Information
1	Category
2	HT Action
3	MIMO Control
4	CSI Report

Figure 8.3: CSI frame elements

We have already seen the contents of the MIMO Control field but what is in the CSI report? The CSI Report field is used by the CSI frame to carry explicit channel state information to an HT transmit beamformer. The structure of the field depends upon the value of the MIMO Control Channel Width subfield. The CSI Matrix subfields in the CSI Report field are matrices whose elements are taken from the CHAN_MAT parameter of RXVECTOR. 20 MHz and 40 MHz wide channels have different structures. The CSI Report field for a 20 MHz channel width structure can be seen in Figure 8.4. The structure for a CSI Report field of a 40 MHz wide channel can be seen in Figure 8.5.

Field	Size (bits)	Meaning
SNR in receive chain 1	8	Signal-to-noise ratio in the first receive chain of the STA sending the report.
...		
SNR in receive chain Nr	8	Signal-to-noise ratio in the Nr'th receive chain of the STA sending the report.
CSI Matrix for carrier –28	$3+2\times Nb\times Nc\times Nr$	CSI matrix
...		
CSI Matrix for carrier –1	$3+2\times Nb\times Nc\times Nr$	CSI matrix
CSI Matrix for carrier 1	$3+2\times Nb\times Nc\times Nr$	CSI matrix
...		
CSI Matrix for carrier 28	$3+2\times Nb\times Nc\times Nr$	CSI matrix

Figure 8.4: CSI Report field for a 20 MHz wide channel

Field	Size (bits)	Meaning
SNR in receive chain 1	8	Signal-to-noise ratio in the first receive chain of the STA sending the report.
...		
SNR in receive chain Nr	8	Signal-to-noise ratio in the Nr'th receive chain of the STA sending the report.
CSI Matrix for carrier −58	$3+2\times Nb\times Nc\times Nr$	CSI matrix
...		
CSI Matrix for carrier −2	$3+2\times Nb\times Nc\times Nr$	CSI matrix
CSI Matrix for carrier 2	$3+2\times Nb\times Nc\times Nr$	CSI matrix
...		
CSI Matrix for carrier 58	$3+2\times Nb\times Nc\times Nr$	CSI matrix

Figure 8.5: CSI Report field for a 40 MHz wide channel

Within the multiple transmissions you will find independent unique data streams. Each of these data streams is known as a spatial stream. Each unique spatial stream can contain different data. Each spatial stream travels using a different path. This behavior is due to the separation between the multiple transmitting antennas within the MIMO array.

The multiple streams following different paths to the receiver, because of the space between the transmitting antennas, is called spatial diversity. Transmitting multiple independent streams of unique data using spatial diversity is also called spatial multiplexing or spatial diversity multiplexing. By sending multiple unique data streams throughput is drastically improved.

If a MIMO access point send two unique data streams and a MIMO client station receives both streams, the throughput is theoretically doubled. If a MIMO access point sends three unique data streams to a MIMO client can receive them, the throughput is theoretically tripled.

MIMO diversity can use Maximal Ratio Combining (MRC) and algorithms to join multiple received signals. If receive diversity is used, the signals can be linearly combined. Its algorithms combine multiple received signals by examining each signal and optimally combining the signals using a method that is additive as opposed to destructive, an improvement over SISO. When a MIMO system is using both switched diversity and MRC it effectively increases the SNR level of the received signals.

MRC is most useful when a SISO radio transmits to a MIMO receiver and multipath occurs. The MRC algorithm then focuses on the signal with the highest SNR level. It is

316

possible for the MIMO receiver to combine information from the noisier signals as well. This results in less data corruption, due to the ability to create a better estimate of the original data using reconstruction and resulting in improved RSSI.

HT offered great improvements over both DSSS and OFDM in both the 2.4 GHz and 5 GHz bands by using MIMO, channel bonding, and more efficient modulation. It laid a solid foundation for the improvements found in Very High Throughput(VHT). VHT shares a lot with HT but makes additional enhancements in MIMO, channel bonding, and modulation. VHT did abandon support for 2.4 GHz and only operates in the 5 GHz space.

Most of the differing features found in VHT increase the maximum throughput achievable between two VHT STAs beyond using HT features alone. The VHT features are available to VHT client STAs associated with a VHT access point. Additionally, a subset of the VHT features is available for use between two VHT STAs that are members of the same IBSS. Similarly, a subset of the VHT features is available for use between two VHT STAs that have established mesh peering and a subset of the VHT features is available for use between two VHT STAs that have established a TDLS link. The key is that to fully benefit from the improvements in VHT, the communications need to be between two VHT capable radios.

The support for VHT transmit beamforming, discussed later, sounding, and VHT MU PPDUs in a VHT AP and more than one VHT STA within a VHT BSS enables the optional use of downlink MU-MIMO. With downlink MU-MIMO (sometimes called DL-MU-MIMO) a VHT AP can create up to four A-MPDUs, each carrying MPDUs destined for a different associated MU beamforming capable STA. Basically, a VHT AP can transmit up to 4 data frames destined for MU-MIMO stations as a single transmission, reducing the time needed for contention and transmission. Each MU-MIMO STA to whom this frame is sent will send individual ACKs.

The VHT AP uses what are called group identifiers (GIDs) to signal the potential recipient STAs. The AP then transmits the A-MPDUs simultaneously in separate space-time streams in a way that each recipient can demodulate the space-time streams carrying its A-MPDU. The simultaneous transmission of A-MPDUs in a single VHT MU-PPDU increases aggregate throughput over that achieved by sending the A-MPDUs in separate SU-PPDUs, as would occur with non-MU-MIMO and non-VHT stations.

Implementation of MU-MIMO is more difficult in a high density environment due to the higher requirements of SNR. VHT has simply built upon the foundation laid by HT.

Examine the HT capabilities information in Figure 8.6 and then compare it to Figure 8.7, the VHT capabilities information. You can see that the VHT capabilities information is much more complex because there is more support to convey to the stations involved in VHT communications.

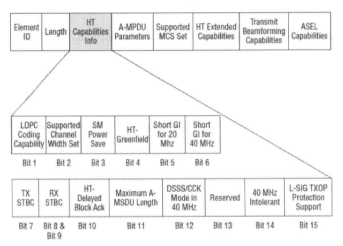

Figure 8.6: HT Capabilities information

So, what are the major improvements made by VHT? Let's look at them. The main PHY enhancements in VHT over HT are:

- Mandatory support for 40 MHz and 80 MHz channel widths
- Mandatory support for VHT single-user (SU) PPDUs
- Optional support for 160 MHz and 80+80 MHz channel widths
- Optional support for VHT sounding protocol to support beamforming
- Optional support for VHT multi-user (MU) PPDUs
- Optional support for VHT-MCSs 8 and 9
- Expanded use of MIMO including MU-MIMO

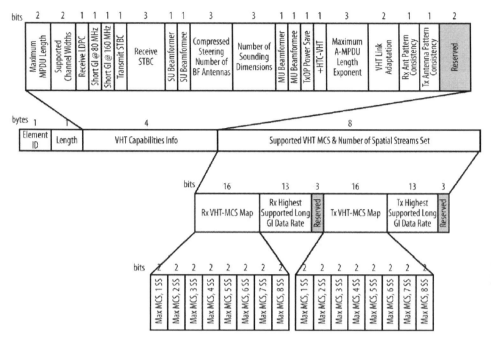

Figure 8.7: VHT Capabilities information

The major improvements made at the MAC layer include these features in a VHT over HT:

- Mandatory support for the A-MPDU padding of a VHT PPDU
- Mandatory support for VHT single MPDU
- Mandatory support for responding to a bandwidth indication (provided by the RXVECTOR parameters CH_BANDWIDTH_IN_NON_HT and DYN_BANDWIDTH_IN_NON_HT) in a non-HT and non-HT duplicate RTS frame
- Optional support for MPDUs of up to 11 454 octets
- Optional support for A-MPDU pre-end-of-frame (pre-EOF) padding of up to 1,048,575 octets
- Optional support for VHT link adaptation

The requirement of 40 MHz and 80 MHz channel widths made the use of 2.4 GHz impractical, due to the channel overlap found in that spectrum. That space also has more

319

legacy devices and noise than the cleaner 5 GHz space, where there are more channels to use without the worry of channel overlap.

VHT also increases the use of MIMO from a maximum in HT of 4X4:4 to a maximum in VHT of 8X8:8. The additional Tx, Rx and spatial stream used means that the throughput could be 8 times that of SISO, due to the improved use of a single channel. It is important to know that the number of spatial streams used cannot be greater than the number of elements used in the antenna array. This means that you are not able to have a MIMO system where the number of spatial streams used outnumbers the Tx and Rx elements. For example, you would not see a 3X3:4 MIMO solution but could see a 3X3:2 MIMO solution. When the count of array elements exceeds the number of spatial streams, as in a 3X3:2 deployment, there is an additional signal used for processing gain that can be used to improve the SNR used in beamforming.

Combine the much larger MIMO use with the use of up to 160 MHz wide channels versus the maximum 40 MHz wide channels in HT and you can quickly see that VHT will produce much higher data rates than HT could, if one were to use the wider channels, which is not the typical case in enterprise deployments.

Beamforming was introduced in HT. However, it was not adopted in any large manner. By using the MIMO antenna array to send purposely phase-shifted patterns, it is possible to guide or "steer" data streams toward a particular receiver. Which is great, so long as the receiver is no moving. VHT takes beamforming farther by allowing multiple simultaneous transmissions for MU-MIMO. This use of beamforming and MIMO allows the same channel to be used in different areas by the same access point. These enhancements mean that the VHT control field, seen in Figure 8.8 below, must differ from that of an HT system, seen in Figure 8.2 above.

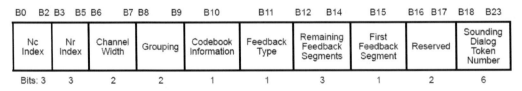

Figure 8.8: VHT Control field

The MIMO Control field used in VHT is similar to that of HT but defines its specific parameters as below:

- **Nc Index** indicates the number of columns, Nc, in the compressed beamforming feedback matrix minus 1.
- **Nr Index** indicates the number of rows, Nr, in the compressed beamforming feedback matrix minus 1.
- **Channel Width** indicates the width of the channel in which the measurement to create the compressed beamforming feedback matrix was made and could be from 20 MHz to 160 MHz in width.
- **Grouping** indicates the subcarrier grouping, Ng, used for the compressed beamforming feedback matrix.
- **Codebook Information** indicates the size of codebook entries for either SU or MU.
- **Feedback Type** indicates the feedback type as either SU or MU
- **Remaining Feedback Segments** indicates the number of remaining feedback segments for the associated VHT Compressed Beamforming frame. In a retransmitted feedback segment, the field is set to the same value associated with the feedback segment in the original transmission.
- **First Feedback Segment** will be Set to 1 for the first feedback segment of a segmented report or the only feedback segment of an unsegmented report; set to 0 if it is not the first feedback segment or if the VHT Compressed Beamforming Report field and MU *Exclusive Beamforming Report* field are not present in the frame.   In a retransmitted feedback segment, the field is set to the same value associated with the feedback segment in the original transmission.
- **Sounding Dialog Token Number** is the sounding dialog token from the VHT NDP Announcement frame soliciting feedback

As stated in the 802.11 standard, the VHT Compressed Beamforming Report field is used by the VHT Compressed Beamforming feedback to carry explicit feedback information in the form of angles representing compressed beamforming feedback matrices for use by a transmit beamformer to determine steering matrices. The size of the VHT Compressed Beamforming Report field depends on the values in the VHT MIMO Control field. The VHT Compressed Beamforming Report field contains VHT Compressed Beamforming Report information or successive portions thereof in the case of segmented VHT Compressed Beamforming feedback. VHT Compressed Beamforming Report information is always included in the VHT Compressed Beamforming feedback. The VHT Compressed Beamforming Report information contains the channel matrix elements indexed, first, by matrix angles and second by data subcarrier index from lowest frequency to highest frequency. How these angles are determined is well beyond the scope of the CWAP exam.

Transmit Beamforming (TxBF)

Transmit Beamforming (TxBF) is the use of multiple antennas to transmit a signal strategically with varying phases so that the communication arrives at the receiver in such a manner that the signal strength is increased. Since transmit beamforming results in constructive multipath communication, the result is a higher signal-to-noise ratio and greater received amplitude. The use of transmit beamforming results in greater range for individual clients when communicating with an AP. Transmit beamforming allows for higher throughput due to the higher SNR. This allows for the use of more-complex modulation methods with the ability to encode more data bits. The higher SNR also allows communications with fewer Layer 2 retransmissions, further improving the efficiency.

All this improvement in communication requires more than wishful thinking on the part of the transmitting STA. This requires communications between the transmitter and receiver about the quality of the signal received and how to improve it for subsequent transmissions. This feedback comes in two forms, Implicit and Explicit methods of calculation.

For an HT or VHT transmitter, called a beamformer, to calculate an appropriate steering matrix for transmit spatial processing when transmitting to a specific HT or VHT receiver, called the beamformee, the beamformer needs to have an accurate estimate of the channel over which it is transmitting. The transmitter knows what it hears but needs to learn from the receiver what it hears to better form the next transmission. When using the implicit feedback method, the beamformer receives long training symbols transmitted by the beamformee, which allow the MIMO channel between the beamformee and beamformer to be estimated. When the MIMO channel being used is reciprocal, the beamformer can use the training symbols that it receives from the beamformee to make a channel estimate which is suitable for computing the transmit steering matrix to be used in the next transmission.

Calibrated radios in MIMO systems can improve reciprocity. The HT TxBF calibration procedure consists of 4 frames.

- **Calibration Start frame** / Position 1 / sent by calibration initiator / TRQ=1: This Sounding PPDU (A QoS Null Data frame) initiates the calibration procedure and is followed by an ACK frame.
- **Calibration Sounding Response frame** / Position 2 / sent by calibration responder: This Sounding PPDU (an ACK+HTC frame) is sent a SIFS after receipt of the Calibration Start frame. This frame is used by the calibration initiator to estimate the MIMO channel.
- **Calibration Sounding Complete frame** / Position 3 / sent by calibration initiator: This Sounding PPDU is sent a SIFS after receipt of the Calibration Sounding Response frame. This frame is a QoS Null+HTC frame, has the CSI/Steering subfield of the HT Control field set to 1, is used by the calibration responder to estimate the MIMO channel.
- A normal ACK frame (the 4th frame in the calibration sequence).

Each calibration sequence has a unique identifier found in the Calibration Sequence subfield in the HT Control field. This identifier remains the same throughout each calibration sequence and is incremented each time a new calibration procedure is started. There are specific requirements for both the beamformer and beamformee when using implicit feedback. The procedures for HT transmit beamforming with implicit feedback use only HT and non-HT PPDUs. The HT Control field, when present, is the HT variant HT Control field.

Transmit beamforming with implicit feedback has the ability to operate in a unidirectional or bidirectional manner. When using unidirectional implicit transmit beamforming, only the HT beamformer sends beamformed transmissions. When using bidirectional implicit transmit beamforming, both STAs send beamformed transmissions. This means that a STA can act as both an HT beamformer and an HT beamformee. Using implicit feedback, the calibration of receive or transmit chains should be done to improve performance of transmit beamforming. Over-the-air calibration is described in 10.32.2.4 of 802.11-2016. For implicit transmit beamforming, only the HT beamformer, which is sending the beamformed transmissions, needs to be calibrated. A device that advertises itself as being capable of being either an HT beamformer, an HT beamformee using implicit feedback, or both will be required to operate as described below.

The beamformer must:

- Set the Implicit Transmit Beamforming Capable subfield to 1 of the
- Transmit Beamforming Capability field of the HT Capabilities element in HT
- Capabilities elements that it transmits.
- Set the Implicit Transmit Beamforming Receiving Capable subfield to 1
- of the Transmit Beamforming Capability field of the HT Capabilities element.
- Be capable of receiving a sounding PPDU for which the SOUNDING
- parameter is SOUNDING and the NUM_EXTEN_SS is equal to 0 in the
- RXVECTOR in the PHY-RXSTART indication primitive, independently of
- the values of the Receive Staggered Sounding Capable and Receive NDP
- Capable subfields.
- Set the Calibration subfield to 3 of the Transmit Beamforming Capability
- field of the HT Capabilities element to advertise full calibration support.

The beamformee must:

- Shall set the Implicit Transmit Beamforming Receiving Capable subfield to 1 of the Transmit Beamforming Capability field of the HT Capabilities element in HT Capabilities elements that it transmits.
- Shall be capable of setting the SOUNDING parameter to SOUNDING and the NUM_EXTEN_SS to 0 in the TXVECTOR in the PHY-TXSTART request primitive when transmitting a sounding PPDU, as a response to TRQ=1, independently of the values of the Transmit Staggered Sounding Capable and Transmit NDP Capable subfields.

Any STA that performs one of the roles related to transmit beamforming with implicit feedback must support the associated capabilities you can see in Figure 8.9. To assist the transmitter and receiver in transmit beamforming the devices use sounding PPDUs which are used to help determine the direction in which the signal is to be steered. It is similar to a Wi-Fi version of the swimming game Marco Polo, where one person says Marco, to ask where you are and the other says Polo, to be found.

In many cases it is desirable to obtain as full a characterization of the MIMO channel as is possible. To do this the transmission of a sufficient number of High Throughput Long Training Fields, HT-LTFs, is required to sound the full dimensionality of the channel. This is referred to as MIMO channel sounding. As stated in the 802.11 standard, if the HT beamformee transmits a sounding PPDU, the SOUNDING parameter in the TXVECTOR in the PHY-TXSTART request primitive shall be set to SOUNDING. If the HT beamformee is capable of implicit transmit beamforming and the HT beamformer can receive implicit transmit beamforming, the sounding PPDU from the HT beamformer may be steered. A STA that acts as an HT beamformer using implicit feedback expects to receive a sounding PPDU from the beamformee in response to a training request. The beamforming STA can then compute steering matrices from the channel estimates obtained from the sounding PPDU received from the beamformee.

Role	Required support
HT beamformee: A receiver of transmit beamformed PPDUs	Shall transmit sounding PPDUs as a response to TRQ=1.
Beamformer: A transmitter of beamformed PPDUs	Can receive sounding PPDUs. Can compute steering matrices from MIMO channel estimates obtained from long training symbols in sounding PPDUs received from the HT beamformee.
A responder in a calibration exchange	Can receive and transmit sounding PPDUs. Can respond with a CSI frame that contains channel measurement information obtained during reception of a sounding PPDU.
An initiator in a calibration exchange	Can receive and transmit sounding PPDUs. Can receive a CSI frame sent by a calibration responder.

Figure 8.9: Transmit beamforming support required with implicit feedback

Implicit transmit beamforming can be either unidirectional or bidirectional. When using unidirectional TxBF, the 802.11 standard states that the PPDU exchange can be summarized as follows:

- STA A initiates the frame exchange sequence by sending an unsteered PPDU to STA B. The PPDU includes a training request (TRQ= 1) in a +HTC MPDU.
- STA B sends a sounding PPDU in response to the training request from STA A.
- On receiving the sounding PPDU, STA A uses the resulting channel estimate to compute steering matrices and uses these matrices to send a steered PPDU back to STA B.
- The steered PPDU transmitted in step c) and subsequent steered PPDUs transmitted by STA A may include training requests (TRQ=1) in a +HTC MPDU. In response to each training request, STA B returns a sounding PPDU to STA A, which enables STA A to update its steering vectors. If the steering vectors

resulting from step c) or subsequent sounding PPDUs are deemed stale due to delay, the sequence may be restarted by returning to step a). Step d) in the above PPDU exchange represents steady-state unidirectional transmit beamforming operation.

During the PPDU exchange neither the receiving nor the transmitting STA should switch antennas.

When using bidirectional implicit transmit beamforming, sounding PPDUs are used that carry MPDUs. STA A initiates the frame exchange, and STA A and STA B alternate in the roles of HT beamformer and HT beamformee. The PPDU exchange in the case of bidirectional implicit TxBF can be summarized as follows:

- STA A initiates the frame exchange sequence by sending an unsteered PPDU to STA B. The PPDU includes a training request (TRQ= 1) in a +HTC MPDU.
- STA B sends a sounding PPDU in response to the training request. In addition, this PPDU includes a training request in a +HTC MPDU to enable implicit transmit beamforming in the RD.
- On receiving the sounding PPDU, STA A uses the resulting channel estimate to compute steering matrices and uses these matrices to send a steered PPDU back to STA B. This steered PPDU is also a sounding PPDU in response to the training request from STA B. Steering matrices with non-orthonormal columns should not be used in transmitting sounding PPDUs for implicit feedback. In general, bidirectional implicit beamforming will not function as described here when the steering matrices have non-orthonormal columns.
- On receiving the sounding PPDU, STA B uses the resulting channel estimate to compute steering matrices and uses these matrices to send a steered PPDU back to STA A. The steered PPDU transmitted in step c) and subsequent steered PPDUs transmitted by STA A may include training requests in HTC. In response to each training request, STA B returns a sounding PPDU to STA A, which enables STA A to update its steering vectors. If the steering vectors resulting from step c) or subsequent sounding PPDUs are deemed stale due to delay, the sequence may be restarted by returning to step a).
- The steered PPDU transmitted in step d) and subsequent steered PPDUs transmitted by STA B may include training requests in HTC. In response to each training request, STA A returns a sounding PPDU to STA B, which enables STA B to update its steering vectors. If the steering vectors resulting from step d) or

subsequent sounding PPDUs are deemed stale due to delay, the sequence may be restarted by returning to step a). Steps d) and e) in the above PPDU exchange represent steady-state bidirectional transmit beamforming operation.

Just as when using unidirectional TxBF, during the PPDU exchange neither the receiving nor the transmitting STA should switch antennas.

When using the explicit feedback method (the only one supported in VHT), the HT beamformee, the receiver, makes a direct estimate of the channel from training symbols sent to it by the HT beamformer, the transmitter. The HT beamformee can prepare Channel State Information, CSI, or steering feedback based upon its observation of these training symbols. The HT beamformee quantizes the feedback and sends it to the HT beamformer. The HT beamformer can use the feedback as the basis for determining transmit steering vectors. An explicit HT beamformer uses the feedback response that it receives from the HT beamformee to calculate a beamforming feedback matrix for transmit beamforming. This feedback response may have one of the three formats listed below. The formats supported by the transmit beamformee, receiver, shall be advertised within the HT beamformee's HT Capabilities element. This allows the beamformer to use a format that is more efficient and that both devices understand.

- **CSI**: The HT beamformee sends the MIMO channel coefficients to the HT beamformer.
- **Non-compressed beamforming**: The HT beamformee sends calculated beamforming feedback matrices to the HT beamformer.
- **Compressed beamforming**: The HT beamformee sends compressed beamforming feedback matrices to the HT beamformer.

As you learned earlier CSI refers to the known channel properties. This information describes how a signal propagates from the transmitter to the receiver. It also represents the combined effect of environmental impacts such as scattering, fading, and power decay with distance. The method used to calculate these influences is called channel estimation. An HT beamformer could even completely discard the feedback response. This can happen if the TSF time when the PHY-CCA indication (IDLE) primitive corresponding to the feedback response frame's arrival minus the value from the Sounding Timestamp field in the feedback response frame is greater than the coherence time interval of the propagation channel. TSF is the timing synchronization function which is specified in the BSS to fulfill timing synchronization among STAs. A TSF keeps the timers for all stations in the same BSS synchronized.

In addition to using CSI, the beamformee may send its calculated beamforming information to the beamformer in either a non-compressed or compressed manner. A Non-compressed Beamforming frame is an Action or an Action No Ack frame of category HT and the format of its Action field can be seen below in Figure 8.10. The Non-compressed Beamforming Report field is used by the Non-compressed Beamforming frame to carry explicit feedback in the form of non-compressed beamforming feedback matrices for use by a transmit HT beamformer to determine steering matrices. The structure of the field is dependent on the value of the MIMO Control Channel Width subfield.

Order	Information
1	Category
2	HT Action
3	MIMO Control
4	Noncompressed Beamforming Report

Figure 8.10: Non-compressed Beamforming frame format

The Compressed Beamforming frame is also an Action or an Action No Ack frame of category HT. Its Action field format is seen in Figure 8.11 below. The Compressed Beamforming Report field is used by the Compressed Beamforming frame to carry explicit feedback information in the form of angles representing compressed beamforming feedback matrices for use by a transmit HT beamformer to determine steering matrices. The size of the Compressed Beamforming Report field depends on the values in the MIMO Control field. These reports and values are well beyond the scope of the CWAP exam. Should you wish to see them, they are in the 802.11-2016 standard Part 11: Wireless LAN Medium Access Control (MAC) and Physical Layer (PHY) Specifications in section 9.4.1.29. It is important to note that the format varies with the channel width used ,20 MHz versus 40 MHz and so on.

Order	Information
1	Category
2	HT Action
3	MIMO Control
4	Compressed Beamforming Report

Figure 8.11: Compressed Beamforming frame format

The use of TxBF in VHT has been simplified when compared to its use in HT. In HT, using TxBF meant that both the beamformer and beamformee had to agree on the method used. Due to the complexity in making such decisions, some vendors decided not to implement TxBF in their products, usually client stations. To avoid the negotiations required by HT, VHT uses a single method called null data packet sounding, NDP sounding, which is a form of explicit feedback.

Rather than transmitting a steering matrix, a VHT beamformee calculates a feedback matrix and compresses it. This allows it to be represented by a smaller frame and actually take up less airtime, making VHT communications more efficient. This single sounding technique used, NDP sounding, is rather complex in its self but is still a better solution than being forced to support multiple methods and negotiate different methods with different clients as in HT. Because VHT uses a single sounding method, the unequal modulation found in HT to support beamforming does not exist in VHT communications.

TxBF use results in each spatial stream having a different SNR. Unequal modulation was designed and used in HT so that spatial streams with a higher SNR values could use higher data rates and more efficient modulation techniques, while spatial streams with lower SNR values could still use lower data rates and less efficient modulation. VHT eliminates unequal modulation. This is to help simplify the use of data rates. This simplification in VHTs use of TxBF requires that all spatial streams be modulated identically.

What does this mean in design? If you need to achieve the most you can out of a VHT deployment, you will need to use smaller cells and more APs, which will impact your channel planning and budget. Keep in mind that VHT only works in 5 GHz. If you are deploying dual radio APs, you may want to look for a large portion of them to be dual 5 GHz capable. This will give you the ability to have multiple 5 GHz cells with fewer cable drops. The remaining dual band APs can support legacy stations in 2.4 GHz as needed while still offering a 5 GHz cell for VHT use.

The most vital part of beamforming is calculating the steering matrix for the channel between the beamformer and the beamformee. When using VHT only explicit beamforming is used. Therefore, A STA shall not transmit a VHT NDP in an NDP sequence that contains an HT NDP announcement. The VHT NDP sounding procedure is not the same as that of HT. A VHT beamformer initiates a sounding feedback sequence by transmitting a VHT NDP Announcement frame. This frame is followed by a VHT NDP following a SIFS. The VHT beamformer includes in the VHT NDP Announcement frame and one STA Info field for each VHT beamformee that is expected to prepare the VHT Compressed Beamforming feedback. It identifies the VHT beamformee(s) by including the VHT beamformee's association identifier, AID within the AID subfield of the STA Info field. The VHT NDP Announcement frame must include at least one STA Info field. When using direct link setup to communicate with a peer, the STA that transmits the VHT NDP Announcement frame to a DLS or TDLS peer learns the AID for the peer STA from the DLS Setup Request, DLS Setup Response, TDLS Setup Request, or TDLS Setup Response frame used in setting up the link.

To further simplify TxBF in VHT, the beamformers shall not transmit either a VHT NDP Announcement+HTC frame or a Beamforming Report Poll+HTC frame that contains an HT variant HT Control field. There is no reason for the legacy HT information when VHT stations communicate with each other. They must support the VHT NDP to communicate using VHT. A VHT NDP Announcement frame is to be followed by a VHT NDP after SIFS. The NDP format can be seen in Figure 8.12.

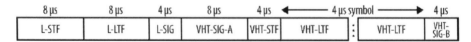

Figure 8.12: Null Data Packet, NDP, Format

In an additional effort to keep things cleaner in VHT, the beamformers that have not received a VHT Capabilities element from a STA or in cases where the last VHT Capabilities element received from a STA has the SU Beamformee Capable field set to 0 shall not transmit a VHT NDP Announcement frame addressed to the STA or that includes the STA's AID in one of the STA Info fields. They may not transmit a Beamforming Report Poll frame addressed to the STA either. This is because the STA has indicated that it is not capable by having set the SU Beamform Capable fields bit to 0, which means it is incapable of this operation.

When using SU-MIMO, a VHT beamformer that transmits a VHT NDP Announcement frame to a VHT SU-only beamformee shall include only one STA Info field in the VHT NDP Announcement frame and set the Feedback Type subfield of the STA Info field to SU, since it is communicating with an SU station and not an MU station.

If the VHT NDP Announcement frame includes more than one STA Info field, the receiver address, RA, of the VHT NDP Announcement frame shall be set to the broadcast address. If the VHT NDP Announcement frame includes a single STA Info field, the RA of the VHT NDP Announcement frame shall be set to the MAC address of the single VHT beamformee. This allows for the use of MU-MIMO stations and communications with a single MU-MIMO capable station and accounts for instances when a SU-MIMO STA is present.

A VHT NDP Announcement frame shall not include two or more STA Info fields with same value in the AID subfield. There is no need to identify the client more than once. Imagine this process as a lot of if then or if not then statements in basic programming. Basically, the beamformee tells the beamformer how to talk to it and the beamformer uses that information to communicate efficiently with the beamformee. SU stations have different requirements than MU stations. Communications with a single MU station is different than communications with more than one MU station. Due to the complexity in the actual data exchanges to get the high speeds found in VHT, everything about the how to communicate needs to be discovered to work properly.

There are also considerations for communicating in ad-hoc mode and with AP mesh STAs. To that end, A VHT beamformer that transmits an NDP Announcement frame to a VHT beamformee that is an AP, mesh STA or STA that is a member of an IBSS, shall include a single STA Info field in the VHT NDP Announcement frame and shall set the AID field in the STA Info field to 0. These are single device to single device communications and must be formatted as such. The TXVECTOR parameter CH_BANDWIDTH of the PPDU containing the VHT Compressed Beamforming feedback shall be set to indicate a bandwidth not wider than that indicated in the RXVECTOR parameter CH_BANDWIDTH of the received VHT NDP frame. Basically, this means that a station should not respond using a wider channel than used by the NDP received.

To address the use of Beamforming Report Poll frames used when a VHT beamformer transmits a VHT NDP Announcement frame with more than one STA Info field, the VHT beamformer should transmit any Beamforming Report Poll frames used to retrieve VHT Compressed Beamforming feedback from the intended VHT beamformees in the same TXOP. If the duration of the TXOP that contained the VHT NDP Announcement frame has insufficient duration to accommodate the transmission of all the feedback reports, the VHT beamformer may poll for the remaining VHT Compressed Beamforming feedback in subsequent TXOPs. The format for a Compressed Beamforming Action frame can be seen in Figure 8.15. This allowance for polling ensure the beamformer is able to acquire all of the feedback information needed to communicate effectively with the corresponding STAs.

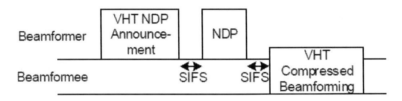

Figure 8.13: A representation of the sounding protocol with a single VHT beamformee

In the event there is difficulty, the standard allows for a worst-case scenario in which a VHT beamformer may use the following worst-case parameters to estimate the duration of the expected frame(s) that contain(s) the feedback response(s): lowest rate in basic VHT-MCS set, no grouping. Using the lowest rate and not grouping is similar to legacy methods of using the lowest rates and least efficient modulations to communicate when necessary. A glimpse into the VHT capabilities supported by a STA can be seen in a frame capture in Figure 8.16.

There are a lot of parameters to be defined in NDP sounding due to the complexity of VHT communications. HT used multiple methods that the STAs and APs had to sort through to determine which one(s) they both supported and which one of them to use. As complex as NDP sounding seems, it is still more efficient to use a single, all be it complex, method that does not require differing methods by client. All VHT capable devices use the same method. Figure 8.13 illustrates the VHT sounding protocol with a single VHT beamformee. An example of the VHT sounding protocol when more than one beamformee is present is illustrated in Figure 8.14. A deep dive into TXBF in VHT can be found in the 802.11-2016 standard Part 11: Wireless LAN Medium Access Control (MAC) and Physical Layer (PHY) Specifications section 10.34.

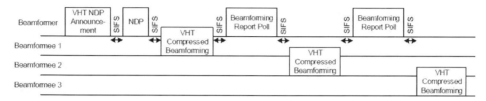

Figure 8.14: A representation of the sounding protocol with more than one VHT beamformee present

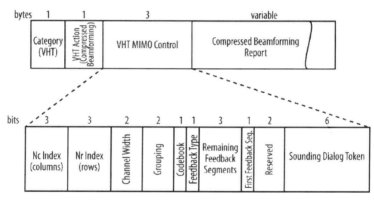

Figure 8.15: The Compressed Beamforming Action frame format

The frame capture in Figure 8.16 is of a beacon frame. It contains information about how this AP is able to use VHT. Notice the references to the number of beamforming antennas, SU Beamformee support and supported channel widths.

HT and VHT have many similarities. However, the higher data rates, extended use of MIMO, MU MIMO and wider channel use make which all help to make VHT much faster also make some parts of its use seem more complex in nature. This perceived complexity is also what makes VHT operations simpler in application. Using a single sounding method saves time but requires more information to be exchanged initially.

Examining what is supported between two stations or an AP and the service set will help you to determine their optimal operations.

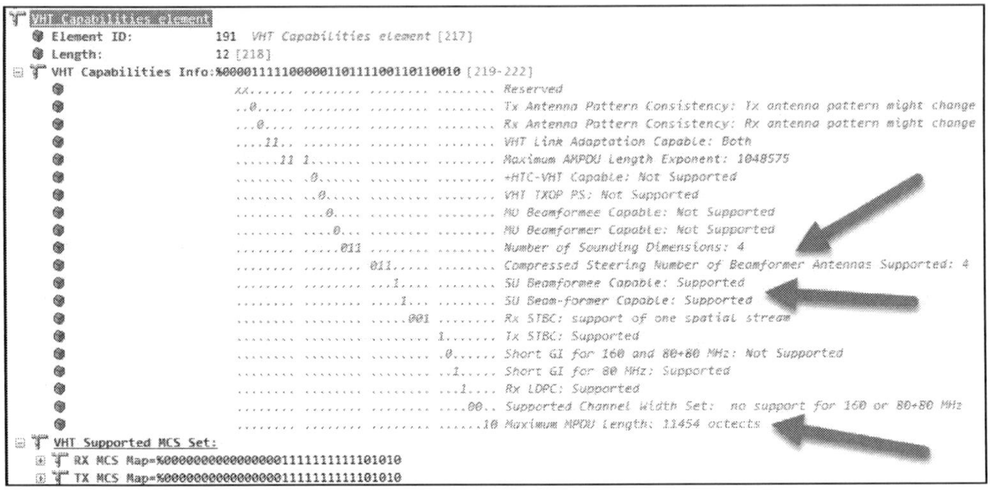

Figure 8.16: A frame capture illustrating the VHT Capabilities Information

MU-MIMO

As stated earlier, VHT builds upon the foundation built by HT. In the previous sections you learned how VHT increases the performance at the Physical layer by expanding the use of MIMO from the 4X4:4 maximum found in HT to 8X8:8. The expanded support increased the complexity of the communications but dramatically increased the potential data rates in doing so. MIMO as introduced with HT was an implementation that used Single User MIMO. VHT did not stop there. It also has provision for using MIMO to improve the downstream transmissions, those from the AP to client STAs. This is accomplished through the use of MU-MIMO.

As you learned in the previous section, there are provisions for beamforming for both SU and MU versions of MIMO. The additional use of multiple streams on the same channel in MU-MIMO is accomplished by targeting multiple users/devices simultaneously. This means that in the access point can transmit multiple streams of data with multiple RAs in the transmission versus a single RA. For the AP to be able to do this it needs to have very accurately estimated radio channel information for each of the intended receivers. This is obtained through the transmit beamforming process described above, NDP sounding. The AP learns how to best communicate with each of the MU-MIMO capable client devices. MU-MIMO takes advantage of transmit beamforming and channel sounding to transmit to multiple client STAs at the same time.

Remember, MU-MIMO is downstream only. To implement MU-MIMO, the AP creates groups that can receive streams at the same time. These groups must contain two or more stations with a maximum of four client STAs. If there is a MU-MIMO capable STA connected and it is the only station to receive a transmission it will be handled as a SU-MIMO transmission to an MU-MIMO capable device. The AP will still learn how to communicate with the single station but will do so as if it were an SU-MIMO STA.

Essentially, MU-MIMO uses the multiple streams that MIMO uses but rather than directing them all to one STA, MU-MIMO can use a single stream for each MU-MIMO capable client in the group and frame aggregation, discussed later, in a single contention and transmission.

This brings up an important compatibility issue. Most implementations are using APs that support more streams than their clients. For example, you may have a 4X4:4 AP servicing 1X1:1 or 2X2:2 stations. If there are four MU-MIMO stations involved in the downstream transmission, each would only use a single stream. If there were two such clients connected and were 2X2:2 or better, each could receive two streams. The performance goal of using MU-MIMO in a downstream manner is to use as many streams as possible. So, if there is a 4X4:4 AP and a single 4X4:4 station, four streams will be used. Also, using the same AP but with four 1X1:1 client stations, four streams will be used. If the station were the only one connected and 3X3:3 capable, three streams would be used.

VHT does support 8X8:8 MIMO but still limits the downstream transmissions used in MU-MIMO to four, see Figure 8.17.

In MU-MIMO conversations the client STA is not required to have multiple antennas to use MU-MIMO. A small client, such as a phone, with only one antenna can still use MU-MIMO. They will only be able to receive a single stream, but it will be in a MU-MIMO conversation that is used to improve throughput within its service set. The successful use of MU-MIMO will largely be dictated by the client capabilities and their environment.

The big impact of MU-MIMO is improved throughput for the service set. The use of MU-MIMO reduces contention for the medium and the time taken by SIFS. The AP can send multiple frames in a single transmission, which requires only a single contention from the AP side versus one for each client to be served.

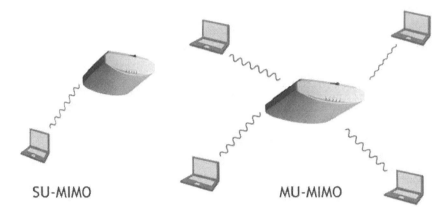

Figure 8.17: An 8X8:8 AP serving 1 SU-MIMO and the same AP serving 4 MU-MIMO client stations

MU-MIMO will work on any VHT supported channel width from 20 MHz to 160 MHz. Obviously, there are other advantages found in using wider channels but they are not required. Many client stations support narrower channels than the APs. Also, in high density deployments, wider channels are not recommended. The improvement in MU-MIMO involves the more intelligent use of the spatial streams not the channel widths. The MU-MIMO will work better when the client stations are stationary than when they are very mobile. This is due to the calculations used in beamforming. The client's environment changes when they move and it is hard for the soundings to keep up with the movement. The stations that do not move or move very little will be able to better use MU-MIMO but the service set as a whole still benefits from its use.

MU-MIMO stations are not magical creatures on your WLAN. They are not able to escape some of the basic rules of W-Fi. They must still acknowledge reception of MU-MIMO transmissions they have received. MU-MIMO is only downstream. So, each station is responsible for acknowledging the frames they receive. To do this in MU-MIMO, a station receiving more than one frame from the AP will use a block acknowledgement. This is because in VHT all data transmissions are A-MPDUs, aggregate MPDUs. When a block acknowledgement is required, the device that sent the frame, the AP in MU-MIMO, may send a block acknowledgement request to the receiving station. The station then replies with the block acknowledgement.

When using MU-MIMO and there are multiple clients within the group that have received data, the AP sends a BAR to one station, waits for it to reply with a block acknowledgement and then repeats the process for each of the remaining stations. See Figure 8.18 for an illustration of a BlockAckReq frame and its control field. The RA field of the BlockAckReq frame is the address of the recipient STA. The TA field value is the address of the STA transmitting the BlockAckReq frame or a bandwidth signaling TA. In a BlockAckReq frame transmitted by a VHT STA in a non-HT or non-HT duplicate format and where the scrambling sequence carries the TXVECTOR parameter CH_BANDWIDTH_IN_NON_HT, the TA field value is a bandwidth signaling TA. When the MU-MIMO transmission is for a single device, the A-MSDU contains multiple MSDUs encapsulated in a single frame with one MAC header and one destination. Therefore, only normal acknowledgments are required when using MSDU aggregation. However, an A-MPDU contains multiple MPDUs, each with their own unique MAC header. Each of the MPDUs must be acknowledged separately; this is accomplished by using a multiple traffic ID block acknowledgment (MTBA) frame. An MTBA is basically a Block ACK frame for an A-MPDU. In a case such as this, the use of a single acknowledgement for multiple frames or aggregated frames reduces MAC layer overhead and therefore improves throughput efficiency by reducing airtime utilization.

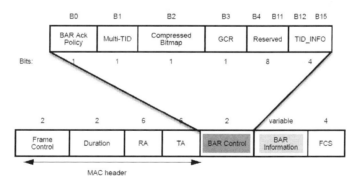

Figure 8.18 BlockAckReq frame format

Block ACKs are used as lists of data frames being acknowledged. Should one of the encapsulated frames need to be retransmitted, there is no need to retransmit all the frames again. Block ACKs allow selective retransmission of data frames, again improving

337

efficiency. For BlockAckReq frames sent under other types of agreement, the BAR Ack Policy subfield is reserved. For BlockAckReq frames sent under Delayed and HT-delayed agreements, the BAR Ack Policy subfield of the BAR Control field will have different meanings and values as seen in Figure 8.19. The values of the Multi-TID, Compressed Bitmap, and GCR subfields determine which of four possible BlockAckReq frame variants is represented, as seen in Figure 8.20.

Multi-TID subfield value	Compressed Bitmap subfield value	GCR subfield value	BlockAckReq frame variant
0	0	0	Basic BlockAckReq
0	1	0	Compressed BlockAckReq
1	0	0	Extended Compressed BlockAckReq
1	1	0	Multi-TID BlockAckReq
0	0	1	Reserved
0	1	1	GCR BlockAckReq
1	0	1	Reserved
1	1	1	Reserved

Figure 8.19 Block ACK Request ACK Policy subfield

Multi-TID subfield value	Compressed Bitmap subfield value	GCR subfield value	BlockAckReq frame variant
0	0	0	Basic BlockAckReq
0	1	0	Compressed BlockAckReq
1	0	0	Extended Compressed BlockAckReq
1	1	0	Multi-TID BlockAckReq
0	0	1	Reserved
0	1	1	GCR BlockAckReq
1	0	1	Reserved
1	1	1	Reserved

Figure 8.20 Block ACK Request frame variant encoding

The BAR Information field of the Basic BlockAckReq frame contains the Block Ack Starting Sequence Control subfield. The Starting Sequence Number subfield of the Block Ack Starting Sequence Control subfield contains the sequence number of the first MSDU for which this Basic BlockAckReq frame is sent. The Fragment Number subfield is set to 0.

Essentially, the use of block acknowledgements improves channel efficiency by aggregating several acknowledgments into one frame, just like the downstream MU-MIMO aggregates data frames to improve efficiency. There are two types of block acknowledgement mechanisms. The first is immediate and is used for latency sensitive applications. Remember, block acknowledgements were initially introduced in the 802.11e amendment to improve quality of service. The second type is delayed, which is more suitable for use with applications that tolerate moderate latency. MU-MIMO uses components of MIMO and QoS combined with the ability to transmit to multiple recipients simultaneously to increase efficacy within a single channel, regardless of its width. Although MU-MIMO has not been largely adopted, it does offer a better means of communication when available and all of the many parameters required are in place – sadly this is rarely a reality and MU-MIMO lacks usefulness in many deployments because of this. For MU-MIMO to really work well, it needs the following:

- STAs positioned well to be un MU groups.
- Frames destined for more than one STA in an MU group.
- STAs that actually support MU-MIMO.

Because it is extremely rare for all three of these to be true (and other constraints exist as well), MU-MIMO is not practical as a benefit today. Will it be more beneficial eventually with the release of uplink MU-MIMO in 802.11ax? Only a very long time (4-5 years – in networking time, that's a very long time) will tell.

Frame Aggregation (A-MSDU and A-MPDU)

Frame aggregation was introduced in Wi-Fi for improvements to QoS transmissions in 802.11e. It is used there and in HT and VHT transmissions as well. It increases throughput by sending multiple MSDU payloads in a single transmission. It is an integral part of MU-MIMO, as discussed above. Its use improves throughput since the fixed MAC layer overhead is reduced, the odds of collision are lowered, and overhead caused by the random back-off timer during medium contention is minimized. Using it you can send multiple MSDU payloads using a single contention. There are two methods of frame aggregation used: Aggregate MAC Service Data Unit (A-MSDU) and Aggregate MAC Protocol Data Unit: (A-MPDU). We will examine them separately.

 While aggregated frames were introduced in 802.11e, they really weren't implemented significantly until the release of 802.11n in 2009. Today, they are used for all 802.11ac PPDUs as they are all sent as A-MPDUs.

A-MSDU is a method used when an AP receives multiple 802.3 frames for transmission to a wireless client STA to get the frames to the station as efficiently as possible. The AP removes the 802.3 headers and trailers then encapsulates the multiple MSDU payloads into a single 802.11 frame for transmission to the client STA. The single transmission containing aggregated MSDUs will have a single destination. An A-MSDU contains only MSDUs whose destination address, DA, parameter values map to a single receiver address, RA, value. Additionally, an A-MSDU contains only MSDUs whose source address, SA, parameter values map to a single transmitter address, TA, value. This means that multiple sources can send to a single destination.

When using a Short A-MSDU, an A-MSDU will contain only MSDUs whose SA and DA parameter values are the same, coming from the same source and going to the same destination. The Short A-MSDU subframe structure is used only between a pair of STAs that communicate directly. The Short A-MSDU subframe structure cannot be used for frame forwarding.

Additionally, the encapsulated MSDUs of an A-MSDU shall all have the same priority parameter value from the corresponding MA-UNITDATA request primitive. This means that the individual MSDUs must all be of the same QoS access category. For example, voice MSDUs are not allowed to be mixed with Best Effort or video MSDUs inside the same aggregated frame.

Stations wishing to transmit an A-MSDU must contend for the medium just as if they were sending a single MSDU. The channel access rules for a Data frame carrying an A-MSDU are the same as a Data frame carrying an MSDU. The block acknowledgement process as described earlier is used to acknowledge this transmission.

The format of an A-MSDU can be seen in Figure 8.21. In an A-MSDU the multiple MSDU packets are combined into a single A-MSDU. The A-MSDU serves as one packet as it is passed down from higher layers to the MAC sublayer. The CRC is calculated for each A-MSDU as if it were a regular data frame. So, if an A-MSDU transmission fails, the entire A-MSDU must be retransmitted reducing its effect.

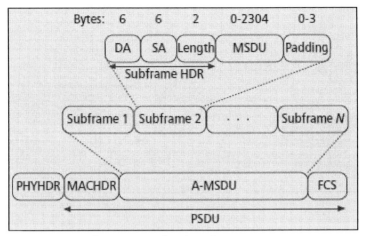

Figure 8.21 The A-MSDU Format

The A-MPDU has the same goal, to make the use of the medium more efficient. The individual MPDUs within an A-MPDU must all have the same receiver address as well. The data payload of each MPDU is encrypted separately. This can be done using either TKIP or CCMP. Individual MPDUs must all be of the same QoS access category. Just as with A-MSDU use, voice MPDUs cannot be mixed with Best Effort or video MPDUs inside the same aggregated frame and so on.

MPDU aggregation has more overhead than MSDU aggregation. This is because each MPDU has an individual MAC header and trailer. CRC errors can be detected within individual MPDU frames. This means that if retransmissions are required an entire A-MPDU does not need to retransmitted. Only the individual MPDU that is corrupted will need to be retransmitted. Having individual headers and trailers means that an A-MPDU transmission is less susceptible to noise than A-MSDU, since only the affected portion needs to be retransmitted in the event of a collision or failed reception. The format of an A-MPDU can be seen in Figure 8.22.

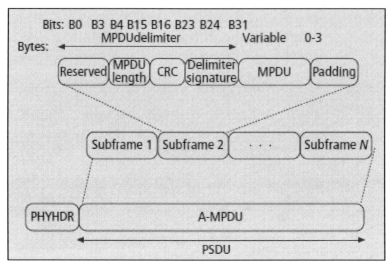

Figure 8.22 The A-MPDU Format

The use of A-MPDU aggregation joins multiple MPDU sub frames with a single leading PHY header. A-MPDU use offers higher overall MAC throughput than the use of A-MSDUs.

Since A-MPDUs are more efficient in retransmission, why shouldn't we just use A-MPDUs all the time and not use A-MSDUs? We could do that but the inclusion of A-MSDUs as a part of A-MPDU use is more efficient over all. This is because the inclusion results in: fewer CRC calculations. CRCs only need to be calculated once per A-MSDU as opposed to once for every encapsulated MSDU in an A-MPDU. This also means that there are fewer MAC headers to build. Most traffic is made of smaller transmissions. Allowing this type of aggregation improves speeds due to the reduced overhead of these calculations. Another advantage attained when using A-MSDUs is the allowance for mixed source addresses. A-MSDUs can contain MSDUs potentially from different source as long as they are of the same traffic identifier, TID.

The size limit of an A-MSDU and an A-MPDU is based on the negotiations between the transmitter and the receiver. The component of negotiation happens in the association process using the association request and association response frames. Each STA or AP will include their supported frame size as 3.8K, 7.9K or 11K bytes in the A-MSDU support element. Once the AP and STA have their maximum A-MSDU size negotiated, the individual transmission sizes are dependent upon implementation.

Chapter Summary

The operations of both HT and VHT have the same goal, to improve the use of the very limited spectrum we have for Wi-Fi use. The overhead of wireless networking creates a rather large impedance to its use. HT and VHT attempt to improve upon how we use the medium once we have won the contention. The ability to transmit multiple spatial streams in a single channel found in MIMO, SU-MIMO and MU-MIMO is a great improvement. Additionally, adding QoS features like aggregate frames and block acknowledgements continues to improve our use of the space.

Facts to Remember

- MIMO takes advantage of multipath to send and receive multiple spatial streams using spatial multiplexing (SM).
- Transmit beamforming can increase the received signal strength at the receiver, but it performed at the transmitter.
- Maximal Ration Combining (MRC) can increase the received signal strength at the receiver and is performed at the receiver.
- MU-MIMO depends on several factors to work, including STA candidates for MU groups, data destined to multiple STAs in MU groups, and STAs supporting MU-MIMO.
- Block Acknowledgements reduce airtime consumption required by individual MPDU acknowledgements.
- Aggregate frames (MSDUs or MPDUs) improve efficiency of airtime usage.

Review Questions

1. When using an 8X8:8 VHT AP and MU-MIMO how many MU-MIMO client stations can be in a single group??

    A. 2

    B. 4

    C. 6

    D. 8

2. When using transmit beamforming in VHT, which technique is used for the AP and STA to determine how the beams are to be formed?

    A. NDP sounding

    B. Beamformee enumeration

    C. Beamformer enumeration

    D. VHT beamform arbitration

3. Upon how many channels can an AP and an associated STA simultaneously use MIMO without changing channel?

    A. One

    B. Two

    C. Four

    D. Eight

4. Within the context of MIMO transmissions, what term is used to describe the known channel properties?

    A. CCI

    B. CCA

    C. CSI

    D. CIA

5. What is the maximum number of client stations that can simultaneously transmit block acknowledgements when using MU-MIMO?

> A. One
> B. Two
> C. Four
> D. Eight

6. Which frame type can contain multiple MSDU payloads from multiple source addresses?

> A. A-MPDU
> B. A-MSDU
> C. Block Acknowledgement
> D. NPD Sounding

7. What kind of beamforming is used in VHT?

> A. MU-MIMO
> B. A-MPDU
> C. Implicit
> D. Explicit

8. Where should you look for the maximum MPDU length supported by a VHT AP in a beacon frame?

> A. In the VHT capabilities
> B. In the MIMO capabilities
> C. In the NPD Sounding Element
> D. In the Channel Width Support

9. True or False: The MIMO channel coefficients are sent to the beamformee by the beamformer.

> A. True
> B. False

10. Why is beamforming difficult in most deployments?

     A. The CSI varies due to non-802.11 noise sources.

     B. The CSI varies because client stations are mobile.

     C. The APs and STAs support different versions of MIMO.

     D. The use of 20 MHz wide channels does not provide enough bandwidth.

Review Answers

1. The correct answer is B. MU-MIMO supports a maximum of 4 downstream clients per group.
2. The correct answer is A. Although HT has multiple methods, NDP sounding is the only method used in VHT.
3. The correct answer is A. MIMO transmissions occur within a single channel. If channel bonding is used, it is still a single channel, just using more space.
4. The correct answer is C. Channel State Information, CSI, refers to the known channel properties.
5. The correct answer is A. MU-MIMO is a downstream use of the channel. Stations must independently acknowledge the reception of frames. Only on STA can transmit a clock acknowledgement at a time.
6. The correct answer is B. An A-MSDU can contain multiple MSDU payloads from multiple sources but they must all be for the same destination address.
7. The correct answer is D. Although HT could use either Implicit or Explicit and had many sounding methods to negotiate, VHT only uses Explicit.
8. The correct answer is A. The maximum MPDU length supported by a VHT AP should be found in the VHT capabilities of a beacon frame.
9. The correct answer is B. The MIMO channel coefficients are sent to the beamformer by the beamformee to determine the CSI.
10. The correct answer is B. The CSI varies because client stations are mobile. The conditions found in one spot are not the same as in others. Stationary clients benefit more from TxBF than mobile clients.

Chapter 9: Spectrum Analysis

Objectives Covered:

2.1 Capture RF spectrum data and understand the common views available in spectrum analyzers

2.2 Analyze spectrum captures to identify relevant RF information and issues

2.3 Analyze spectrum captures to identify various device signatures

2.4 Centralized spectrum analysis solutions

When troubleshooting or conducting a physical site survey, many people often only focus on Layer 2 information that can be seen in a packet capture with a protocol analyzer. This information is very valuable and often points to the issues as desired; however, it only tells part of the story. Since 802.11 communications use both Layer 1 and Layer 2, you really need to examine what is happening at both layers to get the whole story. Spectrum analysis allows you to find out what is happening at Layer 1.

As you know, Wi-Fi uses the unbounded medium of the RF on the air to communicate. This exposure makes the communication process subject to more sources of interference than communications using a bounded medium such as Ethernet cabling. In addition to contending for the medium, the RF, with many 802.11 signals using the same frequencies, 802.11 communications also share the medium with many non-802.11 signals and noises on the same frequencies. These non-802.11 signals, intentional or accidental disruptions, do not contend for the medium in a way that is compatible with 802.11, if they contend at all. If you were merely conducting a Layer 2 analysis using a packet capturing utility, you would not be able to determine the source of any of these very common non-802.11 interferers. With a protocol analyzer, you may see things such as a high retransmission rate or be able to locate hidden node problems but would miss everything at Layer 1. To truly have the whole story of what is happening in your basic service areas (BSAs), you need to examine both Layer 1 and Layer 2.

Adding spectrum analysis and packet analysis to your investigative process will allow you to better understand what is happening in the space, giving you the ability to avoid or remediate issues that could be adversely impacting your WLAN. This chapter will focus on the use of spectrum analysis in planning and troubleshooting WLAN deployments. The topic of spectrum analysis comprises 15% CWAP exam.

Capturing Data and Using Spectrum Analyzers

Gathering information about what is happening in your basic service area at Layer 1 will require specialized hardware and software. Although some vendors have enabled the radios in their APs to report a limited amount of information about RF energy found at Layer 1, the standard Wi-Fi adapters found in client devices are not able to do this for you.

In addition to the specialized radios used to collect the information, you will also need specialized software to interpret what you collect. APs having the ability to collect a limited amount of information about the RF energy and help you locate the general area impacted by the noise faster, since the APs are distributed throughout the network and you are not. APs using spectrum analysis are not able to perform any other AP function using the radio or radios involved in the analysis. They are locked on Layer 1 analysis and are not able to act as a normal AP radio during this use. These APs do not physically appear in any way different from the other APs on your network. This additional functionality is usually just a matter of firmware and licensing to be made available. The licensing is usually priced per AP. The APs can report the noise to your controller or wireless network management system (WNMS) for viewing and analysis.

From the AP monitoring, you can get a rough idea of the device for which you will be looking when you go onsite. Once onsite, you will need to use dedicated hardware and its software to locate the noise source as APs cannot move around the environment like a portable analyzer. Some noise sources are mission critical devices in manufacturing or healthcare, for example, and are not able to be removed. Items that are not mission critical, such as a microwave at the desk of a user, can be found and removed. Using spectrum analysis with your portable analyzer in-hand, you are able to conduct last mile discovery of interference sources or conduct the entire discovery when there are no APs in the area with the ability to help.

Install, Configure, and Use Spectrum Analysis Tools

Spectrum analyzers are used by wireless engineers to capture and display visual representations of raw RF signals, from both 802.11 based and non-802.11 based sources. We will now examine some of the hardware and software commonly used in the wireless industry for spectrum analysis and the software with which it works. Some spectrum analyzers are hand-held devices using self-contained software and a proprietary operating system. Additionally, many spectrum analyzers work only on laptops. However, newer versions of software have enabled the latest generation of spectrum analyzers to work well using tablets. Earlier spectrum analyzers used PCMCIA cards and were laptop-based. Since PCMCIA cards have largely faded from use, these may be hard to find and harder to use. The non-integrated (not part of an AP) spectrum analyzers use USB connections in most cases today. Notice how these commonly used models very closely resemble client Wi-Fi adapters in Figures 9.1 and 9.2.

Figure 9.1: NETSCOUT AM/C1097

Figure 9.2: Metageek Wi-Spy DBx

These adapters connect in the same way you are most likely used to connecting Wi-Fi adapters and are easily installed directly or by using a cable. Although you would be using them within the same area as the noise for which you are searching, they are still using an omni-directional antenna setup. You can use your body as a shield and block some of the signal from reaching the antennas. Using this method, you would need to turn around slowly until the signal became weaker, indicating the source was behind you. You could also use a directional antenna to help you locate the noise source. With this method, a stronger signal would indicate that the source of noise is in the direction your antenna is facing (the intended direction of propagation of the directional antenna and therefore the most sensitive receiving side of the antenna). The image in Figure 9.3 shows a spectrum analyzer attached to a laptop and using a directional antenna.

You can also use an all-in-one client device for locating the noise source. See Figures 9.4 and 9.5. These have integrated Layer 2 radios as well as an integrated spectrum analyzers and integrated batteries to power the radios, saving battery life on your laptop or tablet so you can survey and or troubleshoot longer. Keep in mind that these devices use an omni-directional antenna configuration. You will need to turn about to find the direction in which the noise source is located as described above. Additionally, since these devices do not hang from your laptop or tablet you may be tempted to have them in a backpack.

Do not do this. They will overheat, potentially damaging the device, creating a hazardous situation, and may not be able to detect the signals as well as needed. Some all-in-one devices require the use of a laptop or tablet. Others have their own screen for viewing collected data. How they report the information gathered will vary based upon the proprietary software interface used.

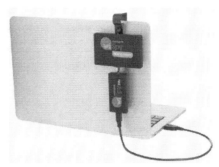

Figure 9.3: Metageek Wi Spy DBx with Device Finder antenna

Figure 9.4 Ekahau Sidekick

Figure 9.5 NETSCOUT AirCheck G2 Wireless Tester

Spectrum analysis hardware has evolved over time as our client devices have changed and as our use of Wi-Fi has changed. Some early spectrum analyzers only scanned 2.4 GHz. Today, that seems rather limited. However, at the time they were popular, because very few networks were using the now needed 5 GHz and were still supporting many old 2.4 GHz only clients. Most of the non-802.11 sources of noise you will encounter reside in the 2.4 GHz space as well.

However, today's networks utilize the 5 GHz band, either in addition to the 2.4 GHz band or on its own. Therefore, you should be using a spectrum analyzer that is capable of scanning both bands. Some spectrum analysis adapters scan both bands but only one at a time. The adapter must be "locked" onto the band you wish to scan. Others scan both bands, first scanning one and then the other. Many people conducting spectrum analysis use two cards at the same time, one locked on 2.4 GHz and the other locked on 5 GHz. This method greatly reduces the time it takes to fully scan an area, since you are scanning both bands at the same time.

You will find that some of the spectrum analyzers are able to sweep the bands faster than others or offer the ability to scan for user defined durations in their sweeps. "Sweeping the band" is not some new way to get a bad musical group out of a club. In this case, it is passing across the frequency range (band) specified and reading the energy on the frequencies as it passes across them. It is sometimes called the *sweep cycle*.

If you have determined that the noise source is on a specific channel, it is useful to lock your spectrum analyzer on that channel. This allows your adapter to spend all its time sweeping the single channel and reducing the time it takes you to find the noise source.

The APs, adapters and software you select for your work may be a matter of brand loyalty or budget. An important thing to know about the tool you are using is resolution bandwidth (RBW). It is a reference to the smallest frequency that can be resolved by the receiver. RBW should be low enough to resolve spectral components of the transmissions being measured. Frequency hopping devices typically represent the smallest transmit shape that should be recognized by a spectrum analyzer in the Wi-Fi domain. If the resolution is low, your sweep times decrease (it sweeps faster). If the resolution is high, your sweep times increase (it sweeps slower). Remember, higher RBW is a narrower frequency inspection and lower RBW is wider frequency inspection, though it is typically set in kilohertz, it can be thought of as higher resolution when narrower kilohertz values are used and lower resolution when wider kilohertz values are used. This may impact your sampling across the entire band. Remember, you really need to scan all channels in both bands today. So, select hardware and software combinations that will enable you to perform thorough analysis.

The software interfaces used to visualize the RF signals detected by the spectrum analyzers vary by manufacturer. Some only show a graphical representation of the RF energy. See Figure 9.6. Some only show you what the software believes the source of the RF energy to be based upon known signatures being compared to the RF signals reported through the spectrum analyzer. See Figure 9.7. Some try to do both things, display a graphical representation of the RF energy detected and provide the user with what the software believes to be the source of the RF signal.

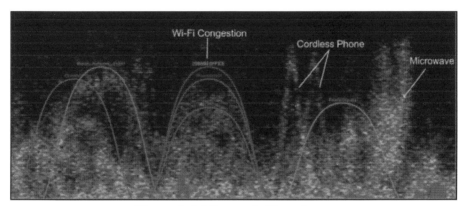

Figure 9.6: Metageek Chanalyzer

Figure 9.7: NETSCOUT AirCheck G2

Although some RF sources may have a similar impact on your WLAN, their signatures vary enough to allow you to find the source using the suggested source signatures. Advances in hardware have allowed some to use a single spectrum analysis radio to scan Layer 1. The newer radios are able to sweep the spectrum much faster, reducing the need to use two radios and saving battery life. The faster sweep also allows for a smoother graphical representation of the detected noise, making the user interface more appealing. See Figure 9.8.

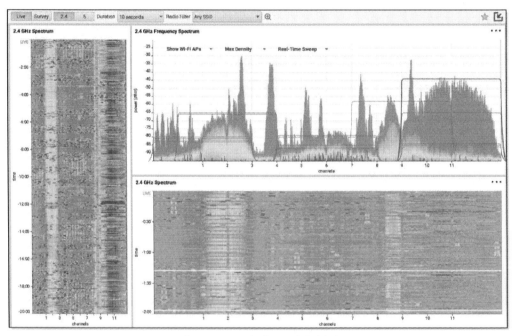

Figure 9.8: Ekahau Sidekick

Distributed use of spectrum analysis is quite useful. This is the use of either a purpose-built spectrum analysis radio or an 802.11-based radio within an access point for determining the source of and location of interferers. This use will usually be a separate purchase or an additionally licensed feature from your WLAN vendor and is part of the WLAN infrastructure. However, the time savings in locating problems and solving them faster will soon make up for the cost. These radios do not need to be assigned in every access point. They can be enabled or installed in at risk or key usage areas. When users report a problem that you cannot find using Layer 2 analysis and believe the source to be a Layer 1 interferer, you simply enable the spectrum analysis function from the controller or WNMS on an AP in the impacted area.

Keep in mind, when an AP radio is functioning as a spectrum analysis radio, it cannot service clients, nor can it perform other AP or Layer 2 functions. Also, if a dedicated radio is used for spectrum analysis, the other AP radios may stop functioning to prevent their use from ruining the Layer 1 diagnostics on the spectrum analysis radio. Since the users in that service set area are already having problems, this should not be a major concern in many cases. Their client radios should be able to roam to another AP, allowing them to still work but at a lower data rate, assuming your WLAN is designed properly. See Figure 9.9. For a look at the spectrum analysis display provided by a distributed/infrastructure utility see Figure 9.10.

Figure 9.9: Aerohive Warning

Finding the source of interference is not hard, if the interferer is active. It should take no longer than a couple of minutes for a trained eye to see the problem when using spectrum analysis. Once you have determined what the source of the interference is, you can take corrective measures. If needed, you can then go into the area with your portable spectrum analyzer for the last mile of locating the source. When using a distributed spectrum analysis method, you can approximate the location of the noise source prior to or in many cases instead of traveling to a location. This is a growing method of finding interferers, since it allows you to reduce truck rolls - physical visits by an administrator or specialist. This method gets users back up and working quickly, increasing productivity and reducing expense. The major down side is that when using 802.11 based radios for spectrum analysis, the graphical display in the user interface is not as precise as when using a dedicated spectrum analysis radio. However, you are still able to determine the source of the noise by looking at the information displayed.

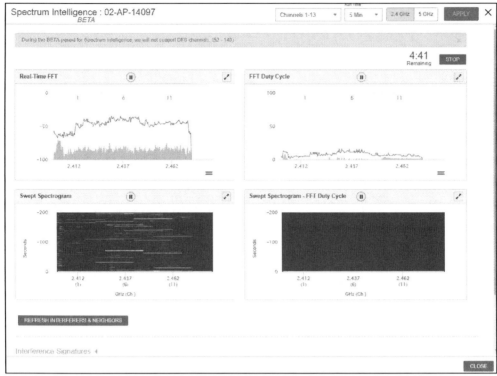

Figure 9.10: Aerohive Spectrum Intelligence

Some portable and some distributed spectrum analysis utilities have a database of known interference signatures. They compare what you are capturing with this database and will display an estimation of the interference source, such as a camera, Bluetooth, or other non-802.11 noise source.

Capturing RF Spectrum Data

To capture Layer 1 noise using a spectrum analysis tool, you will first need to decide which tool to use. If you have access to both portable and infrastructure-based methods of capture, you may use both or could have a specific use case for only using one. If the problem requires immediate diagnosis and you are remote, the infrastructure spectrum analysis is the best choice. If you are onsite or need to conduct last mile locationing of the source yourself, a portable spectrum analyzer is the better choice.

When using both, you will start with the infrastructure spectrum analysis. You will need to navigate to the desired tool in the controller or WNMS interface. Some have this as an

358

option you select and then browse to the desired AP for use. Others have you select the AP and then the spectrum analysis function. You will most likely receive a warning, reminding you that while the AP is scanning Layer 1, it cannot function at Layer 2. The verbiage will vary. You will then select to continue. At this point you should start seeing the visualization of the noise detected by the radio.

You may need to switch bands to find the noise. Often the systems using a single dual-band radio will default to scanning and displaying 2.4 GHz. This is because the majority of non-802.11 noise sources reside in this band. If your noise is in 5 GHz, you will need to change bands and wait for the user interface to populate.

Once you have determined what the noise source is, you will need to determine where it is located. Many infrastructure spectrum analysis utilities work with your network maps. They will display the noise, most often in red, on the map where it is believed to be located. This is normally within a 10-meter radius of the source. The accuracy of this estimation is directly related to the proximity of the APs detecting the noise and the number of APs that can hear the noise. A high-density deployment will allow you to better estimate the location of the noise source because you have more APs in each area. If you can work with someone at the location to remove the noise source, do so. If not, you will now need to go to the location and use your laptop-based, portable, spectrum analysis tool. You will have a much better idea of where to start looking for the noise source, having used the infrastructure tool first.

Should you either not have or not be able to use an infrastructure tool, you will need to visit the location. You will start your investigation within the same physical area as the users reporting a problem. For in-person locationing and or last-mile locationing using your laptop-based or portable spectrum analysis tool, you will need to scan both the 2.4 GHz and 5 GHz bands. Most users think wireless networking is just something that works. They have no idea of which band they are using. Scanning both bands while you are there is a best practice.

If you are not using a directional antenna, you will need to use your body to shield the antenna as discussed previously. Remember, most spectrum analysis radios use omni-directional antennas. When using this method and slowly turning about, the noise should become weaker when the antenna is on the opposite side of your body from the source of the noise. Humans are mostly water and water absorbs 2.4 GHz waves exceptionally well. If you are using a directional antenna, the noise source will be in the direction where it is detected with the strongest signal facing the antenna.

Once you have determined which tool or tools to use, finding and mitigating or remediating the source of the noise is easy. If the noise is not on your property or is from a mission critical source, you will need to work around the noise. You will need to plan your channel and band usage to allow both the noise and your WLAN to coexist within the dame physical area. If the noise is on your property and is not mission critical, you may decide to still work around it. You may also decide to remove it or use another device for its purpose that does not interfere with your Wi-Fi.

Using Spectrum Analyzer Views

Different spectrum analysis products have different user interfaces and views. Some are very simple, and others are more complex. The hand-held all-in-one devices tend to have smaller screens and therefore simpler interfaces. Laptop-based and infrastructure-based tools tend to have richer feature sets and therefore offer a more complex interface. You will need to understand what you are being shown and how to use that information. This section will cover some of the information you will encounter when conducting spectrum analysis and will teach you what it means as well as how to use it in diagnosing Layer 1 issues.

 Understanding the purpose of different spectrum analyzer views is important for the CWAP exam. Make sure you know the kind of information shown in common views and the use of those views.

The first piece of information we are going to discuss is *real-time FFT*. A real-time spectrum analyzer does not have any blind time, since it is feeding the information gathered into the user interface as it is collected. A Fast Fourier Transform (FFT) is an algorithm that samples a signal over a period of time (or space) and divides it into its frequency components. These components are single sine wave oscillations at distinct frequencies. Each will have their own amplitude (power) and phase. The spectrum analyzer can capture the incoming RF energy within the time domain and convert the information to the frequency domain using the FFT process which is then processed in parallel, gapless, and overlapped so there are no gaps in the calculated RF spectrum and no information is missed. To see how this is represented in some spectrum analyzers, see

Figure 9.11.

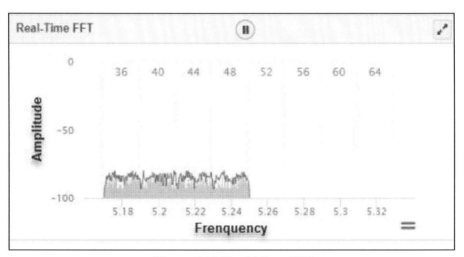

Figure 9.11: Real-Time FFT

The *swept spectrogram* shows you the RF energy present at a particular frequency over the course of time. This is essentially the same information as the Real Time FFT, but it is presented in a different format and tracked over time. It will display the frequency and signal strength (amplitude) of the detected RF signals. You can see the similarity in Figure 9.12, which displays a transient, non-persistent, interference source. A *waterfall view* displays the same information as a swept spectrogram but vertically versus horizontally. Some tools use only one view while others use both, either in the same interface or in different portions of the products interface. Figure 9.13 is an image displaying an RF noise in a waterfall view.

Another measurement displayed in spectrum analysis software is the *power spectral density*. This displays the strength of the detected energy as a function of frequency. In other words, it shows at which frequencies any detected RF energy variations are strong and at which frequencies these variations are weaker. See Figure 9.14.

Historic views can be useful in diagnosing troubles as well. If you are not able to visit a site, another person can conduct the capture for you. They can send you the capture file for your analysis. You can open the file using your spectrum analysis tool and review the capture. This will be historical information versus a live view.

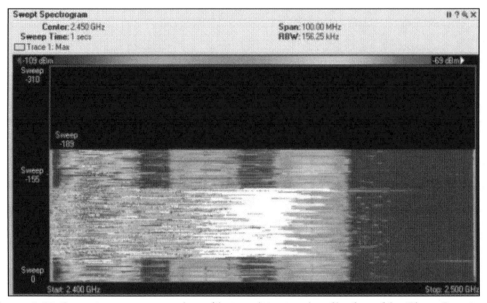

Figure 9.12: Swept spectrogram vies of intermittent noise displayed in Cisco Spectrum Expert

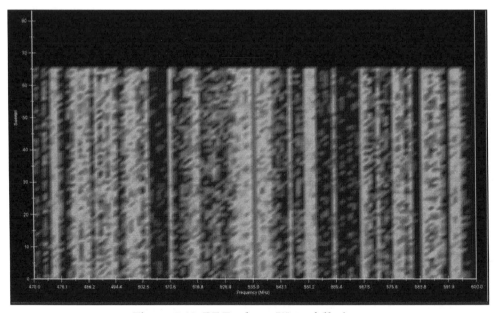

Figure 9.13: RF Explorer Waterfall view

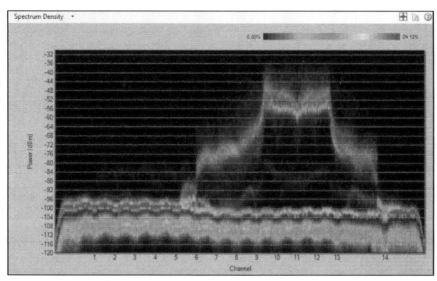
Figure 9.14: Spectrum Density Aruba Networks an HPE company

Some infrastructure systems allow you to trigger a frame capture or spectrum analysis capture to happen automatically based upon an alarm configuration. For example, you could configure an alarm to trigger if the noise flor in each area reaches a certain level. Based upon this alarm triggering, actions can be taken automatically by the system, such as sending an email to an administrator or beginning a capture. You can then access the controller or WNMS to view the captured data in an historical context. This type of capture and view is useful in locating the source of an intermittent interferer. Often, by the time a user has a problem and the report reaches the correct administrator, the noise is gone. Having the ability to capture what is happening at Layer 1 and store it for historical analysis is a great feature. Most portable tools allow you to save your capture for future analysis as well.

The *spectrum utilization* and *duty cycle* are also important pieces of information displayed by spectrum analysis tools. The spectrum utilization reporting allows you to determine how much airtime is being used on a given frequency. This should include both 802.11

transmissions and non-802.11 based noise. If you have a very low-density deployment generating a small number of Wi-Fi transmissions, you could still have a very high spectrum utilization due to noise. This will cause a high retransmission rate and lower throughput. Users will complain of a slow network, even when there are no high QoS demands from applications like voice or video. At Layer 2, you will see many retransmissions. You may not find any hidden node or CCI problems. Once you turn to Layer 1 analysis, you will see a lot of noise in the frequency. The noise is using the same spectrum as your WLAN. It's just not contending for the use of the medium with your devices and causing problems. The 802.11 radios may be able to detect the noise but not being able to read any 802.11 information, transmit and collide with the noise. This will cause the transmitting device to retransmit, because it never receives an acknowledgement. 802.11 stations will retransmit up to 32 times before giving up, in most devices. When you are looking at airtime utilization, you must include non-Wi-Fi sources of RF energy on your channels. See Figure 9.15. Spectrum utilization views can help you see the entire picture, not just what Wi-Fi is doing.

Figure 9.15: Spectrum and Channel view in Ekahau Site Survey

The duty cycle is traditionally calculated for a specific signal and is defined as the pulse duration divided by the pulse period. Many spectrum analyzers calculate the duty cycle as the amount of time the measured amplitude is above the noise floor or another arbitrary threshold. A high duty cycle indicates that the noise source could be causing measurable problems for your WLAN. A very low duty cycle indicates that the noise is causing some type of problem but is likely a negligible amount of interference. Imagine you are in a classroom with someone that is playing a radio loudly all day. That would be a high duty cycle and would have a negative impact on the class. Compare that to someone that whispers to a fellow student 3 or 4 times over the entire class. That would be a negligible amount of interference and may not warrant investigation or remediation. The display of an RF transmissions duty cycle in spectrum analysis shows this to you in an easy to read graph, enabling you to determine which signals to act upon. See Figure 9.16. FFT Duty Cycle measurements are often an important way to determine the potential impact of an RF transmitter on WLAN operations. The duty cycle measures the duration of time a signals amplitude is above some arbitrary threshold, such as -95 dBm.

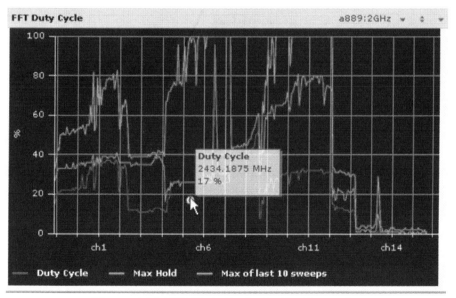

Figure 9.16: FFT Duty Cycle Aruba Networks

Detected devices have their own signatures. A Wi-Fi door bell will not use the spectrum the same way that a microwave does. Spectrum analyzers will detect noises of all types within the frequencies they are designed and enabled to work. Some will have a detection library and will display what they think is causing the noise based upon the stored signatures. Others do not offer this feature and leave the interpretation of the displayed noise up to the user. It will take you some time and experience to be able to tell what is causing the noise simply by looking at the spectrograph found in your spectrum analysis tools. However, once you have seen the signature a few times and tracked down the offending devices, you will be quite good at estimating the source of the noise, because you will have your own internal library of signatures. When looking at information displayed by spectrum analyzers, you will see many signals, even if locked on a single frequency. That is due to the number of devices placing RF energy into the space. You will need to determine which devices are supposed to be there and which devices are not. Device identification will be covered later in this chapter.

WLAN integration views will allow you to see both the RF energy visualized in the spectrum analysis and the SSID and in some cases the MAC address of detected APs. This is useful in helping you decide if an offending AP is yours or a neighboring one. It is also useful in helping you determine if your APs are causing the problems you are troubleshooting. See Figure 9.6 above.

Analyzing Spectrum Captures

Once you have captured data using spectrum analysis tools, you will need to interpret the information gathered. You will need to determine what is relevant to your design work or troubleshooting efforts.

RF Noise Floor

One of the first things you will need to determine is the signal strength of the noise floor. This is an important piece of knowledge to be used in your design and in any troubleshooting. For our purposes, the noise floor is the combination of all RF signals or energy created by all the noise sources and unwanted signals within a requirement area, where noise is defined as any signals or energy other than that being created by your WLAN devices.

Why is the noise floor such an important thing to us in Wi-Fi? Many applications require a signal strength that is based upon a measure above the noise floor to work properly. Conventionally, people try to maintain an RSSI from the APs of -80 dBm for basic connectivity, -70 dBm for high speed data, - 67 or -65 dBm for voice (based upon vendor recommendations) and - 62 dBm for RTLS. These numbers all assume a standard noise floor of -95 dBm exists. What if your noise floor is higher than -95 dBm? Some applications may fail to work. You may need to adjust the transmit power on your APs to compensate for the higher noise floor.

Basic Connectivity	-80 dBm coverage recommended
High Speed Connectivity	-70 dBm coverage recommended
Voice	-67 to -65 dBm coverage recommended
RTLS	-62 dBm coverage recommended

 It is a great point of frustration to many new WLAN administrators that vendors list data rate capabilities and performance capabilities based on received signal strength (such as RSSI) instead of SNR. These administrators eventually learn that SNR is the key to both data rate achievement and performance achievement. When a vendor says you need -65 dBm, remember, they are saying you need an SNR of 30 dB in most cases.

If you are not able to obtain the needed RSSI value for the devices or applications you are using, they will not be successful. Suppose your requirements are only for high speed data transmissions. You would normally only need an RSSI value of -70 dBm or better to achieve the desired use. That will change if the noise floor is higher than -95 dBm. If the noise floor is -80 dBm, 15 dB higher than the expected norm of -95 dBm, you would need to increase the transmit power on your APs to compensate for the noise or install more APs, which can in turn increase the overall noise floor (yes, it can be a vicious cycle). You may need an RSSI value of -55 dBm or better. For high speed transmissions you should have an RSSI value that is 25 dB stronger than the noise floor.

Some noise is created by mission critical devices. So, you are not going to be able to remove the noise source. You may see a situation in which the clients are older single band 2.4 GHz only devices. This means that you are not able to simply move to 5 GHz to avoid the noise. Some interferers are broadband RF noise makers (like microwave ovens). This means that simply changing the channel used within the 2.4 GHz band will not work. You are then left with increasing the transmit power of the APs to compensate for the noise. This will only serve as a mitigation. The clients may not be able to have the transmit power increased. So, what do you do? You have to break some of the best practice rules by adding more APs than you would normally want and just deal with the increased CCI to support the applications and clients in that area. Throughput will be degraded but the network will be able to function versus having no Wi-Fi or replacing the legacy 2.4 GHz only stations. Fortunately, the legacy stations are usually not running any applications that are network intensive except for legacy VoIP phones. These situations are increasingly rare, due to hardware and application refreshes. Another option would be to use directional antennas, focusing the beams to better support the clients and possibly reducing the exposure to noise. You may need to shield the noise source or find budget to upgrade equipment if you are unable to coexist with the noise in the band the legacy devices support. Not every deployment is a walk in the park; some of them are more like a walk in a muddy park.

SNR

The SNR is a comparison of the level of signal power to the level of noise power. See Figure 9.17. SNR is most often expressed in decibels (dB). SNR is the difference in decibels between the received signal and the background noise level. Higher values mean a better specification, since there is more of the intended signal than there is unwanted noise. Data corruption and re-transmissions will occur if the received signal is too close to the noise floor.

SNR is a great way to judge the quality of signal. This is because SNR also takes the ambient noise of the RF environment into account. To determine the SNR, you will need to measure both the signal strength from wanted transmissions and the signal strength from the unwanted transmissions. This can be done using a spectrum analyzer.

As you learned earlier, some applications require a stronger signal than others to operate properly. Generally, a signal with an SNR value of 25 dB or more is recommended for high speed data networks where as an SNR value of 28 to 30 dB or more is recommended for networks that use voice applications.

Remember that a signal with an RSSI value of -67 dBm is twice as strong as one of -70 dBm since it is 3 dB stronger. So, voice communications require at least double the signal strength of high speed data transmissions. Transmissions requiring higher SNR values are more susceptible to noise related problems than those requiring lower SNR values.

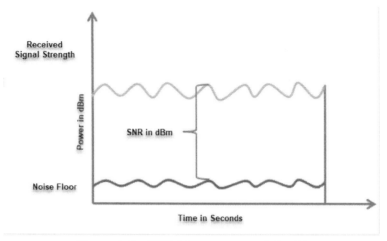

Figure 9.17: SNR Measurement: Meraki

Interference

When you believe that the problem an WLAN is experiencing is due to interference or as part of your physical site survey you determine that there is non-802.11 interference in the space, you will need to identify and locate the source of the unwanted RF energy. As discussed earlier, you can use a distributed detection or detection from a portable spectrum analyzer to find the source of the noise.

When using an integrated solution, you will know the area in which the source of the RF noise is most likely located but will not be able to do a last-mile discovery of the source. You can start with the integrated solution and then use your portable spectrum analyzer for last-mile locationing, or simply begin your search for the source within the area where any problems indicating noise are reported.

Identifying the source requires a knowledge of the signatures different noise sources have or a spectrum analyzer with a definition library that can tell you what it believes to be the source. You should make yourself familiar with the more common signatures. The actual signatures of various noise sources will be covered later in this chapter.

If possible, spend some time scanning with a spectrum analyzer to find even more RF noise sources before you go into the field or take the exam.

A common RF interferer is a microwave oven. They leak energy even though they are designed to keep as much of it in as possible. They operate in the 2.4 GHz band as these frequencies absorb well into water and, therefore, food. Some microwave ovens leak more than others, but must leak at a level lower than the average AP. Still, if the user is near the microwave oven, it can wreak havoc on their 2.4 GHz WLAN link.

 Do not turn on a microwave without food in microwave safe containers in the microwave. This may cause the microwave to fail and need to be replaced. You may want to run spectrum analysis at meal or break time in an office.

Channel Utilization

When using a spectrum analyzer, you can identify the sources of many different non-802.11 RF signals. You can also identify Wi-Fi devices and the channels upon which they are transmitting. This information is easily found in a packet capture since the channel upon which the transmission occurred is identified in the header information. Switching back and forth between tools is a time-consuming task. If you are already using spectrum analysis, why switch to packet analysis just to determine which channels are being used in your requirement area? Spectrum analysis software will show the channels being used in either the swept spectrogram, the waterfall view or in both. Some just show the channel number while others display the frequency. Figure 9.18 below illustrates multiple APs on separate channels in the 5 GHz space. Notice that the 20 MHz wide channels they are using are labeled under each APs RF energy visualization in the swept spectrogram.

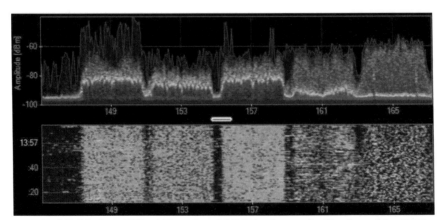

Figure 9.18: Multiple 5 GHz APs using 20 MHz channels displayed by Metageek

In Figure 9.19 you see a single 5 GHz 802.11ac access point using an 80 MHz wide channel. You can tell that this is the case because the guard space that exists between the RF signals from the APs shown in Figure 9.18 above are being ignored and used to transmit data by the single AP in Figure 9.19 below. Radios ignore the guard space between consecutive channels used in channel bonding. This gives the radios more frequency space for data transmissions and is one of the ways in which newer technologies can achieve such high throughput.

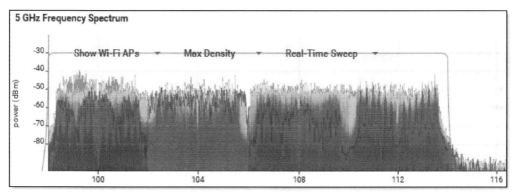

Figure 9.19: An OFDM AP using an 80 MHz wide channel and 4X4:4 MIMO displayed by Ekahau Site Survey

Non-Wi-Fi Transmitters

When more than one 802.11 device is operating within the same space and on the same channel, they contend for the medium. This helps to ensure that every device gets a chance to transmit, even when using QoS. However, non-802.11 devices operating in the same space will not contend for the medium like the 802.11 devices. When non-Wi-Fi transmitters are in the area, Wi-Fi usage will be negatively impacted. The degree to which the WLAN is disrupted will vary based upon the type of device that is creating the non-802.11 RF energy. As you learned earlier, Bluetooth devices do operate in the same space as 2.4 GHz Wi-Fi devices and can cause problems if enough of them exist to disrupt Wi-Fi (such as 20 or more in a space and "hear-shot" of each other). It is unlikely that there will be enough Bluetooth use to dramatically impact Wi-Fi in most cases. If someone is streaming music or video over Bluetooth and they are very close to an AP, that may be a problem.

You can use spectrum analysis to determine the cause and locate the offending device. An office filled with Bluetooth headsets, keyboards and mice could be a problem if they were all in use at once and all close to Wi-Fi devices but the volume of user devices it would take to cause a serious disruption in Wi-Fi is too high to be practical. Other interferers are more likely suspects. However, you will not know what is causing the noise until you perform spectrum analysis.

Microwaves only impact 2.4 GHz Wi-Fi transmissions since they only work in the 2.4 GHz space. Wi-Fi devices using 2.4 GHz, on any channel, near microwaves, will have connectivity issues when the microwaves are in use. Look for this problem around meal and break times but expect it anytime the microwaves are in use. A leaky microwave can disrupt Wi-Fi usage across a large area if the microwave is not well insulated. If the microwaves are causing a significant problem, look for better insulated models with which to replace them. You can also implement band steering to move as many clients in the area to 5 GHz as possible. You can also try updating critical clients to dual-band from 2.4 GHz-only if indicated. There is not much you can do for IoT (Internet of Things) devices in this situation. They are mostly 2.4 GHz only and are not able to be updated or steered to 5 GHz. The microwave itself will have to be removed or replaced with a model using better shielding. Important devices and users may need to be moved out of the area, if possible.

Cordless phone base stations can cause problems for Wi-Fi if they are located too close to an AP. However, the phone usage will only impact Wi-Fi when the phone is in use and has hopped to the channel being used by the AP or an overlapping adjacent channel if they are in 2.4 GHz. You can find the base station using spectrum analysis. This problem is an older one that has largely disappeared. Cordless phones have a usable range that is rather limiting when compared to cellular phones and VoIP wireless phone usage. Most users have cell phones and do not need a cordless phone in the office. Also, many offices have moved away from cordless phones to VoIP wireless phones. You may still see these in SOHO deployments. If you encounter this problem, you should examine the use of the cordless phone and search for an approved better option.

Many people like the idea of using wireless surveillance cameras since they cost less to deploy than a wired system. These are found mostly in the 2.4 GHz space. Unlike Bluetooth and cordless phones, wireless cameras are not frequency hoppers. They are typically locked on a single channel. Finding them using a spectrum analyzer is easy. See their signature in Figure 9.24. Once you locate them, you can determine the channel they

372

are using, then hard code the APs closest to a camera to use other non-overlapping channels. If there are a lot of these cameras using channels 1,6 and 11 or the channels you need, you may need to go back to wired security cameras or migrate your Wi-Fi usage to 5 GHz to completely remediate the problem.

Overcoming non-Wi-Fi interference boils down to some very simple things, though they may be time-consuming.

- Locate the offending devices.
- If possible, remove the interference source.
- Change channels.
- Change frequency bands.
- Shield the noise.
- Move the Wi-Fi devices away from the noise.
- Replace the offending devices with non-offending ones.
- Increase the Wi-Fi transmit powers to overcome the noise.
- Use directional antennas on the APs to increase the signal at the receivers and increase the received signal at the APs.

Not all these options are always doable. Sometimes you can combine work arounds to coexist with the noise. Other times you must tolerate it because you have done the best you can do in the given situation. Limiting factors include device capabilities, available frequency space, time and budget. However, most situations have a resolution.

Overlapping and Non-Overlapping Channel Interference

As you know, there are overlapping, and non-overlapping channels used in Wi-Fi. In 5 GHz, the channels are considered to be non-overlapping, when channel bonding is not in use. In 2.4 GHz, the channels overlap with their adjacent channels. A good channel plan avoids the use of overlapping channels within audible range of each other. However, you have no control over what the neighboring WLANs are doing in terms of channel use nor in terms of power usage. A physical site survey using spectrum analysis will help you locate the neighboring devices and identify the channels upon which they are operating and the channels with which they overlap. You plan your AP placement and channel usage around the neighboring devices and all is well, until the neighbors make changes. Now you need to go back into the area and troubleshoot. It is not uncommon to find devices on overlapping channels in the 2.4 GHz space. They have been deployed by people that do not know how to plan their channels or the auto-channel feature they are using has been configured to use these channels. Either way, you now have a problem.

Co-channel and overlapping channel interference are two of the names commonly used to describe what happens when two or more APs are using the same channel within the same physical area (also called an overlapping BSS (OBSS)). What is happening here is not really interference. What is happening is an increase in contention for the medium across service sets on the same channel. For this reason, a newer more accurate term is being used by many industry leaders, co-channel cooperation or co-channel coordination. Most people in Wi-Fi believe that most of the co-channel interference is caused by the APs. However, the majority of this "interference" is caused by the client stations around the perimeter of the overlapping coverage cells in most networks.

In addition to the increased contention caused by this problem, there is usually an increase in the hidden node problem. The hidden node problem will further degrade the throughput of the service sets due to an increase in retransmissions.

When using spectrum analysis to diagnose the problem, you may start by looking for a non-802.11 noise source. You will not find one but will see the energy from the APs centered on the same channel. The APs will most likely not have the same detected signal strengths due to their relative proximity to your spectrum analysis tool. You will be able to see independent representations of each APs RF energy in the interface of your spectrum analysis tool. Wi-Fi aware spectrum analysis tools also allow you to see the channel being used in addition to the RF energy representations by frequency. This is nice, because most controller and AP interfaces only show the channel number and not the frequency being use, for example Ch1 versus 2.412 GHz. See Figure 9.20. This can be used as an additional indicator of the overlapping channel coverage problem, when you see multiple APs on the same channel using different SSIDs. If they are all using the same SSID, you will need to determine if the network is using a single channel architecture, SCA. If it is, there is not a CCI problem, because the controller will not allow APs that can hear each other to transmit at the same time. Since most adoptions of SCA have been migrated to a multi-channel architecture, MCA, finding an SCA network is rare, but they are out there and many of them work quite well.

The CCI problem occurs when more than one WLAN or BSS is attempting to co-exist in the same coverage area on the same channel. When good WLAN design is used, the CCI problem should be minimized within the same network. However, neighboring and rogue device use still cause this problem. Both packet analysis and spectrum analysis can find this issue. Once found, the issue can be addressed. To resolve this issue within your WLAN, you can ensure the output power is not higher than is needed on your networks APs. This will reduce CCI.

Spectrum - WiFi Summary				
Channel Summary				
Ch... ▲	Curr...	Avg	Max	Duty Cycle
Band 2.4 GHz				
1	-106	-99	-39	22.02%
2	-105	-99	-39	20.70%
3	-104	-99	-40	16.32%
4	-106	-100	-30	12.94%
5	-109	-96	-9	8.78%
6	-109	-96	-9	10.60%
7	-110	-96	-9	21.13%
8	-109	-96	-9	11.48%
9	-106	-103	-14	19.09%
10	-105	-102	-29	24.70%
11	-104	-102	-34	17.69%
12	-105	-102	-34	12.88%
13	-108	-102	-34	10.10%
14	-114	-109	-62	0.32%

Figure 9.20: Channels and duty cycles displayed for 2.4 GHz

Overlapping adjacent channel interference is truly interference. This occurs when two or more APs within the same area are using adjacent overlapping channels such as 1 and 2 or 6 and 7 in 2.4 Ghz. Remember that the channels in 2.4 GHz overlap with each other. See Figure 9.21 for an illustration of the channel overlap in 2.4 GHz.

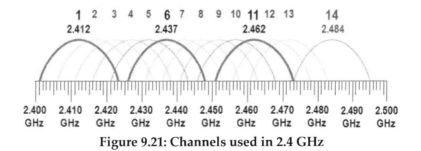

Figure 9.21: Channels used in 2.4 GHz

DSSS channels are 22 MHz wide and OFDM channels have a 20 MHz width. There are 14 channels in the 2.4 GHz space used in Wi-Fi at the above widths that must exist within roughly an 83 MHz wide space. The first non-overlapping channel pair is channel 1 and

6, the next 6 and 11. Most WLANs use a three-channel plan in 2.4 GHz: 1, 6 and 11. More information about channel use can be found in the Certified Wireless Network Administrator (CWNA) materials.

To resolve CCI, you will need to remove offending APs or change the channel so that there is more separation in frequencies. Because so many APs default to channel 6, if only two APs are required in a coverage area to provide the needed capacity and there are no other nearby WLAN cells, you can usually get the best results by simply setting the APs to channels 1 and 11. In most cases, CCI cannot be completely avoided in 2.4 GHz, due to capacity requirements and neighboring networks. When possible, try to use 5 GHz channels. There are more of them and they theoretically do not overlap. If you must remain in 2.4 GHz, for legacy support and supporting 2.4 GHz only devices such as IoT and Machine-to-Machine (M2M) usage, plan 2.4 GHz only as needed in specific requirement areas. Use only the number of APs required to provide capacity in 2.4 GHz. Implement band steering to encourage dual band clients to use 5 GHz. Upgrade as many clients to 5 GHz support as possible. Shape the coverage using antennas and the building materials as possible. Having done all that you can to mitigate the problem, properly set user expectations for the space.

Adjacent Channel Interference (ACI) exists primarily in 2.4 GHz and can be identified by a high rate of frame retransmissions. Remember, 5 GHz channels are considered to be non-overlapping. Retransmission rates above 10% can result in significant degradation of throughput and above 1-2% for VoIP can be problematic.

When you conduct spectrum analysis in this scenario, you will see APs on separate channels that overlap with each other. This is overlapping adjacent channel interference and is truly interference. Stations on one channel most likely are not able to decode the frames from the overlapping channel but must still contend with the noise, RF energy, within their space. You can also find the AP causing this problem using a protocol analyzer by looking within the header of a captured frame to find the MAC address of the AP and the channel upon which the frame was transmitted, should you want to validate your spectrum analysis findings at Layer 2. See Figure 9.22 for details.

Within a single WLAN, you can completely avoid ACI from your own devices by using a three-channel plan such as 1, 6 and 11. Some auto-channel feature sets use plans resulting in ACI. If this is the problem, you can configure the controller or RF profile in the WNMS to use a three-channel plan instead of using any channel. This capability is not available in most consumer devices.

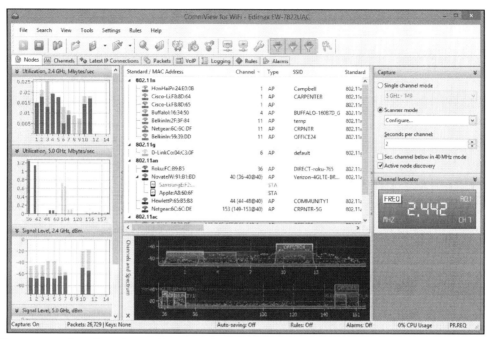

Figure 9.22: Overlapping Adjacent Channel Interference, channels and SSIDs seen in CommView for WiFi

Neighboring and rogue devices on overlapping channels are not as easily mitigated. A rogue device can be located and removed from you space. Neighboring devices cannot be so easily removed. You will need to adjust your channels around neighbors as best as you can with a hope the problem is mitigated in doing so.

Proper design can prevent many issues in WLAN deployment. However, you will find, in densely populated areas, that you may not be able to remediate the problems created by CCI nor the problems presented by ACI. This is especially true in shared office spaces. Short of turning your buildings into Faraday cages, degraded performance, due to over congestion and poor channel planning, in the band may be out of your control.

Radio Problems: Poor Performance and Faults

Hardware, no matter how well manufactured, is still made by humans and can be shipped in faulty condition, improperly configured, or can develop problems due to use or damage. Hardware issues are not uncommon in Wi-Fi. The number one problem in WLAN use is poor design. The number two problem seems to be driver or firmware related. Interference and user created problems run a distant third and fourth. Hardware problems can exist on WLAN clients, APs, controllers, WNMSs, and even on the wired side of the network. We will now address some of the more common problems you may encounter when troubleshooting as they relate to poorly performing or faulty radios.

As mentioned above, the number one problem in WLANs is poor design. The design may be completely wrong or could have been great but the use of Wi-Fi or the environment changed without the design being updated. For the purpose of this discussion, we will stipulate that the design is spot on. Interference and Denial of Service attacks can be found and remediated or mitigated. That leaves us with hardware and users as the most likely causes of our problems.

Users have less and less to do with their connections as their interfaces are restricted by the devices or their devices are configured for them by an IT professional. Gone are the days of asking the user if their Wi-Fi card is inserted correctly or the more humorous question is it plugged in at all (though this problem does still exist as laptops and mobile devices allow users to turn off Wi-Fi). The WLAN cards are not only pre-installed but are most likely integrated into the system board of their devices.

Not all adapters are created equally. Users may complain that they are not getting the lightning fast speeds promised by the new 4X4:4, 160 MHz wide channel access points you deployed (which, of course, we hope you didn't, at least not the 160 MHz wide channel). They do not understand that their client device must support the same things and have a great signal to get the magic speeds promised on the box.

If the radio is not built to support something, it will not be able to do so. There are limitations to the functionality of Wi-Fi adapters. For example, a single-band adapter simply cannot operate outside of its frequency capabilities. In most cases, single-band adapters are 2.4 GHz only. If they are using a legacy 2.4 GHz-only client device or even a new wearable 2.4 GHz-only device, they will not be able to connect to the new dual-5 GHz access point. You will find that many new client devices are still being sold having only internal 2.4 GHz radios: cameras, speakers, projectors, fitness devices, M2M clients and more. Older dual-band clients were configured to prefer 2.4 GHz. If this is the case, you may be able to change that in the devices management interface. Newer dual-band clients are set to prefer 5 GHz.

While most newer devices are configured to prefer 5 GHz, they are also often configured to scan 2.4 GHz first and then 5 GHz when looking for APs. In many devices, if the organization uses the same SSID for both bands, they will connect to that first AP seen in 2.4 GHz. To prevent this, use different SSIDs for 2.4 GHz networks and 5 GHz networks. This can also help prevent the rare, but real problem, of band roaming.

Client devices have limitations beyond just being single band. Some of these include:

- Supported PHYs (802.11n supported but not 802.11ac)
- Number of supported spatial streams (1X1:1 versus 2X2:2 or higher)
- Support for security features
- Interface type (USB, mini-PCIe, etc.)
- Receive sensitivity (there is no industry standard for calculating RSSI values)
- Antenna gain (clients usually have internal only that unchangeable)
- Output power (most have a factory set max Tx that is not user adjustable)
- Support for WMM or QoS
- Excessive roaming

Non-hardware-specific features are enabled within firmware. If a user is unable to use such a feature, their firmware may be out-of-date and in need of an upgrade. Drivers/firmware can often be the root of a client adapter's problem. Disabling and reenabling the adapter causes the driver to reinitialize, which often solves the problem. The same thing happens when a USB adapter is removed and reinserted. It is not uncommon for a helpdesk employee to ask the user to reboot their device. This also causes the device driver to reinitialize and often solves the problem.

The wrong driver can also cause problems for the devices. If the user has recently updated the driver and now reports that the device is not working properly, they may have installed the wrong driver or an outdated version of the driver or a new version that is faulty. Sometimes the driver provided by the chipset manufacturer is needed to resolve the issues encountered when using the driver provided by the client devices operating system, such as through Windows Update. Optimal performance can be impacted by using the wrong drivers as well.

New drivers offer many things that can help or hurt. Let's be honest, firmware and driver updates often cause problems forcing you to roll back to the old version. The intent of new drivers is to offer things such as bug fixes and feature enhancements.

Wireless radios can stop working correctly and warrant replacement because of hardware issues as well. If that is the case, replace the radio or the clients as needed. However, it is far more likely that there is an issue with the driver or firmware. Poorly performing devices may need to be replaced if their unacceptable performance is due to a limitation of their hardware.

You can optimize many clients by using the latest firmware or driver and ensuring their configurations meet the needs of the user. However, there are far more client devices out there that you are not able to configure than those you are able to configure. This is because phones, tablets, wearables, door bells, cameras and every other thing under the Sun people have demanded have a wireless adapter are locked so that the user has no control over the adapter short of turning on and of Wi-Fi. This was a measure taken by the manufacturers to reduce user-created problems for the device.

If the device is not damaged, you will need to research the device having trouble to find out if the trouble is something that can be addressed by firmware/driver changes or configuration settings you can change.

An older configuration problem was excessive roaming (and it still exists in many environments). Users would adjust the roaming aggressiveness too high and would cause their client device to bounce between APs too often. Most clients today do not allow the user to change this setting, but they may still not have an optimized roaming algorithm. This may be solved through driver updates or it may be something requiring hardware replacement.

On the opposite side of this is a sticky client, a device that will not roam away fast enough. This could be a configuration issue, if it is a configurable option, or just a legacy client issue. You should examine the minimum supported data rates on the APs and make changes if needed.

Of course, WLAN cards can go bad. They may stop working completely or have intermittent problems. One problem bad cards share on both wired and wireless clients is that they become chatty. They just start dumping nonsense onto the network. This can cause collisions and a decrease the throughput for the WLAN.

If you determine the configuration is a problem, reconfigure it. If the firmware needs changed, change it. Lastly, if the device is damaged or incapable of providing what the user needs, you may need to replace it.

Identifying Signatures

Although 802.11 and non-802.11 RF energy is found within the same frequency range, their signatures vary greatly. Within this section, we will examine some of the more common RF energy sources found in the 2.4 GHz and 5 GHz bands and their signatures. It is important for you as a Wi-Fi professional to be able to identify both Wi-Fi and non-Wi-Fi signatures. Within Wi-Fi signatures you should be able to distinguish between DSSS and OFDM signatures as well as 20 MHz channels versus wider channels using channel bonding. You should also be able to identify the base channel of a bonded channel use AP.

Frequency Hopping Devices

Bluetooth devices operate in the 2.4 GHz band. These devices use frequency hopping, moving from one frequency to another 1,500 times per second across the entire 2.4 GHz space. See Figure 9.23. This means that you do not have the option of changing channels to avoid it. However, it will only bother you for 1/1500 of a second when it lands in your channels frequency. Also, Bluetooth devices are relatively low-powered. It would require several Bluetooth devices simultaneously active in your space before you would likely have any trouble with your WLAN. Additionally, modern Bluetooth devices use Adaptive Frequency Hopping (AFH), which means that when they are interfered with on a frequency in their hopping pattern, they avoid that frequency in the future. In the end, this also prevents them from interfering with your Wi-Fi signals as much as possible, though their goal is to prevent your Wi-Fi signals (or whatever interfered on that frequency) from interfering with them. Obviously, there is only so much space in 2.4 GHz so some interference cannot be avoided, but AFH helps.

Cordless phones are also frequency hoppers. However, they can be found in both the 2.4 GHz space and the 5 GHz space. See Figure 9.24. Cordless phones create a constant peak in amplitude while on a given channel. They normally do not hop while in an active call unless they detect noise. Older versions had a button which allowed the user to change channels if they were having trouble communicating. Some models may hop across the entire band. Cordless phones may change their frequency each time they are used. Channel changes can be seen in the swept spectrogram or waterfall. These are based upon a sweep. The sweep is the period of time it takes to scan the desired band, 2.4 GHz or 5 GHz. Some tools sweep faster than others. Many tools allow you to adjust the sweep time or lock them on a specific channel.

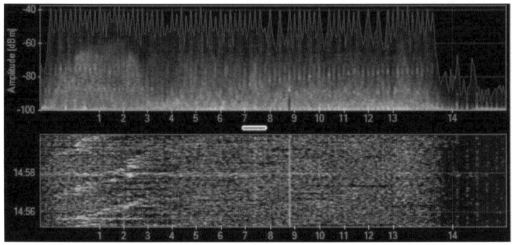

Figure 9.23: Bluetooth displayed by Metageek

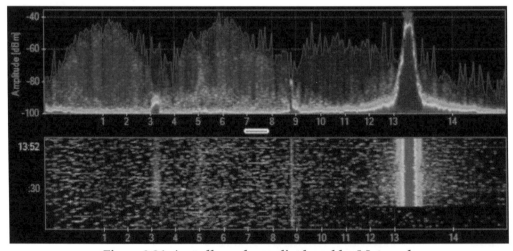

Figure 9.24: A cordless phone displayed by Metageek

802.11 PHYs

802.11 devices also have distinctive signatures. An AP using Direct Sequence Spread Spectrum (DSSS) as seen in Figure 9.25, legacy 802.11 and 802.11b, will have a bell curve shaped signature, a width of 22 MHz and will only be found in the 2.4 GHz space. An AP using Orthogonal Frequency Division Multiplexing (OFDM), 802.11a/g/n/ac/ax, will have a more box shaped pattern and, with the exception of 802.11g which exists in 2.4 GHz only and 802.11ac which exists in 5 GHz only, be found in either the 2.4 GHz or 5 GHz band. See Figure 9.26 below. If channel bonding is used, the box shape elongates to the width of the channel being used, from 40 MHz to 160 MHz in width.

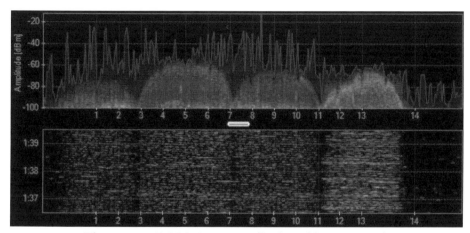

Figure 9.25: DSSS AP usage displayed by Metageek

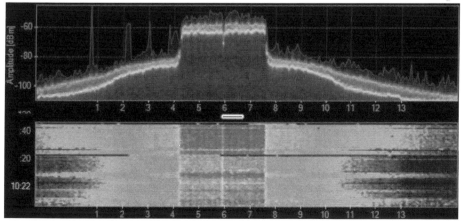

Figure 9.26: An OFDM AP using a 20 MHz wide channel displayed by Metageek

The image above, Figure 9.26, could be an 802.11g or an 802.11n access point on channel 6. A packet capture would let you know which modulation technique is in use, ERP-OFDM or HT-OFDM. Additionally, if the spectrum analyzer supports Wi-Fi integration, it can inform you have the actual PHY in use.

Figure 9.27 could be an 802.11n or an 802.11ac access point using channels 44 and 48 in 5 GHz to transmit data. You can tell that it is a 40 MHz wide channel being used for data transmission because, not only are the two channels being used, but so is the guard space between them. If this capture were of two 20 MHz wide channels being used independently, the guard space would be observed and space would exist between the RF energy visualizations. Figure 9.28 is an 802.11ac access point transmitting data using an 80 MHz wide channel.

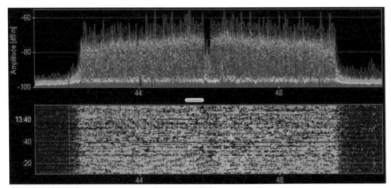

Figure 9.27: An OFDM AP transmitting data on a 40 MHz wide channel in 5 GHz displayed by Metageek

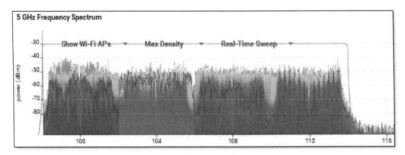

Figure 9.28: An OFDM AP using an 80 MHz wide channel and 4X4:4 MIMO displayed by Ekahau Site Survey

When using channel bonding and transmitting data all bonded channels are used. Additionally, the guard space between the channels is ignored and used for data transmissions. Management and control frame transmissions only use the primary channel. To determine the primary channel using spectrum analysis, simply look for the single channel being used in every transmission. It will look like a regular 20 MHz OFDM signal. Some spectrum analysis interfaces will show a box or some other type of line across the bonded channels, even when only detecting the primary channel in use. Examine Figure 9.28 which shows a 4X4:4 data transmission using an 80 MHz wide channel. Notice the box around the entire channel and the guard space being used to transmit data versus separating channels. An AP using 802.11ac on a 160 MHz wide channel can be seen in Figure 9.29.

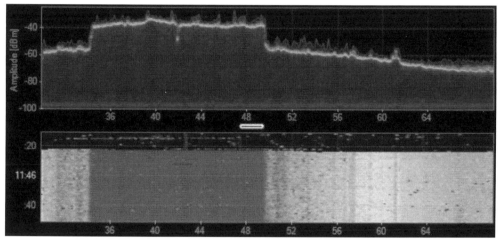

Figure 9.29: An 802.11ac access point using a 160 MHz wide channel seen in Metageek

Many implementations use dynamic channel width allowing the administrator to assign the maximum width. Channel bonding should never be used in 2.4 GHz, due to the limited number of channels and vast number of interference sources. Channel bonding should be carefully used in 5 GHz. APs can usually use wider channels than most clients. Given that fact, bonding wider than the clients support wastes channels. Also, you should not bond using channels in use by neighboring APs, even if they are yours. The bonded APs will not be able to function as desired if this is the case. The problem faced by users of bonded channels is often that their environment and or capacity demands will not allow bonding to work as desired.

Non-802.11 Devices

Remember that Wi-Fi operates in unlicensed frequency ranges. This means that any device can create RF energy either as a direct part of its function or as a side effect of its function so long as it is not being used to purposely disrupt the signals of other devices. Many such devices exist in the frequency ranges used by WLANS. When conducting physical site surveys and troubleshooting WLAN problems, spectrum analysis is used to find the source of non-802.11 RF signals. Within this section we will examine some of the more common non-Wi-Fi interference sources.

Microwave ovens operate in the 2.4 GHz band. Early in their use they were called Radar Ranges, because they use RF energy to warm food and drink. The normally create a large and widespread peak shape in the swept spectrogram or waterfall. See Figure 9.30.

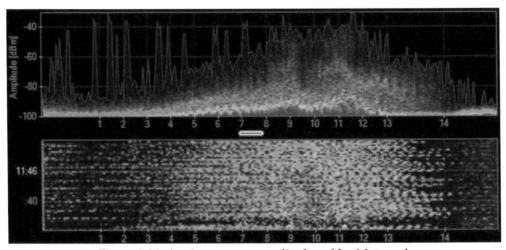

Figure 9.30: A microwave oven displayed by Metageek

Microwaves are used in minutes and seconds, normally. This makes them easy to see in the spectrum analysis software. The power levels (amplitude levels) displayed for microwave oven use will vary depending on their power setting, age, shielding, attenuation of building materials and distance from your spectrum analyzer. Commercial microwaves are better insulated than consumer grade microwaves. You can expect them to create problems around break and meal times for those using 2.4 GHz near their locations. It is not uncommon for users to have a microwave at their desk. These are usually the inexpensive, lower powered and less shielded types. They may cause problems throughout the day. Many organizations have policy restricting their use outside of designated areas to reduce power consumption and reduce interference. Notice the width of the disruption caused by microwave oven in use captured in Figure 9.30. If you are closer to the microwave, the amplitude of its RF energy will appear stronger. 2.4 GHz clients and APs near a microwave in use will have high retransmission rates. Many older clients will stop working and require a reboot.

Other increasingly common noise sources you may find are wireless cameras and wireless audio devices. See Figure 9.31. They usually create three spikes in the 2.4 GHz band. These devices do not contend for the medium like 802.11 based devices. They are constantly transmitting and are usually locked on a single channel or rarely change channels.

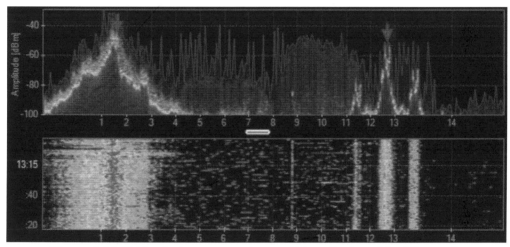

Figure 9.31: X.10 wireless camera transmitting displayed by Metageek

An RF signal generator, the politically correct name for RF Jammer, as seen in Figure 9.32, can create constant noise on a single frequency or can be a broadband jammer and create noise across the entire band. These are used in a denial-of-service attacks, hijacking attacks and due to the amount of noise they create, will prevent other wireless technologies from fully operating within the given range. Their use is illegal in most countries. In some, it is even illegal to have one in your possession. RF jammers are not just a problem for communications but are also an indication that your network is at risk when they are detected. Intrestingly, USB 3.0 interference can look like an RF jammer that is some distance away from you. It does not radiate with the energy of an RF jammer, but within 1 meter, it has a similar signature, usually sweeping across the entire 2.4 GHz band starting with lower power on the low-end of the band and higher power on the high-end of the band.

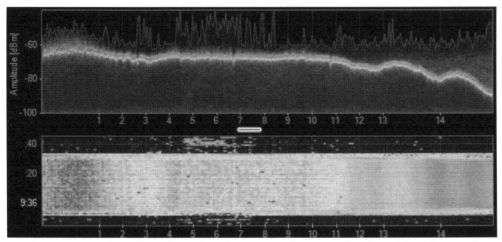

Figure 9.32: A broadband RF signal generator/jammer displayed by Metageek

Baby monitors, like the signature seen in Figure 9.33, are also a source of noise that impacts Wi-Fi. However, they are most often found in residential environments. Similar video monitoring devices may be deployed in business spaces.

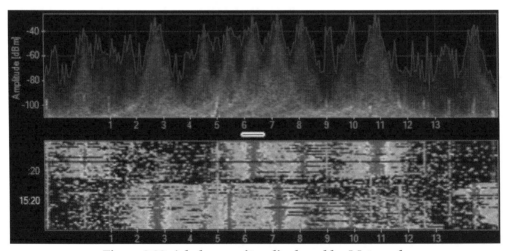

Figure 9.33: A baby monitor displayed by Metageek

In addition to the more common sources of interference you will find others such as:

- Alarm systems
- Remote control toys
- Speaker systems
- Projectors
- Video game controllers
- Motion sensors
- Weather Radar

A listing of many of these and their related visualizations can be found here:

```
https://cwnp.link/rfsigs
```

Centralized Spectrum Analysis

Time is a precious resource. So, having a distributed way to collect information about your network is a popular, if not required, method of diagnosing problems found in WLANs. Spectrum analysis can also be done using distributed radios versus portable/handheld methods. Some vendors offer the ability to use your access points and their 802.11 based radios for spectrum analysis while others offer a dedicated sensor solution. The choice between the two is usually made based upon one of two deciding factors: cost and functionality. The integrated solutions found by using existing APs usually costs less but may not provide the detail found when using purpose-built spectrum analysis radios. The dedicated sensor solution offers more detail but costs more to buy and implement. No matter which of the two is used, you will be able to save a great deal of time in diagnosing Layer 1 issues, since you do not need to travel to the location to collect the needed information. As discussed earlier, many people use a combination of methods, distributed and portable/handheld, for spectrum analysis. If you can solve the problem remotely using a distributed method that is great. If not, at least you are able to narrow down the affected area. Then when you do go onsite you will be able to use your portable/handheld solutions more efficiently.

AP-Based Analysis

AP-based spectrum analysis uses the standard 802.11 AP radios. This usually requires specific firmware to enable the functionality. Additional licensing may be required. This licensing can be tied to specific access points or limited to several simultaneous uses.

Licensing models vary greatly among AP vendors. Some even include this feature at no additional cost.

When using spectrum analysis from an AP, there are options. First, you can run it in a background mode. This means that the AP will conduct Spectrum analysis when the AP is not transmitting and is not awaiting an acknowledgement from another radio. This method collects the least amount of information and is often referred to as time slicing. If you are using this method in a busy network, you will collect little to no information from spectrum analysis.

Another method is to use one radio for spectrum analysis and another to service clients as an AP. This method allows you to collect more information than the first but also has issues. The radio acting as the AP will cause interference for the radio acting as the spectrum analyzer on the channel being used and if in 2.4 GHz the overlapping channels. AP vendors offering this method have measures in place to subtract the noise they know their AP radio makes from the views presented in the interface. This makes the interface cleaner but does nothing to prevent the radio being used as an AP from preventing the spectrum analysis radio from hearing things on the impacted frequencies that may be at distance from the AP or that may have a weaker signal.

Many of the same arguments for and against these methods exist when using an integrated Wireless Intrusion Prevention System (WIPS). They are lower costs solutions but are missing full functionality.

Another method of AP based spectrum analysis allows the AP to suspend all AP functions to use the radios strictly for spectrum analysis. This method yields the best results possible when using 802.11 radios for spectrum analysis. However, there is still an issue. When the AP radios are dedicated to spectrum analysis, they are not able to service clients. If there is already a problem in the area, a couple of minutes of using the radios for analysis should not be a significant issue. The clients should be able to roam away to another AP and roam back when you are finished.

When you elect to begin spectrum analysis from an AP you may should be given some type of warning reminding you that the users may be impacted by your use of the APs radio. See Figure 9.34 as an example of the warning. If you are already working within your controller or WNMS you do not need to switch tools to begin your analysis. You simply navigate to the desired AP and begin your diagnostics. The interface will vary from vendor to vendor. Some require you to select the function then the AP while others require you to select the AP and then the function.

Figure 9.34: Warning message presented when beginning spectrum analysis from an Aerohive AP

Figures 9.35 and 9.36 show spectrum analysis views from vendors using an AP based solutions. Having even a limited ability to do spectrum analysis remotely saves both time and money. It also gives you a chance to get the users back up and working faster, reducing downtime in your WLAN.

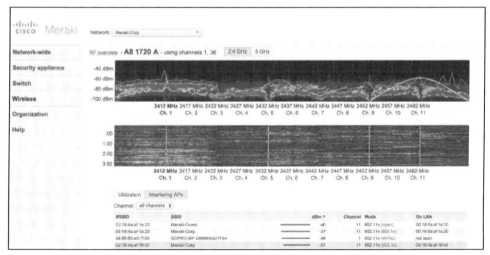

Figure 9.35: RF Spectrum page in Cisco Meraki dashboard

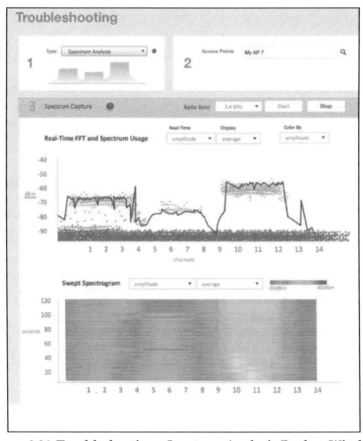

Figure 9.36: Troubleshooting - Spectrum Analysis Ruckus Wireless

Sensor-Based Analysis

Sensor-based spectrum analysis uses dedicated hardware. This can be in a form factor like an AP or the same as your laptop-based tools but set up to report to a remote interface. Often the sensors are APs dedicated to sensor-only functionality and use the same 802.11 radios for spectrum analysis that they would normally use as an AP radio. There are also a few spectrum analysis-only sensors that have been produced. The radios used in these sensors are purpose-built for spectrum analysis, just like the ones you use in your handheld/portable spectrum analyzers. They can better detect RF noise sources and identify them in their interface than AP-integrated options. They do cost more to implement. They require additional hardware be deployed throughout the WLAN as needed. That means you will have additional design and mounting costs as well as additional cable runs. If you experience Layer 1 issues on a regular basis or have areas of your network that require more up time than others, a dedicated sensor solution may be just what you need. These may also have a WIPS component available for increased security monitoring.

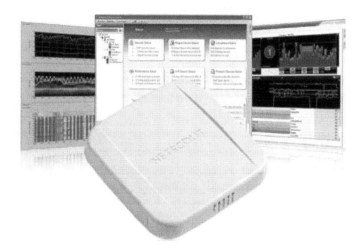

Figure 9.37: The Sensor4-R2S1-I from NETSCOUT

Spectrum Analysis Report Generation

Many spectrum analyzers provide built-in report generation. Report generation is a useful feature of spectrum analyzers. Figure 9.38 shows the report builder in Chanalyzer. This tool allows you to build reports from the different views in the Chanalyzer software. You can also format the header, report title, author, location, and data. You can add custom blocks as well, where you might include photos or screenshots from other software.

Spectrum XT also includes report building features. According to NETSCOUT:

> *AirMagnet Spectrum XT's integrated report engine makes it easy to turn RF spectrum analysis sessions into professional reports. Customization features allow this Wi-Fi spectrum analyzer to generate reports on the RF spectrum graphs, Wi-Fi charts and the list of RF interference sources for the current environment. With the wireless spectrum analyzer, reports can be exported in the Word, RTF, PDF, HTML formats for handoff.*

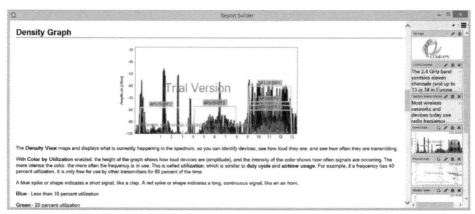

Figure 9.38: Chanalyzer Report Builder

The Chanalyzer report builder can save reports in the Wi-Spy Report Format only; however, you can export the report in PDF, Rich Text, or HTML formats as shown in Figure 9.39.

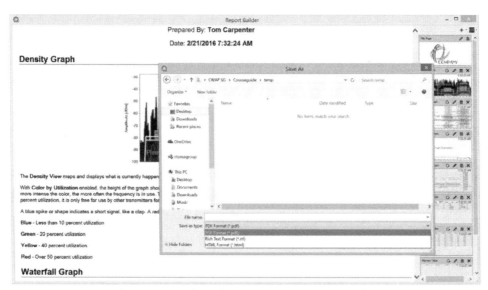

Figure 6.19: Chanalyzer Report Export Dialog

Finally, Figure 6.20 shows a report generated from Spectrum XT

WiFi Spectrum Environment Overview

2.4 GHz

This report provides information on channels 1, 2, 3, 4, 5, 6, 7, 8, 9, 10, 11, 12, 13, 14 operating in the frequency range 2.402 GHz to 2.842 GHz. The Maximum and the Average Power represents the maximum and average power levels across all channels in the 2.4GHz Band. This table also provides the number of APs, stations and phones found on the respective channels. Duty Cycle is defined as the percentage of time that a signal power above that of the noise floor is detected by the application.

Channel	Average Power (dBm)	Maximum Power (dBm)	Average Duty Cycle (%)	Number Of APs	Number Of Stations	Number Of Phones
1	-100	-41	26.86	22	1	0
2	-100	-29	22.15	1	0	0
3	-100	-10	12.93	0	0	0
4	-100	-10	10.82	0	0	0
5	-97	-10	17.57	1	0	0
6	-97	-10	8.26	15	1	0
7	-97	-11	9.09	7	0	0
8	-97	-12	5.83	0	0	0
9	-103	-12	6.37	0	0	0
10	-103	-14	12.27	0	0	0
11	-103	-17	11.17	29	4	0
12	-103	-36	14.82	0	0	0
13	-103	-36	8.84	0	0	0
14	-108	-36	0	0	0	0

Spectrum Density Snapshot

The Spectrum Density graph shows the "popularity" of a particular frequency /power reading over time . The X-axis shows the frequency or channel for the 2.4GHz radio band; the Y-axis shows the minimum and maximum power readings in dBm .

Figure 6.22: Spectrum XT Report with Wi-Fi Integration Information

Chapter Summary

To understand the entire Wi-Fi story, from pre-deployment physical site survey to troubleshooting, you need to perform analysis where Wi-Fi exists, at both Layer 1 and Layer 2 of the OSI model. There are many ways to collect and display the information needed to determine what is happening within the frequencies used in Wi-Fi that may impact your use. Just like conducting protocol analysis at Layer 2, you must be able to interpret the information displayed in the interface of your spectrum analysis tools. Non-802.11 sources of RF energy, noise, in the frequencies you are using will have a negative impact or your WLAN. Spectrum analysis allows you to find this noise and either design around it or remove it from your space. Network issues can exist on the wired network or in the air. Radios can have hardware and or software issues. Users and administrators make mistakes. Determining the source of any trouble and applying the correct remediation or mitigation techniques as quickly as possible reduces downtime within your WLAN. Spectrum analysis is one of the most valuable tools a wireless professional has in designing, building and troubleshooting wireless networks.

Facts to Remember

- The duty cycle shows the amount of time RF energy is detected above the noise floor or some arbitrary threshold.
- The sweep cycle is the amount of time required to scan the frequency range monitors.
- The real-time FFT view shows the energy for each frequency in real-time.
- The swept spectrogram view shows the energy each frequency over time and provides a historical view of activity.
- Common interferers include other Wi-Fi networks, Bluetooth, microwave ovens, cordless phones, video cameras, and other non-Wi-Fi devices.
- AP-based spectrum analysis may require that the AP cease serving clients during the analysis.
- Sensor-based spectrum analysis may use specially designed radios that five a more precise view of the RF activity
- Laptop-based and portable spectrum analyzers are excellent for locating sources of interference or identifying low-power interferers that may not be seen by distant sensors or AP.

Review Questions

1. What is the name of the measurement defining the amount of time in which the amplitude of RF energy in a frequency range is above an arbitrary threshold??

    A. Channel Impact

    B. Sweep Cycle

    C. Amplitude Duration

    D. Duty Cycle

2. When a spectrum analyzer shows the SSIDs detected on specific channels in the spectrum views, what feature is being used??

    A. Wi-Fi Integration

    B. WLAN discovery

    C. Protocol Analysis

    D. SSID Arbitration

3. When using a spectrum analyzer, which view shows you the RF energy present at a particular frequency over the course of time?

    A. The Real Time FFT

    B. The Power Spectral Density

    C. The Swept Spectrogram

    D. The Persistent BSSID

4. What is used to display the strength of the detected energy as a function of frequency?

    A. The Power Spectral Density

    B. The Waterfall View

    C. The Swept Spectrogram

    D. The Real Time FFT

5. What is the name given is a comparison of the level of signal power to the level of noise power.

    A. Noise Floor

    B. SNR

    C. SINR

    D. Airtime utilization

6. What can be determined based upon the information displayed in this image?

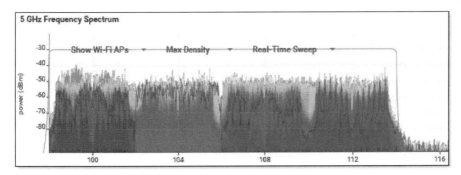

    A. VHT/OFDM is being used

    B. HT OFDM is being used

    C. Channel Bonding is being used

    D. 4X4:4 MIMO is being used

7. What could lead you to spectrum analysis after conducting protocol analysis of a troubled service set?

    A. Excessive retransmissions

    B. HT Greenfield mode not in use

    C. Low data rates being observed

    D. 160 MHz channel widths in use

8. What is the source of the noise displayed in this image?

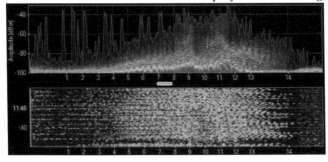

    A. A cordless phone

    B. Bluetooth

    C. A VHT AP using a 160 MHz wide channel.

    D. A microwave oven

398

9. True or False: The image below is a representation of a DSSS AP in use on channel 1.

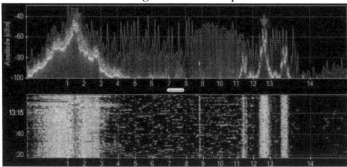

    A. True

    B. False

10. What is seen in this image?

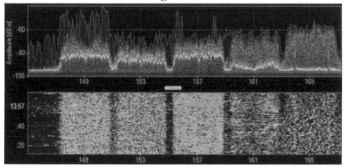

    A. A VHT AP using a 100 MHz wide channel

    B. A microwave oven disrupting channels 161 and 165

    C. A cordless phone in use

    D. Multiple OFDM APs being used on separate 5 GHz channels

Review Answers

1. The correct answer is D. Duty cycle is a reference to the RF energy measured above a given threshold. It is a time domain measurement.

2. The correct answer is A. Wi-Fi integration is being used. It requires the use of an 802.11 adapter in addition to the spectrum analysis adapter and is used to show information that would be revealed at Layer two from beacon frames or other 802.11 transmissions.

3. The correct answer is C. The Swept Spectrogram shows you the RF energy present at a particular frequency over the course of time. This is essentially the same information as the Real Time FFT, but it is presented in a different format and tracked over time.

4. The correct answer is A. The Power Spectral Density displays the strength of the detected energy as a function of frequency. In other words, it shows at which frequencies any detected RF energy variations are strong and at which frequencies these variations weaker.

5. The correct answer is B. The signal to noise ratio, SNR, is calculated by subtracting a signal strength in dBm from a measured noise, also in dBm.

6. The correct answer is C. Channel bonding is being used. Neither the PHY not the MIMO variation used are determinable in this image. Also, notice that the guard interval is being ignored.

7. The correct answer is A. Excessive retransmissions are often an indication that there is a source of non-802.11 RF energy causing problems. Retransmissions beyond a 5% rate warrant investigation. If protocol analysis does not indicate hidden node issues, spectrum analysis should be used to find the source of the problem.

8. The correct answer is D. This image displays a microwave oven in use.

9. The correct answer is B. This image is of an X10 camera transmitting. A DSSS AP on channel 1 would display a more even bell curve and would not also have energy detected as far away as channels 11-13.

10. The correct answer is D. This is multiple APs using separate 5 GHz Channels. There are no 100 MHz wide channels defined in VHT. Microwaves operate in the 2.4 GHz spectrum. Cordless phones use only one channel at a time.

Glossary: A CWNP Universal Glossary

40 MHz Intolerant: A bit potentially set in the 802.11 frame allowing STAs to indicate that 40 MHz channels should not be used in their BSS or in surrounding networks. The bit is processed only in the 2.4 GHz band.

4-Way Handshake: The process used to generate encryption keys for unicast frames (Pairwise Transient Key (PTK)) and transmit encryption keys for group (broadcast, multicast) (Group Temporal Key (GTK)) frames using material from the 802.1X/EAP authentication or the pre-shared key (PSK). The PTK and GTK are derived from the Pairwise Master Key (PMK) and Group Master Key (GMK) respectively.

802.11: A standard maintained by the IEEE for implementing and communicating with wireless local area networks (WLANs). Regularly amended, the standard continues to evolve to meet new demands. Several Physical Layer (PHY) methods are specified and the Medium Access Control (MAC) sublayer is also specified.

802.11a: An 802.11 amendment that operates in the 5GHz band. It uses OFDM modulation and is called the OFDM PHY. It can support data rates of up to 54 Mbps.

802.11aa: An 802.11 amendment that added support for robust audio and video streaming through MAC enhancements. It specifies a new category of station called a Stream Classification Service (SCS) station. The SCS implementation is optional for a WMM QoS station.

802.11ac: An 802.11 amendment that operates in the 5GHz band. It uses MU-MIMO, beamforming, and 256 QAM technology, up to 8 spatial streams and OFDM modulation. Support is included for data rates up to 6933.3 Mbps.

802.11ae: An 802.11 amendment that provides prioritization of management frames. It defines a new Quality of Service Management Frame (QMF). When the QMF service is used, some management frames may be transmitted using an access category other than the one used for voice (AC_VO). When communicating with stations that do not support the QMF service, the station uses access category AC_VO to transmit management frames. When QMF is supported, the beacon frame includes a QMF Policy element.

802.11ah: An 802.11 draft that specifies operations in the sub-1 GHz range. Frequencies used vary by regulatory domain. The draft supports 1, 2, 4, 8 and 16 MHz channels with OFDM modulation.

802.11ax: An 802.11 draft that will support bi-directional MU-MIMO, higher modulation rates and sub-channelization. It is too early to know the final details of this amendment at the time of writing; however, it is planned to operate in the 2.4 GHz and 5 GHz band.

802.11b: An IEEE 802.11 amendment that operates in the 2.4GHz ISM band. It uses HR/DSSS and earlier technology. It can support data rates of up to 11Mbps.

802.11e: An 802.11 amendment, now incorporated into the most recent rollup, that provided quality of service extensions to the wireless link through probabilistic prioritization based on the contention window. The Wi-Fi Multimedia (WMM) certification is based on this amendment.

802.11g: An IEEE 802.11 amendment that operates in the 2.4GHz ISM band. It uses ERP-OFDM and earlier technology. It can support data rates of up to 54Mbps.

802.11i: An 802.11 amendment, now incorporated into the most recent rollup, which provided security enhancements to the standard and resolved weaknesses in the original WEP encryption solution. It provided for TKIP/RC4 (now deprecated) and CCMP/AES cipher suites and encryption algorithms.

802.11n: An IEEE 802.11 amendment that operates in the 2.4 ISM and 5GHz UNII/ISM bands. It uses MIMO, HT-OFDM and earlier technology. It can support data rates of up to 600Mbps.

802.11k: An IEEE 802.11 amendment that specifies and defines WLAN characteristics and mechanisms.

802.11r: An IEEE 802.11 amendment that enables roaming between access points.

802.11u: An IEEE 802.11 amendment that adds features for mobile communication devices such as phones and tablets.

802.11w: An IEEE 802.11 amendment to increase security for the management frames.

802.11y: An IEEE 802.11 amendment that allows registered stations to operate at a higher power output in the 3650-3700 MHz band.

802.1X: 802.1X is an IEEE standard that uses the Extensible Authentication Protocol (EAP) framework to authenticate devices attempting to connect to the LAN or WLAN. The process involves the use of a supplicant to be authenticated, authenticator, and authentication server.

802.11 State Machine: The 802.11 state machine defines the condition of the connection of a client STA to another STA and can be in one of three states: Unauthenticated/Unassociated, Authenticated/Unassociated, or Authenticated/Associated.

802.3: A set of standards maintained by the IEEE for implementing and communicating with wired Ethernet networks and including Power over Ethernet (PoE) specifications.

AAA Framework: Authentication, Authorization, and Accounting is a framework for monitoring usage, enforcing policies, controlling access to computer resources, and providing the correct billing amount for services.

AAA Server Credential: The AAA server credential is the validation materials used for the server. When mutual authentication is required, a server certificate is typically used as the AAA server credential.

Absorption: Occurs when an obstacle absorbs some or all of a radio wave's energy.

Access Category (AC): An access category is a priority class. 802.11 specifies four different priority classes – voice (AC_VO), video (AC_VI), best effort (AC_BE), and background (AC_BK).

Access Layer Forwarding: Data forwarding that occurs at the access layer, also called *distributed data forwarding*. The data is distributed from the access layer directly to the destination without passing through a centralized controller.

Access Point: An access point (AP) is a device containing a radio that is used to create an access network, bridge network or mesh network. The AP contains the Distribution System Service.

Access Port: An AP used for mesh networks and that connects to the wired or wireless network at the edge of the mesh.

Acknowledgement Frame: A frame sent by the receiving 802.11 station confirming the received data.

Access Control List (ACL): ACLs are lists that inform a STA or user what permissions are available to access files and other resources. ACLs are also used in routers and switches to control packets allowed through to other networks.

Active Mode: A power-save mode in which the station never turns the radio off.

Active Scanning: A scanning (network location) method in which the client broadcasts probe requests and records the probe responses in order to determine the network with which it will establish an association.

Active Survey: A wireless survey conducted on location that involves measuring throughput rates, round trip time, and packet loss by connecting devices to an AP and transmitting data during the survey.

Ad-Hoc Mode: The colloquial name for an Independent Basic Service Set (IBSS). STAs connect directly with each other and an AP is not used.

Adjacent Overlapping Channels: Adjacent overlapping channels are channels whose bands interfere with their neighboring channels on the primary carrier frequencies. Non-overlapping channels are channels whose bands do not interfere with neighboring channels on the primary carrier frequencies.

Adjacent Channel Interference (ACI): ACI occurs when channels near each other (in the frequency domain) interfere with one another due to either partial frequency overlap on primary carrier frequencies or excessive output power.

AES (Advanced Encryption Standard): The encryption cipher used with CCMP and WPA2 providing improved security over WEP/RC4 or TKIP/RC4.

AID: Association ID (AID) is an identification assigned by a wireless STA (AP) to another STA (client) in order to transmit the correct data to that device in an Infrastructure Basic Service Set.

AirTime Fairness: Transmits more frames to client STAs with higher data rates than those with lower data rates so that the STAs get fair access to the air (medium) instead of having to wait for slower data rate STAs.

Aggregated MAC Protocol Data Units (A-MPDU): A-MPDU transmissions are created by transmitting multiple MPDUs as one PHY frame as opposed to A-MSDU transmissions, which are created by passing multiple MSDUs down to the PHY layer as a single MPDU.

Aggregated MAC Service Data Unit (A-MSDU): See *Aggregated MAC Protocol Data Unit*.

Amplification: The process of increase a signal's power level.

Amplifier: A device intended to increase the power level of a signal.

Amplitude: The power level of a signal.

Antenna: A device that converts electric power into radio waves and radio waves into electric power.

Association: The condition wherein a client STA is linked with an AP for frame transmission through the AP to the network.

Announcement Traffic Indication Message (ATIM): A traffic indication map (sent in a management frame) in an Ad-Hoc (IBSS) network to notify other clients of pending data transfers for power saving purposes.

Attenuation: The loss of signal strength as an RF wave passes through a medium.

Attenuator: A device that intentionally reduces the strength of an RF signal.

Authentication: The process of user or device identity validation.

Authentication and Key Management (AKM): The protocols used to authenticate a client STA on a WLAN and generate encryption key for use in frame encryption.

Authentication Server: The authentication server validates the client before allowing access to the network. In an 802.1X/EAP implementation for WLANs, the authentication server is often a RADIUS server.

Authenticator: The device that provides access to authentication services in order to allow connected devices to access network resources. In an 802.1X/EAP implementation for WLANs, the authenticator is typically the AP or controller.

Automatic Power Save Delivery (APSD): APSD is a power saving method which uses both scheduled (S-APSD) and unscheduled (U-APSD) frame delivery methods. S-APSD sends frames to a power save STA from the AP at a planned time. U-APSD sends frames to a power save STA from the AP when the STA sends a frame to the AP. The frame from the STA is considered a trigger frame.

Autonomous AP: An AP that can perform security functions, RF management, and configuration without the need for a centralized WLAN controller or any other control platform.

Azimuth Chart: A chart showing the radiation pattern of an antenna as viewed from the top of the antenna. Also called an H-Plane Chart or H-Chart.

Backoff timer: The timer used during CSMA/CA to wait for access to the medium, which is selected from the contention window.

Band Steering: A method used by vendors to encourage STAs to connect to the 5 GHz band instead of the 2.4 GHz band, which is more congested. Typically implemented by ignoring probe requests for some period of time before allowing connection to the 2.4 GHz radio by clients known to have a 5 GHz radio based on previous connections to the AP or controller.

Bandwidth: The frequencies used for transmission of data. For example, a 20 MHz wide channel has 20 MHz of bandwidth.

Basic Service Area (BSA): The coverage area provided by an AP wherein client STAs may connect to the AP to transmit data on the WLAN or through the AP to the network.

Basic Service Set (BSS): An AP and its associated STAs. Identified by the BSSID.

Basic Service Set Identification (BSSID): The ID for the BSS. Often the MAC address of the AP STA. When multiple SSIDs are used, another MAC address-like BSSID is generated.

Beacon Frame: A frame transmitted periodically from an AP that indicates the presence of a BSS network and contains capabilities and requirements of the BSS. Also colloquially called a beacon instead of the full phrase, beacon frame.

Beamforming: Directing radio waves to a specific area or device by manipulating the RF waveforms within the different radio chains.

Beamwidth: The width of the radiated signal lobe from the antenna in the intended direction of propagation. It is usually measured at the point where 3 dB of loss is experienced.

Bill of materials (BOM): A list of the materials and licenses required to assemble a system, in the case of WLANs, including APs, controllers, PoE injectors, licenses, etc.

Bit: A basic unit of information for computer systems. A bit can have a value of 1 or 0. Used in binary math.

Block Acknowledgement: An acknowledgement frame that groups together multiple ACKs instead of transmitting each individual ACK when a block transmission has been received.

Bridge: A device used to connect two networks. Wireless bridges create the connection across the wireless medium.

BSS Transition: Roaming that occurs between two BSSs that are part of the same ESS.

Byte: A basic unit of information that typically consists of 8 bits. Also called an octet.

Capacity: The number of clients and applications a network or AP can handle.

Captive Portal: Authentication technique that re-routes a user to a special webpage to verify their credentials before allowing access to the network. Commonly used in hotel and guest networks.

Guest Networks: A segregated network that is designed for use by temporary visitors.

CardBus: A PCMCIA PC Card standard interface that supports 32-bits and operates at speeds of up to 33 MHz. It is primarily used in laptops.

Carrier Frequencies: The frequency of a carrier signal or the frequencies used to modulate information.

Carrier Sense Multiple Access (CSMA): CSMA is a protocol that allows a node to detect the presence of traffic before sending data on a shared network. Used in CSMA/CA.

Carrier Sense Multiple Access with Collision Avoidance (CSMA/CA): CSMA/CA is the method in 802.11 networks in which a node only sends data if the shared network is idle in order to avoid collisions.

CCMP: Counter Cipher Mode with Block Chaining Message Authentication Code Protocol (CCMP) is an key management solution that provides for improved security over WEP.

CCMP/AES: CCMP used with AES, as it is in 802.11 networks, is a key management and encryption protocol that provides more security than WEP. It is based on the AES standard and uses a 128 bit key and 128 bit block size.

Centralized Forwarding: Every forwarding decision is made by a centralized forwarding engine, such as the WLAN controller.

Certificate Authority (CA): A server that validates the authenticity of a certificate used in authentication and encryption systems. The CA may issues certificates or it may authorize other servers to do the same.

CompactFlash (CF): Originally produced in 1994 by SanDisk, CF is a flash memory mass storage device format that can support up to 256 GB. CF devices can also function as 802.11 WLAN adapters.

Channel: A specified range of frequencies used in the 802.11 standard used by devices to communicate on the network.   Channels are commonly 20, 40, 80 and 160 MHz in width in WLANs. Newer standards will support 1, 2, 4, 8 and 16 MHz channels in sub-1 GHz networks.

Channel Width: The range of frequencies a single channel encompasses.

Clear Channel Assessment (CCA): CCA is a feature defined in the IEEE 802.11 standard that allows a client to determine idle or busy state of the medium based on energy levels of a frame or raw energy levels as specified in each PHY.

Client Utilities: Software installed on devices that allows the device to connect to, authenticate with and participate in a WLAN.

Co-Channel Interference (CCI): Congestion cause by the normal operations of CSMA/CA when multiple BSSs exist on the same channel. Commonly called co-channel congestion (CCC) today as well.

Collision Avoidance (CA): A method in which devices attempt to avoid simultaneous data transmissions in order to prevent frame collisions. Used in CSMA/CA.

Coding: A process used to encode bits to be transmitted on the wireless medium such that error recovery can be achieved. Part of forward error correction (FEC) and defined in the modulation and coding schemes (MCSs) from 802.11n forward.

Containment: A process used against a detected rogue AP to prevent any connected clients from accessing the network.

Contention Window: A number range defined in the 802.11 standard and varying by QoS category from which a number is selected at random for the backoff timer in the CSMA/CA process.

Control Frame: An 802.11 frame that is used to control the communications process on the wireless medium. Control frames include, RTS frames, CTS frames, PS-Poll frames and ACK frames.

Controlled Port: In an 802.1X authentication system, the virtual port that allows all frames through to the network, but only after authentication is completed.

Controller-Based AP: An AP managed by a centralized controller device. Also called a lightweight AP or thin AP.

Coverage: 1) The colloquial term used for the BSA of an AP. 2) The requirement of available WLAN connectivity throughout a facility, campus or area. Often specified in minimum signal strength as dBm; for example, -67 dBm.

Clear-to-Send (CTS) Frame: A CTS frame sent from one STA to another to indicate that the other STA can transmit on the medium. The duration value in the CTS frame is used to silence all other STAs by setting their NAV timers.

Data Frame: An 802.11 frame specified for use in carrying data based on the general frame format. Also used for some signaling purposes as null data frames.

Data Rate: The rate at which data is sent across the wireless medium. Typically represented as megabits per second (Mbps) or gigabits per second (Gbps). The data rate should not be confused with throughput rate, which is a measurement of Layer 4 throughput or useful user data.

dBd (decibel to dipole): A relative measurement of antenna gain compared to a dipole antenna. Calculated as 2.14 dB greater than dBi as a dipole antenna already has 2.14 dBi gain.

dBi (decibel to isotropic): A relative measurement of antenna gain compared to a theoretical isotropic radiator. When necessary, calculated as 2.14 dB less than dBd.

dBm (decibel to milliwatt): An absolute measurement of the power of an RF signal based on the definition of 0 dBm = 1 milliwatt (mW).

Distributed Coordination Function (DCF): A protocol defined in 802.11 that uses carrier sensing, backoff timers, interframe spaces and frame duration values to diminish collisions on the wireless medium.

Elevation Chart: A chart showing the radiation pattern of an antenna as viewed from the side antenna. Also called an E-Plane Chart or E-Chart.

Deauthentication Frame: A notification frame sent from an 802.11 STA to another STA in order to terminate a connection between them.

Decibel (dB): A logarithmic, relative unit used when measuring antenna gain, signal attenuation, and signal-to-noise ratios. Strictly defined as 1/10 of a bel.

Delay: The time it takes for a bit of data to travel from one node to another. Also called latency.

Delivery Traffic Indication Message (DTIM): A message sent from an AP to clients in the Beacon frame indicating that it has data to transmit to the clients specified by the AIDs.

Differentiated Services Code Point (DSCP): A Layer 3 QoS marking system. IP packets can include DSCP markings in the headers. Eight precedence levels, 0-7, are defined.

Diffraction: The bending of waves around a very large object in relation to the wave.

Direct-Sequence Spread Spectrum (DSSS): A modulation technique where data is coupled with coding that spreads the data across a wide frequency range. Provides 1 or 2 Mbps data rates in 802.11 networks.

Disassociation Frame: A frame sent from one STA to another in order to terminate the association.

Distributed Forwarding: See *Access Layer Forwarding*. Also called, *distributed data forwarding.*

Distribution System (DS): The system that connects a set of BSSs and LANs such that an ESS is possible.

Distribution System Medium (DSM): The medium used to interconnect APs through the DS such that they can communicate with each other for ESS operations using either wired or wireless for the DS connection.

Domain Name System (DNS): A protocol and service that provides host name resolution (looking up the IP address of a given host name) and recursive IP address lookups (finding the host name of a known IP address). Also, colloquially used to reference the server that provides DNS lookups.

Driver: Software that allows a computer to interact with a hardware device such as a WLAN adapter.

Duty Cycle: A measure of the time a radio is transmitting or a channel is consumed by a transmitting device.

Dynamic Frequency Selection (DFS): A setting on radios that dynamically changes the channel selection based on detected interference from radar systems. Many 5 GHz channels require DFS operations.

Dynamic Rate Switching (DRS): The process of reducing a client's data rate as frame transmission failures occur or signal strength decreases. DRS results in lower data rates but fewer transmissions required to successfully transmit a frame.

Encryption: The process of converting data into a form that unauthorized users cannot understand by encoding the data with an algorithm and a key or keys.

Enhanced Distributed Channel Access (EDCA): An enhancement to DCF introduced in 802.11e that implements priority based queuing for transmissions in 802.11 networks based on access categories.

Equivalent Isotropically Radiated Power (EIRP): The output power required of an isotropic radiator to equal the measured power output from an antenna in the intended direction of propagation.

Extended Rate Physical (ERP): A physical layer technology introduced in 802.11g that uses OFDM (from 802.11a) in the 2.4 GHz band and offers data rates up to 54 Mbps.

Extended Service Set (ESS): A group of one or more BSSs that are interconnected by a DS.

Extensible Authentication Protocol (EAP): An authentication framework that defines message formats for authentication exchanges used by 802.1X WLAN authentication solutions.

Fade Margin: An amount of signal strength, in dB, added to a link budget to ensure proper operations.

Fast Fourier Transform (FFT): A mathematical algorithm that takes in a waveform as represented in the time or space domain and shows it in the frequency domain. Used in spectrum analyzers to show real-time views in the frequency domain (Real-time FFT).

Fragmentation: The process of fragmenting 802.11 frames based on the fragmentation threshold configured. Fragmented frames have a greater likelihood of successful delivery in the presence of sporadic interference.

Frame Aggregation: A feature in the IEEE 802.11n PHY and later PHYs that increases throughput by sending more than one frame in a single transmission. Aggregated MSDUs or aggregated MPDUs may be supported.

Frame: A well-defined, meaningful set of bits used to communicate management and control information on a network or transfer payloads from higher layers. Frames are defined at the MAC and PHY layer.

Free Space Path Loss: The natural loss of amplitude that occurs in an RF signal as it propagates through space and the wave front spreads.

Fresnel Zones: Ellipsoid shaped zones around the visual LoS in a wireless link. The first Freznel zone should be 60% clear and would preferably be 80% clear to allow for environmental changes.

Frequency: The speed at which a waveform cycles in a second.

Full Duplex: A communication system that allows an endpoint to send data to the network at the same time as it receives data from the network.

Gain: The increase in signal strength in a particular direction. Can be accomplished passively by directing energy into a smaller area or actively by increasing the strength of the broadcasted signal before it is sent to the antenna.

Group Key Handshake: Used to transfer the GTK among STAs in an 802.11 network if the GTK requires updating. Initiated by the AP/controller in a BSS.

Group Master Key (GMK): Used to generate the GTK for encryption of broadcast and multicast frames and is unique to each BSS.

Group Temporal Key (GTK): Used to encryption broadcast and multicast frames and is unique to each BSS.

Guard Interval (GI): A period of time between symbols within a frame used to avoid intersymbol interference.

Half Duplex: A communication system that allows only sending or receiving data by an endpoint at any given time.

Hidden Node: The problem that arises when nodes cannot receive each other's frames, which can lead to packet collisions and retransmissions.

High Density: A phrase referencing a WLAN network type that is characterized by large numbers of devices requiring access.

Highly-Directional Antenna: An antenna, such as a parabolic dish or grid antenna, that has a high gain in a specified direction and a low beamwidth measurement as compared to semi-directional and omnidirectional antennas.

High Rate Direct Sequence Spread Spectrum (HR/DSSS): An amendment-based PHY (802.11b) that increase the data rate in 2.4 GHz from the original 1 or 2 Mbps to 5.5 and 11 Mbps while maintaining backward compatibility with 1 and 2 Mbps.

High Throughput (HT): An amendment-based PHY (802.11n) that increased the data rate up to 600 Mbps and added support for transmit beamforming and MIMO.

Hotspot: A term referencing a wireless network connection point that is typically open to the public or to paid subscribers.

Independent Basic Service Set (IBSS): A set of 802.11 devices operating in ad-hoc (peer-to-peer) mode without the use of an AP.

Institute of Electrical and Electronics Engineers (IEEE): A standardization organization that develops standard for multiple industries including the networking industry with standard such as 802.3, 802.11 and 802.16.

Intentional Radiator: Any device that is purposefully sending radio waves. Signal strength of the intentional radiator is measured at the point where energy enters the radiating antennas.

Interference: In WLANs, an RF signal or incidental RF energy that is radiated in the same frequencies as the WLAN and that has sufficient amplitude and duty cycle to prevent 802.11 frames from successful delivery.

Interframe Space (IFS): A time interval that must exist between frames. Varying lengths are used in 802.11 and a references as DIFS, SIFS, EIFS and AIFS in common use.

Internet Engineering Task Force (IETF): An open group of volunteers develops Internetworking standards through request for comments (RFC) documents. Examples include RADIUS, EAP and DNS.

Isotropic Radiator: A theoretical antenna that spreads the radiaton equally in every directon as a sphere. None exist in reality, but the concept is used to measure relative antenna gain in dBi.

Jitter: The variance in delay between packets sent on a network. Excessive jitter can result in poor quality for real-time applications such as voice and video.

Jumbo Frame: An Ethernet frame that contains more than 1500 bytes of payload and up to 9000 to 9216 bytes.

Latency: The time taken data to move between places. Typically synonymous with delay in computer networking.

Layer 1: The physical layer (PHY) that is responsible for framing and transmitting bits on the medium. In 802.3 and 802.11 the entirety of Layer 1 is defined.

Layer 2: The data-link layer that deals with data frames moving within a local area network (LAN). In 802.3 and 802.11, the MAC sublayer of Layer 2 is defined.

Layer 3: The network layer where packets of data are routed between sender and receiver. Most modern networks use Internet Protocol (IP) at Layer 3.

Layer 4: The transport layer where segmentation occurs for upper layer data and TCP (connection oriented) and UDP (connectionless) are the most commonly used protocols.

Lightning Arrestor: A device that can redirect ambient energy from a lightning strike away from attached equipment.

Line of sight (LoS): When existing, the visual path between to ends. RF LoS is different from visual LoS. RF LoS does not require the same clear path for the remote receiver to hear the signal. When creating bridge links, visual LoS is often the starting point.

Link Budget: The measurement of gains and losses through an intentional radiator, antenna and over a transmission medium.

Loss: The reduction in the amplitude of a signal.

MAC filtering: A common setting that only allows specific MAC addresses onto a network. Ineffective against knowledgeable attackers because the MAC address can be spoofed to impersonate authorized devices.

Management Frame: A frame type defined in the 802.11 standard that encompasses frames used to manage access to the network including beacon, probe request, prober response, authentication, association, reassociation, deauthentication and disassociation frames.

Master Session Key (MSK): A key derived between an EAP client and EAP server and exported by the EAP method. Used to derive the PMK, which is used to derive the PTK. The MSK is used in 802.1X/EAP authentication implementations. In personal authentication implementations, the PMK is derived from the pre-shared key.

Maximal Ratio Combining (MRC): A method of increasing the signal-to-noise ratio (SNR) by combining signals received on multiple radio chains (multiple antennas and radios).

Mesh: A network that uses interconnecting devices to form a redundant set of connections offering multiple paths through the network. 802.11s defined mesh for 802.11 networks.

Mesh BSS: A basic service set that forms a self-contained network of mesh stations.

Milliwatt (mW): A unit of electrical energy used in measuring output power of RF signals in WLANs. A mW is equal to 1/1000 of a watt (W).

Mobile User: A user that physically moves while connected to the network. The opposite of a stationary user.

Modulation: The process of changing a wave by changing its amplitude, frequency, and/or phase such that the changes represent data bits.

Modulation and Coding Scheme (MCS): Term used to describe the combination of the radio modulation scheme and the coding scheme used when transmitting data, first introduced in 802.11n.

MPDU: A MAC protocol data unit (MPDU) is a portion of data to be delivered to a MAC layer peer on a network and it is data prepared for the PHY layer by the MAC sublayer. The MAC sublayer receives the MSDU from upper layers on transmission and creates the MPDU. It receives the MPDU from the lower layer on receiving instantiation and removes the MAC header and footer to create the MSDU for the upper layers.

MSDU: A MAC service data unit is a portion of transmitted data to be handled by the MAC sublayer that has yet to be encapsulated into a MAC Layer frame.

Maximum Transmission Unit (MTU): The largest amount of data that can be sent at a particular layer of the OSI model. Typically set at layer 4 for TCP.

Multi-User MIMO (MU-MIMO): An enhancement to MIMO that allows the AP STA to transmit to multiple client STAs simultaneously.

Multipath: The phenomenon that occurs when multiple copies of the same signal reach a receiver based on RF behaviors in the environment.

Multiple Channel Architecture (MCA): A wireless network design using multiple channels strategically designed so that the implemented BSSs have minimal interference with one another.

Multiple Input/Multiple Output (MIMO): A technology used to spread a stream of data bits across multiple radio chains using spatial multiplexing at the transmitter and to recombine these streams at the receiver.

Narrowband Interference: Interference that covers a very narrow band of frequencies and typically not the full with of an 802.11 channel when used in reference to WLAN interferers.

Near-Far: A problem that occurs when a high powered device is closer to the AP in a BSS and a low powered device is farther from the AP. Most near-far problems are addressed with standard CSMA/CA operations in 802.11 networks.

Network Allocation Vector (NAV): The NAV is a virtual carrier sense mechanism used in CSMA/CA to avoid collisions and is a timer set based on the duration values in frames transmitted on the medium.

Network Segmentation: The process used to separate a larger network into smaller networks often utilizing Layer 3 routers or multi-layer switches.

Noise: RF energy in the environment that is not part of the intentional signal of your WLAN.

Noise Floor: The amount of noise that is consistently present in the environment, which is typically measured in dBm.

Network Time Protocol (NTP): A protocol used to synchronize clocks in devices using centralized time servers.

Octet: A group of eight ones and zeros. An 8-but byte. Sometimes simply called a byte.

Orthogonal Frequency Division Multiplexing (OFDM): A modulation technique and a named physical layer in 802.11 that provides data rates up to 54 Mbps and operates in the 5 GHz band. The modulation is used in all bands, but the named PHY operates only in the 5 GHz band.

Omni-Directional Antenna: An antenna that propagates in all directions horizontally. Creates a coverage area similar to a donut shape (toroidal). Also known as a dipole antenna.

Dipole Antenna: An antenna that propagates in all directions horizontally. Creates a coverage area similar to a donut (toroidal) shape. Also known as a omni-directional antenna.

Open System Authentication: A simple frame exchange, providing no real authentication, used to move through the state machine in relation to the connection between two 802.11 STAs.

Opportunistic Key Caching (OKC): A roaming solution for WLANs wherein the keys derived from the 802.1X/EAP authentication are cached on the AP or controller such that only the 4-way handshake is required at the time of roaming.

OSI (Open Systems Interconnection) Model: A theoretical model for communication systems that works by separating the communications process into seven, well-defined layers. The seven layers are Application, Presentation, Session, Transport, Network, Data Link and Physical.

Packet: Data as represented at the network layer (Layer 4) for TCP communications.

Passive Gain: An increase in strength of a signal by focusing the signal's energy rather than increasing the actual energy available, such as with an amplifier.

Passive scanning: A scanning (network location) method wherein a STA waits to receive beacon frames from an AP which contain information about the WLAN.

Passive survey: A survey conducted on location that gathers information about RF interference, signal strength and coverage areas by monitoring RF activity without active communications.

Passphrase Authentication: A type of access control that uses a phrase as the pass key. Also called personal in WPA and WPA2.

Phase: A measurement of the variance in arrival state between to copies of a wave form. Waves are said to be in phase or out of phase by some degree. The phase can be manipulated for modulation.

PHY: A shorthand notation for physical layer which is the physical means of communication on a network to transmit bits.

Physical (PHY) Layer: The physical (PHY) layer refers to the physical means by which a message is communicated. Layer one of the OSI model.

PLCP: Physical Layer Convergence Protocol (PLCP) is the name of the service within the PHY that receives data from the upper layers and sends data to the upper layers. It is the interaction point with the MAC sublayer.

PMD: Physical Medium Dependent (PMD) is the service within the PHY responsible for sending and receiving bits on the RF medium.

PMK Caching: Stores the PMK so a device only has to perform the 4 way handshake when connecting to an AP to which it has already connected.

Pairwise master Key (PMK): The key derived from the MSK, which is generated during 802.1X/EAP authentication. Used to derive the PTK. Used in unidirectional communications with a single peer.

PoE Injector: Any device that adds Power over Ethernet (PoE) to ethernet cables. Come in two variants, endpoint (such as switches) and midspan (such as inline injectors).

Point-to-Multipoint (PtMP): A connection between a single point and multiple other points for wireless bridging or WLAN access.

Point-to-Point (PtP): A connection between two points often used to connect two networks via bridging.

Polarization: The technical term used to reference the orientation of antennas related to the electric field in the electromagnetic wave.

Power over Ethernet (PoE): A method of providing power to certain hardware devices that can be powered across the Ethernet cables. Specified in 802.3 as a standard. Various classes are defined based on power requirements.

PPDU: PLCP Protocol Data Unit (PPDU) is the prepared bits for transmission on the wired or wireless medium. Sometimes also called a PHY Layer frame.

Preauthentication: Authenticating with an AP to which the STA is not intending to immediately connect so that roaming delays are reduced.

Pre-shared Key (PSK): Refers to any security protocol that uses a password or passphrase or string as the key from which encryption materials are derived.

Primary Channel: When implementing channels wider than 20 MHz in 802.11n and 802.11ac, the 20 MHz channel on which management and control frames are sent and the channel used by STAs not supporting the wider channel.

Probe Request: A type of frame sent when a client device wants information about APs in the area or is seeking a specific SSID to which it desires to connect.

Probe Response: A type frame sent in response to a probe request that contains information about the AP and the requirements of BSSs it provides.

Protected Management Frame (PMF): Frames used for managing a wireless network that are protected from spoofing using encryption. Protocol defined in the 802.11w amendment.

Protocol Analyzer: Hardware or software used to capture and analyze networking communications. WLAN protocol analyzers have the ability to capture 802.11 frames from the RF medium and decode them for display and analysis.

Protocol Decodes: The way information in captured packets or frames is interpreted for display and analysis.

PSDU: PLCP Service Data Unit (PSDU) is the name for the contents that are contained within the PPDU, the PLCP Protocol Data Unit. It is the same as the MPDU as perceived and received by the PHY.

PTK (Pairwise Transient Key): A key derived during the 4-way handshake and used for encryption only between two specific endpoints, such as an AP and a single client.

Quality of Service (QoS): Traffic prioritization and other techniques used to improve the end-user experience. IEEE 802.11e includes QoS protocols for wireless networks based on access categories.

QoS BSS: A BSS supporting 802.11e QoS features.

Radio Chains: A reference to the radio and antenna used together to transmit in a given frequency range. Multi-stream devices have multiple radio chains as one radio chain is required for each stream.

Radio Frequency (RF): The electromagnetic wave frequency range used in WLANs and many other wireless communication systems.

Radio Resource Management (RRM): Automatic management of various RF characteristics like channel selection and output power. Known by different terms among the many WLAN vendors, but referencing the same basic capabilities.

RADIUS: Remote Authentication Dial-In User Service (RADIUS) refers to a network protocol that handles AAA management which allows for authentication, authorization and accounting (auditing). Used in 802.11 WLANs as the authentication server in an 802.1X/EAP implementation.

RC4 (Rivest Cipher 4): An encryption cipher used in WEP and with TKIP. A stream cipher.

Real-Time Location Service (RTLS): A function provided by many WLAN infrastructure and overlay solutions allowing for device location based on triangulation and other algorithms.

Reassociation: The process used to associate with another AP in the same ESS. May also be used when a STA desires to reconnect to an AP to which it was formerly connected.

Received Channel Power Indicator (RCPI): Introduced in 802.11k, a power measurement calculated as INT((dBm + 110) * 2). Expected accuracy is +/- 5 dB. Ranges from 0-220 are available with 0 equaling or less than -110 dBm and 220 equaling or greater than 0 dBm. The value is calculated as an average of all received chains during the reception of the data portion of the transmission. All PHYs support RCPI and, though 802.11ac does not explicitly list its formulation, it references the 802.11n specification for calculation procedures.

Received Signal Strength Indicator (RSSI): A relative measure of signal strength for a wireless network. The method to measure RSSI is not standardized though it is constrained to a limited number of values in the 802.11 standard. Many use the term RSSI to reference dBm, and the 802.11 standard uses terms like DataFrameRSSI and BeaconRSSI and defines them as the signal strength in dBm of the specified frames, so the common vernacular is understandable. However, according to the standard, "absolute accuracy of the RSSI reading is not specified" (802.11-2012, Clause 14.3.3.3).

Reflection: An RF behavior that occurs when a wave meets a reflective obstacle large than the wavelength similar to light waves in a mirror.

Refraction: An RF behavior that occurs as an RF wave passes through material causing a bending of the wave and possible redirection of the wave front.

Regulatory Domain: A reference to geographic regions management by organizations like the FCC and ETSI that determine the allowed frequencies, output power levels and systems to be used in RF communications.

Remote AP: An AP designed to be implemented at a remote location and managed across a WAN link using special protocols.

Resolution Bandwidth (RBW): The smallest frequency that can be extracted from a received signal by a spectrum analyzer or the configuration of that frequency. Many spectrum analyzers allow for the adjustment of the RBW within the supported range of the analyzer.

Retry: That which occurs when a frame fails to be delivered successfully. A bit set in the frame to specify that it is a repeated attempt at delivery.

Return Loss: A measure of how much power is lost in delivery from a transmission line to an antenna.

RF Cables: A cable, typically coaxial, that allows for the transmission of electromagnetic waves between a transceiver and an antenna.

RF Calculator: A software application used to perform calculations related to RF signal strength values.

RF Connector: A component used to connect RF cables, antennas and transmitters. RF connectors come in many standardized forms and should match in type and resistance.

RF Coverage: Synonymous with coverage in WLAN vernacular. Reference to the BSA provided by an AP.

RF Link: An established connection between two radios.

RF Line of Sight (LoS): The existence of a path, possibly including reflections, refractions and pass-through of materials, between two RF transceivers.

RF Propagation: The process by which RF waves move throughout an area including reflection, refraction, scattering, diffraction, absorption and free space path loss.

RF Signal Splitter: An RF component that splits the RF signal with a single input and multiple outputs. Historically used with some antenna arrays, but less common today in WLAN implementations.

RF Site Survey: The process of physically measuring the RF signals within an area to determine resulting RF behavior and signal strength. Often performed as a validation procedure after implementation based on a predictive model.

Roaming: That which occurs when a wireless STA moves from one AP to another either because of end user mobility or changes in the RF coverage.

Robust Security Network (RSN): A network that supports CCMP/AES or WPA2 and optionally TKIP/RC4 or WPA. To be an RSN, the network must support only RSN Associations (RSNAs), which are only those associations that use the 4-way handshake. WEP is not supported in an RSN.

Robust Security Network Association (RSNA): An association between a client STA and an AP that was established through authentication resulting in a 4-way handshake to derive unicast keys and transfer group keys. WEP is not supported in an RSNA.

Rogue Access Point: An access point that is connected to a network without permission from a network administrator or other official.

Rogue Containment: Procedures used to prevent clients from associating with a rogue AP or to prevent the rogue AP from communicating with the wired network.

Rogue Detection: Procedures used to identify rogue devices. May include simple identification of unclassified APs or algorithmic processes that identify likely rogues.

Role-Based Access Control (RBAC): An authorization system that assigns permissions and rights based on user roles. Similar to group management of authorization policies.

RSN Information Element: A portion of the beacon frame that specifies the security used on the WLAN.

Request to Send/Clear to Send (RTS/CTS): A frame exchange used to clear the channel before transmitting a frame in order to assist in the reduction of collisions on the medium. Also used as a backward compatible protection mechanism.

RTS Threshold: The minimum size of a frame required to use RTS/CTS exchanges before transmission of the frame.

S-APSD: See *Automatic Power Save Delivery*.

Scattering: An RF behavior that occurs when an RF wave encounters reflective obstacles that are smaller than the wavelength. The result is multiple reflections or scattering of the wave front.

Secondary Channel: When implementing channels wider than 20 MHz in 802.11n and 802.11ac, the second channel used to form a 40 MHz channel for data frame transmissions to and from supporting client STAs.

Semi-Directional Antenna: An antenna such as a yagi or a patch that has a propagation pattern which maximizes gain in a given direction rather than an omni-directional pattern, having a larger beamwidth than highly directional antennas.

Service Set Identifier (SSID): The BSS and ESS name used to identify WLAN. Conventionally made to be readable by humans. Maximum of 32 bytes long.

Signal Strength: A measure of the amount of RF energy being received by a radio. Often specified as the RSSI, but referenced in dBm, which is not the proper definition of RSSI from the 802.11 standard.

Single Channel Architecture (SCA): A WLAN architecture that places all APs on the same channel and uses a centralized controller to determine when each AP can transmit a frame. No control of client transmissions to the network is provided.

Single Input Single Output (SISO): A radio transmitter that supports one radio chain and can send and receive only a single stream of bits.

Signal to Noise Ratio (SNR): A comparison between the received signal strength and the noise floor. Typically presented in dB. For example, given a noise floor of -95 dBm and a signal strength of -70 dBm, the SNR is 25 dB.

Space-Time Block Coding (STBC): The use of multiple streams of the same data across multiple radio chains to improve reliability of data transfer through redundancy.

Spatial Multiplexing (SM): Used with MIMO technology to send multiple spatial streams of data across the channel using multiple radio chains (radios coupled with antennas).

Spatial Multiplexing Power Save (SMPS): A power saving feature from 802.11n that allows a station to use only one radio (or spatial stream).

Spatial Streams: The partitioning of a stream of data bits into multiple streams transmitted simultaneously by multiple radio chains in an AP or client STA.

Spectrum Analysis: The inspection of raw RF energy to determine activity in an area on monitored frequencies. Useful in troubleshooting and design planning.

Spectrum Analyzer: A hardware and software solution that allows the inspection of raw RF energy.

Station (STA): Any device that can use IEEE 802.11 protocol. Includes both APs and clients.

Supplicant: In 802.1X, the device attempting to be authenticated. Also the term used for the client software on a device that is capable of connecting to a WLAN.

Sweep Cycle: The time it takes a spectrum analyzer to sweep across the frequencies monitored. Often a factor of the number of frequencies scanned and the RBW.

System Operating Margin (SOM): The actual positive difference in the required link budget for a bridge link to operate properly and the received signal strength in the link.

Temporal Key Integrity Protocol (TKIP): The authentication and key management protocol supported by WPA systems and implemented as an interim solution between WEP and CCMP.

Transition Security Network (TSN): A network that allows WEP connections during the transition period over to more secure protocols and an eventual RSN. An RSN does not allow WEP connections.

Transmit Beamforming (TxBF): The use of multiple antennas to transmit a signal strategically with varying phases so that the communication arrives at the receiver such that the signal strength is increased.

Transmit Power Control (TPC): A process implemented in WLAN devices allowing for the output power to be adjusted according to local regulations or by an automated management system.

U-APSD: See *Automatic Power Save Delivery*.

Uncontrolled Port: In an 802.1X authentication system, the virtual port that allows only authentication frames/packets through to the network and, when authentication is successfully completed, provides the 802.1X service with the needed information to open the controlled port.

User Priority (UP): A value (from 0-7) assigned to prioritize traffic that correspond to different access categories for WMM QoS.

Virtual Carrier Sense: The 802.11 standard currently defines the Network Allocation Vector (NAV) for use in virtual carrier sensing. The NAV is set based on the duration value in perceived frames within the channel.

Voltage Standing Wave Ratio (VSWR): The Voltage Standing Wave Ratio is the ratio between the voltage at the maximum and minimum points of a sanding wave.

Watt: A unit of power. Strictly defined as the energy consumption rate of one joule per second such that 1 W is equal to 1 joule per 1 second.

Wavelength: The distance between two repeating points on a wave. Wavelength is a factor of the frequency and the constant of the speed of light.

Wired Equivalent Privacy (WEP): A legacy method of security defined in the original IEEE 802.11 standard in 1997. Used the RC4 cipher like TKIP (WPA), but implemented it poorly. WEP is deprecated and should no longer be used.

Wi-Fi Alliance: An association that certifies WLAN equipment to interoperate based on selected portions of the 802.11 standard and other standards. Certifications include those based on each PHY as well as QoS and security.

Wi-Fi Multimedia (WMM): A QoS certification created and tested by the Wi-Fi Alliance using traffic prioritizing methods defined in the IEEE 802.11e.

Wi-Fi Multimedia Power Save (WMM-PS): A power saving certification designed by the Wi-Fi Alliance and optimized for mobile devices and implementing methods designated in the IEEE 802.11e amendment.

Wireless Intrusion Prevention System (WIPS): A system used to detect and prevent unwanted intrusions in a WLAN by detecting and preventing rogue APs and other WLAN threats.

Wireless Local Area Network (WLAN): A local area network that connects devices using wireless signals based on the 802.11 protocol rather than wires and the common 802.3 protocol.

WPA-Enterprise: A security protocol designed by the Wi-Fi Alliance. Requires an 802.1X authentication server. Uses the TKIP encryption protocol with the RC4 cipher. Implements a portion of 802.11i and the older, no deprecated TKIP/RC4 solution.

WPA-Personal: A security protocol designed by the Wi-Fi Alliance. Does not require an authentication server. Uses the TKIP encryption protocol with the RC4 cipher. Also known as WPA-PSK (Pre-Shared Key).

WPA2-Enterprise: A security protocol designed by the Wi-Fi Alliance. Requires an 802.1X authentication server. Uses the CCMP key management protocol with the AES cipher. Also known as WPA2-802.1X. Implements the non-deprecated portion of 802.11i.

WPA2-Personal: A security protocol designed by the Wi-Fi Alliance. Does not require an authentication server. Uses the CCMP key management protocol with the AES cipher. Also known as WPA2-PSK (Pre-Shared Key).

Wi-Fi Protected Setup (WPS): A standard designed by the Wi-Fi Alliance to secure a network without requiring much user knowledge. Users connect either by entering a PIN associated with the device or by Push-Button which allows users to connect when a real or virtual button is pushed.

Index

NOTES

436

NOTES

NOTES

NOTES

NOTES

Made in the USA
Lexington, KY
18 February 2019